Philosophies of Nature after Schelling

PHILOSOPHIES OF NATURE AFTER SCHELLING

IAIN HAMILTON GRANT

continuum

Continuum International Publishing Group

The Tower Building
11 York Road
London SE1 7NX

80 Maiden Lane
Suite 704
New York, NY 10038

www.continuumbooks.com

First published 2006
Paperback edition 2008

British Library Cataloguing-in-Publication Data
A catalogue record for this book is available from the British Library.

ISBN-10: 0-8264-7902-2 (HB) 1-8470-6432-9 (PB)
ISBN-13: 978-0-8264-7902-0 (HB) 978-1-8470-6432-5 (PB)

Library of Congress Cataloging-in-Publication Data
A catalog record for this book is available from the Library of Congress.

Typeset by Free Range Book Design & Production Ltd
Printed and bound in Great Britain by MPG Books Ltd., Bodmin, Cornwall

Contents

Preface to the Paperback Edition

The two years since its initial publication have afforded me the opportunity of reviewing this book at a distance, aided by the observations, reviews and criticisms of those generous enough to offer them. I would like here to draw attention to those features of the present work that warrant emphasis, as well as to those that prompt further work.

The book was intended to accomplish two tasks. First, to introduce Schelling's extraordinary philosophical and conceptual inventiveness into the context of a European philosophy still beset by the same problems Kant bequeathed Schelling 200 years ago. I would hope this has been achieved in a manner sufficiently interesting to warrant a reconsideration of his corpus. Secondly, to recommend Schelling's naturalistic solutions to these problems, and to construct from them a contribution to the metaphysics of nature. This in turn involves two subordinate tasks. First, to examine the sources of the problems, naturalistic and philosophical, that engaged Schelling, in order to demonstrate that their naturalistic basis is no orgy of Romantic metaphor, but rather a necessary consequence of any metaphysics that takes the problem of nature seriously. Secondly, to analyze the conceptual architecture of the 'antiphysics' philosophically preeminent not only in Schelling's age, but equally in our own. While these subordinate tasks are, I take it, completed here, the metaphysics of nature is anything but, and for several reasons.

First, the metaphysics of nature has become again a contemporary focus of philosophical attention, buoyed by its rediscovery of powers. The prospect of a *field theoretical* ontology to supplant metaphysics' attachment to substance preoccupied Schelling and Whitehead, amongst others, but has been curiously absent from the metaphysics of powers as contemporarily treated. Essential to such a theory is the temporality (or temporalities) and historicity of an ontology of powers, which is what transformed natural history from comparative anatomy into a science of transformation. Contemporary powers ontologists would do well, it seems to me, to draw on a time- rather than a substance-based naturalism, and would learn a lot from Schelling in this regard, and, I hope, from the quite full account of this offered here.

Secondly, the problem of a naturalism attaching to reason, also explored here, has become a focus for a broad range of philosophical inquiry, from neuroscientism and evolutionary epistemologies, on the one hand, to new accounts of the problem of sufficient reason and causality on the other. As explored in what follows, this problem extends at least as far back as Platonism reaches, and probably to Parmenides. It certainly extends to Schelling and to another underexploited philosophical resource, the paradoxical naturalist idealism of Bernard Bosanquet. It is, however, this problem that requires to be further drawn out. A naturalism regarding reason, for instance, entails that the problem of sufficient reason does not exhaust that of ground, which must also include, at a minimum, ground as causal; yet how does 'nature' resolve this problem? What is the ground of ground? While this problem strikes the majority of post-Kantian philosophers as recursively insoluble, the profusion of contemporarily operative solutions to it – Heidegger's transcendentalism, Meillassoux's post-metaphysical rationalism, Harman's extraordinary reworking of causal occasionalism – has returned it to centre stage in contemporary metaphysics. The question, therefore, of what a temporalising, field-theoretical, powers ontology such as Schelling offers is discussed below, will therefore form the subject of my next contribution to the philosophy of nature, tentatively titled *On Grounds, After Schelling*. I hope the reader will be sufficiently stimulated by what follows to consider such an undertaking worthwhile.

Bristol, June 2008

Preface

The present book is entitled *Philosophies of Nature after Schelling*. There are many candidates to fulfil such a role: Bergson, Whitehead and Merleau-Ponty, for example, all extend their engagements with nature *beyond the epistemological concerns of the philosophy of science*. Even Heidegger's self-conscious revivification of Classical German philosophy entailed a flirtation with naturephilosophy, and its nonconsummation there has remained decisive for the trajectory of contemporary philosophy, notwithstanding a recent upsurge in phenomenological naturephilosophy in Böhme and Schiemann (1997) and Courtine (1990). Rescher (2000), unaffected by Heideggerianism, does naturephilosophy, while Ellis (2001) designs a philosophy of nature to undo Humean damage. The sciences have their indigenous philosophers of nature: Schrödinger (1954), for instance, and the works of Prigogine and Stengers (1984), contribute towards this project, which René Thom (1978), recently echoed by Roland Omnès (1999), demanded be revived 'after the late eighteenth century model'. The problem, in other words, with naturephilosophy is not that it died out in the 1830s, but that there are too many approaches to cover in any single volume. Since, however, for my part, the work of Deleuze and Guattari tends most overtly in this direction, it should be taken as a constant counterpoint to the present work, and surfaces from time to time, like Protagoras momentarily emerging and disappearing from the earth in Plato's *Theaetetus*.

Two principles govern this decision. Firstly, among the most opaque parts of an unusually motile and profligate philosophy, Schellingian naturephilosophy requires considerable, text-consuming reconstruction. Of the growing Schellingian literature in English – Bowie (1993), Snow (1996) and Beiser (2002), for instance – few make the naturephilosophy their focus. Beiser bucks this trend, but, like the philosophically inclined historians of science who have given considerable attention to that philosophy, he tends as a consequence of the historical remit to enfold the context of the work within a reducibly local problem-field, rather than evolving it along the broader one of what Schelling called 'the eternal and necessary bond between philosophy and physics' (VII, 101). For the historians of science (e.g., Lenoir 1981, 1982; Sloan 1992; von Engelhardt 1976), the context is supplied by the development of the sciences, while Beiser's context is that of German Idealism. Esposito (1977), whose work remains the only volume in English devoted to Schelling's naturephilosophy, repeats both problems by presenting the speculative excess of the philosophy as responsible for its failure to resolve the problems animating what Schelling called the 'universal palingenesis of all science' at the turn of the nineteenth century. Similarly, while admirable historical labour underpins the *Historical Critical Edition* of Schelling's works currently underway, this has tended to be the focus of the massive body of German literature on the subject, with some exceptions: Heuser-Kessler (1986) and Küppers (1992) adopt critically opposed perspectives on the actuality of Schellingianism in contemporary non-linear dynamics and biology, respectively. However, as Warnke (1998) remarks, critically seconding Heuser-Kessler's productive anachrony, this approach risks losing philosophy to a Popperian propaedeutic to positivization in natural science.

Thus, secondly, the context in which I here present Schellingianism-as-naturephilosophy takes neither its immanent historicity nor its transcendent anachrony as its focus. Rather, it is an argument of this book, as it was of Schelling's work, that metaphysics cannot be pursued in isolation from physics. To reject this isolationism entails the reconstruction not only of Schelling's naturephilosophy, therefore, but the repairing of the context from which it begins. The very idea of a Platonic physics removes the ground from the self-conception of post-Nietzschean philosophy's constant inversions of Platonism; it follows, however, from that physics that it is these very inversions that create the two-worlds metaphysics that made them necessary in the first place. Once introduced, the turbulences Platonic physics effect in philosophy's self-conception are therefore immense.

In addition to overhauling the concepts of nature, becoming and being, Platonism is also a contemporary problem, lying at the heart of philosophy becoming capable once again of metaphysics. Both because this is the case, and because the concept of non-eliminative Idealism proposed by Schelling (of which no trace remains in Hegel, as becomes most egregiously apparent in his own naturephilosophy) derives from the conjoint productivity of nature and Idea introduced in Plato's philosophy of nature as *non-finite becoming*, Schelling's Platonism simultaneously necessitates the reconstruction of the latter's physics and, in so doing, is an irrevocably contemporary problem. Since again the enemy in all this is *all* post-Cartesian European philosophy's elimination of the concept, even the existence, of nature, a deficiency common equally to Kant and the postkantians, the antithetical couple Kant–Plato continues to pose a problem to the '*aphysia*' of contemporary philosophy, as Badiou attests, albeit for exactly the opposite reasons. And since, finally, against Badiou's stipulations of the contemporary 'impossibility' of a 'philosophy of or as nature', Deleuze and Guattari's repeated attempts to construct a philosophy capable equally of nature and the Idea prompted the reengagement of naturephilosophy alongside the return of Schelling, Schellingian naturephilosophy is not only a contemporary problem, but an unfinished project of the most consistent metaphysician of the last century. Insofar therefore as the antithetical couple 'Plato–Kant' that lay at the heart of the immediate postkantian context continues to organize metaphysics, contemporary philosophy is importantly and immediately postkantian, as attested, for instance, by Alliez's recent (2004) recovery of the Fichtean project. At stake, therefore, are two models of metaphysics: a one-world physics capable of the Idea, and an eliminativist practicism. The contrast could be neither more overt nor more pressing: ethicism is purchased at the cost of the elimination of nature.

The book then is entitled *Philosophies of Nature after Schelling* not because it explicates the immense body of work carried out under that rubric, but because it engages in those reconstructions necessary in order that the project reveal its contemporary necessity. That naturephilosophy succeeds Schelling is evident at the level of the profusion of works that continue to appear under that rubric; that it remains massively unacknowledged as a core philosophical problem, however, equally so. The title is therefore more of an incitation than a narrative indicator.

The largely unread works of the *Naturphilosophen* themselves – especially Kielmeyer, Steffens, Windischmann and Eschenmayer – are discussed at some length in what follows. Two things are important to remember: that naturephilosophy was synthetic with regard to the departments of the special sciences entails not that naturalists' work submitted to the imperatives of their philosophical master's 'encyclopaedism', but rather that *naturalistic enquiry is indissociable from philosophizing*. Nor, secondly, is their philosophizing trivial – Steffens' 'Review of the editor's recent naturephilosophical writings', published in Schelling's *Journal for Speculative Physics*, is the most philosophically astute account I have read, while Eschenmayer's 'Spontaneity = Worldsoul', from the same source, is a sophisticated critique of Schelling, all the more remarkable for its tenacious support of Fichteanism *in the context of physics*. These are not simply largely ignored resources (there are of course exceptions, amongst which I must mention Bach's (2001) study of Kielmeyer), but examples of a practice that extends well beyond the armchair, and into the laboratories; most importantly, however, is the basic realism with which all the philosophical naturalists, including Schelling, extend to the philosophy of nature. Since the natural sciences occupy too vast a canvas even to be scanned by a single gaze, it seems to me, as to Schelling, that this cooperative model for naturephilosophy is to be encouraged; all too often, the finite intellect degenerates into practical (in both senses) and analytical atomism, rather than embracing the synthetic as an operating premise for large-scale naturephilosophical projects.

These remarks aside, chapter 1 sets out the problems to be engaged in the work, first amongst which is the rescue of Platonism from modern antiphysics, which illuminates the extent to which modernity's often vaunted incapacity for metaphysics stems from what Carus called its '*aphysia*', and forms the subject matter of chapter 2. Schelling's reconstruction of dynamic physics follows from the core of transcendental territory in Kant and Fichte, of course, but also in the naturalists such as Oken and Carus, whose works are assessed for their capacity for nature in chapter 3. The fourth chapter pursues the problem-sources and attempted solutions of transcendentalism in naturephilosophy, both from the perspectives of the philosophers and the 'physicists'. Chief amongst these are the problem sources driving Kielmeyer's multiphasic dynamics of generative nature, from which Schelling famously dated a 'new epoch in natural history', and the diverse conceptions of the naturephilosophical project ensuing from Schelling's inquiries are investigated in chapters 5 (nature) and 6 (intelligence). The work concludes by engaging the Schellingian alongside the most remarkable of contemporary naturephilosophies in Deleuze.

Throughout the work, references are principally to Karl Friedrich Schelling's edition of his father's *Sämmtliche Werke* (Stuttgart and Augsburg: J. G. Cotta'scher Verlag, 1856–61), which for brevity's sake are reduced to the roman numerals identifying the volume (I–XIV) and page numbers. Works not included in the *Sämmtliche Werke* are cited as per the bibliography. Where possible, existing translations have been referenced, while all other translations are mine unless otherwise noted.

Acknowledgments

Whole crowds of persons, events, institutions and objects have aided this project in untold numbers of ways, so, perhaps not unexpectedly, acknowledging them all presents a daunting task. I would however like to thank Keith Ansell Pearson for his encouragement and support, in particular during the initial stages of the project. The interest in this work shown by many has been as welcome as it has been unexpected: requests for papers, comment, and offers of support have come from Andrew Bowie, Ray Brassier, Judith Norman, Andrea Rehberg, Damian Veal, Alistair Welchman, James Williams and David Wood, although my own responses to many have fallen short of adequate; in this regard, I would like in particular to thank Dale Snow for her enthusiastic willingness to aid a 'fellow Schellingian' in distress at a crucial juncture in the preparation of the manuscript, and hope that this work compensates in some measure for the silence that met that enthusiasm. I would like to thank my colleagues at the University of the West of England, especially Jane Arthurs and Martin Lister, for their support over a not inconsiderable period. My work has benefited extraordinarily, however, from those involved in the philosophy programme there, and who have created a stimulating and vital environment, amongst whom I must mention Allison Assiter, Peter Jowers, Mark Paterson, Simon Thompson and Sean Watson, along with our superb and rewarding philosophy students. At Continuum, Sarah Douglas and Tristan Palmer were supportive and tolerant to a heroic degree, for which I thank them. Finally, my love and thanks to Karin Littau, for everything.

I would also like to thank those who have commented on and supported this work following initial publication, in particular Jeremy Dunham, Graham Harman, Robin Mackay, Joseph Lawrence, Dustin McWherter, Quentin Meillassoux, and Eugene Thacker.

CHAPTER 1

Why Schelling? Why Naturephilosophy?

And with this the author delivers over these Elements of a System of
Speculative Physics to the thinking heads of the age, begging them to make
common cause with him in this science – which opens up views of no mean
order – and to make up by their own powers, knowledge and public
connections, for what, in these respects, he lacks. (III, 326; 2004: 232)

The thinking or striving to discover a system of human knowledge, or,
otherwise and better put, to view human knowledge as a system, in
coexistence, naturally presupposes that originally and of itself, it is not a
system – that it is therefore an asystaton, *something non-coexistent, but*
rather something conflictual. [. . .] [T]*his conflict has an objective ground*
[*which*] *is grounded in the very nature of things, in the primary roots of*
all existence. (IX, 209–10; cf. 1997: 210–11)

[*W*]*e require to know how and why it* [*nature*] *originally and* necessarily
grounds everything that our species has ever thought about nature. (II, 55;
1988: 41)

Schelling is not an easy thinker. His several systems, each of which is a
philosophy of the Absolute or unconditioned (*das Unbedingte*), are compli-
cated by the obligation to start from scratch, to rethink the All absolutely
as a precondition of thinking the All repeatedly, that is: time and again, and
each time, absolutely. The philosophical exposition of the unconditioned, or
Absolute, is not like the analysis of a concept or state of affairs; rather, the
exposition of the Absolute occurs within the Absolute, as the medium of its
own exposition: 'Philosophy is entirely and thoroughly only in the Absolute'
(IV, 388). Such a philosophical system does not therefore seek a fixed point
from which to gain leverage on an external world, nor to rise above it, but
is itself a 'genetic' (II, 39; 1988: 30) movement of and on this world, unconditionally. Philosophy does not, according to Schelling, consist in a
redescription of otherwise available phenomena, but launches 'thought-
operations' in the 'medium of the universal and the impersonal' (Jaspers
1955: 85). It is 'not [a] demonstrative, but [a] *generative [Erzeugende]*'
process (XI, 330) through which productive nature *itself* acts on, or produces,
itself: 'to philosophise about nature means to *create* nature' (III, 13; 2004:
14). Even the later, 'positive philosophy' will have 'the concept of creation'
as its 'true aim' (1989a: 117). On the other hand, nor is the task of

philosophy simply to fabricate its own objects, in the *conditioned* manner that Kant stipulates: '*He who would know the world must first manufacture it* – in his own self, indeed' (*Ak.*XXI, 41; Kant 1993: 240). For Schelling, nature necessarily 'grounds everything *our species* has ever thought about nature' (II, 55; 1988: 41; my emphasis), undercutting any supposition of voluntarism as underlying 'manufacture'. Thus, when Lavoisier instituted modern chemistry as 'creating its own object . . . manufacturing a universal transparent to reason' (Bensaude-Vincent, in Serres (ed.) 1994: 671), what calls for explanation is not the miraculous coincidence of natural and voluntaristic, arbitrary invention, but rather the impersonal coincidence of the transcendentally generated universal and self-generating nature. Schelling's hypothesis is, in other words, that there is a naturalistic or physicalist ground of philosophy: 'For what we want is not that Nature should coincide with the laws of our mind *by chance* . . . but that *she herself*, necessarily and originally, should not only express, but even *realize*, the laws of our mind, and that she is, and is called, Nature only insofar as she does so' (II, 55–6; 1988: 41–2). From this perspective, the invention of an '*Ich*' or ego *behind* or *causing* the manufacture of the universal, of concepts in general, seems an arbitrary add-on by means of which to explain the assumption of a non-coincidence of nature and idea. It is not even the *Ich* or ego, transcendental or empirical, that thinks in the passage just cited, nor, by extension, in philosophizing as such, but rather the *species*, just as Schelling holds philosophy to be 'nothing other than the natural history of mind' (*SW* II, 39; 1988: 30). Yet surely 'species' is a highly conditioned and contingent condition of intellection?

If *what a given species thinks* or *can think* about nature were the limit of Schelling's naturephilosophy, then it would be simply a prototype of recent naturalized epistemologies. Moreover, the philosophy of the unconditioned would then be conducted under the strict conditions imposed upon it by the neurophysiological constraints specific to that species, and would therefore a priori fail to be an unconditioned philosophy, forming instead just another conditioned philosophy of the unconditioned, with false a prioris furnished a posteriori according to empirically discovered species-specific physiological and/or ideational constraints, as opposed, say, to Kant's transcendentally deduced critical laws. If, in other words, 'to philosophise about nature means to create nature', the latter cannot be a nature restricted a priori by the particular physiological means by which it philosophizes. Instead, nature philosophizing must itself be unconditioned, so that the range of instances of natural philosophy must extend beyond the remit of physiologically conditioned particulars such as species, or even phylla. This is why, following a proceedure of successive unconditioning performed by thought-operations upon nature, Schelling arrives at a conception of '*nature as subject*' (III, 284; 2004: 202): this infamous characterization is not a 'senseless . . . Romantic anthropomorphism' (Krings, in Heckmann, Krings and Meyer (eds) 1985: 111–12),[1] but affirms the *autonomy* of nature; nature, then, not as it appears to Mind, but *nature itself*.

The present book is devoted to explicating the problems of Schellingianism *as naturephilosophy*. It does so not only in order to rewrite a chapter that, until recently, has lain largely unwritten in the *history* of philosophy (although, until relatively recently, this was indeed the case),[2] but because these problems remain problems for contemporary metaphysics and philosophy of nature, and do so because these latter remain caught within the epistemologizing-analytic confines imposed upon philosophy by Kant's Copernican revolution. If Kantianism had as its consequence the excision of the 'in itself' from metaphysics, or its functional reduction to 'the mathematical X' (XIII, 49), the general replacement of metaphysics with epistemology, and of philosophical systematizing with conceptual and logical analysis, then this revolution continues to incapacitate philosophy in its attempts to *make*, rather than merely criticize, systematic metaphysics. Further, if this revolution and its consequences adequately characterize both Kantianism and postkantian philosophy (taking this designation in its broadest possible, i.e., chronological and philosophical, sense), then it provides an instructive and enticing clue to the nature and difficulty of Schellingianism that it should define the function of philosophy precisely *against* the consequences of the Kantian revolution: 'By way of philosophy . . . humanity is to be carried beyond simple representation' (Schelling 1989a: 20). This provides the philosophical – or strictly speaking, the *metaphysical* – context in which the present work seeks to demonstrate the continuing relevance of naturephilosophy.

Within contemporary Schelling scholarship's endless discussions of whether there is 'only one Schelling'[3] or 'no one Schellingian philosophy' (Fuhrmans, in Hasler (ed.) 1981: 227), just serial outlines, sketches, and so forth, scant attention is paid to the deep vein of naturephilosophy running through it. Two things clearly emerge from this: firstly, that commentators' reluctance (demonstrated in the mid-twentieth century in particular by Jaspers' (1955) synopsis of Schelling's philosophy) to consider the naturephilosophy *core* to Schellingianism, rather than just a *phase*, vitiates any coherent conception of that philosophy; and secondly, that the periodizing tendency reproduced in virtually every account of Schelling's philosophy is therefore at best misleading.

According to this latter schema, the first of these periods is called 'Fichtean' to the extent that it is held to develop a theory of the subject; yet Schelling's analyses demonstrate that to limit, as Fichte does, the theory of the subject to the axiomatization of the subjective in philosophy is to render the latter incapable of a theory of the subject itself, that is, the subject absolutely or without conditions, *auto to auto*, which continues to be a major concern throughout all phases of Schelling's philosophical development. Moreover, bookended as it is by the 1794 *Timaeus* essay's concern with 'the becoming of being' ([1794] 1994a: 63) and the Platonic physics of 'productive nature [*e tou poiountos phusis*]' (*Philebus* 26e6; cited in Schelling [1794] 1994a: 48) at one end, and the *Treatise Explicatory of the Science of Knowledge* at the other, which recapitulates the earlier Platonic material (cf.

I, 356f; 1994c: 71f) and therefore the inquiry into 'self-organising nature' (I, 386; 1994c: 92, t.m.), it becomes clear that Schelling is explicitly pitting the philosophy of nature against Kanto-Fichtean philosophy. In short, the 'Fichtean' period is not Fichtean to the extent that its central concern with the theory of the subject is necessary precisely to combat the Fichtean restriction of the subject to that available to reflective human consciousness.

Following the extended series of works belonging to the naturephilo-sophical period held to supersede the Fichtean – the *Ideas for a Philosophy of Nature* (1797), *On the World Soul* (1798), *First Outline of a System of Naturephilosophy* (1799), *Introduction to the Outline* (1799) and *Universal Deduction of the Dynamic Process or the Categories of Physics* (1800) – naturephilosophy continues to occupy the larger portion of those works, from 1801–6, commonly categorized as constituting the third phase of Schelling's philosophical development, the Identity Philosophy or 'Identity System', which was, as Schelling reports in both *On the History of Modern Philosophy* (in the chapter on *Naturphilosophie*: X, 107; 1994b: 114), and in the *Philosophy of Mythology*, 'a designation that in any case the author himself used just once' (XI, 371). The occasion Schelling is referring to occurs in the *Presentation of My System of Philosophy* (IV, 113), which has as its remit the systematization of 'the absolute identity of mind and nature' already affirmed, although not developed in the *Ideas for a Philosophy of Nature* (II, 56; 1988: 42). Although apparently downplaying the significance of that system, by the late 1840s Schelling would refer to its grounding as 'the discovery of my youth' (1977: 95). It is clear therefore that while the identity *system* diminishes in importance, *identity itself* does not. Why then the above dismissal? 'Solely to differentiate [my philosophy] from the Fichtean, which accords nature no autonomous being' (XI, 371). While the 'autonomy of nature' becomes an explicit theme in the *First Outline of a System of Naturephilosophy* (1799), it is already evident in the *Ideas'* demand that 'nature itself should . . . not arbitrarily, but *necessarily* . . . not only *express*, but even *realize*, the laws of our mind' (II, 55–6; 1988: 41–2). The so-called identity philosophy does not therefore constitute one of many separate *systems* in Schelling's corpus, but rather an intra-naturephilo-sophical development that accordingly prompted not only in the major re-editions of the *Ideas for a Philosophy of Nature* (1797/1803) and *On the World Soul* (1798/1806), but also explains the publication both of the initial manifestos for the 'identity philosophy' – the *Presentation of My System of Philosophy* (1801) and the *Further Presentations from the System of Philosophy* (1802) – in the *Journal* and *New Journal for Speculative Physics* (1800–2), respectively, and the two sets of *Aphorisms on Naturephilosophy* in the *Annals of Scientific Medicine* (1806–7). Finally, alongside the critical-polemical *Exposition of the True Relation of Naturephilosophy to the Improved Fichtean Theory* (1806), the major developed statement of this philosophy presented in Schelling's Würzburg lectures of 1804 as *System of Philosophy as a Whole* not only specifies its concern with *Naturephilosophy in Particular* in its title, but devotes two thirds of its attention to the topic.

4

Schelling confirms the preponderance of naturephilosophy throughout this period in the *Philosophical Inquiries into the Essence of Human Freedom* (1809), which states that he had until then 'confined himself exclusively to naturephilosophy' (VII, 333; 1986: 3). This does not entail, as is frequently thought, that with the 'philosophy of freedom', naturephilosophy is finally abandoned; rather, that work reverts to the territory covered in the 1797 'Is a philosophy of history possible?' (I, 466–73), to argue that nature must furnish, rather than vitiate, the only possible basis for a philosophy of freedom it then rendered inconceivable for Schelling, and to generate a first 'geology of morals'. Even by 1830, with the *Introduction to Philosophy*, which claims finally to have found the 'Ariadne's thread' of history running through the 'true Proteus' of nature (1989a: 142), naturephilosophy remains 'the substrate of the entire system' of philosophy (1989a: 55), and continues this service even in Schelling's last, unpublished works.[4] The intertwining of geology, ethology and history is amplified in the development of the 'system of times' (1946: 14, 211; 1997: 123), which progresses from 'magnetic time' through the 'electrical' until the 'organism of times' is achieved (VIII, 310; 2000: 82), throughout the various versions of the *Ages of the World*.[5]

Finally, while Schelling's late return to naturephilosophy, in the 1844 *Presentation of the Process of Nature* (X, 301–90), may seem to be an isolated instance given the contemporaneous *Philosophy of Mythology* (1842–54, XI–XII) and *Philosophy of Revelation* (1842–54, XIII–XIV), Schelling defines the 'Positive Philosophy' that grounds both these projects as an 'empiricism with regard to matter, only an aprioristic empiricism' (XIII, 102). This materialist empiricism is not aprioristic in the sense that, like Kant's transcendentalism, it regulates possible cognition for a transcendental ego; rather it is a priori in the sense that it is governed by precisely that 'innate and indwelling logic of nature' (XIII, 103) that made it possible for Schelling to define philosophy as the 'natural history of our mind' in the *Ideas for a Philosophy of Nature* (1797, 1803; II, 39; 1988: 30).[6] One definition of naturephilosophy therefore runs: naturephilosophy is a naturalistic 'empiricism extended to the absolute' (III, 24; 2004: 22; t.m.).

In contrast *firstly*, therefore, to Jaspers' judgement that the 'ill-fatedness [*Verhängnis*]' of Schellingianism is demonstrated in that, despite its 'greatness', it 'produced no school, no movement, no followers' (1955: 213), therefore, the present work asserts firstly that Schellingianism is resurgent every time philosophy *reaches beyond the Kant-inspired critique of metaphysics, its subjectivist-epistemological transcendentalism, and its isolation of physics from metaphysics*. It is precisely because this latter, in particular, has constituted an unacknowledged two-worlds metaphysics for the present age, that Schellingian naturephilosophy remains not only 'examplary', but a definitive problematic for contemporary postkantian metaphysics. In contrast *secondly*, therefore, to the adherents of the Hegelian judgement that Schelling produced 'no finished philosophical system', but only 'a series of its developmental stages' (1955; III, 513), precisely because Schellingianism *is* naturephilosophy throughout, varying only according to its objects, we further assert that the unrecognizability of such a trajectory in postkantian philosophy is consequent upon the success of Kant's critical revolution in legislating the *conditioning and production* of appearances for finite rational intellects. An exposition of Schellingianism therefore entails the systematic undoing of the critical revolution. Accordingly, since we do not consider Schelling's own works the exhaustion but rather the inception of naturephilosophy, 'Schellingianism' designates the philosophical project of *unconditioning* the metaphysics of nature.

1.1 POSTKANTIAN NATUREPHILOSOPHY

[T]he φυσιολογοι are neither 'physiologists' in the contemporary sense of physiology as a special science of general biology . . . nor are they philosophers of nature. The φυσιολογοι is rather the genuine primordial title for a questioning about beings as a whole, the title for those who see that it is spoken out, who bring it to revealedness. (Heidegger 1995: 28)

The unconditioned necessity of *appearances* can be called natural necessity. (CPR A419/B447)

Heidegger here offers an exemplary account of why, for postkantian philosophy, i.e., all philosophy that draws on Kant for the matrix of its problems, naturephilosophy is a problem. In line, that is, with the Copernican revolution in philosophy whereby, sanctioned by the 'primacy of pure practical reason' (*Ak.* V, 119ff) over speculative reason, 'the unconditioned necessity of appearances' determines nature *subjectively* (rather than *substantially*; cf. Schelling 1989a: 5) in accordance with what becomes a 'natural necessity' (CPR A419/B447). Setting aside for the moment the ethico-practical engine driving the critical philosophy, not only, as Badiou succinctly puts it, does Kant's 'logic of appearance depose ontology' (2004: 171); rather, *natural* necessity alibis the excision of nature *itself* from metaphysics, leaving only a nature now determined as 'the whole of appearances' (*Ak.* IV, 467; Kant 1970: 3). The same excision underwrites Heidegger's account of the ancient 'physiologists': neither life-scientists nor philosophers of nature, the physio*logist* brings the 'whole of beings' *primordially* to language, which means that language, insofar as it is spoken out, supplants nature as the substrate in which beings inhere. Yet nature disputes that 'where word breaks off, no thing may be'; deep, geological time defeats a priori the prospect of its appearance for any finite phenomenologizing consciousness. This is why Schelling's postkantian confrontation with nature itself begins with the overthrow of the Copernican revolution; why, that is, it must refashion the theory of the subject and engage nature 'beyond simple representation' (Schelling 1989a: 20); why the primacy of the practical, rather than finding its alibi by analogy with organic nature, is ceded to a *geology* of morals, and why nature, *phusis*, is core to postkantian philosophy.

There is a further, intra-naturephilosophical sense in which Heidegger's statement advertises its postkantianism: the determination of nature in terms of '*beings* as a whole'. At the outset of the *Metaphysical Foundations of Natural Science*, Kant defines nature as 'the sum total of all things', before adding the familiar Copernican caveat, 'insofar as they can be objects of our senses' (*Ak*. IV, 467; Kant 1970: 3). At stake here is a further ground for the elimination of nature itself from philosophy, insofar as the latter is nominalistically reduced to natural *things*: 'Existentia est singulorum', as the Scholastic nominalists had it (cf. XI, 279). It is a short step from this nominalistic metaphysics to the physics of simples, to the atomisms of various kinds that continue to play a defining role in the metaphysical grounds of the natural sciences as the 'mildest form of reductionism', the 'basic tenet of science', i.e., that it investigate *not nature itself*, but rather 'an isolated part of the world' (Omnès 1999: 229). Far from being the originator of this twofold nominalization of nature – its linguistic determination on the one hand, and its reduction to entities on the other – Kant, and Heidegger, along with postkantian philosophy in general, follow Simplicius' account of Aristotle's physics as 'the physics of all things [*ta physika panta pragmata*]' (*In Physicam* 198.28), which stands opposed to Plato's 'physics of the all [*tou pantos phuseos*]' (*Tim.* 47a9, 27a5). As a result of this divergence, Aristotelianism generates considerable trouble with the nature of 'the ultimate, underlying subject [*hypokeimenon*, "subjectum"] common to all the things of nature' (*Phys.* 192a), just as the antinomy of teleological judgement drives Kant to seek a substrate 'underlying' nature and freedom (*Ak.* V, 176; Kant 1987: 15).[7]

The problem of the substrate brings us to a further determination of the philosophical nature of postkantianism. It forms, for example, one of the elements of the rejection of Kantianism proposed by Badiou as 'rethinking the concept of ground' (2000: 44–5). Having made nature into (a) the totality of natural bodies and (b) *one pole* of the two united by a substrate underlying both, it is clear that for Kant, nature cannot be that substrate (*hypokeimenon* or *sub-jectum* – the subordinate or 'sub-jected [*das Unterworfene*]' (XI, 319, 333–5) *itself*. Kant's conclusions in the third *Critique* are presaged in the polarity between the 'merely logical concept of ground' (Schelling 1989a: 5) Kant advances in the *Nova dilucidatio* (1755) and the *Only Possible Argument in Support of a Demonstration of the Existence of God* (1763), on the one hand, and the naturalistic concept of ground articulated in the essays on volcanism and cosmogony, on the other. Noting that Kant's philosophy unsatisfactorily 'segregated organic nature from general natural science' (VI, 8) and therefore failed to transform his piecemeal considerations of natural science into a general naturephilosophy, Schelling reexamines the question of ground throughout his corpus, reengineering the concept of the subject from its post- to its pre-kantian acceptation as *subjectum*, thus aiding our understanding of the 'nature as subject' thesis.[8] The naturephilosophical rethinking of the concept of ground is particularly evident, however, in the *Philosophical Inquiries into the Nature of Human Freedom*. That work draws on the naturalistic concept of ground examined in Kant's precritical essays on volcanism and the age of the earth, i.e., on *geology* or 'geophilosophy', in order to resolve the antinomy of teleological judgement. Schelling repositions this antinomy as 'the ungrounding that precedes all ground' (VII, 406; 1986: 87, t.m.) and 'the self-operation of the ground' (VII, 379; 1986: 56, t.m.), the dynamic combination of the two giving rise to nature as 'the ground of existence' (VII, 358; 1986: 32, t.m). Schelling's resolution of the antinomy is premised on the abolition of the restriction of agency to consciously purposive rational beings, on the one hand, and the consequent location of activity to nature itself, on the other. This in turn clearly opposes the Aristotelian and Kantian accounts of physics as 'the physics of all *things*' or 'bodies' (somatism),[9] since it proposes that 'things', beings or entities, are consequent upon nature's activity, rather than this latter being inexplicably grounded in the properties or accidents of bodies. The philosophy of nature itself, in other words, is no longer grounded in somatism, but in the dynamics from which all ground, and all bodies, issue: 'matter is precisely just matter, that is, the ground of bodies, but immediately therefore, not corporeal' (X, 328).

Contemporarily, Deleuze has revisited the Schellingian resolution of the antinomy of nature and freedom by positing a 'geology of morals',[10] having initially reexamined that resolution in an inquiry into the overtly Schellingian 'dynamic process of construction' that 'must embrace all the concepts of nature and freedom' (1994: 19). In this latter work, Deleuze makes a great deal of the concept of 'ungrounding' and its relation to geology, borrowing passages from geologist and naturephilosopher Heinrik Steffens' 'On the oxydation and de-oxydation process of the Earth' (*Journal for Speculative Physics* (1800) 1.i.: 152–3; Schelling 2001: 101–2), along with Schelling's commentary thereon from the *Further Presentations from the System of Philosophy* (IV, 504; *New Journal of Speculative Physics* (1802) 1.ii.: 172–3), in order to establish a 'transcendental volcanism' (Deleuze 1994: 230). While therefore Deleuze's philosophical impetus is clearly postkantian, and while the 'geology of morals' clearly points towards the 'philosophy of nature' he and Guattari were working on shortly before the latter's death (Deleuze 1995: 140), the idea of a *transcendental* volcanism clearly proposes a radicalization of transcendental philosophy that differs substantially not only from Schelling's geophilosophy, running from the commentaries on Steffens to the *Philosophical Inquiries*, but also from his overtly neoplatonizing 'physics of the All'. Kantian versus Platonic geophilosophy: in either case, the Deleuzian example makes clear that postkantianism marks the horizon of contemporary philosophy exactly as it did in the early nineteenth century, and draws particular focus onto what Schelling considered the 'utterly natural and conceptually secure . . . result of Kantian critique', namely, 'the transition to naturephilosophy' (1989a: 37).

Accordingly, we accept Badiou's counter-Deleuzian view that philosophy ought to have done with overturning Platonism (although not for the same reasons), and must reject Kantianism in its stead (insofar as the transcendental in Kant becomes the merely logical ground of phenomena).[11] This view

is premised on the characterization of the philosophical present as importantly postkantian, not merely in the historical sense of succeeding Kant, but
philosophically, in that it is defined by the coordinates set by Kant for philosophical activity. However, we reject the basis of Badiou's neoplatonism, in
that it forsakes *physis* for formalism. This is not merely to rehearse the
'number or animal (= Plato or Aristotle)?' problem by which Badiou, in his
polemical essay on Deleuze's *The Fold* (Badiou 1997), sought to differentiate
his own from the latter's philosophy, and to conclude, with (Badiou's)
Deleuze, in favour of animal, since, as is argued below, this is itself to
recapitulate one of the central themes of the immediate postkantian response
to the philosophical problem of nature. The view that nature extends no
further than animality owes a great deal to Fichte's radicalization of Kant's
antinomic conclusions regarding teleological as opposed to mechanical
causality in the 'Antinomy of Teleological Judgment'. However, because
physis, nature, extends beyond animality, or beyond *organized bodies in
general*, the polarity Badiou establishes remains inconclusive with regard to
Deleuze's own 'philosophy of nature'. Further, in opposing his own Platonism
to Deleuze's alleged Aristotelianism in terms of number and animal, Badiou
seems to leave the *Timaeus*' dealings with both number and animal out of
account. This is because Badiou regards the *Timaeus* as 'a novel, a fabulous
and eccentric narration' (2000: 70), rather than, as Proclus understood it, a
work of physics that 'embraces the whole of physiology and . . . pertains to
the theory of the universe' (1997: 1). In other words, whereas Badiou,
buying into the 'likely story' account of Plato's *Timaeus*, wants a mathe-
matizing neoplatonism bereft of nature as an ontological problem, Schelling
constructs a Platonic physics of which Badiou remains unaware,[12] and in
which initial inquiries into the central naturephilosophical problematic of the
genesis of matter, or the materiality of becomings, are launched.

The contemporary inconceivability of a Platonic physics, and of a modern
philosophy of *nature* grounded on it, demonstrates a lacuna in any understanding of metaphysics premised on the 'two-worlds' thesis that, since
Nietzsche, has been understood as deriving from Platonism. But the centrality
of *phusis* to metaphysics demonstrated in the *Timaeus*, and embraced by
Schelling's naturephilosophy, demonstrates that the two-worlds thesis is
derived from elsewhere. In *Treatise Explicatory of the Idealism in the Science
of Knowledge* (1797), Schelling will argue that it is the critical revolution
itself that 'locates the standpoint from which to examine the world itself not
within the world but outside of it' (I, 400; 1994c: 102), and thus establishes
a two-worlds metaphysics. Fichte's *Science of Knowledge*, which self-
consciously presents itself as building on the foundations of Kant's 'yet-to-
be-completed whole' (*W* I, 479n, 485; 1982: 51, 57), obligingly confirms
Schelling's diagnosis: 'Intellect and thing . . . inhabit two worlds between
which there is no bridge' (*W* I, 436; 1982: 17). Schelling, however, will locate
the source of Kanto-Fichteanism's two worlds in Kant's 'segregation of
organic nature from general natural science' (VI, 8), making it appear as if
'the animal itself is no longer matter, but an entity of quite another kind, as

if from another world' (XI, 334). In other words, it is Kant's 'failure' to transform his *Metaphysical Foundations of Natural Science* into the basis of a *'philosophy* of nature' (VI, 7–8) that produces a two-worlds *physics* from which Fichte will derive his two-worlds *metaphysics*, renouncing all philosophical claim on nature (see chapter 3, below). It is for these reasons that Schelling's naturephilosophy begins with a study of the one-world physics presented in Plato's *Timaeus* ([1794] 1994a), set against the background of problems from Kant's critical philosophy (chapter 2).

Postkantian philosophy has repeatedly reverted to organism, to the phenomena of *life*, precisely to head off naturephilosophical incursions. In other words, inherent in the problem of organism, as we have seen, is a *two-worlds physics*. Life acts as a an Orphic guardian for philosophy's descent into the physical. This is because life provides an effective alibi against accusations of philosophy's tendency to 'antiphysics', while centralizing ethico-political or existential problematics as philosophy's true domain. For such philosophies, it is a short step from 'biocentrism' to 'logocentrism', as Bernouilli and Kern (1926: viii) falsely – but significantly – characterize the poles of Schelling's naturephilosophy. While seeming to constitute a metaphysics capable of nature, the philosophy of organism, therefore, carries with it the danger of a metaphysics premised on a 'great gulf fixed' between nature and freedom, as Kant had it (*Ak.* V, 174; 1987: 14; see also, *Ak.* V, 195; 1987: 35), and it is along this rift that all postkantian naturephilosophies are aligned. The persistence of this problem stems almost entirely from the ambivalent position Kant's third *Critique* accorded reflective judgements of purpose in natural phenomena: in brief, Kant's scepticism regarding the prospects for a naturalistic science of life facilitated the assimilation of the phenomena of life and organic nature to the realm of mind alone. Amongst the first fruits of this are Fichte's 'Propositons regarding the Essence of Animals' (1811), which argues that organic matter is as far down the *scala naturae* that Mind may descend, since 'life is autonomy in the realm of appearance', as Schelling characterizes the phenomenological roots of that philosophy (I, 249). Despite the naturephilosophy disputing this one-sidedness, the metaphysical dissymmetry that retains biology as a philosophical science while rejecting geology or chemistry from its remit has haunted the philosophy of nature ever since, finding expression, in varying ways, in Nietzsche, Bergson, and (particularly in Badiou's criticisms of) Deleuze.

By contrast, it had been an integral element of Schelling's naturephilosophy since *On the World Soul* (1798) that the perimeter dividing organic from 'anorgic' nature be eliminated as naturalistically untenable and philosophically vicious, in order that organization become not an exception to a mechanistic natural order, but rather the *principle* of nature itself. This was already implicit in the early attention Schelling gave the concept of 'self-organizing nature' (I, 386; 1994b: 92, t.m.). While this solution to the problems of subjectivity and organization in nature invites Schelling's reevaluation as a precursor of developments regarding non-linearity, self-organization and complexity in the natural sciences (as Heuser-Keßler (1986), Mutschler (1997) and Warnke (1998) have done), from the earliest works on naturephilosophy, Schelling was clear that it was no part of that philosophy's purpose to engage in the 'pitiful, mundane occupation' of 'apply[ing] philosophy to natural science' (II, 6; 1988: 5). To provide such reevaluations in the light of later developments in the natural sciences is not only anachronistic, but also positivistically reduces, as Popper recommends, philosophical interventions into nature to a theoretical resource to be raided as and when the natural sciences deem it necessary, stripping the usable core of naturephilosophy from the 'neomedievalising obscurantism' (Depew and Weber 1996: 55) of its metaphysics.

Given that Bernouilli and Kern's (1926: viii) characterization of naturephilosophy's 'biocentrism' has become the dominant mode of understanding Schelling's in particular, but *Naturphilosophie* in general (cf. Jaspers 1955, Ayrault 1976, Esposito 1977, Gould 1977, Bach 2001, Jardine 2000, Beiser 2002), the problem of organization warrants attention before we proceed. When Kant, in the *Critique of Teleological Judgment*, circumscribes phenomenal access to 'organic causality', or natural teleology, to reflective consciousness alone, he prepares the way for the ontologically quietist vitalism of the Kant–Blumenbach research programme, where the 'maxim' of our reason, that we should restrict judgements of purpose to subjective reflection, and consider them void of objective purchase (see *Ak*. V, 397–401), is transformed into a merely *formal* principle for the restriction of the philosophical inquiry into nature to the contents of 'natural' consciousness.[13] In the name of 'transcendental philosophy', this merely formal vitalism refuses the 'reduction' of life to matter as much as it rejects the accessibility of matter to consciousness. Since Schelling rejects precisely this quietism regarding nature, and eliminates what Blumenbach (1781: 81), earning Kant's approval (*Ak*. V, 424; 1987: 311), characterized as the 'gulf' between organic and 'anorgic' nature, this elimination does not merely entail a transcendental or ideal organicism applied *all the way down* to so-called inanimate matter, as the cliché regarding Romantic naturephilosophy would have it; it also entails an uninterrupted physicalism leading from 'the real to the ideal' (cf. III, 272f; 2004: 194f; III, 342–3; 1978: 6–7). In other words, rather than a projection of organicism 'downstream' in the scale of nature, organization is a power or *Potenz* of 'the self-construction of matter' (IV, 4). Accordingly, what the first of Schelling's trilogy of early naturephilosophical works, the *Ideas for a Philosophy of Nature* (1797), refers to as 'organic physics' (II, 8; 1988: 7), does not simply mean that organism is the dominant paradigm of all physics, but especially that there is, *pace* Kant's sceptical conclusions in this regard, a *physics of organization*.

Yet there are instances in Schelling's philosophy where the physicalistic treatment of the problem of organization seems to give way to the practical-philosophical problematic of *the evaluation of organism*, that has dominated the philosophical determination of nature from Kant and Fichte on. The problematic arises in Schelling's search for a system of philosophy that

11

'would be strong enough to withstand the test of life' (XIII, 177). There are two ways of understanding this test: as testing philosophical systems against their capacity for explaining the entire range of the phenomena of organic life, from non-organic matter through to ideation, so that it can be assessed whether or not philosophy has indeed 'become genetic' (II, 39; 1988: 30); or as testing philosophical systems against their *utility* for life, as Nietzsche will do. Jaspers' strong foregrounding of the *Lebensprobe* in Schelling (1955: 114, *passim*) clearly aligns it with this latter, existentialist-*Lebensphilosophische* trajectory, whereas the former account is in accord with the general development of Schelling's naturephilosophy from the *Ideas for a Philosophy of Nature* (1797) on, which Jaspers almost entirely ignores. Nevertheless, Schelling's focus on *life* in this context is indicative of a tension within the naturephilosophy, a tension, itself naturalistically grounded, between a *linear* and a *non-linear* use of the theory of recapitulation. Schelling draws this theory from natural historian and comparative anatomist Carl Friedrich Kielmeyer's *Discourse on the Continuous Development of Organic Forces throughout the Series of Organizations* ([1794] 1938: 59–101), a text from which, as *On the World Soul* (II, 565) famously asserts, 'future times will doubtless reckon the advent of a new era in natural history'. The linear use of the concept places a single natural product at nature's summit, this product generally being humanity (e.g., XI, 400). As Schelling puts it in the first issue of the *Annals of Medical Science* (1806), 'The science of medicine is the crown and blossom of all the natural sciences, just as the organism in general, and the human organism in particular, is the crown and blossom of the world' (VII, 131). Such instances, however, are relatively rare; conversely, therefore, the 'Foreword' to the first issue of the *Journal of Speculative Physics* ([1800] 2001: 5) announces that the second issue will 'continue the critique of theories of organic nature begun in the present, interrupted, essays'. The essays interrupted here include[14] Schelling's *Universal Deduction of the Dynamic Process* (1800), in which Schelling does indeed undertake a critique of the two-worlds physics attendant upon the isolation of organic from inorganic matter, or organized from non-organized bodies: 'Since organic nature as such is nothing other than the self-recapitulation of the inorganic at a higher power [*Potenz*], with the categories of the construction of matter in general, those for the construction of the organic product are also given' (IV, 4).

The theory of recapitulation remained controversial throughout the major debates in the early nineteenth-century life sciences between Kielmeyer's pupil, Georges Cuvier, and the 'transcendental morphology' of Etienne Geoffroy Saint-Hilaire in France, between Richard Owen and Darwin in England, and between Johann Friedrich Meckel and Karl Ernst von Baer in Germany.[15] Picking up directly from Kielmeyer's argument that recapitulation applied throughout nature, and not just to its organic part, *Naturphilosophen* such as Lorenz Oken ([1802–10] 1847) in the life sciences, Karl Joseph Windischmann (1805)[16] in general physics, and Heinrik Steffens (1801) in geology, broadened the problematic, and introduced the naturephilosophical as well as the natural scientific problems it raised. Following especially from Kielmeyer's argument that recapitulation operated not solely in the organic, but also in the inorganic realm, i.e., from cosmogony through to the production of the higher mammals, the passage cited above demonstrates Schelling adopting a *non-linear* use of the theory of recapitulation, whereby *the unit of recapitulation* is the 'dynamic process' itself, the 'continuous self-construction of matter . . . recapitulated at various levels' (ibid.). In other words, in keeping with Schelling's physicalism regarding the genesis of organic matter, organism – or organization – results simply from matter acting on its self-construction, or from increasingly complex organizations of the inorganic. Nothing, however, suggests that there is a given *terminus* of recapitulation, which is rather 'continuous' and 'variant'. Indeed, rather than *resulting* in the formation of 'humanity' as nature's highest product, 'naturephilosophy conceives matter as . . . unrestricted being' (1989a: 52), as 'the *material* of the universal' (XI, 313) which, in its dynamic activity, will repeatedly bring about 'a new race equipped with new organs of thought' (1989a: 57). What Schelling's naturephilosophical treatment of recapitulation achieves, then, is a successive unconditioning of the concept of recapitulation as regards the *unit of recapitulation*, which, rather than being located in a particular body, whether an atom, a chemical compound, an organism, or a planet, is itself the dynamic process of the self-construction of matter. This has far-reaching consequences concerning the reducibly naturalistic use of the concept of recapitulation: identifying a recapitulation event, in other words, is dependent upon first identifying what it is that is being recapitulated. As Clark and Jacyna note concerning the emergence of neuroanatomy, this was a live issue in the sciences of the era: 'Romantic theoretical assumptions . . . presented the student of the nervous system with a central problem: to identify the "type" – the basal element – of nervous organization [and] how this type became progressively elaborated' (Clark and Jacyna 1987: 44).

The identification of a *physically instantiated* type is not simply resolved by such devices as Goethe's *Urtyp*; for having identified, say, the 'primal type' for a given plant, the question then arises as to the basal element of the primal plant-type in turn: does the primal plant arise, as it were, *ex nihilo*, or are the elements from which it has itself developed themselves developed instances of more basic types? The task of identification is in principle as limitless as naturephilosophy conceives matter to be (1989a: 52), provoking a debate between Kielmeyer and Windischmann as to whether or not the basal element of recapitulation *can* be circumscribed within a given natural class of entities. In this way, the theory of recapitulation is the basis of the naturephilosophical theory of identity that assumes centre stage in Schelling's work after 1801 (see ch. 4, below).

The theory of recapitulation cannot a priori, but only on theoretical-instrumental grounds, be reduced to the naturalistic applications made of it in the internal histories of the special sciences (Omnès' 'mildest form of reductionism'), or in contemporary debates that may be said to owe something to these, such as the 'unit of selection' problem that divides neo-Darwinism and

13

population genetics.[17] Nor, however, is the nature*philosophical* residue reducible to a 'world 3' stockpile of ideas for Popperian scientistic exploitation.[18] As we have noted above, the principal method of naturephilosophy consists in 'unconditioning' the phenomena. In this instance, therefore, Schelling will work through successive unconditionings of the unit of recapitulation in order to reach the self-construction of matter, which is nothing other than 'recapitulation itself', which will be the focus of our attention in chapter 4.

Accordingly, Schelling certainly problematizes the relation between *linear* and *non-linear* recapitulation in nature by way of the 'test of life', which *apparent* reversion to Kanto-Fichteanism seems similarly implicit in the late *Exhibition of the Natural Process* (1844): 'organic nature begins where the blind principle first sees itself as free, no longer being a blind and unconscious entity, but rather one that is conscious of itself', and becomes its own 'goal, aim and purpose' (X, 375–6). Yet, as in the *Timaeus* essay at the beginning of Schelling's oeuvre, so in the works of his last decade, Kantianism is set against a Platonic backdrop, with continuous referencing of the Platonic theory of matter (e.g., XI, 324, 392, 398, 401, 423–4). Even in the *Philosophy of Revelation* (1854), where the 'test of life' is propounded, Schelling continues to assert the 'indwelling and inborn logic in nature' (XIII, 102), to advocate a naturalistic empiricism (XIII, 103), and to reject any naturephilosophy premised on the determination of nature in accordance with its appearing-to-consciousness (XIII, 4–6), all of which contravene Kantian critical injunctions. While, therefore, the similarities between Schelling's late naturephilosophical turn to life, organism, and the practical determination of nature and the Kanto-Fichtean critical programme may be initially striking, the crucial difference, even at this stage, remains that, unlike the critical philosophy of organism, Schelling is concerned with *bodies*, i.e., with *physically* determinable units of recapitulation.

1.2 THE NATURE OF POSTKANTIANISM

For Schelling, Kant is the turning point, Fichte's idealism the foundation, and he himself the completion of the philosophy of freedom. (Jaspers 1955: 178)

Jaspers here provides the basic type of the frequently reiterated and erroneous proposition that naturephilosophy amounts to an extension of Kant's or Fichte's critical philosophies.[19] Schelling, by contrast, takes repeated pains to distinguish critical- from nature-philosophy. As the exchange of letters between Schelling and Fichte, which ran from 1800 until the appearance of Hegel's highly critical *Difference between the Fichtean and the Schellingian Systems of Philosophy*, shows,[20] Fichte himself originated the claim that, whatever 'differences of opinion' there might be between them, these did not constitute 'obstacles to a common project' (Fichte to Schelling, 27 December

1800, in Schulte-Sasse 1997: 79). Ironically, after asserting insurmountable differences between the two philosophers in the *Difference* essay, it was Hegel himself who, in the *Lectures on the History of Philosophy*, notoriously cemented Fichte's 'common project' claim by making Schelling nothing more than Fichte's successor. The *Difference* essay, meanwhile, differentiates between Fichte and Schelling *precisely* on the grounds of their respective capacities for a naturephilosophy. While 'Fichte comes closer than Kant to managing the antithesis of nature and freedom and exhibiting nature as an absolute effect and as dead' (Hegel 1977a: 143), Schellingian nature *itself* 'has freedom[, f]or nature is not a stillness of being, it is a being that becomes' (Hegel 1977a: 168). Moreover, Hegel finds the roots of Fichte's dead nature in his 'deduction' of the organic or 'material body' as 'nothing more' than the *objectively posited limit* segregating 'the sphere of all the person's possible free actions' (Fichte W III: 59; 2000: 56) from the 'atomistic lifelessness' of external nature (Hegel 1977a: 142). In other words, as we have already found, the basis of two-worlds metaphysics lies in a two-worlds physics: the inert, inorganic world of external nature, and the organic world from which 'nature has withdrawn her hand', leaving humanity free to articulate the organic body (W III: 79–80; 2000: 74). Again, it is therefore ironic that it is Hegel himself who, in his *Philosophy of Nature*, sets the seal on the exteriorization of nature from philosophy.[21] Organism does not provide the ground uniting nature and freedom, but merely the locus of a failed attempt to accommodate physics. Thereafter, this failure will no longer occasion, for Fichte, the scepticism it did for Kant, who despaired of finding a 'Newton of the blade of grass' (*Ak.* V, 400; 1987: 282–3), but will instead become a triumphalistic *antiphysics* that celebrates and polices the inadequacies of physics: the 'natural law [*Naturrecht*]' now runs 'nature is determined immediately by and for intelligence' (Hegel 1977a: 143). This naturephilosophical contradiction will subsequently inform the bedrock of most phenomenological and all ethico-political philosophy, alongside the linguistic idealism that represents 'nature' as determined solely in and for language.

By contrast, no sooner is it accepted that Schelling shares the Kanto-Fichtean transcendental-critical account of organism, than it becomes a simple matter to combine Schelling's transcendental philosophy with his early, so-called 'Fichtean' works, thereby reducing naturephilosophy to a means whereby consciousness attains insights into a nature *of its own manufacture*. Frequent citations from Schelling concerning the role of the *Ich* are held to demonstrate this, such as the concept of the 'transfer of the I onto nature' that the *Ideas for a Philosophy of Nature* acknowledges as a 'peculiarity of our power of conception'[22] only to dismiss (but that remains a stubborn refrain in accounts of Schelling's naturephilosophy),[23] or what Vater suggestively calls the 'transfinite mentality' of the *System of Transcendental Idealism* (Vater, in Schelling 1978: xxxiii),[24] and which Schelling will later, in the *Introduction to Philosophy* (1830), designate 'subjectobjectivity'.[25]

The Schellingian theory of the subject itself (see ch. 4. below), of the *auto kath' auto*, has little or nothing to do with issues of selfhood and consciousness. The theory of 'nature as subject' (III, 284; 2004: 202), therefore, does not entail the projection of the familiar furniture of first-person reflective consciousness onto the interior of an actually intentional nature, which would amount to transforming Kant's *reflective* into *constitutive* judgements of natural purpose, but is more akin to the Leibnizian 'nature itself'. In other words, there is no forced or analogical export of the *conditions* (transcendental or physiological) of consciousness onto an entity called 'nature'. As William Wallace noted in 1894, the 'excess of objectivity' (1931: 107) characteristic of Schelling's philosophy means that the *Ich*, as the ideal principle, has, like matter, 'no interiority' and 'no predicates'; neither are *in themselves* 'a thing' (III, 368; 1978: 26–7). On the contrary, 'they' are *unthinged* (*unbedingt*), leaving open for the moment the plausibility of the differentiation or numerical identification of unpredicables. The only 'self' there is, is misconstrued in both the transcendental- and the nature-philosophy when viewed as empirical, reflective, or transcendental consciousness; rather, the self as principle is the *itself*, the *to auto*, of the unconditioned (*das Unbedingt*) which cannot be a thing (*Ding*; cf. I, 166; 1980: 74). The *auto* has the irremediable externality of the automatic, the autonomic, its only 'in itself' deriving exclusively from the irreversibility of dependency relations stemming *from* it, rather than extending *to* it. As Camilla Warnke notes, 'Schelling's autopoietic systems could equally be *technical systems, machines*, to the extent that they fulfil the determinant conditions of autopoiesis' (1998: 233). In other words, the foundational relation, for Fichte, of the absolute to the empirical I, is transformed in Schelling: on the one hand, the production of an empirical I is merely a conditioning of the unconditioned; on the other hand, the unconditioned I has a nature which, rather than empirical consciousness, corresponds to the self-acting of a *subjectnature*. This concept has, of course, a long history, from Plotinus (III.8.iv) to Kielmeyer (1938: 63ff), von Uexküll (1965: 90) to Merleau-Ponty (2003: 177). In none of these cases have we to do with an ascription of 'subjectivity' to nature that would be recognizable from the standard post-eighteenth-century philosophical concept of 'the subject'.

The critical reduction of naturephilosophy thus fatally obscures the transformation Schelling undertook in the nature of the subject itself, the '*to auto*', and leaves the naturephilosophy prey to subsumption under the general clichés surrounding Idealism: that it *anthropomorphizes* nature, or that it consists solely in the determination of nature by intellect, so that nature is reduced to a nature of the phenomenalizing conscious subject's own manufacture *in accordance with essentially ethico-practical ends*. This principle, inherited from the ontological quietism attendant upon the Kant-Blumenbach restriction of organic causation to subjective judgement alone, informs the vast majority of postkantian developments in the philosophy of nature: Schopenhauer's 'world as will and appearance'; Nietzsche's 'physiological philosophy'; Marx's restriction of agency to the social body as the sole actor on 'the earth, man's inorganic body' (Marx 1993: 488); Bergson's demonstrations of the continued dominance of mechanics over biology in science and philosophy; *Lebensphilosophie*, and so on, all of which extend the possibility of activity and cognition only so far as the limits of the organic reach.

In this sense, the framework within which the philosophical encounter with nature takes place remains, after two hundred years, that established by Kant's *Critique of Teleological Judgment*. Even contemporarily therefore, we find the exclusive disjunction 'number or animal' dominating the metaphysics of nature: pure formalism versus organicism. Yet both the formal critique of the organic and the organic critique of the formal, operate on a shared basis: the suppression of inorganic externality established in Hegel's *Philosophy of Nature*. The reason for this tacit enforcement of such a restriction of naturephilosophy is simple: it provides the alibi for the maintenance of politics and ethics, or for the preservation of the 'ancient (Greek) division of philosophy into physics and ethics' (IV, 92). On one side, the field of human action must remain the sole locus of autonomy, possessing no substrate but the ethico-practical; on the other, autonomy is enshrined in nature itself, as 'its own lawgiver' (III, 17; 2004: 17). In other words, the antinomy of teleological judgement, i.e., the mutual exteriority of nature and freedom, remains the axis around which philosophy is organized. Postkantian philosophical inquiry must therefore, as Deleuze writes, 'embrace all the concepts of nature and freedom' (1994: 19).

Along this axis therefore, the *Philosophical Inquiries into the Essence of Human Freedom* occupies a crucial position. This is not, *pace* Jaspers, insofar as Schelling therein turns away from the early naturalism towards a later proto-existentialism or *Lebensphilosophie*, but rather, insofar as it constitutes a naturalistic resolution of the antinomy of nature and freedom, it exemplifies the above Deleuzian injunction regarding the nature of postkantianism. On the one hand, the *Philosophical Inquiries* responds to the concerns raised in the earliest works regarding the possibility of a philosophy of history, to which Schelling now returns on the grounds that, rather than a naturalistic grounding constituting the elimination of history, history cannot be history unless it has precisely such a grounding. Despite therefore the author's categorization of *all* his earlier work as belonging to naturephilosophy (VII, 333; 1986: 3), to infer that the *Freedom* essay constitutes a break with this philosophical past would be precipitate: the work remains a contribution to the naturephilosophy to the extent that it lays the groundwork for the 'system of times' (the magnetic, the electrical, and the organic) that occupy the *Ages of the World* (1811–20) through to the *Philosophy of Revelation* (1854). Its concern with the 'self-operation of the ground' (VII, 379; 1986: 56, t.m.) is a geological eruption in the midst of the philosophy of freedom (cf. Krafft 1993: 12), and an incursion of the system of times into the construction of matter. Rather than a substantive turn from naturephilosophy, the *Freedom* essay again demonstrates the persistence of naturephilosophy throughout his work, linking the emergence of the later philosophies of time, mythology and revelation, with naturephilosophy as the 'substrate' of philosophy in general, as Schelling says in 1830. Precisely the conjunction of nature and time had, of course, been a problem that Kant developed out of the late eighteenth century's fright in the face of natural history:

> How many such [natural] revolutions (including, certainly, many ancient organic beings, no longer alive on the surface of the earth) preceded the existence of man, and how many (accompanying, perhaps, a more perfect organization) are still in prospect, is hidden from our inquiring gaze – for, according to Camper, not a single example of a human being is to be found in the depth of the earth. (*Ak.* XXI, 215; 1993: 67)

The terror provoked by the fossil record – a 'sublime of time' – rearticulates the antinomy of nature and freedom by acknowledging the dependency of reason on catastrophic species-change, and thus requires Kant to produce the *Transition from Metaphysics to Physics* to make good the expulsion of non-organic nature from his earlier naturephilosophy.[26] Similarly, in the 1797 essay 'Is a Philosophy of History Possible?' (I, 466–73), Schelling had proceeded antinomically: history is possible only where there is freedom; there is no freedom, but only necessity, in nature; 'nature is the embodiment [*Inbegriff*] of everything that has happened and thus qualifies as the object of history' (I, 466); therefore, a 'philosophy that begins from *freedom* thereby eliminates everything outside us' and so '*a philosophy of history is impossible*' (I, 473). The *Philosophical Inquiries*, conversely, begin with the *conjunction*, rather than the disjunction, of nature and history, now that nature is itself subject, and ground naturalistically conceived as 'self-operative' (VII, 379; 1986: 56). Natural history, then, does not consist solely in empirical accounts of the development of organizations on the earth's surface, nor in any synchronic cataloguing of these. Its philosophical foundations make it a science that attempts to straddle the gulf between history, as the product of freedom, and nature, as the product of necessity, as Schelling's analysis shows. That it had such philosophical impact can be seen from Kant's discussions of it in *On Using Teleological Principles in Philosophy* (*Ak.* VIII, 161–2) and *Critique of Teleological Judgment* (*Ak.* V, 428n; 1987: 315), and from Girtanner's attempt to subject this science to 'philosophical scrutiny' in *On the Kantian Principle in Natural History* (1796).[27]

Naturephilosophy rejects the vitalist alibi that maintains the isolation of organic from inorganic matter. To the extent that any naturephilosophy retains a *particular* kind of physical organization – any body whatever – as its 'primal type', it remains necessarily Kanto-Fichtean. Schelling gives the implications of this particularization with particular poignancy in the form of the 'test of life', which has retained enormous value in subsequent naturephilosophies, from Nietzsche to Bergson, from existentialism to Deleuze: such naturephilosophies, that is, have invariably given the vital instance as the particular physical organization, or contingent physical product, from which philosophy may ascend to action and consciousness *independent of the motions of matter in general*.[28] It is the argument of the present work that this has been the prevailing case wherever the philosophy of nature has suffered even the slightest return to philosophical prominence, so that the situation of contemporary philosophy, from this perspective, remains that of the immediately postkantian period. By way of the naturephilosophy, Schelling provides a rare instance of the as yet mostly untried consequences of exiting the Kantian framework which has held nature in its analogical grasp for the two hundred years since its inception.

Naturephilosophy accordingly rejects these Kantian constraints, and pursues nature beyond the merely analogical relation established by the third *Critique* between nature and intellection. In more contemporary terms, naturephilosophy, that is, disputes the logico-linguistic or phenomenal determination of nature; rejects the primacy of the practical; reworks the theory of the subject as a theory not of 'self', but of *the itself*, the subject '*kath' auto*', and a corresponding theory, therefore, of 'nature as subject'. It thus *unconditions* the construction of concepts with regard to the 'self-construction of matter' (IV, 4); conceptual genesis and natural genesis become one and the same; or, in other words, *nature autoproduces its self*. The further unconditioning of *time* as the merely subjective a priori form of inner sense that is therefore *implicit* in Schelling's injunction that 'philosophy become genetic' (II, 39; 1988: 30), in accordance with the polar externalities of the *auto* and matter, is made precisely explicit by the equally disorienting externality of the 'system of times' in the *Ages of the World*, and the geology of morals that becomes possible due to the *Philosophical Inquiries*' embracing of natural history.

These themes, then, become the central contexts in which the naturephilosophical challenge can be posed not merely to postkantian philosophy as an episode in the history of philosophy, but to the postkantianism that remains foundational for contemporary philosophy. In consequence of the philosophical currency therefore attaching to the naturephilosophical programme, Schelling is a contemporary philosopher.

1.3 THE HISTORY OF PHILOSOPHY AS THE COMPARATIVE EXTENSITY OF PHILOSOPHICAL SYSTEMS

The transcendental idealist . . . must have the courage to assert the strongest idealism that has ever been taught, and not even to fear the charge of speculative egoism. (Jacobi [1787] 2000b: 175)

Our account opens with investigations in the history of philosophy. These investigations are essentially premised around a test Schelling first conducted in his 1794 commentary on Plato's *Timaeus*, and the Platonic 'physics of the All' (*Tim.* 47a4) remains the basis for all subsequent testing of philosophical systems. Schelling specifies the basis of the test as follows 'true philosophical science is cognition of the universe [*das All*]' (VIII, 50). Philosophy, accordingly, is 'the infinite science' (II, 56; 1988: 42), and cannot therefore be 'conditioned [*bedingt*]' by eliminating anything a priori from its remit. It is in this sense that Schelling's is a philosophy of the absolute, or the 'unconditioned [*das Unbedingte*]', and no other. Moreover, 'let the absolute be thought of, to start with, purely as matter, as pure identity, as sheer absoluteness' (II, 62; 1988: 47), writes Schelling, indicating that the primary condition vitiating the unconditioned science, 'common to all modern philosophy', is that 'nature does not exist for it' (VII, 356; 1986: 30).

Naturephilosophy is not the partial and one-sided science Hegel presents in his *Difference* essay; Schelling always 'starts with' naturephilosophy because 'nature IS *a priori*' (III, 279; 2004: 198). Accordingly, the systemic relations between naturephilosophy and the transcendental philosophy, even in the identity philosophy, are dynamic, which dynamics – the 'grounding science of a theory of nature' (II, 6; 1988: 5) – derive from the naturephilosophy that continues to underlie, as we have seen, all Schelling's work. Yet neither therefore does Schelling propose a simple naturalistic or scientistic reductionism: the infinite science must test itself against the All, which lacks neither nature nor Idea. It is the *extensity* therefore, the *range* and *capacity* of philosophical systems that is being tested, and it so happens that historically, the principal symptom of their failure is the elimination of nature.

It is against this backdrop that Schelling conducts the 'testing of all previous systems' (II, 56; 1988: 42), beginning with the *Timaeus* commentary. This is, in one sense, an obvious starting point, insofar as it is the source-book of Platonic physics; in another, however, as a starting point for a modern philosophical physics, it seems at best strange: Plato, the very paradigm of the two-worlds metaphysician! Yet the 'physics of the All' demonstrates that Plato is in fact a one-world physicist, proposing, as natural science, the science of becoming, or dynamics. It is from this that the *Ideas for a Philosophy of Nature* will propose that 'philosophy become genetic' (II, 39; 1988: 30). The clear problem with the Platonic programme becomes that of the 'physics of the Idea', however, to which the *Timaeus* commentary allots considerable space. It is precisely because Platonism is capable of both nature and the Idea that the Kantian system is held against it. The results of this test are the conditioned reality Kant accords the Idea, and the irreality to which he ascribes nature. Schelling's testing of transcendental philosophy therefore continues in the *Ideas* with an examination of the incapacity of the philosophy of freedom for nature, and further continues with the series of works on Fichte's 'science of knowledge', provoking the latter to pursue an abortive naturephilosophy. Encompassing the empirical and the philosophical, however, Schelling equally pursues those theories of the naturalists that seek to conceive nature under various restricted rubrics: *On the World Soul* (1798), for example, examines among other things the dualism of organic and inorganic nature that Blumenbach derived from Kant, a procedure all but reversed with the late *Lebensprobe* (XII, 177), and which Jaspers (1955: 114) exploits to precisely that effect, using it to eliminate the naturephilosophy. Similarly, while the *Ideas* examines the dualism of force and body that Kant, in turn, absorbs through Newton, the *First Outline of a System of Naturephilosophy*, the *Introduction to the Outline* and the *Universal Deduction of the Dynamic Process* all pursue the hybrids of somatic and dynamic physics that vitiate the prospect of a true dynamics. As we shall see, Schelling's test of the naturalists sets them against Kielmeyer's dynamic natural history, which the naturephilosophy will seek to extend, in pursuit of 'the unconditioned in nature' (III, 11; 2004: 13), to the Idea.

Schelling's testing of systems for their comparative extensity – a dynamics rather than a mechanics of the concept – does not emerge in a vacuum: the dawn of philosophy as science is accompanied by the constant issuing of tests and challenges, such as Jacobi's momentous challenge to Kant. Such procedures echo the extreme objectivism, the scientificity, that characterizes German Idealism's inaugurated philosophical science. When, therefore, Schellingian naturephilosophy is raised, it does not merely sit episodically amongst other systems and artifacts of the antiquarian intellect, but challenges systems to reveal what they eliminate. Insofar as philosophy still leaves nature to the sciences, it continues to fail Schelling's test, and becomes a conditioned, that is, a compromised antiphysics, an Idealism so 'powerful', in Jacobi's lexis, as to eliminate nature.

Notes

1   I am here arguing against Krings' view that 'nature as subject . . . does not designate a property of nature insofar as it emerges and is given as existence, but rather a *condition of the possibility of nature* . . .' (Krings, in Heckmann, Krings and Meyer 1985: 112; my emphasis). Krings effectively Kantianizes Schelling here, insofar as the function of the transcendental argument for Kant is to arrive at irremediable conditions, whereas I here present Schelling's proceedure as a constant, but 'patient', as Châtelet (1993: 139) says, and *absolute* unconditioning. As Schelling writes in the *First Outline*, wherein 'nature as subject' first appears, 'nature has unconditioned reality' (*SW* III: 17; 2004: 17).

2   Until the fairly extensive treatment Beiser gives the *Naturphilosophie* in his *German Idealism* (2002), Esposito's *Schelling's Idealism and the Philosophy of Nature* (1977) was the only recent *philosophical* examination of the topic in English, although there has been considerable attention paid by historians of science to *Naturphilosophie*, albeit generally offering, as Beiser (2002: 508) notes critically, unreflectively positivistic accounts of it. A flavour of such works can be gleaned from Cunningham and Jardine (1990), while an excellent counter-example is offered by Clark and Jacyna (1987). In French, Judith Schlanger (1966), Roger Ayrault (1976) and Gilles Châtelet (1993) have offered fascinating accounts of Schelling's and others' naturephilosophy, while the *Historical-Critical Edition* of Schelling's works in German (1976ff) has meant that a large industry of commentary and analysis has recently arisen. As well as the immense scholarly undertaking represented by the Supplementary Volume to vols 5–9, *Scientific Commentary to Schelling's Naturephilosophical Writings 1797–1800* (1994), there have been innumerable philosophical studies, of which Heuser-Keßler (1996), Bach (2001), Heckmann, Krings and Meyer (1985), Hasler (1981) and Zimmerli, Stein and Gerten (1997), offer a broad cross-section.

3   See Walter E. Ehrhardt, 'Nur ein Schelling', in *Studi Urbinati di Storia, Filosofia e Litteratura*, 51 (1977): 111–22 and 'Die Naturphilosophie *und* die Philosophie der Offenbarung', in Hans Jörg Sandkühler (ed.), *Natur und geschichtlicher Prozess. Studien zur Naturphilosophie F. W. J. Schellings* (Frankfurt am Main: Suhrkamp, 1984): 337–59:

(339); see also Heidegger (1996) and Jaspers (1955), both of whom assert the essential consistency of Schellingian philosophy. Heidegger presents Schelling as a thinker 'who fought so passionately ever since his earliest periods for his one and unique standpoint' (1996: 6), which precisely entailed that 'Schelling had to give up everything again and again, and again and again bring it back to a new ground', citing Schelling's own statement of this necessity from 'On the nature of philosophy as a science' (*SW* IX: 218–19). Jaspers, by contrast, retains the sense of consistency, but ascribes this in turn to the fact that, 'From the first, Schelling's thinking is in a never overcome antinomy' (1955: 110), citing Schelling's account (from the same source as Heidegger, *SW* IX: 214) of the essential 'asystasy' presupposed by philosophical systems. Amongst recent secondary literature on Schelling, Baumgartner and Korten (1996) argue from the outset against the 'philosophy in becoming' (Tilliette 1970) for the unity hypothesis, while Sandkühler, ed. (1998) contrariwise, affirms the 'work in process' thesis. Bowie (1993), following Frank (1975), cautiously recommends the former route through Schelling's corpus, while Snow (1996) complicates the unity thesis by arguing, with Jaspers, that while Schelling was indeed aiming to construct a single philosophical system, he 'never finally arrives at such a system' (3).

4   The same point is made almost verbatim in the second book of the *Philosophical Introduction to the Philosophy of Mythology, or Presentation of Pure Rational Philosophy* (*SW* XI: 372): while '. . . there is no special theory or science that even *could* be a universal science . . ., some permit themselves to call that science *Naturphilosophie*, although it has been explained often enough that this latter is only one side thereof'. The same point is more thoroughly considered in the 1803 'Supplement to the Introduction' to the *Ideas for a Philosophy of Nature*: 'The whole from which the naturephilosophy issues is *absolute* idealism. Naturephilosophy does not take precedence over idealism, nor is it in any way opposed to it as far as it is absolute, but certainly is opposed, so far as it is relative idealism, and accordingly grasps only the one side of the absolute act of cognition, which, without the other, is unthinkable' (*SW* II: 69; 1988: 51). The consistency in the treatment of *Naturphilosophie* from one end to the other of Schelling's work is clearly manifest here.

5   Schelling's *Berliner Nachlass* contains versions and fragments of the *Ages of the World* dating between 1810 and 1821, which have been edited by Klaus Grotsch (Stuttgart-Bad Cannstatt: Frommann-Holzboog, 2002). The edition printed in *SW* is the 1815 version, translated into English by Frederick de Wolfe Bolman (New York: AMS Press, 1942), and again by Jason M. Wirth (New York: State University of New York Press, 2000). Frank's edition of Schelling's *Ausgewahlte Schriften* (Frankfurt am Main: Suhrkamp, 1985) prints the 1811 version from Manfred Schröter's edition of that manuscript (Munich: Biederstien, 1946) in the *Nachlassband* to the *SW*, where it appears alongside a version from 1813, translated by Judith Norman (Ann Arbor: University of Michigan Press, 1997).

6   Schelling accordingly and repeatedly refers to Kant's critical philosophy as constituting 'the critique of natural cognition' (*SW* XI: 526). This naturalism is no stranger to German Idealist philosophy of nature. In 1828, for example, the professor of medicine and philosophy, Ignaz Paul Vital Troxler's *Naturlehre des menschlichen Erkennens, oder Metaphysik* (Aarau: Heinrich Remigius Sauerländer, 1828; Hamburg: Meiner, 1985), clearly equates meta*physics* with natural history.

7   'So there must after all be a basis *uniting* the supersensible that *underlies* nature [*Also muss es doch einen Grund der Einheit des Übersinnlichen, welches der Natur zum Grunde liegt*] and the supersensible that the concept of freedom contains practically, even though the concept of this basis does not reach cognition of it either theoretically or practically . . .'. See also *Ak.* V, 195–6n, 1987: 36n; *Ak.* V, 255, 1987: 112, *Ak.* V, 345–6, 1987: 219; *Ak.* V, 409, 1987: 293–4; *Ak.* V, 414, 1987: 299; *Ak.* V, 422, 1987: 308; *Ak.* V, 429, 1987: 316–17; *Ak.* V, 449n, 1987: 338.

8   Discussing the becoming of nature, Schelling notes particularly clearly in the 1830 *Introduction to Philosophy*, that 'I assume that my terminology is already known, such that by "materialization" not "becoming-corporeal", but rather "becoming-

hypokeimenon=subject", will be understood' (1989a: 128). The distinction between matter becoming body and matter becoming subject is central to his understanding of naturephilosophy in general, and nature as subject in particular.

9   The designation 'natural science', writes Kant, 'in the strict sense belongs to the doctrine of body alone' (*Ak*. V: 471; 1970: 8–9).

10   The full title of this text runs: '10,000 B.C.: The Geology of Morals (Who Does the Earth Think It Is?)' (Deleuze and Guattari 1988: 39–74). The parenthetical question clearly indicates the reopening of the inquiry into nature as subject or *The Life of the Earth*, as the title of naturephilosopher S. C. Wagener's 1828 text has it, and asserts the geological source of activity that is Schelling's resolution of the Kantian antinomy of nature and freedom. Given Deleuze's propensity to cite von Uexküll, it is likely that the intermediary source of these conceptions is the latter's *Subjektnatur*, which, as Merleau-Ponty notes (2003: 177), von Uexküll's *Streifzüge durch die Umwelten von Tieren und Menschen – Ein Bilderbuch unsichtbarer Welten* (Berlin: Springer, 1934) derives from Schelling. Accordingly, it forms a component of Deleuze's long-standing philosophical inquiries into ethology.

11   Badiou writes: 'it is not Platonism that has to be overturned, but the anti-Platonism taken as evident throughout the entire [twentieth] century' (2000: 101), before turning the tables on Kant: 'Any philosophy may be qualified as classical that does not submit to the critical injunctions of Kant. Such a philosophy considers . . . the Kantian indictment of metaphysics as null and void . . .' (45). The 'Deleuzian view' is neither a summative critique of Deleuze's philosophy in general, however, not least because Deleuze's *Kant's Critical Philosophy* is explicitly a philosophical of Kant as the 'great enemy'. Nor is the 'view' in question restricted to Deleuze alone. Rather, 'Deleuzian' in the present context involves the Nietzschean bedrock upon which much of the twentieth century's 'overturnings of Platonism' were based.

12   Nor need this fragmented *Timaeus* lead Badiou to the 'anti-physics' account he offers, as the naturephilosopher Lorenz Oken demonstrated: 'the world is the reality of mathematical ideas' (1847: 1). We discuss the number and animal dichotomy – the antinomy of a formalist Platonism – in chapter 2, below.

13   Throughout Kant's discussions of reflective judgement, he clearly notes that although such judgement is only subjectively rather than objectively valid, the basis of this subjectivity is itself naturalistic:

> If at any rate we are to judge by what our own nature grants us to see (subject to the conditions and bounds of our reason), then we are absolutely unable [to account] for the possibility of those natural purposes except by regarding them as based on an intelligent being. This is all that conforms to the maxim of our reflective judgment and so to a ground [*dem . . . Grunde*] that, though in the subject, *attaches inescapably to the human race*. (*Ak*. V: 400–1; 1987: 283, t.m.)

Schelling is one of the few consistently to have noted this naturalism in Kant, and repeatedly describes the purpose of the critical philosophy in general as 'Kant's critique of natural cognition' (e.g., *SW* XI: 526), or the forms of intuition as grounded 'in the nature of our cognitive powers' (*SW* X: 81; 1994b: 99). In Grant 2000b, Schelling's contention that naturephilosophy follows 'naturally and conceptually' from the results of Kant's critique (1989a: 37) is reversed to examine the consistent thread of naturalism running from Kant's *Universal Natural History* through to the *Opus postumum*.

14   The other interrupted essay is Steffens' 'Review of the editor's recent naturephilosophical writings'. Steffens describes these writings as researching 'the primordial natural law' (in Schelling 2001: 9), and pursues it in a variety of forms: in time as 'nothing other than the original type of all continuous development' (2001: 11); in life, as 'nothing other than the recapitulation of the construction of nature as such' (27); and in consciousness, which is 'nothing other than the self-cognition and in cognizing, the self-reproduction of

nature' (173).

15 Georges Cuvier studied under Kielmeyer at the Karlshochschule in Stuttgart. His debate with Saint-Hilaire is discussed in Appel (1987), and remains a crucial juncture for Deleuze and Guattari 1988: 45–8, 254–5; Deleuze 1993: 144n; 1994: 184–5). On Owen, Cuvier and Saint-Hilaire, see Rehbock 1983: 75–7, and Sloan 1992: 39–43. On Owen and Darwin, see ibid.: 52–6, and Appel 1987. On Oken, Meckel, von Baer and the 'Meckel-Serres law' account of recapitulation, see Gould 1977: 35–63.

16 See also Kielmeyer's response in a letter to Windischmann of 25 November 1804, concerning the latter's inquiries concerning the universality of recapitulation (Kielmeyer 1938: 203–10), and Windischmann's own assertions concerning the universality of physics in 'Outlines towards a presentation of the concept of physics' (*Neue Zeitschrift für speculative Physik* 1.i.: 78–160), which precedes this exchange. Windischmann's tendency in the latter work is, while Schellingian in expression, rather Fichtean in content.

17 See Bowler's (1984: 322–6) and Depew and Weber's (1996: 377–84) discussions of neo-Darwinism and 'punctuated equilibrium' theorists.

18 Popper's three-worlds hypothesis presents the 'third world' as containing 'philosophical systems . . . problems, or problem situations' (1972: 106) the 'value' of which is demonstrated when they are cashed in as scientific theory (1972: 180–3).

19 Beiser (2002) provides the most recent example of this tendency, while von Engelhardt and Bonsepien (in Hasler (ed.) 1981: 77, 169) provide accounts of naturephilosophy as the 'extension of Fichte[anism] to nature'.

20 Fichte's last letter to Schelling was written on 15 January 1802, while Hegel's *Difference* essay appeared in September of the previous year. The Fichte-Schelling letters have been collected by Walter Schulz, *Briefwechsel Fichte-Schelling* (Frankfurt am Main: Suhrkamp, 1968), and selections translated in Jochen Schulte-Sasse *et al.* (eds), *Theory as Practice* (Minneapolis: University of Minnesota Press, 1997): 73–90. On the effect of Hegel's critique of Fichte in the *Difference* essay on the latter's relations with Schelling, see H. S. Harris and Walter Cerf's translation (Hegel 1977a), and Harris' 'Introduction' (ibid.: 3, 67 n10).

21 'For all externality is non-organic . . . The earth is a whole, as a system of life, but, as crystal, it is like a skeleton, which can be regarded as dead because its members seem still to subsist formally on their own, while its process falls outside it' (*Encyclopaedia* §338 *Zusatz*; Hegel 1970: 278) Hegel explains, citing the formal-vitalist principle noted above: '. . . the organism makes itself into its own presupposition . . . The inwardisation [*Erinnerung*] of the Idea of Nature within itself to subjective vitality . . . is the judgement or partition [*Urteil*] of the Idea into itself and into this processless immediacy' (§338; 1970: 277): judgement, as in Kant, continues to divide Nature (or its Idea) for 'subjective vitality' and to expel the self-expelling inorganic only the better to 'bring back [the] different members [of Life] into unity' (§337, *Zusatz*; 1970: 275), since 'it is only in the Idea that they are *one* Life, one organic system of Life' (§337; 1970: 273).

22 'The peculiarity of our power of conception lies so deep in the nature of our mind that we transfer it, involuntarily, and by a well-nigh universal agreement, to nature herself (that ideal being wherein we think of ideation and production, concept and act, as identical)' (*SW* II: 269; 1988: 214).

23 'Certainly there are philosophers who have *one* universal answer . . . which they repeat at every opportunity . . . That which is form in things, they say, we first transfer onto things' (*SW* II: 43; 1988: 33, t.m.). The passage I paraphrase in the text above is derived from Schelling's characterization of what Krings argues constitutes that text's 'Kantianized Plato' (in Schelling 1994a: 122f). Schelling writes: 'The key to explaining all Plato's philosophy is the remark that he *always transfers the subjective onto the objective*' (1994a: 31). Krings's accompanying essay, 'Genesis und Materie – zur Bedeutung der Timaeus-Handschrift für Schellings Naturphilosophie', therefore argues that Schelling remains critically and transcendentally Kantian here, making nature a product of reason's autonomy,

so that nature has yet to become its own lawgiver, as it does in the *First Outline* (*SW* III: 17; 2004: 17). Further, in *On the True Concept of Naturephilosophy and the Proper Means of Resolving its Problems* (1801), Schelling argues against 'the common understanding' in general and Karl August Eschenmayer's essay 'Spontaneity = World Soul' (*Zeitschrift für Speculative Physik* Bd.2 H.1 (in Schelling 2001: 233–72) in particular, in that it views 'the human mind as nature's lawgiver', whereas 'in naturephilosophy, nature is its own lawgiver' (*SW* IV: 96). The gravity therefore attaching to Schelling's dismissal of the 'transfer' thesis in the *Ideas* (1797) amounts to little more than an epistemological voluntarism or antiphysics deriving from Kanto-Fichteanism. See chapter 3, below. Manfred Baum (in Sedgwick (ed.) 2000: 199–215) and Werner Beierwaltes (in Reydams-Schils (ed.) 2003: 267–89) offer counterarguments against Krings in their discussions of the place of Schelling's *Timaeus*-text in the development of the *Naturphilosophie*.

24 The phrase is suggestive, since it opens the issue of *how* 'transfinite' mentality might be: in other words, if this is taken to mean that the mentality in question is indifferent to particular organic platforms, or at least universalizable for a specific class thereof, then we have transcendentalism; but why does Vater consider it necessary to coin another term? If therefore it is instead taken to imply that the finitude with respect to which mentality is transfinite is precisely that of organic nature, then 'thinking nature' ceases to be a transcendental task, and becomes instead an autonomous activity on the part of nature itself in many, or indeed all, its forms.

25 'Fichte conceived of the I as the substance of the human being alone, so that everything else in the sense- or external world would exist only through the representations of this same I. Such a one would here become quite clear that subjectobjectivity cannot lie exclusively in human consciousness, for although man, alone amongst the nature of things, may be the only one that can say to himself: "I am", it does however follow from this that I alone exist, i.e., that I, man, am the sole existent' (1989a: 41).

26 There is considerable debate on this matter. Förster (2000) argues the case for a continued development rather than a break, between the *Metaphysical Foundations*, the third *Critique* and the *Opus postumum*, and is echoed in this regard by Edwards (2000). See also the essays collected in Blasche (1991), amongst which Tuschling (ibid.: 105–45) argues the case for Kant rejecting the criticist shortcomings of his earlier works and embracing a transcendental idealism, possibly on Schelling's model. See also my 'Physics of Analogy and Metaphysics of Nature' in Jones and Rehberg (eds) (2000): 37–60, which argues that Kant's considerations of the shockingly homo-sapiens free fossil record prompts a 'sublime of time' whereby the 'preservation different in kind' that the sublime proffers mind is an acknowledgement of the contingency of species, and the requirement, therefore, that practical philosophy assume responsibility for the maintenance of mind despite the possible obliteration of reducibly human finite rational beings. This sublime, although it remains undeveloped in Kant's text, would, in conjunction with the sublime of space in the *Critique of Aesthetic Judgment*, render the two parts of the third *Critique* symmetrical.

27 Christoph Girtanner, *Über das Kantische Prinzip für die Naturgeschichte* (Göttingen: Vandenhoek & Ruprecht, 1796).

28 I note here that this is a possible trajectory, not a necessary one. While, for example, existentialism and the phenomenological hermeneutics of Being pursue it, Bergson and Deleuze do not.

CHAPTER 2

The Powers Due to Becoming:
The Reemergence of Platonic
Physics in the Genetic Philosophy

That there really exist two distinct and totally opposite regions, each of which occupies one half of the All – the one termed 'below' towards which move all things possessing any bodily mass, and the other 'above', towards which everything goes against its will – this is a wholly erroneous supposition. (*Tim.* 62c6–d1)[1]

No inquiry has been surrounded, for the philosophers of every age, by so much darkness as that concerning the nature of matter. And yet insight into this question is necessary for all true philosophy, just as all false systems are shipwrecked from the very outset on this reef. Matter is the general seed of the universe, in which is concealed everything that evolves in later developments. (II, 223; 1988: 179)

We begin the account of the philosophy of nature, as does Schelling, with Platonism, and particularly the Platonic *Timaeus*. By singling out the *Timaeus* for a commentary, Schelling joins company with the ancient and pre-Thomist traditions of commentator-philosophers for whom Platonism as a whole simply was 'the theory of the universe' presented in the *Timaeus* (Proclus, *In Tim.* 1.1).[2] Because for that tradition, to be a commentator was to be a Platonist, by setting the transcendental philosophy against the 'physics of the All' (*Tim.* 27a5, 47a8–9), Schelling's *Timaeus* simultaneously signals its Platonism even as it absorbs Kant's transcendental philosophy. Commentary, therefore, is less the 'series of footnotes to Plato' that worried Whitehead, than it is a *collaborative* ideating,[3] a species of 'co-mentation', not merely with regard to 'meanings', but rather to the *objects* of thought. Accordingly, Schelling's commentary is not motivated by interpretive values or disputes, but rather grounds collaborative thinking in the nature of thought and its objects: 'created from the source of things and the akin to it, the human soul has a co-science [*Mitwissenschaft*] with creation' (VIII, 200; 2000: xxxvi, t.m; 1946: 112; 1997: 114). The objects of this science – 'speculative physics' or 'the physics of the All' – are twofold and inseparable, for 'philosophers of every age': matter and Idea, or 'the material of the universal' (XI, 313).

Amongst all possible objects, Platonism gives the Idea alone the status of '*auto kath'auto*', the *absolute*, 'itself according to itself' (*Tim.* 51a1). With the advent of transcendental philosophy, the Idea becomes the 'unconditioned' or the 'unthinged' (*das Unbedingte*) that, according to Kant, it is a 'necessary idea of reason' (CPR Bxxi), rather than a merely contingent historical affectation, 'to demand' (CPR A564/B592). Embedding the transcendental philosophy into the orbit of Platonism, Schelling therefore pits the former's pursuit of *conditions* against the latter's pursuit of the *unconditioned* in terms of the Idea. While therefore Kant 'must be credited with restoring the word *Ideas* to language', Schelling finds that the transcendental philosophy 'accords the Ideas no reality except insofar as they are moral by nature' (VI, 186; 1994c: 173–4). Kant, in other words, attaches conditions to the unconditioned, or restrictions to the absolute. To pursue the unconditioned as such, *auto kath'auto*, entails however that it be subject to no restrictions, but must encompass everything. Accordingly, Schelling defines 'the Idea [as] the infinite concept', but continues: 'the infinite concept is itself the concept of the universe [*das All*]' (VI, 185; 1994c: 173), echoing the *Ideas for a Philosophy of Nature* (1797) in its attempt at 'the absolute [*das Absolute*] thought purely as matter' (II, 62; 1988: 47). Without settling the Platonic problem of the materiality of the Idea, we may note that it follows from the definition of the Idea as the 'infinite concept' that it cannot be made finite with respect to any particular domain of being. Accordingly, not only must the Idea *include the physical universe*, it must do so on condition that this same physical universe be capable of ideation.

We can now see the scope of the problem of the practically restricted absolute that dominates the conclusions of the critical philosophy not only in Kant, but also and especially in Fichte. Apart from the necessary problem of the possibility of freedom in nature, practical transcendentalism is conditioned first by virtue of lacking a physics. It is this charge that Kant sought to make good in his late *Transition from Metaphysics to Physics*, and that Fichte tried to defend the *Wissenschaftslehre* project against in 'Propositions on the Essence of Animals' (cf. 3.3). By embedding the restrictions of the transcendental philosophy in the Platonic context, Schelling tests philosophy against both nature and the Idea. Whereas Jacobi had challenged postkantian idealism to become 'the strongest yet' in the direction of 'speculative egoism' (Jacobi [1787] 2000b: 175), Schelling, by 'tak[ing] physics as his point of departure' (VIII, 337; 1986: 8), challenges idealism with its strategic avoidance of nature and its self-restriction to the practical. In other words, setting Kant against Plato, Schelling contests the *eliminativism* of Kanto-Fichtean idealism with the 'physics of the All'. Unlike Kant's procedure in the transcendental philosophy, therefore, the *Timaeus* commentary seeks to establish 'not merely forms of our understanding, but universal world-concepts [*Weltbegriffe*]' (1994a: 63) or 'nature-concepts [*Naturbegriffe*]' (1994a: 36). Further, in a sense that will become important later in this work, the Idea in no way 'represents' its content; neither the Platonic nor the Schellingian Idea, as we shall see, has as its extension an object or a state of affairs; rather, for Schelling's 'genetic philosophy' (II, 39; 1988: 30) as for Plato's, the Idea provides the means by which 'we must think the *emergence* of the world' (1994a: 63, my emphasis).

Its 'non-objectivity' notwithstanding, the centrality of the problem of the 'physical existence of the Idea' (Schelling 1994a: 34) becomes increasingly clear precisely as nature assumes philosophical 'apriority'. By noting that the task is not simply to establish the necessary 'forms of our understanding', Schelling remoulds this Platonic problem around the axes of Kantianism. While the prospect of a physics of the Idea in Kantianism might seem remote, this is due only to the transcendental philosophy's elision of the *nature of the transcendental* itself, which conditions the possibility of a separably *transcendental concept of nature*. Taking the second part of this problem first, it is because the transcendental philosophy follows the Aristotelian restriction of the field of physics to the study of 'bodies and magnitudes, the beings possessed [thereof] and the cause of these things' (*Heav.* 268a5–6) by restricting nature itself to 'the doctrine of body alone' (*Ak.* IV, 471; Kant 1970: 9), that it operates a *somatic* theory of matter. Plato (*Stat.* 273b5; *Tim.* 31b5) precisely criticizes the 'somaticist' account of matter as overly reductive on grounds later specified by Giordano Bruno: 'matter may be considered in two ways: firstly as power; second as substrate [*subjectum*]' (1988: 65, t.m.). Accordingly, neither Alcinous' 'natural concept formation [*phusike ennoia*]' (1993: 7–10; 67), Plotinus' 'universal substance of the Ideas' (VI.6.vi.6), nor the Platonic theory of matter consider this reducible to somatism; rather Plato follows the first of Bruno's definitions: 'I hold that the definition of being is simply power [*dunamis*]' (*Soph.* 247e4).

It is only so long as the supplanting of somatics for dynamics goes unnoted that the 'widespread prejudice' against the very idea of a Platonic theory of nature (Böhme 2000: 161–2; 18) can be sustained. That this prejudice does in fact remain widespread is a further reason for examining the beginnings of Schelling's philosophy of nature in the *Timaeus* commentary,[4] as contemporary commentators continue to present the *Timaeus* as an ethico-political allegory,[5] despite its subtitle: *On the Nature of Physics.*[6] Platonic physics has as its task to explain the 'emergence' or 'coming into being' of this universe (*Tim.* 28b9–c4). Since it is only in the process of its genesis that the universe acquires body, physics is not restricted to somatics, as Aristotle and Kant maintain, but must treat also of the generation of bodies, relegating the latter to regionality with respect to matter. As Schelling writes, 'materiality alone is not yet corporeality' (XI, 424). In the register Schelling takes from the transcendental philosophy, such a physics is absolute or 'unconditioned [*unbedingt*]' insofar as it does not deal with what is 'determined [*bedingt*]' as a 'thing [*Ding*]' (I, 166; 1980: 74). Since, however, unconditionality equally entails 'unthinged' and unrestricted, a physics that deals with the absolute is equally an absolute physics – hence Schelling's insistence that 'the absolute be thought purely as matter' (II, 62; 1988: 47) and that the 'Idea, the infinite concept, is itself the concept of the universe' (VI, 185; 1994c: 173). But this Platonic-Schellingian conceptual work equally proposes therefore a proper means of conducting physics, against Aristotelian-Kantian somatism: since nature eternally becomes, the science of nature must be genetic. 'Natural history [*phuseos istorian*]' becomes not simply the 'wisdom' in pursuit of which a prephilosophical Socrates spent his youth (*Phaedo* 96a8), but the properly genetic science *consequent* upon the Platonic account of 'the coming into being of this universe' (*Tim.* 28b9–c4).

While in the *Ideas for a Philosophy of Nature*, it is precisely by means of extending such a 'natural history' to 'our mind [*Naturlehre unseres Geistes*]' (II, 39; 1988: 30) that Schelling proposes to resolve the problem of the materiality of the Idea, it remains unresolved at the conclusion of the *Timaeus* commentary, despite assembling therein all the means whereby Platonic physics can resolve the problem of the 'physical existence of the Ideas' (Schelling 1994a: 34, 73). While it follows from the Aristotelian partition of 'physics or secondary philosophy' (*Met.* 1037a15–6) from 'the science of being *qua* being' or *primary* philosophy (1003a1), that metaphysics and physics no longer address the same 'nature', Platonism treats of just one nature, composed of powers or becomings, from which being itself is not exempt. For example, the physics of the Idea explicit in the *Sophist*'s definition of being – of what unconditionally *is* – as 'simply power [*dunamis*]' (247e4), opening up the Idea to study not simply according to its 'copies' but to 'the powers accorded it by nature' (*Tim.* 49a4–6; *Phlb.* 29b7), is echoed in the *Philebus*'s account of the 'becoming of being [*genesis eis ousian*]' (26d8; Schelling 1994a: 63; Krings 1994: 117) and 'productive nature [*e tou poiountos phuseos*]' (26e6; cited in Schelling 1994a: 48). Since genetics is the science of becoming, the 'becoming of being' is the manner in which Platonic physics overtly poses the problem of the materiality of the Idea. We thus see that, far from considering Plato's 'secret teachings' (Aristotle, *Phys.* 209b15) an arbitrary and contradictory appendage to a two-worlds Platonic metaphysics, the problem of the materiality of the Idea is made explicit in the *Philebus*, and follows as a logical entailment of a one-world Platonic physics.

Against this background, unless the Kantian transcendental can demonstrate not merely its critical utility, but also its genetic basis in accordance with a natural 'apriority', it remains conditioned precisely by its setting aside of nature. In accordance with this naturalistic apriority, Schelling will not only find Kant's theoretical philosophy riven into its real and formal aspects, but will locate the source of this rift in the corresponding 'complete separation' between Kant's views on 'organic nature from those of universal natural science'.[7] Entirely opposing therefore the conception of transcendental philosophy as merely a method for serving 'Kant's critique of natural cognition' (XI, 526), Schelling's own conception of that philosophy is premised on 'the identity of the dynamic and the transcendental' (III, 452; 1978: 91). For Schelling, 'transcendental philosophy . . . materialises the laws of intelligence into laws of nature' (III, 352; 1978: 14, t.m.), and thus furthers the 'natural history of our mind' proposed in the *Ideas*.

While this is clear by the time of the *System of Transcendental Idealism* (1800), the *Timaeus* commentary remains unable to resolve the problems stemming from the Aristotelian settlement that Kant inherited. Excruciatingly, the commentary ends by conceding everything. Stipulating that 'the further development of the *mechanical* generation and the *physical* continuity of the elements does not belong here' (1994a: 75), the commentary's concluding sentence repeats the isolation of physics from metaphysics – and thus of matter from the Idea – that are the hallmarks of Aristotle's critique of Platonism as 'treating of another universe and other bodies, not sensible ones' (*Met.* 1090a35). In so doing, Schelling falls foul of the de-ontologizing of nature that is the primary error the *Philosophical Inquiries into the Nature of Human Freedom* (1809) identifies in a modern European philosophy for which 'nature does not exist' (VII, 356; 1986: 30). But the reciprocal isolation of physics from metaphysics – of nature from philosophy – is not only metaphysically flawed. In attempting to avoid any question of a scientistic reduction of metaphysical problems, Schelling, like Aristotle, makes the distinction between the two in terms of the *mechanism* that so dominated the eighteenth century's natural sciences, as to have convinced Kant, for example, to rescind all philosophical claim on the territory of nature in favour of the natural sciences. Ultimately, then, it is on mechanical, corpuscularist grounds that Schelling is compelled to reject the 'physical existence of the Idea' (1994a: 34). The lesson to be learnt is that just as no philosophical work is done by simply applying a scientific theory to a philosophical problem (or vice versa; cf. II, 6; 1988: 5); and just as it cannot be the function of a philosophy of nature to *supplant* the natural sciences; so neither can philosophy renounce conceptual custody of nature *to* the sciences without adopting a particular theory *from* them.

2.1 ESSENCES AND APPEARANCES: THE DEPHYSICALIZATION OF GREAT PHYSICS

[F]or if they are willing to admit that any existence, no matter how small, is incorporeal, that is enough. They will then have to tell what that is which is inherent in the incorporeal and the corporeal alike, and which they have in mind when they say that both exist. [. . .] I suggest that everything which possesses any power of any kind . . . has real existence. (*Soph.* 247c9–e4)

Aristotelian philosophy of nature contains the principles common to *all* natural philosophy, and not just to the part that became our physics. (Des Chenes 1996: 2)

The damage done to Platonic physics by its flawed analyses in Aristotle's *Metaphysics* is inestimable, precisely insofar as the axiomatic Aristotelian physics laid down, as Des Chenes (1996) argues by way of demonstrating that there is continuity and not a rupture between Aristotelian and Cartesian natural philosophy, continues to organize the metaphysics of the natural sciences, despite and throughout any number of 'scientific revolutions' and 'paradigm shifts'. Des Chenes' assessment echoes Whitehead, as he traces the application of the 'fallacy of misplaced concreteness', in metaphysics as in the natural sciences, back to Aristotle's theory of matter:

> The unquestioned acceptance of the Aristotelian logic has led to an ingrained tendency to postulate a substratum for whatever is disclosed in sense-awareness, namely, to look below what we are aware of for the substance in the sense of the 'concrete thing'. This is the origin of the modern scientific concept of matter and of ether, namely they are the outcome of this insistent habit of postulation. (Whitehead [1920] 1964: 18)

'Turning to the physicists' (*Phys.* 187a12), Aristotle divides them into two schools: substrate theorists, who consider entities to be modifications of a 'single underlying substance' or macrobody, and element theorists, who consider entities to be produced from mixtures of microbodies (Democritus' *atoma*, Empedocles' *rizomata*, etc.). In the *Physics*, Aristotle places Platonic physics in the first school, since like the Empedoclean cosmic drama of Love and Strife, generating antitheticals by 'condensation and rarefaction', Plato 'makes matter consist in this diversifying antithesis [*aoristas duas*]' and nothing besides. But Aristotle is therefore compelled to acknowledge that Platonic physics is not substrate theoretical, since he 'finds unity in the Idea; whereas the others find unity in the underlying matter and distinctions and forms in the opposites' (187a17–18). Further acknowledging the ill-suitedness of the *Physics*' taxonomy, the *Metaphysics* praises Plato's 'dyad' of the One (the 'cause of substantial existence') and the Unlimited ('the material cause', *Met.* 988a9–11), as an account of being that is 'unique to him' (987b27). In consequence, when the *Metaphysics* argues that the 'elements' extend even to the Ideas, 'since the Ideas are the causes of everything else, he [Plato] supposed that their elements [*stoicheia*] are the elements of all things' (987b19–20), the continuity of the causal chain requires that Plato be set with the atomists. But again, rather than pursuing the 'secret teaching' concerning the materiality of the Idea, Aristotle reduces this multiplicity to the 'material principle' which consists in the 'Great and Small', and opposes this to the One as the 'substantial principle' (987b19–21). It is as if Aristotle sees only two options, not merely for Platonic physics, but for physics itself: whether one all-enveloping body or substrate, or a multiplicity of all-pervading bodies, physics is and remains nothing other than the science of body. The somatism, in other words, enshrined for Schelling's contemporaries in Kant's mechanistic restriction of natural science to 'the doctrine of body alone' (*Ak.* IV: 471; 1970: 8–9), merely reiterates Aristotle's segregation of 'first philosophy' (the science of being *qua* being; *Met.* 1003a1, 1061b4–33) from 'physics or secondary philosophy' (1037a15–6):

> We may say that the science of nature is for the most part plainly concerned with bodies and magnitudes and with their changing properties and motions, as also with the principles which belong to that class of

substance; for the sum of physically constituted entities consists of (*a*) bodies and magnitudes, (*b*) beings possessed of body and magnitude, (*c*) the principles or causes of these beings. (*Heav.* 268a1–6)

It could easily be objected that Aristotle's concern with Plato *qua* physicist is merely a product of an insufficiently developed understanding of the proper field of the philosophical. It is of course a commonplace that before Aristotle, the remit of physics had yet to be segregated from that of metaphysics, the work now bearing that title having received it only by virtue of having stood 'next to' (*meta*) the *Physics* on Aristotle's bookshelves. Rather, however, than this superficial account, it is the constitution of a 'meta-physics' or 'first philosophy' as no longer having *physis*, nature, as its objective that matters here. For Schelling, diagnosing the consequences of this constitution, 'the whole of modern European philosophy since its inception . . . has this common deficiency – that nature does not exist for it' (*SW* VII: 356; 1986: 30). For Schelling's modernity and for ours, the Aristotelian critique of Platonic physics is the matrix underlying philosophy's dephysi-calized constitution. For example, Aristotle does not treat the vexed problem of the 'participation' of the Ideas in nature as a problem regarding the physics of the Idea, but considers it merely as a 'terminological change', lifted from the old Pythagorean problem of the 'imitation' of numbers by sensible things. As such, a critique of Pythagoreanism is sufficient, for Aristotle, for a critique of Platonism:[8] how can 'numbers which have no weight or lightness . . . construct natural bodies which have lightness and weight' (*Met.* 1090a33–4)? Since they cannot, and since the Pythagorean 'number' is functionally identical to the Platonic 'Idea', the Ideas, Aristotle argues, 'contribute nothing to substantial existence or being [*ousian*]' (1090b26). Insofar as Plato continues to hold that 'the Ideas are causes both of being and generation' (1080a2, glossing *Phaedo* 100c3–d9), it becomes clear that he is indeed 'disregarding the physical universe' (987b1–2) and 'treating of another universe and other bodies, not sensible ones' (1090a35). In this way Aristotle sets up the cross on which 'metaphysics' is created: the inclusion of the Idea in nature excludes physics from Platonism, and exiles his philosophy to meta-physics, understood precisely as beyond nature, that is, concerned with other than sensible *bodies*. Insofar as Aristotle exiles these 'other entities . . . called Ideas' (*Met.* 987b8), from the domain of physics, the object of his criticisms is the centrality of the Idea in Platonic physics.

2.1.1 The physics of the All and the physics of all things

Plato himself, like the Presocratics, still has a concept of nature, that is of *phusis*, which means Being itself. And since for him the Ideas are genuine beings, they too are nature in the strict sense. (Böhme 2000: 18)

Plato repeatedly stipulates that physics is 'the physics of *the All* [*phuseos tou pantos*]' (*Tim.* 27a5, 41e2, 47e8–9). Since it is the reciprocal exclusion of the Idea and *phusis* that forms the cross by which Aristotle segregates metaphysics from physics, a physics that includes the Idea, which Böhme demonstrates to be entailed by the Platonic conception of nature, precisely opposes this settlement. Accordingly, Aristotle's assertion that Plato 'disregard[s] the physical universe [*peri de tes holes phuseos outhen*]' (*Met.* 987b1–2) fails to engage on Platonic ground at all, and precisely this lack of commonality between the two is their only commonality. It is a consequence of Aristotle's further determination of physics as 'the physics of all *things* [*ta physika panta pragmata*]' (Simplicius, *In phys.* 198.28), that Platonism becomes susceptible to Aristotle's accusation of its lack of physics. Because, that is, in accordance with a physics of all *things*, 'the universe is composed of a plurality of distinct individual entities' (*Phys.* 187a34), physics is concerned only to discover 'the principles of perceptible body, that is, tangible body' (*Gen.* 329b7). Intangibles and imperceptibles no longer form part of physics, and any philosopher concerned with such 'other than physical *bodies*' is no longer a physicist.

Somatism is reinforced by what appears, in the *Physics*, to be a merely heuristic, or 'convenient' (*Met.* 1029b2–3), empiricism: 'we must advance from the concrete whole to the several constituents which it embraces; for the concrete whole is the more readily cognizable by the senses' (184a24–6). However, the *Metaphysics* transforms this empiricism into a principle of physics in accordance with the share of the study of 'substance [*ousia*]' proper to it. As Schelling noted in the 1854 *Introduction to the Philosophy of Mythology*, 'Aristotle's *ousia* is not essence (*essentia*), as in Plato . . . it is not the existent, but *that of which* "existent" is said (*kath'ou legetai to on*)' (XI, 362). No longer true being as in Platonism, Aristotelian *ousia*, the 'first' among the many 'senses in which being [*to on*] is said' (*Met.* 1028a10), and the principle object of the *Metaphysics*' investigations, then becomes the principle according to which the tasks of physics and metaphysics are distributed: 'substance [*ousia*] is both the concrete thing [*sunholon*] and the formula [*logos*]' (1039b2–21). Concerned with the properties of sensible objects, physics seeks first and foremost the form [*morphe*] of 'concrete things' or bodies, and becomes, accordingly, entirely empirical. But physics is 'secondary' not simply in importance, but in range, to 'primary philosophy', which no longer has substance, but rather *logos* alone as its object. Between this empirical and logical formalism, matter, while a necessary element in the study of physics, is squeezed out of metaphysics, since matter is not a thing of which 'being' can be said: 'there is no definition or demonstration of sensible things because they contain matter whose nature is such that it can both exist and not exist' (1039b28–30).

2.1.2 Matter, body and substance

In the face of the Platonic philosophy of matter, the Aristotelian elimination of matter from metaphysics is startling. Platonic matter consists of two components: the 'difficult and dark Idea', and the medium or 'receptacle of all becoming' (*Tim.* 49a4–7). As Idea, it is always existing and unchanging and imperceptible to the senses; as receptacle, it is generated and that in which all generation occurs, yet like the Idea, it is 'dark', imperceptible. As Lloyd (1970: 74) remarks, at first sight, the latter is *like* Aristotle's definition of 'prime matter': 'what I mean by matter is precisely the ultimate underlying substrate [*hypokeimenon, subjectum*], common to all the things of nature' (*Phys.* 192a32–3). The commonality or universality of matter is however only logical: 'by universal we mean that which by nature pertains to several things' (*Met.* 1038b15). Matter accordingly cedes primacy: 'By "primary" I mean that which does not imply the presence of something else as a material substrate' (1037b3–4). Matter therefore ceases to be *substrate common to all things* as the *hypokeimenon* assumes the logical role of *subjectum*, the merely logical 'subject' as 'that of which things are predicated'. In accordance with this redefinition, matter loses all substantial existence due precisely to its universality: 'the substance of an individual thing is the substance which is peculiar to it and belongs to nothing else; whereas the universal is common' (1038b10–12). What we witness in Aristotle's metaphysics is the extraction of matter from substantial existence, and its reduction to logic, to a purely extensional *logos*; his physics, which begins with the 'concrete whole [*synholon*]' cognizable by the senses, in the end isolates substantiality, in the sense of the 'substance according to the formula' (1037a16), from 'particular sensible substances' (1039b28). Aristotelian somatism, therefore, is empirical only, so that his physics treats a nature without matter, a 'nature spoken of in accordance with form' (1032a23); Aristotle even makes a feature of a matterless nature, exemplified in the insoluble problem of 'the matter of an eclipse' – because there is nothing that it is like to be an eclipse, i.e., because it has no formula, it has 'no matter' (1044b8–10). Matter is even accidental to the generation of plants and animals, for 'that by which they are generated is the so-called "formal" nature' (1032a24–5). Aristotelian metaphysics is that science concerned with substance not insofar as this is particular, sensible or material, but insofar as it is a *predicable essence*, i.e., only insofar as it is the subject or *hypokeimenon* supporting a *logos*.

Aristotelian physics, as an empirical morphology or *phenomenology,*[9] extracts matter from nature, while metaphysics further supplants matter with form, and reduces 'substantial being [*ousia*]' to the merely predicable subject (Fig. 1) insofar as this is a subject of predication alone. Superimposing this schema onto Platonic physics, we can see that the principal tool in the construction of matterless nature is the systematic elimination of matter from form: at the level of primary philosophy, the formula is distinguished from the sensible particular, giving rise to an ontologically grounded prioritization of immaterial over material substance by which it subordinates secondary philosophy, or physics. At the subordinate level of physics, form is 'more essential' than matter, since the nature of the concrete whole under physical investigation depends on its particularity *as* such-and-such, its 'what-it-is-ness'. Accordingly, 'form and the combination of form and matter are more truly substance than matter is' (1029a29–30). Finally, the distinction between the matter and form of a substance ontologically subordinates the *synholon* to the *logos*, since the concrete whole or sensible particular 'admit[s] of destruction and generation', whereas the 'formulae *are*, and *are not*, independent of generation and destruction'. Hence, concludes Aristotle, 'there is no definition or demonstration of particular sensible substances, because they contain matter whose nature is such that it can both exist and not exist' (1039b23–31).

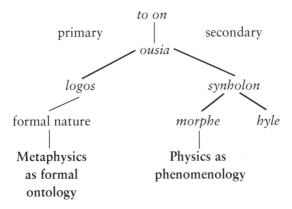

Figure 1 The Desubstantialization of *Ousia* and the Dephysicalization of *Phusis* in Aristotle's Constitution of Metaphysics

2.1.3 *Kosmos noetos*

Having followed the vicissitudes of the dematerialization of form in the emergence, through Aristotle, of phenomenologizing physics and metaphysics as the predication of essences, we will now examine the manner in which Schelling attempts to effect this same operation on the Platonic theory of Ideas, *in order to assess the extent to which the reevaluation of Kantianism entails the presence of a covert Aristotelianism in the early generation of naturephilosophy*. Schelling institutes the distinction in the following terms: 'we must distinguish 2 kinds of Ideas in Plato. 1) those Ideas that ground the world *materially*. 2) those that *formally* ground the world' (1994a: 31). Ideas of the first kind consist in the *zoois noetois* or 'intelligible animals' and the 'world soul originally present in matter' (1994a: 29), which are contained in the *kosmos noetos* or 'intelligible universe' that equally contains those Ideas that ground *only* 'the genus and species [*Gattungen u. Arten*]' (1994a: 30)[10] of all creatures. Against Plotinus' conclusion that 'there must be matter

There too' (II.4.iv) in the *kosmos noetos*, since from where otherwise would the matter of the material world be copied, Schelling argues that, as purely formal, the *kosmos noetos* contains no matter, but does contain the Ideas that ground the materiality of the world, i.e., the 'intelligible creatures' that ground the 'creatures of the visible world' not in terms of the Idea, but, insofar as they are *ensouled*, that is, endowed with 'an original principle of motion' (1994a: 28), and insofar as they are 'animal (*zoon*)', i.e., endowed with 'original moving force' (1994a: 29), and finally, insofar as they are '*noeton*', in terms of the *intelligible forces* of becoming. Schelling's principal strategy here is to elide the somatic Idea he considers in the *Timaeus* essay to be necessarily consequent upon arguments regarding its materiality, by positing the intelligible animate being as mediating the Ideas, which 'by themselves, have no causality' (1994a: 29), by providing an *intelligible* cause of *motion*. Plotinus' argument for Ideal matter shares with Schelling a rejection of the somaticist grounds of Aristotle's dismissal of the substantiality of the Ideas, but departs from him in positing that 'matter, too, is an incorporeal' (III.6.vi). While matter itself – that is, the 'Idea' of matter (*Tim.* 49a4) – appears to be the first casualty of Schelling's non-material argument for the *zoon noeton* as the intelligible motive cause of actual self-moving creatures in the visible world, it does not, despite appearances, reflect an unequivocally Aristotelian-Kantian philosophy of formal or phenomenal nature, since it sketches a dynamics to rival the latter's somaticism. This is not, however, a trajectory the *Timaeus* essay satisfactorily addresses, precisely because it retains the same formalism it fails to understand itself as antithetical to. Insufficiently investigating the dynamics that grounds Platonic antisomatic physics (which we will examine below), the *Timaeus* essay begins an inquiry that will nevertheless be resumed in the naturephilosophical trilogy beginning with the *Ideas for a Philosophy of Nature*.

Although Schelling's claim regarding the two kinds of Ideas is original in Platonism, it has Kantian sources. Citing the same premise from which Plotinus begins, namely, that 'it is wholly necessary that this Cosmos should be a copy of something' (*Tim.* 29b1–2), Schelling writes:

> Since Plato so subordinated the world *qua* visible (*mundum materialiter spectatum*), and even ascribed actual [*vorhandne*] existence to it only in the senses, and since he therefore viewed it (as an object of sensibility alone) as utterly heterogeneous to everything *formal*, he could not possibly consider the *form* of the world, its conformity to rule and to law, as *inherent* in matter, or even as *emergent* from matter. (Schelling 1994a: 26–7)

What Krings (1994: 122) calls the 'Kantianisation of Plato' seems most apparent at this juncture, insofar as the above passage amounts to a paraphrase of Kant's discussion of 'nature regarded materially' at the end of the B edition 'Transcendental Deduction':

Categories are concepts that prescribe laws *a priori* to appearances, thus to nature as the sum total of all appearances (*natura materialiter spectatum*), and, since they are not derived from nature and do not follow it as their pattern (for otherwise they would be merely empirical), the question now arises how it is to be conceived that nature must follow them, i.e., how they can determine *a priori* the combination of the manifold of nature without deriving it from the latter. (CPR B163)

Kant's 'solution' is to demonstrate that 'the necessary ground' of the lawfulness in question is transcendental rather than empirical, and cannot therefore attach to 'nature in general', but only to *natura formaliter spectatum* (CPR B164) – to nature regarded, that is, through the formal lenses imposed by the categories of the understanding. As with Aristotle, we find a phenomenologizing supplanting a somaticizing physics, and a merely predicative metaphysics:

The true method of metaphysics is basically the same as that introduced by Newton into natural science . . . Newton's method maintains that one ought, *on the basis of certain experience* and, if need be, *with the help of geometry*, to seek out the *rules* in accordance with which *certain phenomena of nature* occur. Even if one does not discover the fundamental principle of these occurrences *in the bodies themselves*, it is nonetheless certain that they operate in accordance with this law. (*Ak*. II: 286; 1992a: 259; emphasis added)

Empiricist in its concern with natural *phenomena* rather than with nature itself; somaticist regarding the objects of natural science and the constitution of the physical world; and formalist as regards both naturalistic method and metaphysical outcome, Kant here demonstrates his Aristotelian inheritance, and confirms Des Chenes' thesis (1996: 2) regarding the Aristotelian grounds of all subsequent physics and metaphysics. That Schellingian naturephilosophy constitutes a departure from this transhistorical Aristotelian stasis regarding the metaphysics of *physis* will therefore be clear to the extent to which the *Timaeus* essay opposes the Platonic to the (Aristotelian =) Kantian philosophy of nature.

While imposing the Kantian distinction between matter and form at the level of the Idea, Schelling departs from it at the level of the transcendental grounds Kant ascribes to the lawfulness of nature: for Schelling, Plato 'does not conceive the intelligible world as the ultimate substrate of all appearances'; rather, again paraphrasing Plato against Kant, 'the invisible mother of all things', i.e., matter itself, 'becomes, in some manner difficult to conceive, capable of participation in the form of the understanding' (1994a: 58–9, citing *Tim.* 51a5–b1). Schelling's problem is not therefore how appearances conform to law, or how the formal determination of 'nature materially regarded' is *possible*, but rather the nature of the Ideas expressed in material becomings; that is, it does not concern a transcendental substrate of all appearances, but rather how the Platonic Idea of matter itself exerts dynamizing pressures on the Kantian categorical framework. Therefore the final problem the *Timaeus* essay approaches is the explicitly Platonic concern with the intelligibility of the emergence of order in the *physical* world, 'order itself having been generated out of disorder [*eis taxin auto hegagen ek tes ataxias*]' (*Tim.* 30a5), a concern that returns throughout Schelling's published works, from the *Ideas* to the *Philosophical Investigations into the Nature of Human Freedom*.

It is this emergence of order that Schelling takes Plato's 'becoming of being [*genesis eis ousian*]' (*Phil.* 26d8) to characterize, insofar as this constitutes an attempt to theorize the participation of the Ideas in nature by *physics*, rather than, as in the *Parmenides*, by logic alone. Implicitly indistinct with regard to Platonic doctrine conceived under post-Aristotelian lights, as having nothing whatever to do with the physical universe, the becoming of being is further characterized by the interaction of the four 'kinds [*gene*]' identified in the *Philebus*, and which Schelling will characterize as *categories*. While Schelling explicitly claims that these are 'not merely forms of *our* understanding, but rather universal world-concepts . . . by which the existence of the world must be explicated in its entirety' (1994a: 63) the *Timaeus* essay's focus remains on the cognitive to the extent that the Platonic challenge to Kantianism takes place at the level of an attempted reconception of the nature and range of transcendental philosophy. The nature of this reconception, however, is not reducibly cognitive, but constitutes rather the attempt to open the transcendental method to physics. As becomes clear in the *Ideas*, Schelling's initial strategy is to argue that while Kant establishes the transcendental structure in the emergence of appearances in reflection, this becomes self-eliminating unless the emergence of appearances *in nature itself* can also be accounted for transcendentally. In other words, the 'philosophy become genetic' (II, 39; 1988: 30) the *Ideas* proposes entails a transcendental argument against empiricism in the natural sciences (appearances are products, but how do these arise?), and a physical argument regarding the genesis of entities against the restriction of the transcendental to reflection (the emergence of order is a naturalistic, not a reducibly cognitive problem).

For the *Timaeus* essay meanwhile, the cooperation of the four kinds – unlimited, limit, bond and cause – characterize the 'synthesizing causation [*xunaition*]' (*Tim.* 46c8; Schelling 1994a: 48) by which order emerges, *qua* intelligible, in 'productive nature [*e tou poiountos phuseos*]' (*Phil.* 26e6). The Platonic 'becoming of being' is explicitly said to be the consequence of (1) the introduction of a limit [*peras*] into the unlimited [*apeiron*], (2) generating a common thing [*koinon*] as the 'offspring of these two' (*Tim.* 50d3; *Phil.* 26d8). It will in consequence become clear in Schelling's return to these 'kinds' – three, for the moment – in the *Treatise Explicatory of the Idealism of the Science of Knowledge* (1797), that they are being conceived as fundamentally transcendental, which Schelling at this point defines as arising from the 'self-activity of the intellect' (I, 357; 1994c: 72, t.m.). The *Treatise* therefore identifies the Platonic *apeiron* with space, and *peras* with time; it is only by the 'reciprocal determination and limitation' of these two 'absolutely opposing activities' (I, 356; 1994c: 71) that intellectual self-activity 'creates and brings forth a third, common entity (*koinon* in Plato)' (I, 357; 1994c: 72). The conclusion of this argument provides the key to Schelling's solution to the problem of the materiality of the formal: 'Space and time, however, are merely *formal*, they are originally modes of mind's activity, universally conceived. But they can therefore serve as a principle according to which the *material* of the original modes of mind's activity can also be determined in intuition' (I, 356–7; 1994c: 71–2). 'The material' is not conceived somatically, i.e. neither as substrate nor corpuscle, in accordance with the Aristotelian dichotomy; rather, it is *dynamically* conceived as *consisting only* in actions: 'the substance is composed of its powers', as Faraday put it (1839: 362). Although, as we shall see, this conception has Kantian sources, it does not have a Kantian destination. Schelling's argument, that is, does not amount to the formal programme he accuses the dynamics Kant develops in the *Metaphysical Foundations of Natural Science* of reducing to (*SW* II: 240; 1988: 192), but rather *materializes* the transcendental in an ironic mirror-image of the ' "proofs" that . . . Plato's Ideas are actual substances [*wirkliche Substanzen*]' against which Schelling continues to rage in the *Treatise* (I, 406; 1994c: 106, t.m.), and which the *Timaeus* essay equally vehemently rejects. We will return to this account of the materiality of the transcendental below (3.1, 5). For the moment, however, it is important to note that the *Treatise*'s transcendental account of the kinds elides *cause*. Since, in other words, nothing yet assumes the place of Plato's 'productive *nature*' (*Phil.* 26e6) in Schelling's asomatic physics of ideation, the genetic philosophy here operates with a restricted ontology.

Now Plato's concern, both in the *Timaeus*' and the *Philebus*' discussions of the kinds, is twofold: firstly, they are *generated*: 'these kinds must be declared to be two, for their becomings are unlike in nature [*xoris*]' (*Tim.* 51e1–2); 'the first kind, then, I call unlimited, the second limit, and the third something generated by a mixture of the two' (*Phil.* 27b7–9). The key issue here is the relation between 'kind [*gene*]' and 'idea [*idea*]'. While often argued to be synonymous (e.g., Cornford 1997: 186 n1), they are differentiable at once logically (kinds have the greater extension), and ontologically: of all the things that can be said of the Ideas, the most certain is that they themselves are unchanging and ungenerated, whereas the kinds are *by nature* generated and changeable. The second core Platonic focus is in turn twofold: the 'compound becoming of this cosmos' (*Tim.* 48a1–2), i.e., the physical universe and matter, and 'the becoming of being' (*Phil.* 26d8), directed in turn at 'all the entities [*onta*] in the universe' (*Phil.* 23c3) *including the Ideas*, on the one hand; and the metaphysics of generation as such, on the other. The *Timaeus* essay attempts to combine these Platonic focii in order to produce a logical and material, ontic and metaphysical, account of the *becoming of being*. In other words, Schelling's *Timaeus* commentary is an essay in the philosophy of dynamics. To preface our examination of the development of

Schellingian dynamics in naturephilosophy as in transcendental philosophy, we will first follow the dynamics Plato develops by way of the theory of kinds.

2.2 THE BECOMING OF BEING:
'GENE' AND DYNAMICS IN PLATONIC PHYSICS

If these premises be granted, it is wholly necessary that this Cosmos should be a copy of something. Now in regard to every matter, it is most important to begin in accordance with the natural beginning . . . Accordingly, the reasoning [logous] must be of the same kind [suggeneis] as the entities [ontas] of which it is the logic. (Tim. 29b2–6)

At the outset of the Timaeus essay, Schelling cites two uncontroversial Platonic propositions. The first runs: What is existent always [ti to on men aei] and has no becoming is apprehensible by thought and reason, while what is becoming always [ti to gignomenon aei] and never is existent is an object of opinion and of an 'intuition . . . contrary to the idea [den Ideen wider-sprechenden] (alogou)' (1994a: 23). Since the Ideas are ousiai, true being, for Plato, then if a 'becoming of being [ousian]' is possible and, crucially, kata phusin, 'according to nature', then nature consists in the combination (to koinon) or 'synthetic causation [xunaitia]' (Tim. 46c8) of being and becoming. Despite being 'eternal' like being, there is no Idea of becoming in Plato, a 'becoming itself', auto kath'auto, an 'absolute becoming' reproduced in the world that 'eternally becomes' because, as Schelling's rendering of alogou as 'contrary to the Ideas' emphasizes, being and becoming are not 'of the same kind [suggeneis]'. Moreover, an Idea of becoming would not resolve but merely reproduce the fundamental problem of Platonic phusis, namely, the participation of the Idea, or true being (ousia), in nature as such, and, specifically, in the generation of the physical cosmos. Perhaps the Idea from which becoming that becomes is copied could be the 'infinite', so that physical becoming would be the 'embodied image of the infinite', as time is said to be 'the moving image of eternity' (Tim. 37a7–9)? Becoming would thereby become intelligible, but at the cost of its axiomatic physical immanence. Thus to resolve the problem by way of granting becoming an ousia would produce a merely formal solution rather than a logic of physis of a kind with the All, and therefore simply replicate the dephysicalization of the Idea that is the Aristotelian legacy. That said, we may add to Böhme's 'widespread prejudice' concerning the impossibility of a Platonic physics, a second prejudice: the failure to confront Platonism as a 'physics of the All' leads not only to the occlusion of Plato's dynamic alternative to the assumed somatism of ancient physics, but therefore entails a systematic devaluation of the modalities of becoming in Platonism. In brief, while it is true that everything sensible is a mode of becoming, it is not true that all becoming is sensibly apprehensible, which is especially apparent in two areas, which we explore conjointly below: the dynamics of ideation and the generation of the cosmos.

Schelling's second Platonic proposition states that 'all becomings and destructions must of necessity become owing to some cause' (1994a: 24, citing *Tim.* 27d5–28a6).[11] Before addressing the complexities of 'the various kinds of causes' (*Tim.* 69a6) in Platonic physics, it is clear throughout the dialogues that while there is no Idea of becoming, it does have a principle (*arche*), which Plato calls 'soul': 'the entity which we all *call* soul is precisely that which is defined by the expression "self-generating motion"' (*Laws* 896a2–3), as Schelling reiterates: '*psyche* means nothing other than: *original principle of motion, arche kineseos*' (1994a: 28). That 'soul' is simply a name for 'autokinesis' (cf. Mohr 1985: 171–3) is clear in the elimination of the picture-language[12] in the *Laws*: 'the prime origin of motion is what moves itself', and this arises not only in the animate creature (*zoon empsuchon*) (*Tim.* 30b8), but, by virtue of the world soul (*kosmon psychon*) (34b4ff), in the world itself and in 'any object made of earth, water or fire' (*Laws* 895c4–6), and indeed in the whole 'autarchic cosmos [*to kosmou . . . autokratora*]' (*Stat.* 274a5–6). Autokratic and autokinetic *phusis* is *like* the Ideas precisely because, being '*auto*', it 'can neither be destroyed nor come into being', on the preeminently physical grounds that 'otherwise the whole universe and the whole creation would collapse and come to a stop' (*Phdr.* 245e4–8). On the other hand, autokinesis *itself*, as a principle of visible, generated and generative *physis*, is *alogou* or 'contrary to the Ideas', therefore necessarily a 'discordant and disorderly motion' (*Tim.* 30a4–5). The question therefore arises as to whether, given the 'ataxia of forces' that is matter, becoming without ideation *yet qualifies* as *auto*-kinesis, rather than, for example, being a mere 'errant cause' (*Tim.* 48a8). In other words, as the *Philebus* asks, is a 'contra-rational [*alogou*] and aleatoric power [*dunamis*]' (*Phil.* 28d7) sufficient to 'steer or govern [*diakubernan*]' the 'setting into order this Universe' (*Tim.* 53a8–b1), or what other cause might be necessary? Accordingly, Platonic physics concerns the emergence of order from disorderly and unceasing motion, which creates a post-Aristotelian conception of Platonism: no longer a formal or moralizing two-worlds metaphysics, but a one-world physics. Always centred around the nature of the 'participation' of Ideas in becoming, Platonic physics is the investigation of the 'mixture' of Ideas and *ataxia* involved in the 'generation of the heavens' (48a9–b4).

It thus emerges that the fundamental relevance for Platonic physics of the autokinetic principle lies in its confrontation with the principles (*archai*) underlying the somatic physics of its predecessors, to which Aristotle infamously reverts in book III of *On the Heavens* (289a24ff). Whereas Empedocles, for example, postulated earth, air, fire and water as the 'principles [*archai*]' of nature, or 'the four roots [*rizomata*] of all things' (Barnes 1987: 173–4; DK B6), the Platonic soul is explicitly accounted 'incorporeal' as opposed to the 'solid bodies from which things can . . . be moulded' (*Epon.* 981b3–9). In line with the *Laws*' above-noted elimination of picture-langage and 'bastard reasoning' (*Tim.* 52b3), the primordiality of soul means nothing other than: *the ceaseless becoming that is motion is by nature prior to somatic becomings*. Hence *kata physin* – 'in accordance with nature' – is always *kata dunamin* – 'in accordance with power'. This is one sense of the *Timaeus*' much-repeated *o ti malista*, 'as far as is possible', and *kata dunamin*, 'according to power', with regard to the sciences of nature. Even the demiurge can only fashion order out of disorder *so far as possible*, in accordance with the powers of *things* (30a2, 37d3), because the 'universal soul [*tou pantos psuchen*]' (41d5) is not an absolute, but rather only a 'homeostatic' pilot (*kybernetou*; *Stat.* 273c3; cf. Mohr 1985: 171), i.e., steering between degrees and dynamically balancing contraries.[13] *Kata dunamin* does not therefore reducibly define the scope and possibility of the natural sciences, or 'probable reasoning concerning nature' (*Tim.* 29d2, 57d6–7), in an epistemological sense, but also characterizes *nature itself*: 'I set up as a definition of beings [*onta*] that they are nothing else than power [*dynamis*]' (*Soph.* 247e3–4). This is why the Platonic question directed at natural entities is always: 'with what powers *due to nature* are we to suppose them endowed?' (*Phil.* 29b7; cf. *Tim.* 49a4–6).

It is because of the changing proportions of the powers due to becoming that the Platonic address to nature always involves 'kinds' or *gene*. A kind, composed of 'plurality of being and unlimited not-being' (*Soph.* 256e5–6), neither *is* nor *is not*. Thus, following the architecture of the *Timaeus*, which introduces (27e5) 'the two ideas' of Being and Becoming, only to add a 'third kind' (48e5) 'filled with powers [*dunameon*] neither similar nor balanced' (52e2), the two major Platonic propositions with which the *Timaeus* essay opens are immediately followed by a third, which Schelling naturalistically specifies as 'invisible . . . primordial matter' (1994a: 24). Since it is proper to the kinds 'by nature' that they are mixed or conjoint [*echei koinonian allelois e ton genon physis*] (*Soph.* 257a7), the logic proper to nature is composed of kinds, *gene*, compounds of being and becoming, *genesis*. 'Filled with powers neither equal nor balanced', the *Timaeus*' 'third kind' is paradigmatic: invisible like Being, yet comprising the 'unlimited [*apeiron* . . .] diversity' (*Stat.* 273d7) of 'not-Being' (*Soph.* 256e6), or becoming *sub specie aeternatis*. It is on this basis that the *Philebus*' ontogenetic, the *Timaeus*' cosmological and zoological, and the *Statesman*'s geological dynamics, are developed.

While the *Timaeus* operates three types of kinds, one consisting of Being, Becoming and the 'third kind' (50c9–d1), another of the animal kinds or species (39e9f), and the last of the 'four kinds' generated from matter to form the constituents of physical entities (56c9f), Schelling, with the exception of the *Timaeus*' 'third kind' (1994a: 41), more consistently cites the *Philebus*' theory of kinds. We shall first consider these latter kinds before locating the precise moment at which Schelling's concern with the transcendental in the *Treatise*'s account of the kinds temporarily sidetracks the proto-naturephilosophy of the *Timaeus* essay. The *Philebus*, then, declares the kinds to be four, with 'cause' the last to be declared: 'The first, then, I call unlimited [*apeiron*], the second, limit [*peras*] and the third a being [*ousian*] generated

by a mixture of these two. And [. . .] the cause of this mixture and generation [I call] the fourth' (27b7–c1). Since this cause has already been designated as 'productive nature' (26e6), and since its product is the '*ousian*
generated by a mixture', the generation of kinds is *kata phusin*, 'by nature',
and involves the 'true being' of the Ideas. This is especially clear in the
Timaeus, since the kinds in question are precisely Being, Becoming, and 'the
nurse of all becoming' or matter, on the one hand, and the geometries of
becomings generated in it, on the other. But it is also clear from the Platonic
conception of causation, which is indissociable from the nature of the kinds,
and is dealt with according to the *Philebus*' theory of kinds: 'by nature
[*kata physin*], production always leads, and the generated product follows'
(27a4–6). The priority of *production* over *product,* which will become a
cornerstone of Schellingian naturephilosophy, is not unequivocal, however,
insofar as it is explicitly and repeatedly the 'fourth kind', and the last to be
added. The problem is whether cause is an emergent property of the conjunctions of the kinds, and therefore 'fourth' precisely in that sense, or whether
production *causes* the conjunction of kinds hitherto separate and unmixed.
Since the kinds are composite 'by nature', an unmixed kind is at best a retrospective abstraction: it is Ideas, not kinds, that are *auto kath'auto.*
Accordingly, the *Philebus*' apparent contradiction in this sequencing of the
Platonic *gene* concerns the self-generation of natural production, where
production is the alpha and omega of the process, and 'leads' in precisely the
sense that it exceeds the becoming and passing-away of the product. In
other words, production is the *auto* of the becoming of being, i.e., production
is what causes becoming to become: 'every power is productive which causes
beings not previously existing, to become' (*Soph.* 265b8–9); and precisely
owing to this 'likeness [*suggeneis*]' of the kinds to the *auto,* natural
production *approximates* to the Idea, just as the becomings of the kinds are
suggeneis with becomings as such. Thus, the infamous Platonic 'copy' is not
a mechanical reproduction, but a dynamic defined with reference to the
becoming's degree of divergence from, and approximation to, the Being a
particular becoming *involves.* As for Protagoras, the problem of measurement
is crucial for Plato, although the latter will not, as linear recapitulationists
do in natural history, make this 'man'.

The 'nature that produces' cannot therefore be reduced to sensible nature
because it is the production of sensible nature that is itself not sensible.
Production exceeds empirically apprehensible becomings on two sides:
firstly, as the *Sophist* says: 'nature' cannot 'generate' its products (animals,
plants, and lifeless substances) 'from a self-acting cause [*tinos aitia
automates*] without productive [*phuouses*] intelligence' (265c1–9). Since,
that is, as 'true beings' or *ousiai,* the Ideas are necessary agents in nature,
production involves the Idea *in some necessarily nonsensible manner:* as the
Philebus says, the core problem the Platonic philosophy of kinds sets out
to resolve is the 'becoming of *being*', not simply particular sensible
becomings. Secondly, the time-frames involved in physical becoming are not
phenomenologically accessible precisely because the autokinetic, autarchic

and self-acting nature neither can nor ever therefore has ceased its motions, 'or the universe . . . would collapse' (*Phdr.* 245e7–8). Two grounds, then, for the 'darkness and difficulty' in matter (*Tim.* 48e4), and why 'the nature which receives all bodies' (50b7) is 'invisible and formless' (51a9), requiring a 'non-aesthetic [*anaeisthesias*]' (*Tim.* 52b3) and therefore non-phenomenological physics. As the *Timaeus* says, despite 'vision . . . giving us means of research into the nature of the universe' (46a6–9), 'becoming . . . attaches conditions to [all] the things which move in the world of sense' (38a3–7), including 'the generation of flesh and the appurtenances of flesh' (61c8–9), i.e., precisely its sensitive powers. The emergence of the generated world challenges the senses to exceed their own genesis, and entails instead a 'gaze fixed on what always is' (29a4f), on the *Idea* in nature, despite the Idea itself being necessarily non-sensible (*anhoraton, anhapton*). It is precisely the excess of physical becoming over the phenomenologically accessible that prompts the *Timaeus* essay's epigraph: 'to discover the producer and father of the universe is a great undertaking, and impossible to declare to all' (1994a: 23, citing *Tim.* 28c3–4). For while it is true that everything visible is becoming, it is not true that all becoming is visible, as the *Timaeus* makes abundantly 'fiery'. Time, for example, is called 'the moving image of eternity' (38a8–9) precisely in order to prevent the identification of sensible temporal processes with the totality of a becoming. Similarly, nature is not reducibly its sensible products, but also powers: 'every power is productive which causes becomings to bring into being what did not first exist' (*Soph.* 265b7–9).

What then is the nature of the Platonic *gene*? If they constitute a simply logical generation, then the kinds would indeed constitute the 'categories' Schelling characterizes them as. Yet kinds necessarily co-articulate Ideas and becomings. If we recall that the primary question of Platonic physics is: 'with what powers are they endowed by nature?', then the problem of their reducibility to Idea *or* matter disappears. 'By nature capable of conjunction [*echei koinonian*] one with another' (*Soph.* 257a8), the kinds, involving the generation of *ousiai*, generate, by nature, that nature that mixes Being and Becoming: 'Every kind [*panta ta gene*]', says the *Sophist*, 'has a plurality of Being and infinity of Not-being [*polu men esti to on, apeiron de plethei to me on*]' (256d9–e7). Precisely because they are not reducible to one or another of a series of contraries, the kinds do not stipulate motion *or* rest, same *or* other, but comprise series, each of the form of an 'indefinite dyad': being *and* not-being, motion *and* rest, limit *and* unlimited, and so on. Being thus by nature composite, no one kind is paradigmatic of the kinds as such; rather, what is important is their capacity, logically and *kata physin*, to generate conjunction (*echei koinonian*). It is therefore a consequence of a physics addressing the genesis of matter and of being, a physics that includes the Idea, that, as Parmenides points out in the eponymous dialogue, there is the risk that 'all things think' (*Parm.* 132c8), or that 'nature itself' is 'intelligent' (*Tim.* 46d9–e1). Accordingly, the mixtures of Idea, matter, being and not-being, are necessarily Ideal *and* material, and therefore neither are nor are not, but by nature, the 'becoming of being'. Becoming itself, therefore, *approximates* the eternity proper to the Idea insofar as it is 'unlimited [*apeiron*]', while *particular* becomings approximate the Idea – the *auto* or 'its self-ness' – their becoming involves. Becoming is therefore in permanent motion between absolutes that never themselves *are* become. The 'measure effected by the limit [*peras*]' therefore introduces approximations and divergences, by infinite degrees of 'great and small', into the dynamics of the becoming of being. The Platonic *gene* is like a *phase space of the Idea*, diagrammed in the genesis of matter. Perhaps this is how Buffon's overtly Platonizing natural history conceives it:

> The first animal, the first horse, for example, was the external model and internal germ [*moule intérieur*] on which every horse that has been born, all that exist and all that will be born, has been formed; but . . . the original imprint of . . . this model, of which we know only its copies, [. . .] subsists in its entirety in each individual. ([1753] 1985: 188)

We are now in a position to characterize the Platonic gene: it is a phase space of the Idea in unlimited not-being, that is, the always-becoming, in which the Idea acts as the limit-attractor towards which becoming never ceases to become, the *auto* or absolute approximated but never realized in the generated particular, the whole caused by and causing productive and intelligent nature.[14] We will examine later the *extent* and nature of 'intelligent nature' (*Tim.* 46d9–e1), since despite the grammar (*the* intelligent nature, not *intelligent nature itself*), it is only habit that reduces the phrase to a characterization of particular intelligences. Moreover, granting the core Platonic axiom of the objective existence of the Ideas, alongside the equally objective account of the kinds we have developed from their deployment in the context of the becoming of being, the conjunction of being and becoming, of Idea and matter, forms a dynamics of ideation that is, so to speak, substrate-independent. This, we affirm, is a problem to be confronted by any philosophy *of* nature, insofar as it rejects a priori the reduction of its elements to the phenomenological envelope attendant upon the Aristotelian-Kantian formal or phenomenal natures. The materiality of ideation is not a contingent problem given Plato's proto-Schellingian postulation of 'nature's autarchy' (*Stat.* 274a5–6; III, 17; 2004: 17), precisely because, as one-world physics both, neither the external limits of physical nature nor the internal limits of thinking nature *contain* the Idea, which must in both cases arise objectively (the becoming of *being*). The transcendental problem of the locus of the Idea thus becomes the naturephilosophical one of the physical conditions of its emergence; accordingly, 'philosophy is nothing other than a natural history of our mind' (II, 39; 1988: 30).

2.3 NATURAL HISTORY

'When I was young, Cebes, I was tremendously eager for the kind of wisdom which they call natural history [περι φυσεωη ιστοριαν].' (*Phaedo* 96a8)

While considerable attention has been paid to Schellingian historicism, the *nature* of the history in question has been paid considerably less. There are, for example, those historicists who, following Ernst Bloch's *The Problem of Materialism*, claim Schelling as a precursor of historical materialism (cf. Sandkühler (ed.) 1984; Hasler (ed.) 1981). Equally, there are those who wish to establish Schellingian historicism as the foundation of a 'system of freedom' (Peetz 1995), or who propose that the 'historicity of the Absolute' is 'the Schellingian problem *par excellence*' (David 1998). The first must reduce propositions concerning nature from an ontological to an epistemological status, in order to make an historical consciousness foundational with regard both to nature and knowledge, and shares with the second the requirement that this epistemological subject become in turn a practical one. In other words, both are essentially Fichtean, although the former, in particular, dresses this up with Marxian flourishes. The third at least acknowledges the problematic status of the claim that the Absolute may possess a history, which pits Schelling's verdict that 'there could be *no* history of' an Absolute (I, 473) against his assertion that the Absolute has the double structure of 'nature and history' (V, 111).

Of the modes of the Platonic kinds, one is particularly pertinent to the development of the genetic philosophy through natural history. This is the account of the 'animal kinds' in the *Timaeus*, which Schelling discusses in the *Timaeus* commentary (1994a: 29–31). The portrait of the cosmos as a spherical and limbless but nevertheless constantly mobile animal Plato gives at the end of the work (*Tim.* 92c4–8; cf. 30b9–d5) could be taken to anchor the animal kinds as species or *natural* kinds, much as we find in Aristotle's furnishing each necessary individual with an unchanging substance. Plato does indeed talk of 'animal kinds' in the *Timaeus* (91d6–92c2; cf. 39e4–40a9); insofar, however, as the kinds *in general* are composed of a 'plurality of being and infinite not-being' (*Soph.* 256e6–7), and insofar as nature is 'what endlessly becomes', then particular becomings cannot be *fixed* in nature. Pursuing this paradox will take Schelling to the heart of the problem of natural history, not merely as Plato outlines it, but in contemporary natural history as well. To preempt: if nature necessarily consists of endless becomings, then generated approximations of the Ideas in each kind – of whatever nature – must run through an infinity of becomings in its turn. Applied to natural history, *there is therefore no fixity of species*, so that speciation can only be conceived as infinite change: 'both then and now', Plato's 'discourse concerning the All' concludes, 'living creatures keep passing into one another' (*Tim.* 92b9–c3). The generativity of kinds, each with its own 'infinity of not-being', must itself be infinite. If this is so, then the kind cannot present a *copy* of the Idea, because the Idea has no correlate in nature. Therefore, pursuing the paradoxical account of the Ideas *in* kinds has consequences not only for a genetic account of natural history, but also the genetic account of the Ideas, or being itself. The being of the Idea must be conceived in terms that do not invite phenomenal correspondence with natural becomings. This, then, eliminates the prospect of a 'microcosm/macrocosm' reading of the relations between the cosmic animal and the individual animal kinds, and opens the problem of a genetic, non-phenomenal account of the Idea that nevertheless explains its actuality *in* kinds, i.e., the enveloping of being in becoming. Before dealing with these issues in greater detail, we must first look at the account of history as necesssarily natural history that Schelling initiates in his 1798 essay, 'Is a philosophy of history possible?'

Posed in overtly transcendental form, the question 'Is a philosophy of history possible?' begins to specify the nature of history. From the outset of this essay, Schelling demonstrates from the nature of history that all history is necessarily the history of nature. Since, that is, '*history* [*Geschichte*] is *knowledge of what has passed* [*des Geschehenen*]', and since 'nature is the aggregate of everything that has passed', then nature necessarily 'qualifies as the object of history' (I, 466). The first step in Schelling's deduction, then, is to remove freedom, the 'pleasant dream that deflects us from our limited nature' (I, 473), from history. At the same time, Schelling argues that 'what must be judged *a priori* and what takes place in accordance with necessary laws, is not an object of history' (I, 467). The problem of the nature of history first therefore confronts the problem of the 'nature of nature': does nature consist in the straightforward repetition of necessary laws, or does it act in ways recalcitrant to '*a priori*' determination?

The essay sketches two solutions to this problem. The first consists in the observation that it is only when a natural phenomenon – a comet, say – has yet to be understood in terms of necessary laws that it figures in history, as a 'harbinger of Caesar's death', for example. Comets, meteors, eclipses, eruptions and the like therefore enter history as mythology, 'an historical schema of nature', or a 'doctrine concerning things in the insensible world (because we have no laws of nature for that world)' (I, 472). The importance of this conclusion is demonstrated not merely in its late (1847–52) echo in the *Philosophy of Mythology*'s definition of myth as an 'unconscious, naturalistic . . . kind of philosophizing (*autophysis philosophia*)' (XI, 258). Rather, when this definition is added to the second of the essay's propositions, namely, '*where there is mechanism there is no history, and conversely, where there is history, there is no mechanism*' (I, 471), it becomes clear that mythology enters history not from the side of the science of nature, but rather as self-articulating nature. Accordingly, we may add to Schelling's propositions a third: *what cannot be defined according to natural law is precisely therefore narrated in accordance with it.* That is to say, 'natural philosophizing' is so by virtue not of its *content*, but of its *matter*. The particular *form* in which a myth is given is unimportant precisely because myth, unlike science, has no reflexive recoil such as compels science to account not only for its object, but also for the principles in accordance with which it generates this account (rather than dividing cognitive from natural production, the *System of Transcendental Idealism* (III, 397; 1978: 49) will note that it is the specific nature of philosophical science that it proceeds by this 'double series'). If mythology, then, swells history's coffers to the extent that its objects remain irreducible to nature due 'only to men's ignorance' (I, 466), it follows that 'the more the limits of our *knowledge* are extended, the narrower become the limits of *history*' (I, 472).

If the first solution, addressed almost entirely from the epistemological perspective, graphs the varying proportions of cognition, history and mythology as they struggle over nature, Schelling's second solution sets natural history as the necessary solution to the problem of the nature *of* history. The mechanism assumed under the first solution's theory of nature is properly historyless: that is, there is only a cyclical repetition of events, with no 'has happened' that is not also necessarily a 'will happen'. The segregation of history from nature is therefore a challenge to the philosophy of nature. A philosophy of natural history will resolve the problem of the nature of history to the extent that it makes 'progressivity' not aberrant with regard to a mechanically repeating nature, but necessary to a nature that acts quite otherwise. While the mutual exclusivity of mechanism and history entails that 'history, in the proper, true sense, only exists where it is *absolutely impossible . . .* to determine *a priori* the trajectory of a free activity' (I, 470), the same exclusivity ascribes, by default, a natural eternity to mechanism and thus fails as a natural history. The same premises, meanwhile, also entail that, as the first of the essay's propositions runs, 'whatever is not progressive is not an object of history' (I, 470), and thus make a *natural* history possible. 'How do mechanisms arise?' becomes one of several problems confronted by natural history, while the *philosophy* of history must begin with a philosophy of natural history, precisely insofar as it is only as a *philosophy* of nature that a philosophy of history, as 'the *a priori* science of history' (I, 473), is possible.

Schelling's realism or 'geocentrism' (Kirchhoff 1982: 47)[15] with regard to grounds is the simple and crucial basis of his theory of a priority: natural history exceeds and grounds the possibility of history insofar as the deposition of a ground over time is necessary to any later prosecution of events upon it. Accordingly, apriority cannot apply solely to what is necessary to our representations, since the power of representing presupposes physical and physiological conditions. As 'firstness' therefore, apriority applies to what is unconditionally necessary in order that there be species capable of representing at all. Yet 'necessity' cannot be straightforwardly concluded from apriority: while an earth is a necessary a priori for human history, nothing determines the necessity of *that* history as opposed to any number of others. If the earth, therefore, has only a contingent apriority with respect to its dependents, nature itself, by contrast, has unconditioned apriority. The extent to which the apriority of nature is to be understood here is made clear by Schelling's solution to a second strand of exclusivity attaching to mechanism. As the favoured theory of nature of the dogmatists, mechanism made 'freedom' inconceivable for Spinoza, for example, other than as 'ignorance of the causes' of an action (*Ethics* P35, *schol.*), just as Schelling accounts freedom a 'pleasant dream deflecting us from our limited natures' (I, 473). Having defined 'progressivity', conversely, as free activity, and the purpose of natural history being 'to consider the trajectories of the free activity in nature' (I, 470), natural history recalls its premise in removing freedom from history *in order that it be replaced there as the freedom of progressive*, rather than non-historical or mechanical, *nature*. Progressive nature is a priori with regard to mechanical – or organic – nature precisely in the sense that it generates the 'individual forms' or *products* of nature. In other words, what 'Is a Philosophy of History Possible?' outlines is an early version of the difference between nature as productivity and nature as product that will dominate the *First Outline of a System of Naturephilosophy*, the *Introduction to the Outline*, and the *System of Transcendental Idealism*.

The essay accordingly sets out the parameters of a philosophy of natural history, or a genetic philosophy of nature. Although Plato has Socrates declare his early naturalism, natural history is the inevitable *consequence* of the genetic philosophy entailed by the ontology of becoming (unlimited not-being), rather than its forerunner. In setting out these parameters, therefore, Schelling contrasts the Platonism reinvested, particularly by Buffon, into the mid-eighteenth natural history that Kant renamed the 'description of nature' (*Ak.* V, 428n; 1987: 315n), precisely because it described the contents but not the transformations of nature, with the emerging dynamic systems of natural history, which play a massive role in the development of Schelling's naturephilosophy. Both hypotheses confront the central problem Schelling had drawn from the initial elaborations of genetic Platonism in his *Timaeus* commentary, namely, the 'becoming of being'. Buffon's theory of reproduction, for example, as the production of 'always degenerating' individuals as 'deviations' from the 'originary impression' that grounds species-identity, seems explicitly grounded in a naturalistic Platonism.[16] By not simply ascribing the theory to Buffon, however, Schelling makes visible its resurgence in contemporaneous naturalists such as Carl Gustav Carus, Lorenz Oken, and Goethe (cf. 4.1, below).

The other natural historical schema by which Schelling prosecutes the genesis of genetic philosophy is that proposed by Carl Friedrich Kielmeyer, the title of whose 1793 'Rede', *On the Proportions of Organic Forces Relative to each other in the Series of Various Organisations*, is dissolved almost verbatim into the fabric of the 'History' essay (I, 469). Thus Schelling outlines the two 'hypotheses, highly daring from the perspective of physics' regarding 'the current system of nature'. According to the Kielmeyer hypothesis,

we would think nature in its freedom as it evolves along all possible paths in accordance with an original organisation (which for that very reason cannot now exist anywhere), wherein now one force, at the cost of suppressing the others, has here a lower, and there a higher intensity, and thus an equilibrium is attained amongst these same organic forces; this would even have the advantage over the [other hypothesis] of being able to reduce the external variations amongst the Earth's creatures as regards the number, magnitude, structure and function of the organs to an original, inner variation in the interrelations of organic forces (of which these were only the outward phenomena). In the [Buffonian] case, we would not of course need to establish a common archetype for all organisations; but we would certainly need common archetypes for the many now separate kinds that owe their origin to a gradual *deviation* [*Abweichung*] from the original, produced by various natural influences. (I, 469)

A system of nature grounded on the second hypothesis provides a schema whereby species consist of constant self-reproduction. Variations amongst individuals arise due to an equally constant 'deviation' from the 'original impression', whereby the 'copies', which are all we know of their 'external model and inner germ [*moule intérieur*]', are generated (Buffon [1753] 1985: 188). Entirely in keeping with Platonism, the degeneration of copies yields the phenomenal order of nature, while 'self-subsistent . . . animal or vegetal species [that] can never be exhausted' ([1748] 1985: 186–7) form its non-phenomenal substrate. Apparently materializing the Idea in accordance with the 'secret teachings', Buffon hazards the hypothesis – daring from the point of view of metaphysics – that it is not Ideas, but rather 'the primary animal[s], for example, the first horse' that are self-subsistent and inexhaustible, and that '*were* the outward model and inner germ' of the phenomenal, degenerating animals that, like 'the beautiful and the good', are 'scattered over the whole earth' in varying degrees ([1753] 1985: 188; my emphasis). Thus Buffon attempts a resolution of Platonic physics by realigning the relation between the generative cause and the degenerating copies not in terms of intelligible and sensible alone, but distributes what is intelligible and what sensible, what causes generation and what degenerates, around temporal generative priority. The primary animal, in other words, is not non-phenomenal because intelligible only, but because it cannot presently be observed; it can neither be exhausted *qua* original impression or outward model, since the impression or model is imprinted precisely in each copy; nor *qua* inner germ, insofar as actual generation transports precisely this germ through successive generations.

Yet the Buffonian hypothesis is troubled by two problems. Firstly the animality of the primals yields a natural history of organic matter alone, positing brute matter as 'not-being' by default. Accordingly, there can be no generative history of organic matter as such, since it cannot derive from non-organic or brute matter. Cementing the point with the hypothesis of 'a permanently active organic matter' ([1748] 1985: 186), Buffon effectively rules out the possibility of a generative natural history of animal being. In place of the former, the 'primary animals' become the 'common archetypes for the many now separate kinds', as Schelling puts it, and assume the status of eternal, self-subsisting and inexhaustible beings that are, accordingly, historyless.

Secondly, the ground for the excision of a natural history of animality as such is the distinction between the system and the history of nature. The 'permanent activity' of this 'animate organic matter' that is 'universally extended throughout all animal or vegetal substances' ([1748] 1985: 185), forms a *perpetuum mobile* of flesh, an organic mechanism whose operating parameters never change. Appearances to the contrary, the Buffonian system shares with universal mechanism the basic premise of the essential timelessness or ideal reversibility of the system of nature itself. The difference, for Buffon, is this system is not ideal or abstract, but actually composed of a continuum of 'productive matter' such as 'we may see under the microscope in the seminal fluids of animals' ([1748] 1985: 182). Animals are not clocks; rather, clocks are animals. Accordingly, history begins only where there is irreversibility, which in nature is limited exclusively to actual animals, which degenerate as they reproduce. Neither systemic nature nor the natural kinds (the 'primary animals') have a history, only individuals.

The task of natural history is therefore twofold: firstly, to unpick the reproductive chains by which productive matter composes the system of nature, and secondly, noting the reproductive blockages along these chains in order to establish the morphological territories of the primary animals. In other words, to the empirical criterion of species-identity through reproductive capacity, the Buffonian system gives the non-phenomenal ground of the ideal or primary animals. The task of identification completed, the natural historian must then reconstruct the portrait of each primary animal by collating the *sum of the differences* between those individuals demonstrated by reproducibility to be devolutions from that species-ideal. To compensate, in other words, for the phenomenological non-availability of that point *in time* when the primary animals made their 'original imprint', the natural historian's ultimate role is to reverse the devolutions of history by the phenomenal reconstruction of the *idia*, the particularity, of the original animals.

Schelling raises four objections against this account of the system of nature with its primary animals. They strike, however, not just at eighteenth-century mechanistic natural histories, but also at those contemporary philosophies that descend no further into nature than animality. Firstly, against Kant's protestations that such systems cannot be properly called natural *histories*, Schelling observes that since 'many kinds of animal and plant can be discovered for which there is no species-concept in the system prior to that point, such a discovery can only be accommodated *historically*' (I, 468). The non-reducibility of the 'many now separate kinds' is a problem not because it *is not reduced* to a single common archetype, but because the precise number of kinds cannot be delimited in advance, but is contingent upon the discovery of new kinds. For Schelling, however, it is precisely this *progressive* aspect to the system's necessarily increasing accommodations that makes it 'not illegitimate' that it be called 'natural history' (I, 467). Secondly, if progressivity defines historicity (I, 470), and if there is to be a legitimately so-called *natural* history, then this must be due to nature's *own* progressivity. In accordance with a system that accommodated nature's progressivity, 'we would think nature in its freedom as it evolves along all possible paths' (I, 469).

From the perspective of a Platonic natural history or philosophy of becoming, it is the third of Schelling's objections that is most telling, however. The central error in any system of nature that arrives at archetypes, whether one or many, consists in the philosophy of matter underlying it. For Buffon, for example, while the primary animals determine the existence and nature of the finite number of species amongst natural organisms, the real existence of such organisms is sustained by the 'permanently active organic matter' that forms their substrate, a meta-organic kind from which all individuals emerge. By what nature, however, is the restriction of the permanent activity of 'active organic particles' (Buffon [1748] 1985: 182) accomplished? The primary animals held by Buffon to explain this restriction cannot participate in the circulation of generative material through seminal and nutritive matters, nor in the degeneration that is the necessary fate of those animals that do so participate. If the system of nature is maintained by productive organic nature, the primary animals or kinds, sharing no common substrate with the organisms devolved from them, cannot be held to intervene in these circulating chains. The eternal, self-subsisting, ungenerated and inexhaustible kinds, therefore, are 'ideal' in the sense of being mere conceptual artifacts of natural historians, who advance their hypothetical existence only insofar as they serve as *just one* possible explanation of the real existence of reproductive barriers. Either therefore 'ideal' in the sense of other-than-nature, resulting in a metaphysics without physics; or mere constructions facilitating explanations of nature that have themselves no necessary, but only a nominal relation to their putative objects, resulting in a physics without a metaphysics in the interests of a merely theoretical reduction. When therefore Schelling writes, in the introduction to *On the World Soul*, written contemporaneously with the 'History' essay, 'I hate nothing more than the striving to eliminate the multiplicity of natural causes by means of constructed identities' (II, 347–8), he is of course objecting to natural scientists' abuse of the Idea as a 'merely constructed identity'; unlike the mere idealism Schelling's detractors argue he perpetrates to the detriment of those sciences, however, the grounds of this objection lie not in the Idea, but in the complexity of natural causation.

In such systems, therefore, we see the same separation of the Idea from nature and the same nominalistic reduction of the former coupled with the same empirical reduction of the latter that we find in Aristotle. Only apparently Platonic, Buffon's system turns out to be Aristotelian *in toto*, with a separable realm of individual and unchanging kinds corresponding not to Ideas, but to what does not change in the substantial forms of their living exemplars. Both offer not so much a Platonic natural history (φυσεως ιστοριαν), therefore, as an Aristotelian *history of animals*, a ζωα ιστορια. When therefore, launching his fourth objection, Schelling raises against the systems of ideal archetypes the groundlessness of a 'history of animals in the strict sense' (I, 470), it is precisely against the Aristotelian reduction of nature to an animal history coupled to, but not explained by, a system of nature that, while it causes change, is itself unchanging. This is the form in which Kant's third *Critique* inherited the problem: if self-organizing nature is inconceivable along the lines of mechanism, then the reassuring certainty of a mechanical eternity is removed by fossil remains of vanished creatures.[17] It is crucial to the very conception of the naturephilosophy, however, that the problem cannot be solved either by theoretical reason, practical reason, or their conjunction. This is because of the unconditional apriority attaching to nature with regard to ideation, on the one hand, and with regard to activity, on the other. Accordingly, the solution to the problem can only be pursued in nature.

Since nature consists in ceaseless becoming (so that Carus, for example, will first of all *describe* nature, in overtly Platonic terms, as a 'sea of becoming' (1944: 19; cf. *Stat.* 273e1), before ontologizing nature as '*das Werdende*', in accordance with the Platonic schema), there can be no *kinds* that are at the same time natural and unchanging. Just as it is a necessary outcome of the Platonic account of nature as 'becoming' that the science 'of the same kind (*suggeneis*)' as nature should be the science of becoming, or natural history; so it follows from this that natural history does not have objects as its field of study, but rather kinds, *gene*, and their becomings, their *genneta* or *gignomena*. What therefore remains constant in Schelling's commentary on the *Timaeus*' 'animal kinds', is that one animal-Idea 'covers all the species and types [*Gattungen und Arten*] of animals' (1994a: 30; *Tim.* 30c1–31a1). In other words, a Platonic natural history cannot entail the existence of an Idea of each individual species and type. That this is not the case is clear from the concluding passages of the *Timaeus* itself: 'Thus both then and now, living creatures keep passing into one another in all these ways, as they undergo transformation' (92b9–c2). That this is so demonstrates clearly that there are no species-Ideas, no 'primary animals' in the Buffonian sense, for Platonic natural history. This being so, in what manner do the Ideas participate in the constant transformations that are the subject of natural history? How, in other words, is a Platonic *philosophy* of natural history possible? Schelling (1994a: 29–31, 39) takes particular note of the manner in which the 'world must contain all the different Ideas that intellect discerns contained in the animal that really is [*o esti zoon*]' (*Tim.* 39e7–8). This latter is the world, which although something generated, is 'animal' precisely because it, as do all intelligible animals [*zoois noetois*] for Plato, 'possesses *original motive force*' (Schelling 1994a: 29). What is intelligible in animality is automotive *force*, not animal kinds; in other words, the Idea contains not species or the blueprints of somatic animals, but the dynamics according to which what moves itself, and thus approximates the intelligible animal, and what is moved, and thus deviates from it, i.e., what approximates the not-being of the somatic animal, are combined. This is why Plato has several animal kinds emerge from one animal kind in the abrupt natural history that concludes the *Timaeus*: the infinity of not-being that the kind contains entails its infinite transformability.

Against the Aristotelian account of the problem of natural history, Schelling writes: 'there is no history of individual animals *as* such. For it comprises a cycle of acts beyond which it never steps; what it is, it is forever; what it will become is prefigured for it by the laws of a higher, but still inviolable mechanism' (I, 470). Naturephilosophy supplants the Aristotelian with a Platonic account, and then reinjects this into contemporaneous natural history. History, according to Platonism, is necessarily *natural* insofar as nature is not *what* is, but is the 'always becoming' (*Tim.* 27e–28a). If there is to be a genuinely *natural* history, then the cyclical repetitions of law in nature's mechanical products, i.e., the generation and corruption of individual animals, cannot form the basis of that history. Natural history must instead consist in that *progressivity in nature* that causes it to become; without this progressive causation, 'the whole universe and the whole of creation would collapse and come to a stop' (*Phdr.* 245e4–8). The existence of such progressivity in nature, if it cannot be found in the individual animals' repetitions of law, is nonetheless found in 'the remnants of now vanquished creatures' and in the discovery of creatures for which there is no currently existing 'species-concept in the system' (I, 468). Progressivity destroys the linearity and reversibility of the Buffonian system since the latter assumes the reconstructibility of the primary animals from the differentia of existing species-members (comparative anatomy). In consequence, natural progressivity is manifest in constant changes at the *species* level. Speciation is not the only index, however, of natural progressivity.

Following the predominantly ethico-practical complexion of postkantian metaphysics, some commentators find in this demonstration of 'progressivity in nature' evidence of a simple '*analogy* between the process of nature and history' (Sandkühler (ed.) 1984: 30). It is not Schelling, however, but rather Kant who advances this moral-natural parallelism, and on *practical* grounds: it is the function of judgement to locate in nature *analogies* of consciously purposive behaviour to serve as indices of the steady progress of the human race. This is why, regardless of whatever 'natural revolutions' may have taken place, Kant 'recommend[s] for practical purposes' the thesis that 'the human species has always been progressing towards the better and will continue to do so' (*Ak.* VII, 88). Schelling's view is, by contrast, entirely naturalistic: precisely because there is 'an infinite *progressivity*' in natural history, 'it cannot be concluded from this that the human race is infinitely perfectible' (III, 592; 1978: 202, t.m.). Such a view mistakes nature's progressivity, which Plato gives as its infinite transformability, for the 'analogue' of a freedom attaching to individuals of a single species. If there is history, states the *System of Transcendental Idealism*, then by virtue of being grounded in nature's progressivity, it attaches not to the individual but to the species (III, 597–9; 1978: 206–8).[18] Subject to the infinite transformability that constitutes the *actual* natural history of kinds, no 'race' or 'species' is perfectible. Although 'the most perfect of all visible creatures' (VII, 368; 1986: 44), because he is nevertheless a creature, man is necessarily transitional. Nature is not therefore completed in the production of man (a conceit to be found throughout the majority of commentary on the naturephilosophy); rather, its progressivity pursues that creature's transformation: 'the time had come for a new species, equipped with new organs of thought, to arise . . .' (Schelling 1989a: 57).

Although we have yet to consider the dynamicist natural history that follows from Kielmeyer's principles in light of the foregoing (cf. 4.1, above), the contingent position of 'man' in both Plato's system, wherein that creature plays the role of the material-intellectual point from which radiate all other animal-becomings brought about 'by loss or gain of reason [*nou kai anoias*]' (*Tim.* 92c1–2), and in Schelling's, wherein again man is a contingent stopover in the evolution of intellect, and like 'all individual organisations, merely indicates different developmental stages of one and the same organisation', demonstrates the problem of the nature of this 'original organisation' that will come to preoccupy natural history. The critique of the false Platonism of the Buffonian system, however, makes it clear that Schelling's candidate for this original organization is dynamicist rather than somatic, irrecuperably non-phenomenal, and Ideal without being non-physical. Whatever therefore *appears* or *bodies forth* in nature is necessarily not an image of its original. Not only do we thus dispose of a tenacious misconception regarding naturephilosophy and early nineteenth-century natural history, we have also demonstrated that far from disabling a physics, Platonic physics necessitates a natural history. In exploring the 'progressivity' entailed by such a natural history, we have equally noted that natural history cannot be reduced to a comparative anatomy, since this mistakes the current forms of nature for the exclusive and necessary forms in which nature appears. Rather, natural history consists in maps of becoming that exceed phenomenal or sensible nature both in the direction of time and in that of the physiology of the senses. Finally, in so doing, we have prepared the ground for the differentiation of the *linear* from the *non-linear* uses of the theory of *recapitulation* that is the 'epoch-altering' contribution of Kielmeyer to natural history (II, 565).

Notes

1   Abbreviations of classical texts used in the following chapter are: Plato: *Crat.*= *Cratylus*; *Epis.* = *Epistles* (I–XIII); *Epon.* = *Eponimis*; *Laws* = *Laws*; *Parm.* = *Parmenides*; *Phdr.* = *Phaedrus*; *Phil.* = *Philebus*; *Soph.* = *Sophist*; *Stat.* = *Statesman*; *Tim.* = *Timaeus*. Aristotle: *De an.* = *De Anima*; *Gen.* = *On Coming to be and Passing Away*; *Heav.* = *On the Heavens*; *Hist.An.* = *History of Animals*; *Met.* = *Metaphysics*; *Phys.* = *Physics*. Plotinus = *Enneads* I–VI. Since many passages I cite are compounds of existing translations, or retranslations to bring out occluded aspects of Platonic physics, references give Stephanus numbers for Plato, Bekker for Aristotle, supplemented by line numbers to aid the reader in finding the passages at issue.

2   For example, Marenbon (1988: 6) writes 'The *Timaeus* was the most popular of Plato's dialogues in antiquity . . . In having [it] as the main source for their knowledge of Plato's thought, the early Middle Ages was the beneficiary, or the victim of the philosophical attitudes of Plato's ancient followers'. For Calcidius' translation of the text and its role in communicating ancient Platonism to the early Medievals, see Dutton in Reydams-Schils 2003: 183–205.

3   Schelling concludes the *Introduction to the Outline of a System of Naturephilosophy or On the Concept of Speculative Physics* (1799) with this directly collaborative appeal on the part of his science: 'And with this the author delivers over these *Elements of a System of Speculative Physics* to the thinking heads of the age, begging them to make common cause with him in this science – which opens up views of no mean order – and to make up by their own powers, knowledge and public connections, for what, in these respects, he lacks' (III, 326; 2004: 232). Schelling pursued his overtly collaborative model of speculative physics through editing the *Journal of Speculative Physics* (1800–1801) and *New Journal of Speculative Physics* (1802), and continued it with his editorship of the *Annals of Medicine as Science* (1805–6), itself formed in response to the overtly Fichtean, Kantian and Brunonian *Magazine for the Improvement of the Theoretical and Practical Healing Arts* (1799ff), edited by Andreas Röschlaub, who dedicated the first edition of the journal to Fichte's 'undying service to true philosophy, and therefore to all science' (cited in Tsouyopoulos 1978a: 93). For Schelling's criticisms of Röschlaub, see 'Preliminary Indication of the Position of Medicine according to the Principles of the Philosophy of Nature', VII, 260–88.

4   Following Krings' 'Genesis und Materie – zur Bedeutung der "Timaeus" Handschrift für Schellings Naturphilosophie' (in Schelling 1994a: 115–55), and against Franz, in *Schellings Tübinger Platon-Studien* (1995: 240–1), we here take it as read that a commentary on Plato's *Timaeus* has a necessary connection with the *Naturphilosophie*. Beierwaltes gives a summarial presentation of the issues in Reydams-Schils (ed.) 2003: 274–5.

5   For ethico-political accounts of the *Timaeus*, see for example Cornford 1935 and Sallis 1999. Amongst the physicalist commentaries on the text, following the lead of Whitehead (1920: 17f) and Taylor 1929, see Brisson and Meyerstein 1991, but especially Böhme 2000.

6   As cited by Diogenes Laertius (3.60): *Timaeus e peri phuseos, phusikos*, the 'physics of physics'. It is this, rather than Aristotle's bookshelves, from which 'metaphysics' arises.

7   The full passage, taken from Schelling's obituary 'Immanuel Kant' (1804), runs: 'To the formal aspect of his theoretical critique of reason he will later add his *Metaphysical Foundations of Natural Science* as its corresponding real aspect, although without being able, following this detachment, to develop a true unity in the principles of the two parts and turning his natural science into a *philosophy of nature*, and without his being able even here to bring the universal into complete harmony with the particular. [. . .] His views on organic nature, as set down in the *Critique of Teleological Judgment*, remained entirely separate from natural science in general'. (VI, 7–8)

8   Although Aristotle references Plato's 'unwritten teachings' fairly regularly (*Physics* 209b15; *De Anima* 404b), Martin (1841: 352) cites *Metaphysics* 985b, 987b–8a, 1028b, 1080, 1090 as further references to these doctrines), his interpretation of them concentrates exclusively on their application to the ontology of number, overlooking the problem of matter contained in 'the great and the small'. Martin (1841: 354) summarizes: 'Now following the testimony of Aristotle, Plotinus (II.4.v–vi) and Proclus (*In Tim.* 182), Plato's secret teachings taught that the ideas themselves were composed of matter, *hyle*, or in other words of an indefinite multiplicity, *duas aoristos*, which has as its elements the great and the small, and as form, unity, *to hen*' (1841: 354). Wicksteed's translation of the *Physics* (187a17) appends the following remarks to Aristotle's mention of Plato's 'great and small' doctrine: 'Alexander (quoted and supported by Simplicius) tells us of Plato's hearers mentioning the *aoristas duas en mega kai mikron elegen* (the indeterminate dyad, which he [Plato] called great and small). Though Plato has nowhere in his written works developed the "great and

small" nomenclature, yet its connexion with the 'indeterminate dyad' (cf. *Philebus*) makes it fairly certain that it stands for the purely dimensional 'not-anything' that occupied in Plato's system the place taken by the conceptually abstracted *hyle* or 'matter' in Aristotle.' Accordingly, the terms of Aristotle's critique of Plato reduce the question of participation to one of causation.

9   'The Aristotelian philosophy of nature as a whole can be designated phenomenological, in the sense, as it were, that for Aristotle, nature in general is an *aiestheton*, something perceptible, or in the sense that the experiences belonging to it are sensible and not instrumentally mediated [*apparative*]' (Böhme and Schiemann (eds) 1997: 14).

10   As Aristotle defines 'essence' or 'what-it-is-to-be-a-thing' (*to ti en einai*) as that by virtue of which a species belongs to a genus: 'Hence essence will belong to nothing except species of a genus' (*Met.* 1030a12–13).

11   I have given the passages as Schelling cites them, not according to Plato's text.

12   Sallis (1999) characterizes the *Timaeus*' *eikos logos* as 'discourse on images' (1999: 107) that is a necessary consequence of the dialogue's attempts to 'reveal in words' what is in itself 'dark' (*Tim.* 49a3–4) due to the attachment of 'human discourse to images' (1999: 55). Sallis therefore declares the 'cosmos' to be an image, and, unconsciously echoing Bergson in *Matter and Memory*, the 'third kind' or *matter* to be an 'image' (89), so that the *eikota logos* in 'the *Timaeus* presents . . . a kind of image of images' (107), to parallel the *eikos muthos* or 'discourse on discourse' (56). Support for such a thesis can be found throughout Plato's *Cratylus* (423a1ff), which interprets language as embroiled in the Heraclitean flux, a 'bodily imitation of that which was to be expressed', and in the VIIth letter (342e4–343a3, 343c1–7), where it is explicitly said to be merely a likeness 'offering the soul either in word or concrete form that which is not sought', and therefore not an appropriate medium of truth. That however this in no way affects the Ideas remains a problem that cannot be elided by means of an imagistic treatment of the dialogues.

13   Taking its impetus from the 'pilot of the universe [*tou pantos . . . kybernetes*]' (*Stat.* 272e3–4), Mohr (1985: 172) qualifies his *cybernetic* account of the world soul in the *Statesman* (272d7–3e4): 'For Plato the homeostatic conditions of the observed world cannot be explained *by* physical theories; rather, they have to be explained *in spite of* physical theories.' Mohr thus reproduces the form/matter distinction by interposing a problem of matter beyond the problem of the emergence of order, and therefore does not note the ontological range of Platonic dynamics.

14   As Böhme writes concerning the Platonic theory of 'pattern', as he accounts the geometrical elements of the *Timaeus*' cosmology, 'we could indeed call this . . . a self-organizing process. This conception may very well aid in understanding Plato, but in fact the relation is the other way round: Plato helps us to gain a fuller understanding of the theory of self-organization' (2000: 306). While Böhme's reversal is welcome, if a naturephilosophy is not to be a redundant redescription of philosophy in scientific terms, or of science in philosophical terms – something Schelling accounts 'a pitiful and mundane business' (*SW* II, 6; 1988: 5) – then even the 'fuller understanding' of scientific concepts must be regarded as an instrumental distraction from the strictly philosophical remit of a universal or 'great physics'.

15   This geocentrism remains throughout Schelling's work, and we will return to it in chapter 5. As even the Marxianizing Hans Jörg Sandkühler notes, 'The real basis of the theory of the *Ages of the World* is modern geology' (Sandkühler (ed.) 1984: 21).

16   Buffon's Platonizing is explicit and undisguised: 'There is in nature', he writes, 'a general protoype within each species on which each individual is modelled.' As natural scientists, however, we do not know this prototype but 'only its copies' that are generated by the 'originary impression' of the prototype and 'degenerate', from individual to individual, through the self-reproduction of the species. Through reproduction, the 'interior germ [*moule intérieur*]' distributes the 'model of the beautiful and the good over the whole earth', although the portion of the beautiful and the good 'always degenerates' until recombined

with stock from other climes ([1753] 1985: 188–9).

17 Kant, in other words, does not ask simply 'how organised beings are possible', but rather, given their actuality, what follows from this for natural histories conceived after mechanical principles? This is why Kant insists that 'matter can receive more and other forms that it can get through mechanism' (*Ak*. V, 411; 1987: 296). For a more developed account of the impact of this problem in the formation of Kant's post-critical philosophy, see my 'Kant after geophilosophy' in Jones and Rehberg (eds) 2000: 37–60.

18 Since I cannot conceive a 'moral world-order . . . as absolutely objective', but require something thus objective to ground the possibility of freedom, writes Schelling, I find this in 'the objective element in willing [. . . i.e., in] the unconcious element [. . .]. Here we are of course talking not of the individual's action, but of the act of the entire species' (III, 597; 1978: 206). This is also why Schelling makes his philosophical inquiries 'into the essence of *human* freedom' (see ch. 5, below).

CHAPTER 3

Antiphysics and Neo-Fichteanism

The transcendental idealist . . . must have the courage to assert the strongest idealism that has ever been taught, and not even to fear the charge of speculative egoism. (Jacobi [1787] 2000b: 175)

Since Kant's *Critique of Pure Reason*, philosophy has been progressively evolving, but is now perhaps in the grip of a final crisis. (XIII, 32)

The question whether Jacobi's forensically targeted challenge proposed an increase or a decrease in philosophy's powers remains contemporarily pertinent, since whether met or not, the terms of that challenge have supplied the history of philosophy with its measure of Idealism. Its insufficiency, however, is apparent when we set Jacobi's testing of Kant against Schelling's: where the former set Kantianism the task of increasing its consistency at the cost of a diminished world, the latter tested the critical philosophy's restrictions against Platonic nature, which includes the Idea.[1] Because the expanded realism of Platonic physics manifestly exceeds speculative egoism both on the side of nature and the Idea, Schelling designated his a 'real' or 'objective idealism' (IV, 109),[2] and thus contested merely conditioned idealisms as thereby *eliminative*.

Yet Jacobi's challenge has played a decisive role in constructing the commonplace idea that Idealism is nothing other than 'speculative egoism'. Since it is precisely as a result of this reduction of idealism to egoism, however, that contemporary philosophy opposes it with its practicist, antiphysicist and 'post-metaphysical' consensus, and since Schelling rejects such a 'subjective idealism', polarizing the Jacobian against the Schellingian challenge will highlight the extent to which the Kantian territory remains 'contempory'.[3] The question is, what is the *nature* of that territory?

'Kant' remains the name of an upheaval in modern philosophy, a seismic shift so intense as to shift the terrain on which philosophy is conducted, to supply, *neither for the first nor the last time*, a philosophical terrain irreducible to the body of the earth, a 'second nature' made 'from the materials primary nature supplies' (*Ak.* V, 314; Kant 1987: 182). This new terrain posed the problem of the relation between metaphysics and physics, between thinking and being, or freedom and nature, in decisive, new ways. Even now, therefore, those who question the contemporary dominance of the critical philosophy deem it 'a necessary task' to 'rethink the notion of ground': the transcendental philosophy's 'ungrounding' creates a problem that animates not just Kant's critical philosophy, but all postkantian philosophy up to and including our own, exercising both its critics and adherents.[4] Since the Kantian philosophy was not merely a decisive feature *of* the philosophical landscape, but rather created it, many elements of that philosophy are indispensible to an account of the philosophers driven to realize, complete or ruin idealist philosophical systems.

Two elements of that philosophy will particularly occupy our attention in this chapter. Firstly, the constant revisions in the concept of nature that, according to Schelling, 'prevented his [Kant's] natural science from becoming a philosophy of nature' (VI, 8). Secondly, Kant's formalism, as ontologized by Fichte. In many respects, both Schelling and Fichte are attempting to resolve the same underlying problems encountered by the transcendental philosophy. Both reject Kant's phenomenalism, and both reject the somatism that underlies his concept of matter. Even the *Metaphysical Foundations of Natural Science*, which outwardly pursues a dynamic understanding of matter, is thwarted by its somatic concept of nature. Accordingly, even Kant was eventually impelled to repudiate that somatism in the incomplete and posthumous work, *Transition from Metaphysics to Physics*, and to attempt, by way of the 'ether proofs' therein, to resolve the problem of *the nature of the transcendental*. In place, therefore, of an a priori somatism, the *Transition* asks, 'how does matter produce a body?' (*Ak.* XXI, 476; Kant 1993: 41). As regards the development of Idealist philosophy, however, the Fichtean and Schellingian routes could not be further apart: Fichte radicalizes Kant's formalism precisely insofar as the formal is non-phenomenal and non-somatic; Schelling, by contrast, entirely rejects the 'critique of natural cognition' (XI, 526) he takes the transcendental philosophy to constitute, and pursues the philosophy of nature Kant could not. Where Schelling's 'natural history of our mind' (II, 39; 1988: 30) naturalizes not only the transcendental but also its 'production' (cf. IV, 109), however, Fichte's 'pragmatic history of the human mind' (*W* I, 222; 1982: 198) pursues the ontologizing of the transcendental as antiphysics. Fichte's science fails for precisely the same reasons as Kant's: the elimination of nature is itself premised on an underlying somatism, which contradicts both Kant's dynamics and Fichte's formalism. In both Fichtean science and Kantian transcendentalism, these contradictions become most apparent in their attempts to 'incorporate' nature into their systems, which end up dividing nature in two. The irony is palpable: rejecting Platonism as a two-worlds metaphysics results, in both cases, in a two-worlds *physics*.

Not only therefore can neither Fichte's 'subjective idealism' – or 'speculative egoism' – nor Kant's critical idealism accommodate the 'natural history of mind' into which Schelling will transform the transcendental philosophy; the grounds of this incompetence are revealed in their attempts at a natural history on the basis of a dualist typology of bodies that 'separates entirely organic nature from natural science in general' (VI, 8). Not solely due to the impact of 'the Kantian principle in natural history', as his naturalist student

Girtanner's 1796 work had it, or to the well-documented exchange between Kant and Blumenbach, nor even to Fichte's champions amongst the natural sciences (such as Windischmann, Eschenmayer and Röschlaub), transcendentalist positions began to be echoed throughout the natural sciences, particularly as regards the problem of organism. While therefore naturalists such as Oken and Carus are held, by virtue of being 'philosophers of nature', to be Schellingians; and while 'organicism' is equally frequently held to be equivalent to *Naturphilosophie*, we will see that neither position is accurate. Timothy Lenoir (1982: 5) is therefore right to note that it is not Schelling's *Naturphilosophie*, but rather Kant's that has the larger influence on the development of the nineteenth-century *life* sciences in particular; Schelling's own – Platonic, as we have seen – naturalism forms instead common cause with Kielmeyer's dynamic natural history, and with Steffens' geological researches (ch. 4).

If these naturalistic differences provide grounds to reject the well-worn thesis that the naturephilosophy does nothing more than to extend Kantian or Fichtean transcendentalism over nature,[5] it is equally a mistake to present Schellingianism in general as a 'philosophy of freedom' in precisely the practicist vein responsible for the 'aphysia' of so much contemporary Kantianism. Although Peterson (2004: xxxiii) has recently repeated that 'the philosophy of nature is an expressly ethical project', Jaspers must be held particularly responsible for this error: 'For Schelling, Kant is the turning-point, Fichte's idealism the foundation, and he himself the completion of the philosophy of freedom that can recreate metaphysics quite otherwise than all prior metaphysics' (Jaspers 1955: 178). To the contrary, Schelling is scathing of philosophies that, like Fichte's, consist of 'nothing but a moralizing of the entire world that undermines life and hollows it out; a true disgust towards all nature and vitality except that in the subject, and a crude extolling of morality and the doctrine of morals as *the one reality in life and science*' (VII, 19; my emphasis).

Nature does not, accordingly, depend on freedom, but rather the converse: 'Anything whose conditions simply cannot be given in nature, must be absolutely impossible' (III, 571; 1978: 186). Absolute idealism does not seek, therefore, to explain nature in accordance with freedom, but, if at all, then conversely: to explain freedom from nature, as the geological researches that ground both the *Philosophical Inquiries* and the *Ages of the World* do.[6] The naturephilosophy does not seek to give an idealistic explanation of nature, but rather a 'physical explication of idealism' (IV, 76).[7]

Clear therefore that Schelling is not extending but undoing Kant, and that, rather than ethically determining nature, he is pursuing a naturalistic possibilitization of freedom, the present chapter begins with Kant's essentially Aristotelian somatic physics prior to examining his late transcendental dynamics (3.1), before pursuing Fichte's attempts to meet that challenge through formalism (3.2). The discussion then shifts territory to the natural history that follows of necessity from the Platonic physics examined in chapter 2, and pursues the integration of the science of knowledge into natural history (3.3), and concludes with an account of the development and problems of 'transcendental morphology' which is the Goethean inheritance (3.4).

3.1 LATE TRANSCENDENTAL PHYSICS AND PHILOSOPHY: KANT AND SOMATISM

The *philosophical* part of this work is concerned with *dynamics* as the grounding science [*Grundwissenschaft*] of a theory of nature . . . My object . . . is to let natural science itself first emerge philosophically [*die Naturwissenschaft selbst erst philosophisch entstehen zu lassen*], and my philosophy itself is nothing other than natural science. (*SW* II, 6; 1988: 5, t.m.)

Conceived as an introduction to the study of naturephilosophy, the two editions (1797 and 1803) of the *Ideas for a Philosophy of Nature* frame the emergence and development of that science, acting as a cloud chamber within which we may observe the trajectories of these 'Ideas' through naturalistic and philosophical terrains. Against the scepticism surrounding the physics of the Idea evident from the *Timaeus* commentary and the *Treatise Explanatory*, the *Ideas* defines 'the ultimate goal of our ongoing natural researches' (II, 56; 1988: 42) as 'the most complete elaboration of the theory of Ideas and the identity of nature with the world of Ideas' (II, 69; 1988: 52). Although by elaborating this 'identity' of nature and Idea, it might be assumed that Schelling is continuing a critique of the physics of the Idea, eliding a physical ground of Ideation by means of a *merely meta*-physical identity, such an assumption is rooted in Aristotelian rather than Platonic solutions regarding the relation of physics to metaphysics (see 2.1, above). As the first attempt to construct the problem-field of naturephilosophy, the *Ideas* insists on what the *Introduction to the Outline of a System of Naturephilosophy* (1799) will argue: 'nature IS *a priori*' (III, 279; 2004: 198). Accordingly, the naturephilosophy 'wants' '. . . not that Nature should coincide with the laws of our mind *by chance* . . ., but that *it itself*, necessarily and originally, should not only *express*, but *even realise*, the laws of our mind, and that it is, and is called Nature only insofar as it does so' (II, 55–6; 1988: 41–2, t.m.).

Against Kant's *Metaphysical Foundations*, then, the naturephilosophical grounding of dynamics does not pursue a critical deduction of the 'a priori possibility of these fundamental forces' (*Ak*. IV, 524; 1970: 78), but rather the genetic philosophy whose Platonic groundworks were examined in the previous chapter. Schelling's 'absolute idealism' (II, 68; 1988: 51), which embraces 'the empirical *and* the philosophical' (II, 4; 1988: 4), consists in the dynamic elaboration of the identity of nature *and* Ideas. Accordingly, it opposes the 'merely relative' (II, 69; 1988: 52) or 'empirical idealism' (II, 57; 1988: 43) that imposes limits on the transcendental philosophy, and sets 'coming-into-being [*entstehen*]' against 'derivation [*ableiten*]' (II, 11; 1988: 9, t.m.), the 'synthetic Idea' against the analysis *of* ideas (II, 64; 1988: 48), and 'construction' against 'deduction' (III, 332; 1978: 3).

While the transcendental philosophy is overt in its denial of 'reason's demand for the unconditioned' (CPR A564/B592), and in establishing *Grenzbegriffe* or 'limiting concepts' (CPR A254–5/B310) to prevent the understanding from 'extravagation' (*Ak*. IV, 316–17; Kant 1971: 78) beyond the bounds of possible experience, Kant conceives the 'highest point that transcendental philosophy can ever touch[,] its boundary and completion' (*Ak*. IV, 318; 1971: 79) to lie with the following questions:

> *First*: How is nature possible in general in the *material* sense, namely according to intuition, as the totality of appearances? [. . .] *Secondly*: How is nature in the *formal* sense possible, as the totality of rules under which all appearances must stand if they are to be thought as connected in an experience? (*Ak*. IV, 318; 1971: 79–80)

The faultline along which these questions divide the remit of transcendental philosophy from what lies outside of it is drawn not simply *around* possible experience, but rather *between* possible experience (nature in the 'material' sense; cf. *Ak*. IV, 295; 1971: 54; *Ak*. IV, 467; 1970: 3) and things 'known according to their nature' (*Ak*. IV, 295; 1971: 54), that is, insofar as they are neither nature in the *material* sense ('the whole of all appearances' *Ak*. IV, 467; 1970: 3), nor in the *formal* ('everything that belongs to the possibility of a thing' *Ak*. IV, 467n; 1970: 3), but rather in the 'real', i.e., 'outside my concept' (*Ak*. IV, 295; 1971: 52). It is precisely because Kant thus 'isolates the formal side of his critique of theoretical reason from its real side [as given in] the *Metaphysical Foundations of Natural Science*' that Schelling argues in his eulogy to Kant (1804), 'his natural science cannot be turned into a naturephilosophy' (VI, 7–8). But Schelling is already working on the transcendental philosophy's incapacity for a philosophy of nature in the 'Introduction' to the *Ideas*. In accordance with the genetic method therein being developed, Schelling will seek to show how Kant's division of the real from the formal and the material – of the world from my concept of it and its appearance for me – is able to generate a nature that is possible only, and a mind entirely independent of it.

There are three main grounds of this separation of nature and the Idea. Firstly, the riven 'base kind' in accordance with which the transcendental field is generated. Secondly, the somatism that persists as the *dependent antithesis* of the transcendental field. Thirdly, the attempt, at the apex of the transcendental philosophy, to supplant nature as the ground of appearances with the transcendental itself as the substrate of a 'second nature' (*Ak*. V, 314; Kant 1987: 182). Since the 'Introduction' to the *Ideas* deals expressly with the first two grounds, we will examine this before looking at the two forms in which the transcendental philosophy seeks to crown its antiphysics with a merely invented nature: nature as analogical purposiveness (the philosophy of organism) and the aether dynamics of the *Physical Monadology* and the posthumous *Transition from Metaphysics to Physics*.

3.1.1 *The genetics of transcendentalism*

Treating intially of 'the problems which a philosophy of nature has to resolve' (II, 11; Schelling 1988: 9), the 'Introduction' begins with the Ideas in the one domain Kant 'grants them reality' (VI, 186; Schelling 1994c: 174), i.e., with the domain of freedom. Although Schelling has already, in effect, argued that freedom is a myth, in the sense that it belongs to a pre-scientific understanding of the actions of the species, the *Ideas* does not yet reach the conclusion that 'anything whose conditions simply cannot be given in nature, must be absolutely impossible' (III, 571; 1978: 186), let alone elaborating the naturalistic grounds of freedom, as in the *Philosophical Inquiries* (1809). The *Ideas* does not consider freedom as a problem in itself, but rather as a *limit* proper to transcendental philosophy which, Schelling argues, having reduced 'nature' to 'experience', has now . . .

> Established that only a *regulative* use can be made of [universal natural laws] in theoretical philosophy. Only our moral nature raises us above the phenomenal world, and laws which, in the realm of reason, are of *constitutive* use are for that very reason *practical* laws. So nothing remains hereafter of what was previously metaphysical in theoretical philosophy, except the practical alone. (II, 3; 1988: 3)

The *Ideas* therefore begins with freedom, the last remaining trace of metaphysics in what the above passage makes clear is the transcendental philosophy and its heirs. Freedom is accordingly the 'leading Idea' (I, 353; 1994c: 69) of contemporaneous philosophy, its greatest achievement, the summit of all its systems, and so affords a vantage point from which to survey those systems in their entirety. This procedure defines the programme of the *Ideas* in general, and its 'Introduction' in particular: 'this essay', writes Schelling, 'does not begin from *above* (with the establishment of principles), but from *below* (with experimental findings and the testing of previous systems)' (II, 56; 1988: 42). The problem at hand, therefore, is not the adequacy of the transcendental account of freedom, but the nature of transcendentalism once freedom has been adopted as its apex. The basic question posed at the outset of the *Ideas* is therefore *Is the philosophy of freedom capable of nature?*, and it is only after the 'testing of previous systems' is completed that naturephilosophy can begin to generate principles.

It would be a mistake, however, to reduce the 'Introduction' to a critique of the critical philosophy. Against the background of Schelling's overtly Platonizing 'infinite science' (II, 11; 1988: 9), the work continues the inquiries into the nature of matter and the Idea begun in the *Timaeus* commentary.

Demonstrating the naturalistic a priori under which the experiment is conducted, Schelling writes:

No inquiry has been surrounded, for the philosophers of every age, by so much darkness as that concerning the nature of matter. And yet insight into this question is necessary for true philosophy, just as all false systems are shipwrecked from the very outset on this reef. (II, 223; 1988: 179)

The critique of the 'materiality of the Ideas' is replaced in the *Ideas* with the beginnings of a genetic account of *natural ideation*, against which the 'Introduction' contrasts the merely conditioned concept of matter and ideation with which the transcendental philosophy works. Generated *from* the question 'How is a world outside us, a nature and with it, experience, possible?' (II, 12; 1988: 10), the transcendental philosophy demonstrates that it is in turn premised on an initial separation of nature and Idea. The import of this grounding question-complex is only apparent, however, when the transcendental procedure whereby the conditions are established under which nature *is* possible, is reversed, and considered instead from the *synthetic* perspective: 'how are a nature, experience, and a world created, that are *possible only*?' From this question, all the conditionality of the transcendental is evident from the outset – *given* the divided ontology of nature and thought, the logical necessity to result from transcendental deductions grounded in the latter alone reduce the former reciprocally to a merely logical possibility – but the precise ground of this conditionality is not yet given. To reach this, the *Ideas* systematically unfolds the series of conditions constitutive of this 'philosophy of reflection', as Schelling characterizes transcendental philosophy in general (II, 14; 1988: 11), probing its concepts for their conditionality. Repeatedly overlaying the axis of this separation, reflection's 'endless bifurcations' eventually reduce nature, insofar as it does not appear in reflection, to a 'thing-in-itself' and matter, insofar as it does appear in reflection, to 'a species of reflection' (CPR A370). The transcendental problem therefore becomes apparent: 'How do representations [*Vorstellungen*][8] arise in us?'

From the division of mind, which provides both the *form* (the a priori laws) and the *material* (intuitions), from world (reality) on the basis of which reflection arises (II, 13; 1988: 10), the 'Introduction', scouring the *Critique of Pure Reason*, the *Metaphysical Foundations of Natural Science* and the *Critique of Teleological Judgment* for the Kantian concept of matter, derives all further divisions that recursively condition the transcendental philosophy on the side of the desubstantialized Idea, mapping, as it were, the *gene* or base-kind of that philosophy. This is why Kant's is a 'merely relative idealism': an idealism conditioned, precisely, by the elimination of nature, and therefore ideal *relative to* nature. Yet every ideational division further conditions the side of nature, in two ways: firstly, insofar as nature is thought at all as other than appearance, it serves only to limit the idea (or, for Kant, the *representation*); secondly, regardless of nature being thought, nature insofar as it is *not* thought, i.e., any nature independent of our thinking of it, necessarily exceeds and grounds all possible ideation. As the *System of Transcendental Idealism* puts it, *reversing* rather than *extending* the Kantian procedure, 'Anything whose conditions simply cannot be given in nature, must be absolutely impossible' (III, 571; 1978: 186).

Having established the base-kind and its 'nature', the *Ideas'* genetic unfolding of the transcendental philosophy proceeds to chart its recursion. The first recursion of the initial division separates nature absolutely from transcendental access, permanently isolating it from possible intellection as a 'thing-in-itself' that 'neither understanding nor reason, intuition or imagination, can reach' (II, 14; 1988: 11). On this basis, the next transcendental question is: 'How do representations of *external things* arise in me?' (II, 15; 1988: 12, my emphasis). Insofar as we are to think any connection between things, this necessarily takes the form of cause and effect. If then the external thing (object) and the representation are placed in like relation to cause and effect, a connection is established in our thinking *by analogy* with our representations of the external world (II, 15; 1988: 12). Since this division acts only on the basis of applying a law of the understanding to experience, and therefore acts exclusively on the side of ideation the better to establish their necessity in our thinking, the recursion of the division in effect eliminates cause and effect from the external world, while having the inestimable benefit, for Kant, of eliminating simultaneously any possibility of posing a question concerning a putative external causation of internal ideation.[9] In place, therefore, of the division between idea and nature, the distinction emerges between 'I' and 'my representations'. Insofar as these are representations of cause and effect, I cannot be affected by these since, in articulating them, I 'raise myself above representation' (II, 16–17; 1988: 13). The stratum 'above' representations supplants that 'below' sensuous experience, transforming the material or substantial *hypokeimenon* or substrate underlying all sensuous experience, but itself inaccessible thereto, into the supersensuous (X, 83–4; 1994b: 101–2). If it cannot lie in external objects as a physical origin, the transcendental origin of representation must therefore lie in freedom as an 'original cause' (cf. Kant, *Ak.* XXI, 20; 1993: 226), and is therefore determined by a one-sided practical absolute (II, 18; 1988: 14). Due to this one-sidedness, freedom is possible therefore at the cost of the absolute elimination of matter from an external world, and the latter's reduction to a misunderstood 'thing-in-itself' (II, 21; 1988: 16). 'Thus mind and matter separate', Schelling continues, 'and I place them in different worlds, between which no connection is possible' (II, 16–17; 1988: 13).[10] Returning to the opening problem of the *Ideas*, then, of what nature, therefore, is the philosophy of freedom capable?

3.1.2 *Transcendental philosophy as relative antiphysics*

Of the two-worlds solution transcendentalism invents, one world contains the formal, the material and the causal, insofar as these have been withdrawn from the other. The first, however, finds form only in the laws of the under-standing, matter exclusively insofar as it is intuitable, and causation only within freedom; while the second, lacking all three, is nonetheless the 'real' nature before which transcendental philosophy reaches its 'highest point' and therefore becomes self-reverting. This is why transcendental philosophy is a 'merely relative idealism' or a *conditioned antiphysics*. And just as Schelling's 'genetic typing' of the transcendental philosophy reveals the recursive elimi-nation of nature on the side of the idea, nature remains the substrate on the basis of which these recursions act. It is therefore possible to ask of the transcendental philosophy, 'What is the nature of the "nature" it eliminates?'

In defining 'material nature' as 'the whole of all appearances' (*Ak*. IV, 467; 1970: 3), Kant proposes to dispel the 'darkness' generated 'for philoso-phers of every age' (II, 223; Schelling 1988: 179) by the problem of 'matter, the darkest of all things, or darkness itself, according to some' (II, 359), precisely because the material is, for the transcendental philosophy, equiv-alent to the sensible, so that the concept of a non-sensible matter is self-contradictory. In this, we note Kant's rejection of the Platonic precept that matter itself must necessarily be non-sensible, because it cannot be considered equivalent to any particular visible body.[11] Yet Kant's definition of the material as a whole comprised of the totality of things insofar as they appear echoes not only of Aristotle's heuristic empiricism, but also his assertion in the *Physics* (187a34) that 'the universe is composed of a plurality of distinct individual entities'. Thus even in the account of the transcendentally deter-mined material presented in intuition, physical precepts exercise an unexamined influence on the a priori laws of the understanding. In other words, Kant's failure to provide a naturephilosophy (VI, 8) entails the deter-mination of even the possible *forms* a nature might take by an ontology derived from the 'Aristotelian philosophy of nature, [which] contains the principles common to *all* natural philosophy, and not just to the part that became our physics' (Des Chenes 1996: 2).

The physics implicit in the transcendental philosophy is made explicit in the *Metaphysical Foundations of Natural Science*. Just as 'Natural science properly so-called presupposes metaphysics of nature' (*Ak*. IV, 469; 1970: 5–6), so the transcendental metaphysics of nature presupposes in turn a particular doctrine of nature.[12] Because, that is 'the general name of natural science . . . belongs in the strict sense to the doctrine of body alone . . . such a doctrine is an actual metaphysics of corporeal nature'. Metaphysics, or 'pure philosophy', however, in order to 'ground the doctrine of body', must conduct a 'complete analysis of the concept of matter' (*Ak*. IV, 471; 1970: 8–9). To ground a concept transcendentally does not mean to ground it in the nature of things, but in the laws governing the possibility of a thing. Failure to ground a concept accordingly entails that the object to which that concept belongs cannot be an object of possible experience, and therefore cannot belong to 'material nature'. When, therefore, the 'Metaphysical foundations of dynamics' notes that while the analysis of the concept of matter has been 'reduced to nothing but moving forces' but adds, 'we cannot comprehend a priori the possibility of these original forces themselves' (*Ak.* IV, 524; 1970: 78), Kant is in effect conceding that while 'material nature' has been shown to be 'corporeal nature', and while this latter can be reduced to moving forces, the forces *themselves* cannot form part of material nature (they do not appear in it), nor of formal nature (the failure of their deduction entails that they cannot be demonstrably necessary to possible experience). Kant has no option but to banish, therefore, these 'newly thought-out forces in nature' to the realm of the 'extravagating understanding' (*Ak.* IV, 317; 1971: 78–9) while equally being unable to rule out that, despite immateriality and formlessness, the *Grundkäfte* are 'real', in the sense of having their 'existence outside my concept' (*Ak.* IV, 295; 1971: 52).[13]

The failure to ground dynamics is due to the transcendental philosophy's theory of 'corporeal nature'. This can be seen equally in Kant's considerations of the nature of matter in the *Metaphysical Foundations*. Defining 'matter [as] divisible to infinity, and indeed into parts each of which is again matter' (*Ak.* IV, 503; 1970: 49), it follows necessarily that no concept of matter can ground the somatist doctrine. As Schelling argues (II, 21–2; 1988: 17), if 'material nature' is 'the whole of all appearances', then insofar as matter itself is infinitely divisible, it cannot form part of those appearances, so matter itself is not part of material nature. Even if matter were only finitely divisible, then division would reach ultimate parts. If however I divide matter, all I discover is bodies, so no simples form part of material nature. Just as Aristotle's 'pragmatic' reduction of nature to a totality of 'concrete wholes' facilitated the further reduction of physics to phenomenology, so Kantian somatism supplants the material with the phenomenal. For transcendental philosophy, therefore, echoing Aristotle's argument that 'it is impossible . . . that matter is substantial being' (*Met.* 1029a27), 'matter, the first foundation of all experience, becomes the most insubstantial thing we know' (II, 22; 1988: 17).

Defining matter as thus a priori sensible first eliminates the non-phenomenal, eternally becoming and therefore in itself formless Platonic matter, specifying the matter retained as a variant of the alternative Aristotelian account, rendering it both phenomenal and somatic. While the former belongs to the 'metaphysics of corporeal nature' both materially and formally, the latter remains the specific province of the 'doctrine of corporeal nature'. Claiming to ground the latter, the 'Metaphysical foundations of dynamics' supplies a non-phenomenal condition of material nature that cannot, accordingly, be itself material. The recursion of the elimination of matter from material nature thus results in a non-material reduction of material nature, or a dualism of body and force. In this, transcendental physics mirrors the dualism in the Newtonian natural philosophy. It is, moreover, because the transcendental philosophy depends upon a concept of matter drawn from empirical natural science, that Schelling christens it a merely 'empirical idealism' (II, 57; 1988: 43).

Examining the empirical realism upon which transcendental philosophy grounds its failed grounding of corporeal nature, Schelling refers to Newton's twenty-eighth query in the *Opticks*:

the main business of natural philosophy is to argue from phenomena without feigning hypotheses, and to deduce causes from effects, till we come to the very first cause, which certainly is not mechanical [. . .]. And does it not appear from phenomena that there is a being incorporeal, living, intelligent, omnipresent? (Newton, in Crosland (ed.) 1971: 123)

The 'so-called philosophy' of empiricism (II, 49; 1988: 35), argues Schelling, 'corrupts' philosophy and natural researches because mechanism exemplifies precisely the kind of hypothetical or 'arbitrary assumption' (II, 70; 1988: 52) Newton decries. Mechanism has not, in other words, been *demonstrated* but only *assumed* to be necessary, from which assumption theories of nature – in the empirical natural sciences as well as in Kant's 'metaphysics of corporeal nature' – are invented to accord with it. The arbitrariness of the assumption is revealed when 'Newton[, seeking] after the *efficient cause of attraction*, saw only too well that he stood at the frontier of nature, and that here two worlds diverge' (II, 24; 1988: 19). The concept of matter both Kant and Newton work with gives rise to a two-worlds metaphysics in the first instance, due to the two-worlds physics of the first. Even Newton's search for an efficient cause of gravitation manifests a dualism that divides 'the principle of motion from the moved' (II, 51; 1988: 38), just as the *Metaphysical Foundations* develops the dualism of body and force.

Schelling's genetic typing of the transcendental philosophy reveals not only that it is a relative antiphysics, but also that as such, it remains conditioned by the physics it rejects as well as the physics whose premises it accepts *as* conditions. The recursive elimination of nature from mind is simply the conditioned and dependent antithesis of the metaphysics of somatic nature, and leads to a metaphysics of material *qua* phenomenal bodies and a physics restricted in turn to the phenomenal and thus incapable of a dynamics. Schelling's philosophy, by contrast, which is 'nothing other than natural science', seeks to ground dynamics philosophically not by way of a transcendental, but rather of a physical apriority. Kant's dualism of bodies and forces, however, undergoes one further and important transformation in transcendental philosophy.

3.1.3 *Megabodies and superstrata*

The *Metaphysical Foundations*, as we have seen, do not achieve their aim. Adding a 'real' to the 'formal' and 'material' natures acknowledged by the critical philosophy, the *Metaphysical Foundations* could never have succeeded: were the deduction of *Grundkräfte* successful it would entail the elimination of the transcendental as the *source* of a phenomenal and rational nature rather than the *copy* of non-phenomenal and, as far as the somatics underlying the appearance of nature as the doctrine of body is concerned, unintelligible nature, bringing it, so to speak, down to ground.

Rather than the theoretical deduction of real nature, which the *Metaphysical Foundations* demonstrated to be impossible, therefore, Kant pursues other means by which to bring freedom and phenomenal somatic nature into harmony while preserving the autonomy and priority of the transcendental. Supplanting the requirement for a material substrate, Kant will therefore seek to develop a transcendental 'superstratum' on which all nature and freedom would depend. There are two such attempts: the first consisting in the epistemological-formal solution, which takes its cue from one aspect of material nature – organism – for which, Kant suggests, we can be justly sceptical of any possible mechanical explanation. The second envelops the transcendental philosophy, consisting in Kant's two principal attempts to formulate a metaphysics grounded in the physics of the aether. The earlier aether studies, in the *Physical Monadology* (twice critiqued in the 'Metaphysical foundations of dynamics', *Ak.* IV, 507, 521; 1970: 55, 74), pursue it under the somatic mode of the Aristotelian 'fifth body' (*Heav.* 369a31), while the second, in the *Transition from Metaphysics to Physics*, is overtly dynamicist, and sacrifices the phenomenality of somatic nature for an intelligible and universally formal nature *in which the intellectual powers interact directly with the natural.*

3.1.3.1 Ground and superstratum in transcendental philosophy

The first transcendental superstratum is painfully constructed around the analogy between organic and purposive behaviours. Its necessity is intimated in two ways: firstly, the heightened sense of the powers of mind that can be provoked by confronting the raw power of nature, and salved by art's demonstration of those powers, drives mind above nature and into its non-sensible destination, that is, into a purpose not given in experience, but created through it. Secondly, the need to secure purpose against elimination by real nature is manifest in the abyssal evidences in the emergent fossil record of periodic and catastrophic species-destruction. The first is given in the *Critique of Aesthetic Judgment*, and explores the elevation (*Erhebung*) of mind above spatially extended nature in the sublime (*das Erhabene*); and the second in the *Critique of Teleological Judgment*, which explores the elevation of purpose above temporally extended nature, and proposes a corresponding sublime of time, or more specifically, of temporal ordering through causation or the 'teleological subordination of all nature' (*Ak.* V, 435–6; Kant 1987: 323). The *Critique of Judgment* as a whole therefore contains the blueprints for the construction of a superstratum, something 'raised up' (*das Erhabene*) to overlay aesthetic or phenomenal access to first nature by constructing a 'second nature out of the material that actual nature gives it' (*Ak.* V, 314; 1987: 182).[14]

The teleological subordination of all nature cannot apply at the level of the understanding, which is the source of the laws in accordance with which material nature is theorized, and therefore of foundations for the natural sciences. The realm thus grounded, on the contrary, once its laws are specified by the critical metaphysician, is exclusively the domain of the natural sciences. Any thing, therefore, considered as a merely 'physical possibility', is to be investigated in accordance with the a priori laws that support mechanical causality. Yet the example of organic being provides us with something we cannot avoid considering as purposive: organic beings *cannot not* be thought by us as 'organized and self-organizing', that is, as beings-for-themselves. While as merely physical things, therefore, they can be considered through 'the connection of efficient causes' (although Kant openly despairs of a 'Newton . . . who would explain to us . . . how even a mere blade of grass is produced', *Ak*. V, 400; 1987: 282–3), they could also 'at the same time be *judged* to be a causation through final causes' (*Ak*. V, 374; 1987: 253; my emphasis). That is, they *may* be so judged, but cannot be so cognized.[15] Further, since it is only humanity ('considered as noumenon') in which a 'causality that is teleological, i.e., directed to purposes' exists, we must judge nature, insofar as it is organized teleologically, as dependent upon that species 'as the final purpose of creation[, f]or without man the chain of mutually subordinated purposes would not have a complete basis [*nicht vollständig gegründet*]' (*Ak*. V, 435; 1987: 323). Finally, in complete agreement with the base-kind of the transcendental philosophy, Kant concludes that 'the ground [*Grund*] for the existence of nature must be sought outside nature' (*Ak*. V, 437; 1987: 325), reintroducing the riven nature into the transcendental superstratum.

Obeying the *formal* or 'subjective' requirement that it conform to laws, albeit those of a 'new law-governed order' (*Ak*. V, 379; 1987: 259), the superstratum makes it possible to consider the thus-generated *material* nature as depending not on the endless causal chains established by the natural sciences; rather, these latter depend on 'an original understanding, as cause of the world' (*Ak*. V, 410; 1987: 294). In so doing, however, the transcendental philosophy promotes a divided nature: 'as set down in the *Critique of Teleological Judgment*', writes Schelling (VI, 8), Kant's 'views on organic nature were entirely divided from the natural sciences in general'. Firstly, transcendental nature is divided *formally*, between two powers – the power of the understanding and that of reflective judgement – and their respective domains. This is in turn because material nature is divided between those phenomenal bodies that we cannot but think as self-organizing and those we can only think as inorganic, mechanical bodies.

Along the axis dividing organic from mechanical nature, transcendental philosophy's base-kind, revealed by Schelling's genetic typing, which consists in the repeated 'isolation' of the formal-material from the real (VI, 7–8), is equally apparent insofar as this wholly dualistic nature leaves mechanical nature *untouched* by purposes, leaving a contest between two sets of causal series: the mechanical and the organo-teleological. The *Critique of Teleological Judgment* presents this conflict in formal terms as the 'antinomy of judgment', consisting in a 'natural dialectic' between the powers of determining and reflective judgement (*Ak*. V, 385ff; 1987: 265ff) over whether mechanism is sufficient to *produce* all natural phenomena.[16] The resolution of this antinomy, which is only 'preliminary', concludes that we have no ground for asserting *either* that a priori reasoning can in fact determine the 'endless diversity of natural laws, because they are contingent for us since we cognize them *empirically*', *or* that a 'causality that acts according to purposes' has any 'reality [*Realität*]' (*Ak.* V, 388–9; 1987: 269).

Thus the conflict of causes is ceded to the natural sciences. Accordingly, on the basis of the *empirical* evidence unearthed in the course of proto-palaeontologist Petrus Camper's 'archaeology of nature', Kant accepts that there *is* a nature that has repeatedly staged precisely such a contest between causalities, *destroying whole species in the process*. Camper's excavations revealed not only that periodic 'devastations' afflict 'land and sea . . . and all creatures living on or in them', but also that 'a meticulous examination of the traces of those natural devastations seems to prove . . . that man was not included' amongst the earlier species. Given therefore that empirical natural history demonstrates that, by way of repeated upheavals in the earth, 'natural mechanism holds sway' over all the earth's creatures, and that 'man too must be considered subject to it', the *Critique of Teleological Judgment* cedes to the natural historical question of the '*production*' of nature, which forms the basis of the antinomy of judgement, the 'reality' of the dependence of purposive causality on a mechanical nature (*Ak.* V, 427–8; 1987: 315–16).[17]

In place of the 'transcendental substrate' the *Critique of Judgment* was to provide in order to bridge the abyss dividing theoretical from practical reason, the requirement for this 'elevated' or *erhabene* substrate, which we have called a 'superstratum' for that reason, must confront the prospect of species annihilation. Against the purposive judgement of natural phenomena that was to articulate the relation between reason in its theoretical and practical uses, natural history demonstrates that the powers themselves are *dependent* on an active and destructive nature. Moreover, because these destructive forces 'look like nature working in a state of chaos' (*Ak.* V, 427; 1987: 315), and because – ironically in a contemporary context – Kant cannot regard chaos as 'self-organizing', this dynamic and chaotic nature exceeds the domain of reflective judgement entirely, while straining the powers of the understanding to grasp the mechanism of nature's destructions, 'because unless we presuppose it [the mechanism of nature] in our investigation, we can have no cognition of nature at all' (*Ak.* V, 387; 1987: 268).

If Kant's first foray into a formalist account of nature is unsuccessful, it will nevertheless fuel not only a late reengagment with the problem of the aether, but will also, by way of the transcendental philosophy's insistence on the role of mathematics in the construction of concepts, provide the basis for Fichte's *Wissenschaftslehre* projects. For the second, Kant attempts precisely the kind of formal dynamics that provides a substrate immanent to force and that dispenses with the somatism that thwarted his earlier, more overtly Aristotelian attempt at an aether physics, in the *Physical Monadology*.

3.1.3.2 Megabodies: Somatic aether physics

While the *Metaphysical Foundations* was explicitly concerned to 'reduce the concept of matter to nothing but moving forces' (*Ak*. IV, 524; 1970: 78), but otherwise claimed only a 'negative' role (*Ak*. IV, 424; 1970: 78), this overtly 'foundationalist' inquiry in effect pursues a critique of his own earlier attempts to formulate a dynamics, combining metaphysics with physics, in the *Physical Monadology*. Echoing Aristotle's own formulation of the nature of the 'fifth somatic substance [*ousia somatos*]', as possessing an 'endlessly cycling' motion, as opposed to the 'upward' motion of fire and air, and the 'downward' motion of water or earth (*Heav.* 369a16–31), Kant likewise argues that the aether is 'the operative matter present in all of space' and 'the cause of the planetary orbits' (*Ak*. II, 113; 1992a: 155). Attempting to derive 'body' from the 'operative matter' of the aether, Kant's *The Use of Metaphysics combined with Geometry in the Philosophy of Nature, the first Specimen of which contains the Physical Monadology* (1756) attempts to resolve the problem of the relation of forces to bodies that continued, for example, to haunt Newton's avowedly post-Aristotelian attempts at dynamic physics:

> Elements are completely impenetrable, that is to say, they cannot be wholly excluded from the space they occupy by any external force, no matter how great that force be. They can, however, be compressed, and they constitute bodies which can also be compressed, since, of course, they yield a little to an external force pressing upon them. This is the origin of the bodies or media which are elastic. And among such bodies one may already legitimately include aether, that is to say, the matter of fire. (*Ak*. I, 487; 1992a: 66)

In common, however, with the mechanistic physics that governed Kant's metaphysics,[18]

> In that it undertakes to explain the physical world by mechanical laws, [it] is obliged, against its will, to presuppose bodies, and thus attractive and repulsive forces. For . . . it views the original particles (*corpuscula*) as absolutely impenetrable and absolutely indivisible. (Schelling II, 196; 1988: 157)

The problem of indivisibility, of the preexistence of a substantial or material substrate on which forces might act as its accidents, forms the central problem of Kant's dynamics in both the *Physical Monadology* and the *Metaphysical Foundations*. The 'Metaphysical foundations of dynamics', for example, while superficially grounding the impenetrability of matter in 'its original force of extension' (*Ak*. IV, 503; 1970: 49), in fact merely ascribes such a force to a matter, making it some*thing* that '*has* forces', as Schelling has the transcendental philosopher report (II, 22–3; 1988: 17–18). Even when Kant affirms that the 'force of extension is only the consequence of the repulsive forces',

73

thus apparently deriving matter from force, he in fact argues that these latter forces *belong in turn* to 'each point in a space filled with matter'. Fundamentally, therefore, forces are added to matter, but neither is derived from the other, creating a simple dualism of force and matter. Similarly, apparently arguing against the 'indivisibility' thesis Schelling associates with the mechanical conception of matter, Kant argues that 'matter is divisible to infinity', that is, as far as can be imagined mathematically. When, however, Kant adds, 'and indeed into parts each of which is again matter' (*Ak*. IV, 503; 1970: 49), he effectively posits a material continuum underlying all division that, because it remains unaltered *qua* continuum by the division, is simultaneously composed of discrete, 'isolationist' substances.[19]

The *Physical Monadology* equally argues for the composition of a continuum from simple and isolationist substances. Defining metaphysics as 'the science [*scientia*] of the nature itself of bodies' (*Ak*. I, 475; 1992a: 51, t.m.), Kant establishes two kinds of bodies: substantial or natural compound bodies and formal or geometrical compound bodies. Since the latter are divisible to infinity, this demonstrates that they contain no 'natural' or substantial, but only 'geometrical' or formal existence (*Ak*. I, 479; 1992a: 55). Space-filling by physical substances, on the other hand – the domain of physics – is the consequence of the 'spheres of activity' of the repulsive and attractive forces that combine these 'simple substances' into compound bodies. Although such monads cannot be excluded from the space they fill by virtue of their 'force of impenetrability', as Schelling remarks, impenetrability and/or indivisibility are definitive of the body for mechanical philosophy, as even the *Metaphysical Foundations* notes:

> A body, in the physical signification, is a matter between determinate boundaries (and such matter therefore has a figure). The space between these boundaries . . . is the body's content of space (*volumen*). The degree of the filling of space of determinate content is called *density*. [. . .] In this sense there is absolute density in the system of absolute impenetrability, namely, if a matter contains no empty intermediate spaces at all. (*Ak*. IV, 525; 1970: 80)

A dynamical system, in other words, cannot be constructed out of a substance *composed* of forces without reverting to the problems of somatism, and thus reintroducing the issue of whether body derives from force, or force from body. This is what the *Physical Monadology* discovers; from the simple spheres of attractive-repulsive activity that are the substantial nature of compound bodies, Kant attempts to generate that body from which a continuum of such forces may be constructed in nature. Thus the aether owes its origin to the compression and elasticity of such a substance which, as in Aristotle, primarily means 'substrate':[20]

> It is with good reason presumed that the expansion of bodies as a result of heat, that light, electrical energy, thunderstorms, and perhaps even the

force of magnetism, are many different manifestations of one and the self-same operative matter present in all of space, namely, the aether. (*Ak*. II, 113; 1992a: 155)

The aether is that body, therefore, 'more divine, and prior' to the 'four in our sublunary world' (Aristotle, *Heav*. 369a32), whose accidents or modifications constitute the finer matters in the universe, the substrate or substantial continuum, the megabody underlying nature as a whole, composed, like Aristotle's universe, of 'a plurality of distinct individual entities' (*Phys*. 187a34). Although the *Metaphysical Foundations* criticizes the earlier monadology for its '*Platonic* concept of the world', it is as clear that the *Physical Monadology*'s 'science of the nature itself of bodies' (*Ak*. I, 475; 1992a: 51) is not Platonic, but rather Aristotelian precisely by virtue of its somatism, its 'two kinds of body' (*Ak*. IV, 507; 1970: 55) echoing Aristotle's differentiation of the fifth body from the 'other sublunary' ones. The dualism it establishes is not between two kinds of bodies (since both constitute objects of metaphysics), but between a dynamic and a transcendental somatism. It is precisely this dualism that Kant's final attempt at an aether physics will attempt to overcome.

3.1.3.3 Dynamic aether physics

Having thus limited the scope of physics to the dynamic substance of the aether, while extending that of metaphysics to include the non-substantial bodies of ideal entities such as infinitely divisible space, the transcendental philosophy will supplant the *Physical Monadology*'s 'substantial' with a merely *material* nature, i.e., one that is sensible only (the 'material' of 'the whole of all appearances'), such that no cognition of it is possible beyond my representations. At the same time, ideal or insubstantial bodies become 'things in themselves . . . the objective reality of which can in no way be cognised', and play a merely *formal* role as 'limit-concepts' for the 'objective validity of sensible cognition' (CPR A254/B310).

If transcendental idealism places both nature and the ideal beyond the matter and form of cognition, however, Kant's postcritical return to Leibnizianism[21] in his 'transition' project will revivify the precritical metaphysics, his 1794–5 *Metaphysik Vigilantus* defining 'Meta-physics [as] physics beyond the empirical cognition of nature' (*Ak*. XXIX, 947; 1997: 419).[22] Just as, in other words, Kant's late metaphysics asserts that the realm of *physis*, of nature, extends beyond the empirical – beyond, that is, sensible nature – so the *Monadology*'s 'science of the nature itself of bodies' extends nature across both substantial and non-substantial bodies, or 'figures between determinate boundaries' (*Ak*. IV, 525; 1970: 80).

The metamorphosis of the problem of the nature of non-substantial bodies – Kant's version of the argument regarding the substantial existence of the Ideas[23] – into that of the elimination of 'matter' and 'nature itself' from 'formal-material nature' constitutes the genesis of transcendental philosophy. Just as for Kant, 'transcendental philosophy is also called ontology, and is the product of the critique of pure reason' (*Ak.* XXIX, 949; 1997: 420), so Schelling argues transcendentalism *ontologizes* what critique eliminates, and thus '. . . makes that separation between man and world permanent, because it treats the latter as a thing-in-itself, which neither intuition nor imagination, neither understanding nor reason, can reach' (II, 13; 1988: 11). The thing-in-itself therefore becomes the weakest point not only in the metaphysics of transcendental idealism, but in the physics underlying it: insofar as I can have no access to nature beyond my representations of it, the 'thing-in-itself' poses not merely the *formal* problem of limiting the validity of empirical cognition, but also the problem of a nature *real* in itself.

Hence the transcendental philosophy's repeated attempts to recover physics under transcendental principles: the *Critique of Teleological Judgment*'s attempt to construct a non-sensible superstratum from which both nature and freedom depend; or the dynamical neurochemistry outlined in *Aus Sömmering: Über das Organ der Seele* that would conjointly treat of thinking and extended nature,[24] despite the doubts Kant had about the status of chemistry as a science.[25] But it is the *Transition*'s attempt at the deduction of a 'material principle of the unity of possible experience' (*Ak.* XXI, 585; 1993: 92) – the 'ether proofs' – that bring the question of the relation between material and formal nature, the thing in itself, and the object of intuition, into sharpest relief.

The *Transition from Metaphysics to Physics* turns from the problem of the thing-in-itself as any kind of 'self-subsisting object' (*Ak.* XXII, 28; 1993: 172) such as might underlie material and formal nature, to a dynamic conception of 'thing' as *action*. 'Existence and actuality' derive, writes Kant, 'from *agere*', from acting. 'The thing is there when and where it acts' (*Ak.* XXII, 121; 1993: 203). Rather, therefore, than asking 'what thing is it that affects my sensibility, and what can I know of it?', allowing the thing-in-itself the status only of a limit-concept with respect to the latter, the *Transition* asks: if my sensibility is affected by some *thing*, it must be that this thing acts upon and *in* sensibility. But such a thing is no mere self-subsisting object, but rather, for experience, nothing but an acting-on-my-sensibility. What acts in experience, however, is the subject, which must, according to transcendental philosophy, provide the *form* and *matter* of intuitions. As regards form, the thing in itself is a mere position posited by the subject as a 'thought-object [which] serves as an object = x in order to represent the object of intuition in contrast to appearance'. The 'material element' of intuition is not therefore supplied by objects outside us, but, insofar as the thing in itself is a product of our spontaneous positing, it is 'the mere representation of *one's own* activity' (*Ak.* XXII, 37; 1993: 176; emphasis added). Hence: 'I am an object of myself and of my representations. That there is something else outside me is my own product. I make myself. [. . .] We make everything ourselves' (*Ak.* XXII, 82; 1993: 189).

This achieves two things. Firstly, the superstratum the *Critique of Judgment* had sought to construct is no longer dependent on the ground it sought to supplant, insofar as it supplies a genetic account of the *production* of bodies – 'we make everything ourselves'. Secondly, the dynamic account of the constitution of things seemingly removes the *a priority* of somatism, and accordingly moves Kant away from dealing with the thing-in-itself as an 'unknowable substantial body'. Instead, the thing-in-itself becomes the subject's representation of a field of actions that, insofar as it cognizes, it constitutes as that field. While formally and materially, however, the nature of experience consists solely in the experiencing, rather than merely blocking the question as to the genesis of that experience, the *Transition* is now able to ask firstly after *matter in general* and then, secondly, 'how does matter produce a body?' (*Ak*. XXI, 476; 1993: 41).

Kant's solution to the material genesis of bodies, however, neither engages natural history on its own ground, nor attempts to provide foundations for a physical dynamics, but remains transcendental, i.e., concerned fundamentally with the conditions of possibility of experience: matter now stands to body as space and time stand to particular intuitions. Just as space and time cannot themselves be objects of intuition since they form intuition, so matter forms an a priori condition of the production of bodies. Conceiving, like the *Metaphysical Foundations*, of matter as nothing other than 'moving forces which can only be known by experience' (*Ak*. XXI, 475; 1993: 40), the *Transition* no longer conceives of 'material nature' as the 'whole of all appearances', begging the question as to what it might be that does the appearing; the materiality of experience now consists in nothing other than the 'agitating forces of matter' insofar as they make themselves felt (*Ak*. XXII, 552; 1993: 88). Thus, 'however diverse the objects of physics may be', writes Kant, 'they are, nevertheless, merely phenomena' (*Ak*. XXI, 476–7; 1993: 41). The difference is, phenomenal nature is no longer considered simply as belonging to 'the science of the nature itself of bodies', but consists rather in the *making itself felt* – the experience – of a priori agitating forces.

Thus, just as we represent *our actions*, the forces we exert, as the thing in itself, so we represent the forces acting upon us as objects of intuition. In late transcendental idealism as in physics, therefore, there are forces that are neither bodies nor possible objects of experience, but that make all bodies and all experience possible. Instead of representations, therefore, being representations *of* physical objects or 'bodies', there are forces that act to produce bodies, and forces that act to produce representations. The world is a world of forces that do not *underlie* things in the manner of a substrate, but *produce* them. The position (or self-positioning) of the subject in that world is to act, thus to exert forces upon it. Such a 'transcendental physicalism', where the transcendental and the physical are physically codeterminant of representations, accounts for Kant's otherwise incomprehensible proto-doctrine that, for example 'seeing is repulsive'.[26] But the 'it' = X upon which it exerts forces, is nothing other than force itself. Hence, however, the thing in itself is no longer the unknowable = X 'object' behind appearances, but rather the manufacturing *subject*: 'He who would know the world must first *manufacture* it – in his own self, indeed' (*Ak*. XXI, 41; 1993: 240). It is by positing *myself* as subject *and* as object that I 'manufacture the world' from forces. Transcendental philosophy thus becomes a dynamics of physical and practical actions, rather than a mechanics of objects and their 'effects' on our receptivity.

Unlike Kant's works published during his lifetime, Schelling could not offer an account of the *Transition* at the point of its author's death, merely noting that 'had his age allowed him to complete it, it would doubtless have been of the greatest interest' (VI, 8). We have yet to assess therefore the *Transition*'s attempts to resolve the problem Schelling's brief review identifies as common to all Kant's works in the natural sciences and philosophy: that Kant constantly provokes a riven nature – between organic and inorganic nature, between the real and the formal, and, Kant himself adds, between 'two kinds of body' (*Ak.* IV, 507; 1970: 55).

Kant's dynamical reconstruction of transcendental philosophy seeks to place matter and possible experience – physics and transcendental philosophy – under one and the same a priori principle, from which the two sciences would spring. In contrast to the *Critique of Pure Reason*, therefore, where the world of physics is simply given over to Newtonianism, with its impenetrable bodies and the forces they impart to each other, the *Transition* 'from metaphysics to physics' seeks 'a material principle of the unity of possible experience' (*Ak.* XXI, 585; 1993: 92). To furnish such a principle, Kant reverts to his earlier attempts at an aether physics, and combines this with the dynamics that remained undeduced with regard to their possibility in the *Metaphysical Foundations*.

The 'aether proofs' attempt to demonstrate that possible experience presupposes a whole of world-material that fills space and is permanently turbulent. Kant's deductions are variations around the following core argument (*Ak.* XXI, 216–17; 1993: 67–8):[27]

1. There can be no experience of empty space (nor can empty space be an object of experience);
2. Therefore 'there are empty spaces' is not a proposition of possible experience;
3. Therefore there must exist a continuum forming the whole of all possible experience;
4. For the same reason, 'there are physical bodies' presupposes 'there is matter whose moving forces and actual motion precedes the generation of a body in time';
5. Therefore there must exist a matter which penetrates all bodies, is permanentaly turbulent, and amounts to a whole of world-material ('caloric' or 'ether').

Experience is therefore dependent upon the forces from which I form it, and upon the forces that generate bodies. The material principle is therefore as proto-phenomenal (generating objects of experience) as it is proto-somatic (generating physical objects). Giving this principle as caloric or aether, the

Transition appears to make experience *depend* on *physis* itself: given the presomatic nature of matter and the non-phenomenal nature of experience, the moving forces of this ceaselessly active matter precede both. On this reading, caloric or aether is a 'primary material' (*Ak*. XXI, 219; 1993: 69) that, at the very least, is 'a matter of experience in relation to the possibility of experience' (*Ak*. XXI, 233; 1993: 78). Kant goes further, however, characterizing 'the original moving matter as a real, existing material . . . not a hypothetical one', a 'universally distributed, all-penetrating world-material, which is in continuous motion in its own location', giving 'objective reality to the concept' (*Ak*. XXI, 225; 1993: 73–4). Conversely, Kant equally often draws attention to the 'merely hypothetical' (*Ak*. XXII, 550; 1993: 86) status of the material principle: although a 'constitutive, formal principle, existing a priori, of the science of nature' (*Ak*. XXII, 240; 1993: 56), it 'is merely *thought*' (*Ak*. XXII, 580; 1993: 90) as the 'formal conditions' of sense experience (*Ak*. XXII, 553; 1993: 89), and is therefore a 'hypothesis of matter . . . a thought-object' (*Ak*. XXI, 230–1; 1993: 77); its 'ground of proof is subjective, and determined from the conditions of possible experience, which presupposes moving forces and excludes the void, in order to fill space with an always active matter which may be called caloric, or aether, etc.' (*Ak*. XXI, 221; 1993: 70–1).

Although the *Transition* therefore achieves its material principle on the basis of positing the aether or caloric as a primary 'world-material', it does so not because of any empirical qualities such a matter may have the power to produce, but rather on account of an a priori necessity of a continuity making experience possible. The 'aether proofs' therefore 'suppl[y] the material for a space which is nowhere empty . . . as the basis for the unification of all outer experience in one object . . . [that is,] for an *a priori* thinkable system of matter' (*Ak*. XXI, 547; 1993: 79). In other words, the 'objective reality of this material' is 'grounded *logically* . . . not *physically*' (*Ak*. XXII, 582; 1993: 90).[28] Yet the '*a priori* thinkable system of matter' also supplies a formal condition under which physics *must* operate, if it is to be consistent with possible experience. Conceived in the strongest terms, the *Transition* has wagered that while there must be a physical basis for experience and its transcendental principles, this physical basis can be deduced a priori, and therefore prescribes a unified-field physics as *necessary* if and only if the transcendental conditions of possible experience are the *actual* conditions of possible experience. In other words, it is because the ground of nature is itself empirically inscrutable that it is accessible only to transcendental philosophy. The *Transition* therefore supplies a material principle of formal continuity without empirical commitments. Whether the physicists call it 'caloric, aether, or whatever' (*Ak*. XXI, 226; 1993: 74),[29] there *must be* 'a matter, distributed in the whole universe as a continuum, uniformly penetrating all bodies and filling [all spaces] (thus not subject to displacement)' (*Ak*. XXI, 218; 1993: 69–70).

When however we look to the *nature* of the 'substance' thus stipulated as *necessary*, Kant does ascribe it 'attributes' (*Ak*. XXI, 605; 1993: 97):[30] that it is 'spontaneously' and internally self-moving (*vis interna motiva*), that is, that it cannot take its principle of motion from outside itself, by mechanical means (*vis locomotiva, Ak.* XXI, 217; 1993: 68); that it is therefore a 'prime matter' as opposed to 'all the other materials (oxygen, hydrogen, etc.)' that are secondary (*Ak.* XXI, 604; 1993: 97), a 'matter whose moving forces and motion precedes the generation of a body in time' (*Ak.* XXI, 216; 1993: 68); that it is not only 'distributed in the whole universe and penetrating all bodies and filling [all spaces]' (*Ak.* XXI, 218; 1993: 69), but is itself a 'self-subsistent whole' (*Ak.* XXII, 612; 1993: 99), i.e., a single, unified 'object of all possible outer experience in general' (*Ak.* XXI, 141; 1993: 79).

In other words, primary matter, all-penetrating, agitating and self-moving, produces not only the discrete bodies that furnish the material and form of experience, but also forms *a single object* that nevertheless exceeds all actual experience. The *Transition* proscribes this One-All from physics, which is 'the science of the coordination of all empirical presentations' (*Ak.* XXII, 583; 1993: 91), and consigns it, exactly in accordance with the Aristotelian schema, to metaphysics, 'physics beyond the empirical cognition of nature' (*Ak.* XXIX, 947; 1997: 419). In other words, the *Transition* adapts the two-body solution of the *Physical Monadology*: whereas the latter extended metaphysics, as 'the science of the nature itself of body' (*Ak.* I, 475; 1992a: 51), across substantial and ideal bodies, Kant's late aether deduction generates a single universal substance that forms the formal principle of metaphysics, and furnishes the material of possible experience with which physics works, but whose nature and actuality are deduced completely a priori. The cost of the *Transition* is the abandonment of a non-phenomenal science of the unconditioned self-movement of forces, capable finally of overcoming the somatism inherent in the 'two-body' solution Kant inherits from the Aristotelian conception of the aether, and which eventually draws the transcendental philosophy back to its source.

Two routes for the development of philosophy as the science of the absolute thus open up. Firstly, to pursue the formalism by which Kant's late aether proofs carried transcendental philosophy to 'its highest point . . . its boundary and completion', which it confronts in the question, 'how is nature itself possible?' (*Ak.* IV, 318; 1971: 79). This will be the path taken by Fichte's *Wissenschaftslehre*, which we will examine next. The second consists in Schelling's genetic exploitation of the consequences of the rejection of a somatic solution not simply to physical nature, but to how 'nature itself, necessarily and originally, should not only express, but even *realise*, the laws of our mind' (II, 55–6; 1988: 41–2).

Ironically, Kant scolded Fichte's *Wissenschaftslehre* in his 'Open letter' on the topic, published in 1799, as being 'a totally indefensible system' insofar as a science that abstracts all matter from knowledge in order to examine its form is *logic*, and 'the attempt to cull a real object out of logic is a vain effort and therefore a thing that no one has ever done' (*Ak.* XII, 370–1). Not only is this exactly what the *Transition* was intended to accomplish, but Fichte's 'science of knowledge' projects shared with their transcendental predecessors a metaphysically eliminativist approach to nature. In consequence, just as Kant's eliminativism entails the adoption of Aristotelian-Newtonian principles in physics, so too Fichte's formalist eliminativism will see him extend nature only so far as organism reaches.

3.2 METAPHYSICS AS ANTIPHYSICS: FICHTEANISM AND THE NUMBER OF WORLDS

Intellect and thing . . . inhabit two worlds between which there is no bridge. (*W* I: 436; Fichte 1982: 17)

We certainly no longer exist in inert nature, but instead remain isolated. (*GA* II, 3: 253n)

The given number is the entirety of experience; the factors are the principle demonstrated in consciousness and the laws of thought; the multiplication is the activity of philosophising. (*W* I: 446; 1982: 26)

Declaring the question, 'How is nature itself possible?' to be 'the highest point that transcendental philosophy can ever touch and . . . also its boundary and completion, up to which it must be taken' (*Ak*. IV, 318; 1971: 79), Kant set *actual* (rather than *possible*) nature higher than transcendental philosophy could reach, while at the same time demanding that it define itself by and as this failure. In its attempt to engineer a *superstratum* on which actual nature, too geologically unreliable to function as ground, would depend, however, the transcendental became an 'intellectual world', a *kosmos noetos*, with its own, 'second' nature. The more dynamics eroded the empirical realism of Kant's physics, the more transcendentalism's 'new earth' became susceptible of a *physis* comprising thought *and* world around a non-phenomenal formalism. Still grounded on an Aristotelian substrate ('substance in the truest sense', *Met*. 1029a2), however, transcendental philosophy struggled to retain its grip on the reality of the phenomenal rather than exploiting the potential of the formalism. What Lloyd therefore said of Aristotle serves equally well to characterize the collapse of Kant's last physics: 'The main shortcoming of Aristotle's dynamics is not so much a failure to pay attention to the data of experience, as a failure to carry abstraction far enough' (Lloyd 1970: 114).

Fichte, as the transcendental philosophy's self-proclaimed successor, therefore radicalizes Kant's formalism, and ontologizes the practical as an actual-abstract world on which nature depends, as so many 'inert particulars'. Challenged by Schelling to provide a naturephilosophy Fichte never considered lacking, transcendental philosophy ran again into the ontological cul-de-sac of organism. Paying equal attention to the powers of abstraction evident in Fichtean formalism as to the impotence of organism in his abortive and ultimately dualistic antiphysics, a clearer image of the necessary failure of the eliminative idealism that transcendental philosophy remains, even (perhaps especially) in Fichte, will emerge.

Antiphysics is best understood as the isolation of a practical dominion from physics. Fichte is the philosopher who first makes this isolation absolute, sundering freedom and mechanical necessity into two worlds (*W* I, 509n; 1982: 78n). Worlds are produced by subtracting from the absolute, which Fichte characterizes as absolute I: the self-positing. Nature, however, is already subtracted from the absolute, since not only is the latter only intuitable for intellect (world 2, 'second nature'), but it is 'manifestly false' that 'intelligence is a higher power (expression) of nature' (*W* XI, 362). Since 'mechanism cannot apprehend itself' (*W* I, 510; 1982: 79), the absolute I can neither be *of* nor *from* nature: nature cannot posit itself as *subject*. We might say that the absolute – the *unconditioned* – which 'is what it is', and 'is not *something*' (*W* I, 109–10; 1982: 109), is therefore conditioned by the two worlds it becomes for intellect, since, as the element of intellect, and the object of rational striving alone, it necessarily cannot exist amid the causal-mechanical *world* of nature. Yet the concept of nature, writes Fichte, 'is not so alien to practical philosophy as it may seem at first glance' (*GA* II, 3: 243). This is certainly true: Fichte does not merely turn his back on physics, but like Jacobi, objects to it. The objection is based not on faith, however, but on freedom. Action cannot, he argues, be 'derived . . . from the dead persistence of matter, nor freedom from the mechanism of nature' (*W* I, 468; 1982: 42). And again: 'The relationship between free beings is interaction through freedom, and not causality through mechanically operative force' (*W* I, 509; 1982: 78). However, the concept of nature with which Fichtean science will deal places it in an inert world of particulars. Before discussing the role of these many particulars in Fichte, it is worth asking why, in a science so clearly dedicated to the I, nature should not be alien. There are two reasons for this. First, because practical metaphysics is premised on, and *demanded by*, a Newtonian world, much as is Kant's critical philosophy. Second, because nature is itself a product of the positing by which the absolute first divides itself; in other words, posited nature is internal to the developmental science of the I, while 'raw' nature pertains to other sciences. Meanwhile, the science of 'the infinite I . . . as one and as all' (*W* I, 144; 1982: 138)[31] is pitched against the number of natural particulars. As we will see, Fichte's practical ontology pits the activity of the one (I) against the inert all (nature), but mediates this conflict by way of an avowedly artificial geometry of infinitesimal magnitudes.

Fichte is often supposed merely to have completed Kant's system,[32] not so much by bridging theoretical and practical reason (as Kant attempted in the third *Critique*), but by subordinating the former to the latter: 'it is not in fact the theoretical power which makes possible the practical, but on the contrary, the practical which first makes possible the theoretical[; . . .] reason itself is purely practical . . .' (*W* I, 126; 1982: 123). While then the supposition is in part true, it is not wholly so. Fichte does undertake the complete and systematic derivation of the categories of the understanding from those of activity, and the grounding of the latter in the principle of the unconditioned, in the project he calls *Wissenschaftslehre*.[33] But this latter also exacerbates the gulf between causal-mechanical nature, and the striving of freedom, driving pure practical reason and nature further apart than ever: 'The relationship between free beings is interaction through freedom, and not causality through mechanically operative force' (*W* I, 509; 1982: 78). This abolition of causality from the world of freedom destroys the Kantian system, which accords freedom the 'sublime quality . . . to be itself an original cause' (*Ak*. XXI, 20; 1993: 226). At the same time, the categorical imperative thus becomes a practically disjunctive ontology: there are free beings, and mechanically determined ones. Only the former is self-determining, and cannot be determined by the latter. Each inhabits a different world, and these worlds are unbridgeable (*W* I, 436; 1982: 17). Between them is a struggle over reality, a war of the worlds. At stake is unconditioned freedom, on the one hand, and *the determinability of nature by freedom*, on the other. The true stakes of Fichte's 'ontological imperative' consist in 'the modification of matter' (*W* I, 307; 1982: 269). The completion of the critical system entails the derivation of things from activity (which, as we have already seen, became Kant's late agenda),[34] the priority of act over fact, and the *morphogenesis of worlds* that respond to freedom, not causality. The dogmatic 'the world *is* . . .' becomes the ideal, 'the whole universe ought to be . . .' (*GA* II, 3: 247).

While this 'ought' expresses an ideal, it does not correspond to one of Fichte's two worlds. The ideal, on the contrary, is never realized, but is an object of striving. On the contrary, the two worlds are separated by a quantitative-qualitative struggle over reality, which the I strives to make (= I, i.e.,) one and undivided. This is the form that the practical takes in reflection. Yet how can a conflict arise between a world determined by causality, and a wholly undetermined, and non-determining world? Practical action, which strives [*streben*] and wavers [*schweben*], cannot effect change without itself being causal, which Fichte repeatedly denies it is or can be. Again, the answer lies in the *form* the real takes for reflection. Fichte's insistence on the importance of form in the science of knowledge led Kant, for instance, to criticize it as *mere* formalism, '*pure logic* [that] abstracts from the content of knowledge' ('Open Letter on Fichte's *Wissenschaftslehre*', *Ak*. XII, 371); but this neglects the importance Fichte ascribes to abstraction as a power of reason, and therefore a practical power: reason is 'an absolute power of abstraction' subject only to the 'mere law of an unrealizable determination' (*W* I, 244; 1982: 216). In other words, theoretical reason is the power that determines the form of the unrealizable, the abstract, while practical reason (which is one and the same), is the power that *strives to realize it*. The abstract-formal is ultimately Fichte's innovation in dealing with the problem of nature. This is especially clear in the distributive algebra of Fichte's practical ontology, as well as in the essentially subtractive (or divisive) method of derivation that characterizes the entire logical architecture of the *Wissenschaftslehre*.

The first principle of Fichte's system is the unconditioned, the absolute. The absolute is self-positing, from which all else – the striving I and its negation, the not-I – will be derived. Importantly, this positing is an act, not an entity. For the science of knowledge, 'the concept of being [Seyns] is by no means regarded as a primary and original [erster und unsprünglicher] concept, but merely as derivative, as a concept derived . . . through counter-position [Gegensatz] to activity, and hence as a merely negative concept' (W I, 499; 1982: 69). That the derived nature of being is clearly counterposited to the 'primary and original' demonstrates not just the activity that forms the basis of Fichte's practical ontology, but also the hierarchical sequencing of its logic. When Kant criticized the Wissenschaftslehre as 'the attempt to cull a real object out of logic' (Ak. XII, 371), he stumbled thus upon its central problem: how is being derived from activity?

Fichte's answer to this consists in examining the proposition A=A. The proposition [Satz] is not merely a formal thing, but is properly also a positing [setzen], a concentration of activity (of positing) and thing (the posited). Fichte says that by successive 'reiteration of positing [Wiederholen des Setzens]', the positing-posited I will fulfil its law: that, in reflecting, it find itself to be 'the whole of reality' (W I, 276; 1982: 243). In other words, positing is the self-generative union of act and form.[35]

What, then, does the positing 'A=A' posit? The copula expresses existence, but not on its own; in order to express existence, it has to be expressed, or posited, so that the terms of the proposition enact a relation between expression and expressed, posited and positor, one which is formally certain, and demonstrates a necessary connection between the two terms. The propo-sition therefore reads, 'in the proposition A=A, the positor = the posited'. The existence (modality) expressed is therefore that of positor and posited, which is realized in the positing. In so doing, the 'act of consciousness' that posits (W I, 92; 1982: 93) affirms the existence and identity of positor and posited, yielding existential and relational, albeit still abstract and formal, content for the proposition: 'A=A' becomes 'I am I',[36] demonstrating how being is derived from activity.

However, the numerical non-identity of the terms of the proposition bears on more than one relation. The 'I' has been derived from an act of pure self-positing (A=A), which necessitates an I that posits. On its first iteration the relational property of the proposition therefore posits an I as derived from the self- (or I-) positing proposition. In other words, of the two Is in the proposition, the first is the being posited of the being that posits ('an I posits the I that posits'), demonstrating the passage from act to being: the first I is pure act, and the second is the I that is.

In the second iteration of the proposition, Fichte derives the 'not-I' from the I that posits. In positing that I am = I, the I that posits is numerically distinct from the posited I; thus the posited I, the one that is rather than the one that acts, becomes not-I insofar as it does not act. The I becomes subject and object to itself. As Fichte puts it:

In the proposition 'A=A', the first A is that which is posited in the I, either absolutely [schlechthin], like the I itself, or on some other ground . . . In this matter the I behaves as absolute subject; and hence the first A is called the subject. The second A designates what the I, reflecting upon itself, discovers to be present in itself, because it has first posited this within itself . . . Thus in the proposition 'A=B', A designates what is now being posited; B what is already encountered as posited. – The *is* expresses the passage of the I from positing to reflection on what has been posited. (*W* I, 96n; 1982: 97n)

Thus the *sequencing* of the proposition alerts us to an unavoidable assertion of this numerical difference as conditioned by time, emphasizing the 'derived' nature of each term in any propositional relation. Since therefore each step is derived from its predecessor, the quanta denoted by '1, 2, 3 . . .', for example, denote succession alongside numerical difference. Since the model is genetic, differentiation is indistinguishable from derivation. Fichte calls this process 'division', and we can therefore say that the 'primary and original' proposition is divided into being and negation (quality).

What is primary and original is therefore the positing of the I as a predicate of the subject *in general* that posits it: 'In this matter the I behaves as absolute subject'. This subject-in-general then *divides* into the particular, positing I, and, since the subject in general has been divided, into the posited not-I. Thus the not-I is counter-posited to the positing I, but posited ultimately therefore by the positing I. The 'divisibility [*Theilbarkeit*]' of the I therefore 'contains' both the I and not-I. Given, however, the activity at the root of derivation, and therefore the sequential nature of I and not-I, the two do not merely coexist, but interact as positing and posited. The two reciprocally determine the real as acting and being acted upon, where a maximum of the one = a minimum of the other. Thus arises a struggle over the *degree of reality and negation* attaching to I and not-I: 'Both I and not-I are posited, in and through the I, as capable of *mutually* limiting *one another*, in such a fashion, that is, that the reality of the one eliminates [*aufhebe*] that of the other, and *vice versa*' (*W* I, 125; 1982: 122).

I and not-I *struggle* over the distribution of reality, with the I striving to be 'the whole of reality' (*W* I, 276; 1982: 243) and thus to determine the not-I as mere negation, as merely 'negative quantity' (*W* I, 133; 1982: 128). The I strives for non-limitation, to regain the infinity from which it was derived. Throughout this conflict, 'the infinite I must alone remain, as one and as all' (*W* I, 144; 1982: 138). Practical ontology: free of everything that is not-I, freedom is the determination of limitation as = 0 (the absence of negation). Positing is not merely theoretical, but inherently practical, setting the stakes for the struggle that is the I. The latter 'is posited as all reality, and is thus necessarily posited as an infinite quantum, a quantum exhaustive of infinity' (*W* I, 274; 1982: 241).

Derived from the absolute, everything conditioned concerns quanta: 'darkness is simply a very minute amount of light'; 'passivity is merely a lesser quantum of activity' (*W* I, 144, 145; 1982: 138, 139). Thus the entire process of Fichte's system generates the multiplication of the reality of the I in practical terms, by reversing the order of division from which it derives, in theoretical terms, and which threatens it with extinction, where extinction is merely a tiny quantum of infinite quantity. The I divides into I and not-I, which divide in turn into degrees of activity and being, where activity strives essentially for the absolution of its dividedness as product or factor and to become 'the whole of reality' (W I, 276; 1982: 243). I and not-I divide time and space between them, reducing the I to a point, and the not-I to a line (*GA* II, 3: 217; W I, 73; 1982: 241), while positing posits both as reciprocating or 'interdetermining' spheres of activity.

What then does Fichte's formalism, the power of abstraction, establish? Firstly, it is the limitation of the I by the not-I that *formally* accounts for the quanta of freedom and determination in reality. This does not pretend to demonstrate how a non-causally construed freedom can act on a causally constituted determinism; rather it imprisons each in its own sphere of activity. Such spheres constitute unbridgeable worlds (their division remains insuperable), but are susceptible of further divisibility themselves. In one world, there is causality; in the other, freedom. The quantitative struggle over the determination as a war of the worlds is the essential activity of the I, and is registered by it as feeling: 'the feeling of force is the principle of all life' (W I, 296; 1982: 261). For itself, then, the I is intensive matter; but between such formed or abstracting matter and 'raw and formless matter', there is no passage.

The unconditioned itself, then, cannot be a factor of a higher division. But the practical imperative must impose division upon the absolute, by the non-finite nature of striving. 'The whole universe must be . . .' (*GA* II, 3: 247). Infinite striving must necessarily encounter the limitation of the absolute, that is, the condition of the unconditioned. The absolute is an object only of striving, i.e, only an object for a subject. Although Fichte does hint on occasion that the absolute subject's non-identity with any particular, or the totality of, empirical Is qualifies I-hood for extension to 'human and *all other* finite intellects' (W I, 283; 1982: 249; emphasis added), he also denies absolutely that nature can form a subject. 'Mechanism', he writes, 'is unable to apprehend itself' (W I, 510; 1982: 79), so 'that intelligence . . . is a higher power (expression) of nature . . . is obviously false' (W IX, 362).[37]

This limitation of the absolute follows from the not-I being posited by the I, as a factor of the absolute which is irrevocably I, of course, rather than the reverse. To posit the reverse would merely be to posit the negation of activity and the affirmation of pure being. Both determinations, however, remain merely formal approaches to the world of 'raw and formless matter'. To get round this, Fichte deploys the Kantian device of proclaiming matter to be the determinable in our intuitions: 'matter is theoretical' (*GA* II, 3: 241), not *real*. The 'modification of matter' in which the practical imperative consists remains therefore a modification of the I by itself. The subordination of things to freedom, therefore, while active in the striving of the I for the 'one and all', remains actual only insofar as it does not *act on* 'raw and formless matter' (W I, 499; 1982: 69) *and* the sequence of causal-mechanical determinations that, Fichte agrees, constitutes nature as another world (W I, 509n; 1982: 78n).

The problem of two orders of causality, inherited from Kant's attempt, in the *Critique of Judgment*, to locate teleology in a mechanical universe, lay at the core of Fichte's problematic from his first published work, *Attempt at a Critique of All Revelation* (1792). This work asks: given two causal orders, the one supramundane and the other mechanical, the former can have no effect on the latter unless the divine is mechanical, in which case it is not supramundane (W V, 109; 1978: 120). This division of causal orders remains between those of freedom and determination in the *Wissenschaftslehre*, and posits the essential failure of the I's striving, its 'aspiration to be a cause' (W I, 286; 1982: 252); without such striving, however, 'no object at all is possible' (W I, 264; 1982: 233).

How then is it possible to maintain the coexistence of two worlds, when this coexistence is posited as the annihilation of one by the other? In which of the two worlds is this annihilation to take place, if freedom cannot impact upon mechanism, nor mechanism upon freedom?[38] But it cannot take place only in one of two worlds, without conditioning the unconditioned, and thus annihilating in turn the system of derivations anchored by it. Fichte's answer is that the I and not-I never coincide in one world, but merely limit the sphere of reality that the I produces as transversal to both worlds. It is only thus that freedom can limit determination without exerting causal pressure.

There are two possible demonstrations of this solution. The first is the problem of determining the point at which the quanta of I become those of not-I. Fichte uses the example of darkness and light:

In a boundless space, *A*, put light at a point *m*, and at point *n*, darkness: then, given that the space is continuous, and there is no hiatus between *m* and *n*, there must necessarily be a point *o* somewhere between the two, which is both light and darkness; a contradiction. – Set between the two a middle condition, *twilight*. If it stretch from *p* to *q*, then at *p* the twilight will march with light, and at *q* with darkness. But by this you have gained only a respite; the contradiction has not been satisfactorily resolved. Twilight is a mixture of light and darkness. Now at *p* the daylight can only march with the twilight, in that *p* is at once light and twilight; and thus . . . in that it is at once both light and darkness. Similarly at *q*. – Hence, the contradiction is soluble in no other way than this: light and darkness are not opposed in principle [i.e., logically], but differ only in degree. Darkness is simply a very minute amount of light. – That is precisely how things stand between the I and the not-I. (W I, 144–5; 1982: 138)

In other words, between darkness and light, I and not-I, there is an inexhaustible continuum in which the smallest quantum of darkness is always = > 0. There is no such thing as a non-divisible quantum, so that Fichte's 'points' are mere limitations or determinations of this continuum, rather than its constituents. In that the continuum is formed by the activity of the I, as the self-limitation of the I by the not-I, the I therefore becomes 'intensive matter' (W I, 312; 1982: 273), and reality is composed of an infinite matter of *degrees*. Moreover, since the quantities of I and not-I are *continuous*, without 'hiatus', as Fichte notes, quanta, while infinitely divisible [*theilbar*], never resolve into parts [*Theilen*], since if they were thus reducible, no matter how infinitesimal the space between the parts, the quanta would cease to be continuous. We will call this the *formal* proof of freedom.

The second solution, which by contrast we will call the *practical* proof of freedom, concerns the problem of negative magnitudes. This problem was posed by Kant in the following form: if two contrary predicates are affirmed of a single subject, this can either be a merely logical opposition, or it can be a real opposition. Real oppositions form when, for example, a sailing ship remains in one place by being driven by easterly and westerly winds, and the two winds cancel each other out. Kant writes: 'A magnitude is negative in regard to another magnitude inasmuch as it cannot be conjoined with it except by an opposition, that is, inasmuch as the one magnitude makes a magnitude equal to itself disappear from another' (*Ak*. II, 174; 1992a: 213–14). Thus, of two forces affecting a single object in contrary directions, the magnitude of the one will be subtracted from the magnitude of the other. Even if the two forces, as in the contrary winds driving the sailing ship, amount to an equilibrium, the resultant zero movement of the ship constitutes not something negative, nor a mere logical contradiction, but a *real* singularity, a 'concrete zero', as Gilles Châtelet puts it (1993: 127). The consequence of this means of articulating the problem of how freedom and causality can impact upon one another is that it turns causality into the negative magnitude of freedom, *only insofar* as the I posits the limitation of its freedom, or the restriction of its striving, in the not-I. Like causality, limitation is regional determination only, since striving is infinite. Thus, intellect and thing never meet in one of the two worlds, but only coincide in the self-determination of the I as a limited product *and* as unlimited productivity. Finally, freedom holds quantitative sway over causality insofar as the I's striving is infinite, and causality is always empirically local (tied to particular products). This means that causality is always a negative magnitude of freedom (following Kant (*Ak*. II, 171; 1992a: 211), a *real* rather than a *logical* opposition) and is registered in the I's self-limitation by the not-I.

It is instructive that Kant's sailing ship example pitches logical contradiction against opposing *forces*, since this tallies with Fichte's practical-theoretical concept of *positing* as activity. Real oppositions are forces. Indeed, without such opposition, direction is unthinkable: 'The concept of direction is a purely reciprocal concept; *one* direction is none at all, and is absolutely unthinkable' (W I, 273; 1982: 241). Since the forces the I expresses as active and resistant (I and not-I) have their source in the I's infinite striving, then by the principle of continuity established in the formal proof above, there is no point at which forces are not operative. The I's continuous forces and quanta of activity produce and form reality. The two proofs together, then, yield the formal-practical proof of the reality *produced by* freedom.

However formally satisfactory such solutions may be, it is at least counter-intuitive to portray freedom in terms of continuous quanta and forces, the very language of the science of mechanics whose characterization of the dogmatists' 'reality' Fichte unqualifiedly accepts. At the same time, however, this formalism is an amplification of the power of abstraction inherent in the mathematized sciences. Accepting, as a Kantian, the inaccessibility of the thing-in-itself, Fichte rejects the dogmatist's understanding of the sciences as sciences of nature, and considers them products of freedom. At root, as he infamously writes, one can only choose as to 'whether the independence of the thing should be sacrificed to the independence of the self, or conversely' (*W* I, 432; 1982: 14). At the same time, however, Fichte cannot exclude the special sciences from the scope of the system: 'The science of knowledge gives form not only to *itself*, but rather to *all remaining sciences . . .*' (*W* I, 51). While Kant, however, sees these latter (in the first *Critique* at least) as lying outside the scope of philosophy to address, Fichte amplifies the power of abstraction he locates at the root of both as the ground of freedom (*W* I, 425; 1982: 8). Thus, an avowed anti-mechanist, Fichte can nevertheless charac-terize the 'system of striving of the human mind' – i.e., practical philosophy – as 'fully commensurate with . . . the Newtonian theory of attraction' (*GA* II, 3: 250).[39] Fichte's characterization of the I as a quantum of force-in-action finds its formal base in Newton's account of the generation of mathematical quanta: 'I don't here consider Mathematical Quantities as composed of Parts *extremely small*, but as *generated by a continual motion*. Lines are described, and by describing are generated, not by apposition of Parts, but by a continual motion of points' (Newton [1692] 1974: 141).[40]

The important point here is the generativity ascribed to continual motion: quanta emerge *from* motion rather than designating parts within it. Quanta are discrete products of a continuous process; but how is it that they are thus generated? In essence, the problem is the same as that generated by the formal proof of freedom from continuous quanta: the question is one of establishing limits, of *positing*. If we ask: 'what posits?', the answer for the system of striving must be: 'the I'; if we ask: 'what is posited?', the answer must again be: 'the I'. Insofar as there is an identity between positing and being posited, the I becomes a 'self-constituting mathematical point' (*W* I, 273; 1982: 241). Insofar as, however, there is quantitative difference between the two terms in the relation, and insofar as one is derived from the other, the posited I must be, for the positing I, the not-I. The difference between the I and the not-I is therefore also the qualitative difference of reality and negation, through which limitation is established: the I limits itself by positing the not-I. So it is for reflection. But the positing I has as its law that it posit itself as infinite. In terms of the generation of quanta, then, the limitation of the continuity is established as the self-limitation of an infinite quantity, through which there arises a determinate quantum. In what amounts to a restatement of the law of the I, 'that it shall reflect on itself and

shall demand that, in this reflection, it be found to be the whole of reality'
(W I, 276; 1982: 243), Fichte writes:

> The I is posited as a reality, and in that there is reflection on whether it has
> reality, it is necessarily posited as *something*, as a [determinate] quantum;
> yet it is posited as all reality, and is thus necessarily posited as an infinite
> quantity, a quantum exhaustive of infinity. (W I, 274; 1982: 241)

It is not enough of a criticism to present Fichte's philosophy as 'merely
formal', as both Kant, in his *Open letter to Fichte* and Hegel's early critiques
do. Mathematics yields Fichte a formal, abstract and *generative* method,
where the 'reiteration of positing' (W I, 276; 1982: 243) – that is, of identity,
difference, reciprocity and continuity – generates an abstract product: the
infinite as 'object' of reiteration (= striving). Being abstract, it is self-determining; being iterative, it is generative: the method itself is formal, certainly;
but it is also the free power of reason (abstraction) as act, *productive* and
independent of all givens, so that its generation is continuous with free
action. Abstraction realizes the power of reason: 'The activity of the form
determines that of the matter'; so free action is the realization of the abstract,
or the modification of *matter, on condition that* it is 'the matter of reciprocity
[*die Materie des Wechsels*]' (W I, 170–1; 1982: 158–9), or the self-limitation
of the 'intensive matter' (W I, 312; 1982: 273), that alone is active.

This is why Fichte can and must deny the possibility – even the conceiv-
ability – of the natural production of mind (W XI, 362); ultimately, were
nature so capable, then there would be a *causality of abstraction*, rendering
it no longer free, and no longer generative; a *product* and therefore no
longer *productive*.

Here, however, the ordinary portrait of Fichte as a merely subjectivist
idealist seems confirmed. The hiatus between productivity and product is
bridged only in the I, which produces products through self-limitation.
Everything else 'is what it is' in that 'it is not posited in the positing' (W I,
165; 1982: 154). Such accidents of productive substance fall outside the
sphere of productivity into that of mere being. The 'one ultimate substance'
that is the I (W I, 122; 1982: 119) takes on the unity of 'the virtue and power
of acting' that Spinoza accorded Nature (*Ethics* III, Preface; 1996: 69). If
Spinozism did not ground its 'transcendent' theory of the unity of things in
the absolute, according to Fichte, then the latter 'systematises Spinozism' (W
I, 122; 1982: 119) by dividing nature from the I and restricting all activity
to the latter. Thus nature simply *is* 'the dead persistency' of 'raw and formless
matter' (W I, 468, 499; 1982: 42, 69). The mechanical laws under which the
world stands are not laws of change, but of constancy, so that: '[O]n its own,
nature . . . cannot really bring about change in itself. All change is contrary
to the concept of nature' (W III, 115; 2000: 105). Thus reproduction merely
reproduces individuals, ensuring the constancy of species, since otherwise,
were the conditions of reproduction always given, i.e., between individuals
of all species, then . . .

nature would be in a state of perpetual flux from one shape to another, and no shape would ever remain the same. There would be eternal becoming, but never any being; and then even flux would be impossible, since nothing would actually be that could pass over into something else; this is an unthinkable and self-contradictory thought. (*W* III, 305–6; 2000: 265)

Underlying Fichte's theory of productive generativity (rather than that of reproductive constancy),[41] there lies a theory of nature that demands antiphysics. As raw being, nature is composed only of particulars that only form anything under the abstractive rule of reason. The world of things *is* mechanical; the world of intellect '*ought to be* an organised whole' (*GA* II, 3: 247). For each of these worlds, Fichte has a different theory of matter: things are inert, causally governed; intellect forms matter through and as the reciprocity of self-limitation. Thus the I is limited not only at the derivative level of the not-I, but even at the non-derivative level of the absolute I: the absolute is thus conditioned by the restricted distribution of intelligence, which restriction is not produced, but only given. That the absolute is divided means not simply that it is logically flawed as a ground or first principle, but that the real absolute is precisely this division: it is itself unconditioned, but conditions everything. Haunting Fichte's generative abstraction is its artifice *opposing* any materiality; inert mechanism is the engine that lies at the base of the system of striving.

Because, however, the underived division between the absolute I (= I *and* not-I) and nature is unconditioned, Fichte's attempt to imprison matter in particulars remains ungrounded. Either, therefore, the absolute I is to remain absolute *but not to incorporate the division*, or raw matter must be, Fichte's logical protestations concerning the circularity of the thesis notwithstanding, straightforwardly capable of ideation. It is, in other words, the formal incompleteness of the theory and practice of generation that creates the prospect of an absolute materialism that is also active.

Both solutions to the problem concern the substrate-independence of I-hood, or, of activity and mentation. There are both abstract and realist grounds for such a thesis, which we will explore below (ch. 4). Running through this problem, however, is the positive element in Fichte: the thoroughgoing constructivism that forms a line of generative abstraction issuing from between the sundered worlds of the one I on the one hand, and an unrecognizable, uncharacterizable multiplicity that determines things beneath the threshold of the I's 'unlimited' positing, on the other. It is on this abstract line that the uncharacterizable can be glimpsed: for example, given the pre-divided absolute, the instability of the unconditioned, in the infinite passage between darkness and light, in the 'wavering [*schweben*]' between the I and not-I as quanta and the infinite quantum itself, nothing ties the determinations of I-hood to a substrate other than activity, on which the infinite quantum depends. Again, determination of the I by negative magnitudes (real opposition) cannot demonstrate its source except retrospectively, in the recursivity of the activated categories of the I's self-generation. In both cases, however, the asymmetry between the absolute I and the posited I from which the system begins yields no positive characterization of the absolute I other than through the derivation of a recognizably empirical I from it. Fichte's postulate of the underlying self-identity of intellect and thing is governed only by recursivity or 'reiteration':

> Thus the activity returns into itself by way of the reciprocating [*des Wechsels*], and the reciprocating returns into itself by way of the activity. Everything reproduces itself, and there can be no *hiatus* therein; from every link one is driven to all the others. The activity of the form determines that of the matter, this the matter of the reciprocating, and in turn its form; the form of the reciprocating determines the activity of the form and so on. They are all one and the same synthetic state [*Zustand*]. The act returns to itself by way of a circle. But the whole circle is absolutely posited. It is because it is, and no higher ground can be given for the same. (W I, 170–1; 1982: 158–9)

There is therefore a fundamental wavering in the absolute; that between matter and intellection, between the irrevocably determinate and the indeterminacy of infinite abstraction. 'Spinoza made systematic' thus yields a fundamental demensuration between the one and the all, wherein the one remains necessarily, as a result of its unconditioned freedom, *an* infinite quantum, and the all remain necessarily, as a result of their various determinations, an endless multiplicity of unconnected particulars.

Even in Kant and Fichte, the most antiphysicalist or subjectivist of Idealists, the materialist pole of the absolute exercises its attraction, even if this is as absolute limit. If Kant's late dynamics presented the prospect of a world of acts, alike practical and cognitive, to be treated in a unified fashion by transcendental philosophy, Fichte's mathematical antirealism offers the immanence of abstraction to ideation at the cost, ultimately, of a dead nature of inert material particulars. In this, Fichte becomes an unrecognized contributor to formalist models in the mathematized sciences, or speculation in mathematics. Indeed, Gilles Châtelet (1993) views *Naturphilosophie* as principally a contribution to what Cantor called 'free mathematics'. Ultimately, that there is egress beyond the confines of the subjective philosophy of reflection even in its most prominent exponents, gives us pause: the inherited models of reflection are not so seamless as we find it convenient to think.

3.3 ORGANICS AS ANTIPHYSICS: FICHTE CONTRA OKEN

A philosophy or Ethicks apart from *Naturphilosophie* is a nonentity, a bare contradiction, just as a flower without a stem is a non-existent thing. (Oken 1847: 656)

Not only has the organicist tendency been evident amongst philosophers of nature – even Leibniz considered intra-particulate matter to be aswarm with animals (*Monadology* §66), while Herder tried further to organicize his 'law of continuity',[42] just as Bergson and Merleau-Ponty's 'new science', premised on organism, finds echoes in Deleuze – and even amongst naturalists (Ritter's 'cosmic animal', 1798: 171; Burdach's 'eternal organism', 1817: 21); so equally natural scientists such as the physicist Windischmann, and the physicians Eschenmayer and Röschlaub pursued overtly Fichtean principles in their researches. Before detailing these, and Schelling's interventions in their naturalized Fichteanisms, we will look at the emergence of the transcendental philosophy of the abstract animal, beginning by comparing two such creatures.

Oken's universal animal is a total-organism made of the totality of individual part-animals: 'the independent animals are but parts of that great animal which is the animal kingdom. The whole of the animal kingdom is but one animal, that is, the presentation of animality with all of its organs, each one of which is a whole' (1847, §214ff). Fichte's own universal animal is generated from the ontological imperative governing the activity of the I, 'act infinitely': 'the entire universe ought to be an organised whole; and every minute part of this universe a whole in turn, belonging necessarily to this organised whole' (*GA* II, 3: 247).

While there are superficial similarities between Oken's and Fichte's Allanimals, the former is constituted as the animal kingdom, while the latter encompasses 'the entire universe'. Oken's animal runs from its kingdom to its organs; Fichte's from the universe to 'every minute part [*jedes Theilgen*]'. Fichte's animal universe gives body to the infinite I, forming a single body with 'one force, one soul, one mind' (*W* XI, 366), ignoring previously well-established strictures concerning the differentiation of the absolute from the empirical I.

The animal therefore becomes the initial battleground in the determination of the metaphysics of nature. At stake is the relation between physics and ethics, mathematics and substance, matter and organism. Embedded in the proposition: 'the universe is an animal totality' therefore is not simply a vitalist conceit, but also the question of the *limits of physics*.

Kant's outlines, in the *Critique of Teleological Judgment*, of reflective organicism sought to provide a formalist bridge to span the 'great gulf fixed' (*Ak.* V, 195; 1987: 35) between the practical and the physical domains. The problem is necessarily raised by any formalist solution, however, as to how far beyond reflection, into matter, can form extend? As Kant's self-proclaimed heir in transcendental philosophy, Fichte thought the problem of the relation between the formal and the material already solved in the *Wissenschaftslehre*: there is, in intuition, no such distinction to be drawn, since intuition is driven fundamentally not by a recognition of the given, but by *desire*.[43] Beyond this, it is not a legitimate question for transcendental philosophy, which denies all access to a matter beyond appearances ('matter is a species of representation', CPR A370). Like Kant's procedure in the

Transition, whatever the matter of appearance (the determinable in our intuitions), it is rigorously separated from 'raw and formless matter' precisely by virtue of form. Fichte asks: *where in nature does this happen*? The answer, like Kant's in the third *Critique*, lay in the theory of organized matter or organism.

Fichte's organicism, although grounded in his 'actuation' of the categories of judgement in the third *Critique*, and taking note of the problematics of real teleology (*GA* II, 3: 255–60), misses the point in the formalist rush properly to systematize the Kantian theory. The crucial, physicalist element of Fichte's antiphysicalist organicism consists in quasi-realist assumptions concerning the formative drive.[44] Three elements constitute the basis of this thesis: (1) what is the relation between mathematical formalism and real or substantial nature? Fichte deploys the principle of continuity to argue that in organism, 'intelligence and nature terminate in each other without *hiatus*'; (2) consequently, a result drawn from 'animal oeconomy' (= physiology): the *Wissenschaftslehre*'s primary division between action and being is no longer carved out *in abstraction* between the ideal totality and inert particulars, but *in actuality*, between a *real reciprocity of forces* and *exhausted force*; (3) the idealism of the absolute I, which would ensure a human head be placed on the universal animal.

3.3.1 *Oken's generative history: Mathematics and the animal*

Of all *Naturphilosophen*, Lorenz Oken is the most notorious.[45] Like Fichte, his strategy for approaching nature is by way of mathematics. Whereas Fichte, however, maintains the principle of continuity, division and reiteration of the division as a *formal* defence against the collapse of being into exhausted particularity, Oken's '*Naturphilosophie* is mathematics endowed with substance' (1847: 4)[46] since 'the universe or world is the reality of mathematical ideas' (1). Just as Fichte generates an ideal infinite quantum from the reiterated positing of the I, so chief among Oken's mathematical ideas is the generative potential of the 0:

> Mathematical singulars or numbers can . . . be nothing else than zero disintegrated, or rendered real by determination [. . .]. Numbers have not issued forth from zero as if they had previously resided therein, but the zero has emerged out of itself . . . and then was a finite zero, a number. (Oken 1847: 7)

Oken's account of zero's generative potential can be rendered in the form of the generation of natural numbers from the empty set. The empty set $\emptyset$, on its own, contains nothing; wrap a set around it, however $\{\emptyset\}$, and this second set allows the empty set to 'emerge out of itself as number', since the set containing the empty set contains thereby one member $\{\emptyset\} = 1$. An infinite number of sets can be added in like fashion.[47] As Oken puts it,

'Multiplicity or *real* infinity is, accordingly, nothing special or particular, but only an arbitrary repetition . . . an incessant positing' of zero (1847: 10), where each positing is an additional iteration. Unposited, zero remains Ideal, 'infinite intensity', since it does not contain number, but number emerges from it; posited, since number has now emerged, it becomes real, 'endless extensity' (1847: 7). But this does not yet exhaust the generative function Oken ascribes to zero. In the process of iterating zero, it can be *posited* or *unposited*, which are represented by + and – respectively. The real is generated therefore by positing, and negated by unpositing. Thus a 'first duality' is derived from the positing and unpositing of zero, of which he writes:

> The first or primary duality is not, however, a double unity, both members of which are of equal rank, but an antagonism, disunion, or *diversity*. Many diversities are *multiplicity*. The Many is thus complex. [This] first form is not therefore a simple division of zero or the primary unity, but an antagonistic positing of itself, a becoming manifold. (Oken 1847: 10)

Oken's generative zero is a mobile point of intensity from which the manifold of particulars are generated. In this way, Oken seems to account for the raw *form* of the productions of nature, rather than their *substance*, just as Fichte accounts for the formal generation of the I. In terms of form alone, however, Oken's system yields a principle that generates complex multiplicities ('0, +, –, +, –, 0, –, – . . . *n*'), not divided unities (I = {I and not-I}). In accordance with the *Naturphilosophisch* principle of the unity of number and substance, however, generativity cannot be formal only, but also substantial. Thus Oken's *Naturphilosophie* prescribes for itself the task of *being* the generation of such complex multiplicities in nature itself. Forming the first principle of Oken's *Naturphilosophie*, the very formulation of the problem removes it from the scope of transcendental philosophy, insofar as for the latter, any such unity must be thinkable only. If we take the number-substance relation *transcendentally*, then like Fichte, we begin with the absolute separation of thought and thing, so that substance could relate to number only in thought. If, on the other hand, the system undertakes to generate substance from number in the way, for example, that proponents of 'artificial life' suggest is true of their digital creatures, then we are asking whether numbers *cause* substance to emerge 'from nothing'. Again, number and substance – intellect and thing – start from a position of mutual isolation, as though what must be demonstrated is a causal link between them. Oken, however, does not treat the structural dimension of his system, which moves from the whole to wholes of singulars,[48] as proceeding from form to matter, whether causally or categorially, but instead treats of the unity of number and substance as a relation constant throughout nature: number is substance as the intense point of the ideal within real extensity. Thus number does not stand somehow outside nature, but is rather the science of itself that nature's ascent through various stages of complexification produces: 'A natural thing is nothing but a self-moving number; and organic thing . . . is a number moving itself out of itself, spontaneously; an inorganic thing . . . is a number moved by another thing' (1847: 27). The task of *Naturphilosophie* is therefore merely to realize this production, as 'the generative history of the world' (1847: 2); and mathesis is the self-realization of nature in its most universal form: 'all realisation . . . is not the origin of something that has not previously been: it is only a manifestation, a process of extension taking place in the idea' (1847: 8).

The generative history of the world, or 'cosmogeny' (1847: 17) therefore seeks the points of intensity where everything reduces to nothing. Thus, for example, 'immateriality . . . is the nothing, the intense point of matter, its ideality' (1847: 38). Everything – or rather, nothing – is a matter of the retrogression of real extensity to intensity, since 'that which holds good of mathematical principles must also hold good for the principles of nature' (1847: 17). However, the insistence on a 'parallelism' between nature and mathematics, which Oken frequently reiterates (e.g., 1847: 2; 491–2), suggests precisely the non-identity between mathematics and substance that *Naturphilosophie* axiomatically rejects. The ideal becomes suspended above the real, as its mathematical mirror-image, rather than being the intensity of real extensity. If the parallelism is to be thoroughgoing, then each branch of 'physiophilosophy' – mathesis, ontology, biology – must accordingly have its own zeros and extensities, forming a multiple series of parallels. However, the hypothesis of a plurality of parallel zeros is a false problem, insofar as the zero itself is neither one nor many: 'Zero is not a singularity, such as the one individual thing, or as the number 1, but . . . a numberlessness in which neither 1 nor 2 . . . can be found' (Oken 1847: 9). In other words, the arithmetical zero and the geometrical zero cannot be said to be the same zero, but neither can they be numbered as two. Instead, zero is 'ideal infinity' before it generates real, extensive infinity by iteration, in the case of arithmetic, or by a vector from a point, in the case of geometry (1847: 27–8). Crucially, therefore, the immaterial, or the zero of matter, continues mathematics into the domain of inorganic singulars, which Oken calls ontology, 'the third part of mathematics' (1847: 39). Thus the science of singulars, or 'the doctrine of matter' (ibid.), remains mathematical since it concerns nothing but extensity, or the 'arbitrary repetition' of the ideal (1847: 14). Comprising a real infinity of singulars, ontology is the field of calculable differences, and admits therefore of retrogression to the ideality of zero. Materiality is not therefore superadded to the mathematical as a framework or ideal structure, nor does it constitute an irreducibly parallel series to the mathematical; rather, ontology and mathesis, matter and form, only *become* parallel[49] following their generation from numberless immateriality.

Thus, in the domain of organics, ideality becomes materiality in two ways. Firstly, the zero of organism, its intense point, is not nothing, but mucus, '*Urschleim*' or protoplasm. Thus 'the primary organic is a mucus point' (1847: 188): 'Every organic has issued out of mucus, is naught but mucus under different forms. Every organic is again soluble into mucus …' (1847: 185). Second, life is fundamentally a synthetic process (1847: 178): addition and subtraction form a cycle marked by the death of organic singulars, their return to mucus. Moreover, mucus, as the primary organic, is contained within the organic as its means of generation through reproduction. Thus, from the mucus point on, the relation between ideality and substance is inverted, since the organic series no longer merely retrogresses towards the ideal, but ascends through the series of organics to the incarnation of the ideal in intelligence: 'Mind [*Geist*] is nothing different from nature, but simply her purest outbirth or offspring' (1847: 656; t.m.), a product of extremely differentiated 'neuro-protoplasmic or mucus mass' (1847: 655). Everything is generated from the ideal, but the ideal is differentiated within nature as its points of real intensity.

By contrast with the generation of number and nature as processes of real extension, Fichte's principle of continuity is formed on the basis of the ideal infinity of the I, and its striving to realize the ideal. Since, however, the ideal is an object of striving only, it remains ideal. This has the consequence that, even within the sphere of the I's striving, continuity remains formal only, since there can be no material content, i.e., intuitions of the ideal real. Thus form and matter remain separate not only from the perspective of the unbridgeable gulf between intellect and thing, but even within the transcendental sphere of the I.

The I thus constantly posits and negates the formula of the ideal, 'I = ¬I' as continuous quanta of reality and negation, striving to form its own ideal sphere as a single, continuous, infinite quantum. The productions of Fichtean generation are therefore limited to the one I or its negation (real opposition). By contrast, Oken's zero does not contain the real infinity of numbers, but is *ideal* only as a singularity, an intense point that becomes extensity as real multiplicity is generated. The only totality is nature.

3.3.2 *Naturphilosophy without nature: Fichte's 'essence of animals'*

Antinomy arises, says Kant, when a subjective law of appearances is ascribed to an objective totality, or vice versa. World, cosmos, infinite divisibility are such totalities only as ideas of pure reason, and thus as guiding principles for our thought, but are not to be discovered in nature itself. The solution of the antinomy consists in allocating the two conflicting (anti-) laws (*nomoi*) their rightful place under reason. As an example, Kant gives the law of continuity (*lex continui in natura*) which 'rests on purely transcendental, not on empirical grounds' (CPR A660/ B688). The antinomy results when this transcendental law is therefore applied to empirical phenomena: 'It is easily seen that this continuity of forms is a mere idea, to which no congruent object can be discovered in experience. For in the first place, the species in nature are actually divided, and must therefore constitute a *quantum discretum*' (CPR A661/B689).

Fichte's animal is precisely antinomic. It arises as animal, i.e., as organized being, only upon the application of the law of continuity to nature:

> What is an animal? As it were, a system of plant-souls. Its soul: its self-unity arising from nature. Its world; partly that of plants (Nutrition, from vegetal nature through synthesis to animal nature through analysis), partly that of the animal . . . The animal grows like a plant, forms itself, precisely in accordance with the higher plants or universal organic nature in it [. . .]. The plant soul is . . . the principle of a determined organisation (penetration and union of various chemical forces). (W XI, 366)

Thus we cannot think individual products at all, but only in relation to a larger whole of which they form not products, but reciprocating parts. The 'fundamental elements' of nature are, contrary to all empiricism, 'inexplicable and inconceivable' (W XI, 363). There are no individual chemicals, only 'circuit[s] of chemical-organic attractions and repulsions' (W XI, 365), forming an 'inner animation' of which the plant is the midpoint. Nor are there individual plants: 'The animal would accordingly be a system of plantsouls, and the plant a separated, isolated animal part' (W XI, 367). Similarly, all individual animals are merely part-animals of one, universal 'system of conjoined organism' (W XI, 366). '*Life*, infinite reciprocity' (W XI, 365): a chemico-vegetal-animal continuum. Thus the ideal eradicates the empirical, since what enters into intuition is not caused by stimuli from outside the I, but a free act of positing by it. The tension of the incorporation of nature into the absolute I fuels the striving for infinite continuity.

True to scientific procedure, 'Propositions for the Elucidation of the Essence of Animals' sets out from the I, and from the principle of continuity on which its ontological imperative is based: 'nature and intelligence . . . terminate in each other without *hiatus*' (W XI, 362). If continuity can be established between nature and the I, this entails that the I extend throughout nature, since otherwise the latter would constitute a permanent limitation of the I, a negation of its absolute reality that no striving could overcome. Drawing support from recent developments in the account of the property of life in organic matter, Fichte embraces incipient biology's rejection of the adequacy of causal-mechanical explanations of the phenomena of life. If it is not causal, life must itself be free action, or at least in continuity with it. This continuity is found in the concept of the drive: 'The highest exhibition of intelligence outside itself, in nature, is the *drive*' (W XI, 363).

The positing of drives in nature provided physiologists with the means of explaining the emergence of organized matter. With the concept of the *Bildungstrieb* (formative drive), for example, organic life could be explained from itself, and without reference to merely external, mechanical causality. Insisting on a material basis for the drive, physiologist proponents such as its inventor, Johann Friedrich Blumenbach, insisted equally that the formative drive was not reducible to mechanical-chemical causation:

[I]n all living creatures, from man to maggot and down, from the cedar to the mould, there lies a specific, inborn, effective drive that acts throughout life to take on from the beginning its determinate form, then to maintain it; and if it be destroyed, where possible to repair it. A drive (or tendency or striving, by whatever term one calls it) that is as wholly distinct both from the general properties of the body in general, as from the other forces of the organised body in particular; the one seems to be the first cause of all generation, nutrition and reproduction, and which, to fend off all misinterpretation and to distinguish it from the other forces of nature, I here give the name of the *Bildungs-Triebes* (*nisus formativus*). (Blumenbach 1781: 12–13; cited in *AA* Ergbd.1: 637)

Distinct from all other forces and corporeal properties, the formative drive is irreducibly specific to living creatures. In this, it echoes precisely modern, Stahlian vitalism. Chemist Georg Ernst Stahl[50] noted in the late seventeenth century that chemically formed bodies had a tendency to decompose, which living things seemed to vitiate. There must therefore be, he reasoned, something inherent, a 'vital force [*Lebenskraft*]' or 'rational soul', in living things that resisted chemical decomposition, things which could not then be explained by chemical-mechanical means. The Stahlian rational soul is rational precisely to the extent that it is purposive, and a force insofar as it maintains purposive organization of material parts, yet at the same time is not itself material.[51] In this, there is little to distinguish *Lebenskraft* from *Bildungstrieb*. Crucially, both establish an absolute divide between living and non-living matter. Thus Blumenbach: 'One cannot be more inwardly convinced of something than I am of the immense gulf that Nature has appointed between animate and inanimate Creation, and between organised and non-organised creatures' (Blumenbach 1781: 71; cited in *AA* Ergbd.1: 644). The *Bildungstrieb* therefore presupposes two types of matter: animate-organized and inanimate-anorganized. Whereas Blumenbach sank the abyss between them into nature itself, for Kant it became a gulf dividing the powers of understanding and judgement, the one presupposing mechanical explanations, and the other locating apparent purposiveness in nature, although merely reflectively. For Fichte, however, merely mechanical causality becomes an abstraction from the reciprocal affinity of organic matter for itself, the 'self attraction of the homogeneous in nature' (cf. *W* XI, 364). Fichte thus eliminates the gulf by eliminating nature.

In one sense, the elimination of nature is a consequence of Blumenbach's assertion of the non-reducibility of the *Bildungstrieb* to mechanical causation: it is merely 'a force, the effects of which we know from experience, but the cause of which is concealed from us' (*AA* Ergbd.1: 644; cf. Blumenbach 1781: 26). The 'primal source' of organized matter is therefore 'inconceivable to the natural scientist', as the Kantian pupil of Blumenbach, Christoph Girtanner, asserted, relegating the explanatory task to metaphysics (*Über das Kantische Prinzip für die Naturgeschichte*, Göttingen 1796: 15; cited in *AA* Ergbd.1: 663). As Jörg Jantzen puts it, 'with the concept of organisation natural science as physics has already been abandoned' (*AA* Ergbd.1: 659); so too has metaphysics, which is conceived by Girtanner as an explanatory resource for the natural sciences. Freed of all ties to physics, the *Bildungstrieb* becomes wholly ideal. Thus in an essay by his pupil August Ludwig von Hülsen, entitled 'On the Formative Drive', which Fichte published in his *Philosophisches Journal* in 1800, 'vital materialism' was finally transmuted into critical antiphysics by way of precisely the explanatory gulf between mechanism and organization: 'We cannot separate being and activity from one another' (Hülsen 1800: 118).[52] The eradication of a causal explanation of organized matter and the consequent rejection of materialism prepare the ground for a wholesale replacement of all concepts of causality with that of free activity, which now alone explains organization.

The inorganic side of Blumenbach's gulf, governed by mechanism, is simply dead: 'what does not grow, dies' (*GA* II, 5: 256). However, according to the Hülsen-Fichte ontology, what does not act, is not. Thus not only is mechanism *dead*, it *does not exist*, or exists only as an abstraction:

> It is clear that the chemical forces in nature, just like the drive in man, remain without expression, that is, are *posited* merely abstractly, if the condition of its actualisation is not posited. 'Raw matter': – really only an (empty) abstraction from the efficacy of the drive; just as the drive *in general* (as not determined through and through) is only an abstraction. (*W* XI, 364)

Organization is not a property of matter, which remains an abstraction, but rather one of action. Fully consonant with Fichte's systematization of Kant under the transcendental categories of activity, then, organization *is* not insofar as it remains abstract, and *is* only insofar as it is actualized. Following Kant's synthetic-dynamic hint as to the productivity of the categories (CPR B: 110–11), Fichte's 'actuated' categories effectively render 'causation' an incomplete, and therefore abstract and inactual, reciprocity:

> Either one-sidedly, mere causality . . . gives rise to a product so that that on which it acts is not determined by itself to retroact, thus remains just an inert residuum of the exhausted force [. . .]. Or reciprocally, that both or all penetrate each other internally, forming a reciprocal solution, and flow together into . . . a new whole, that is neither *a* nor *b c*, etc., but rather the result of the most intimate unity of this all. (One force, one soul, one mind.) (*W* XI, 366)

Fichte need no longer regard the elision between the mathematical and the dynamical application of the law of continuity as a dialectical illusion, in the Kantian sense. Rather, since the ground of empirical determination has passed exclusively to the I, the principle of continuity becomes the substrate of the I, actuated as reciprocity in organization. Thus the total organization that the universe ought to become, according to the cosmic-ontological imperative, 'one force, soul, mind' insofar as it is I. That '[t]he ideal would be – an all-encompassing organised matter; the entire universe ought to be an organised whole; and every minute part of this universe a whole in turn, belonging necessarily to this organised whole' (*GA* II, 3: 247) means: either nature is *actuated* as the I's total organism, or *inactual* as the residua of exhausted forces.

Why is the organic a necessary threshold of the positable? Why is it not possible to descend beneath it, into the inorganic-anorganized? The organic *as such* is not in question here; merely the positability of the inorganic. To posit brute particulars would be to disrupt the principle of continuity, since thought, like force, would be exhausted in its product, and be subtracted from the infinite quantum that is the I, limiting the absolute. It would lose itself outside 'the all' that reproduces itself ('*Alles reproduciert sich selbst*'; W I, 170; 1982: 158), where the 'all' is singular, 'the infinite quantum', 'the whole circle': the A=A from which the entire science of knowledge begins affirms the infinite singular, the One, at the expense of the All. Thus Fichte is wrong to use the formula 'A=A' to signify: 'Every thing is what it is [*Jedes Ding ist, was es ist*]' (W I, 165; 1982: 154). Following the Fichte-Hülsen ontology, being is inseparable from acting, and only the I acts, while things are exhausted. Every non-exhaustive force, meanwhile, is for that very reason inseparable from the I.

With formless matter transmuted into exhausted force, Fichte's critical antiphysics is complete. The animal enables the science of knowledge to address the problem of the absolute conditioned by particulate matter, and removes this as a condition by making 'raw matter' into an inactual abstraction of activity, or better, actuation. But the more fully the 'organized whole' is realized, the more particularity is inactuated. The universal animal not only absorbs nature into the absolute, it also destroys the real opposition by which the I can be derived from the absolute. The systematic dissymmetry from which positing as reiteration is formally derived is materially conditioned by the 'inconceivable' formlessness of raw matter, independent of the I. Fichte has maintained the principle of continuity at the expense of that of real opposition, since all real opposition becomes reciprocity, or is exhausted. Thus, that the absolute is always relational becomes a problem given the absence of relation between the absolute and nature, that is, in confronting exhausted particulars.

Two problems finally emerge from the *Naturphilosophie* of critical antiphysics. Firstly, the indetermination of nature by the absolute I in the *Wissenschaftslehre* created the problem of a conditioned unconditioned, or a non-absolute absolute. Because of the derivation of the not-I from the I, the not-I cannot be determined as nature, which therefore leaves nature out of the system of derivations, and thus conditions the unconditioned. It is the problem of excluded nature that the 'Essence of animals' sets out to overcome. But the absorption through reciprocity of organized matter into the continuity of the I, which effectively unconditions, unthings the absolute, turning it from a system of reiterated positing into the singular infinite (the One), exhausts not only the 'inconceivable' particularity of nature (the All), but thereby divests the absolute of real opposition, cutting the I loose from empirical determination. And if the I thus loses any empirical substrate, then it remains undetermined, a mere formula: act, force and feeling. The second problem therefore consists in Fichte's negotiation of the physical immanence of intelligence and nature; in other words, of the *material* indetermination of the I. While the nature in me, the merely determinable, is the empirical subject, nothing ties this empirical subject to the absolute I precisely because it is 'clearly false', Fichte tells us, 'that intelligence is a higher power of nature' (*W* XI, 363). With the conditions for determining empirical subjectivity in nature dissolved into animal-plant-chemical reciprocity, the determining I that gives a head to this universal animal is divested of all relation to nature beyond this immanent reciprocity. It is precisely this that gives Fichte's categorical-logical refusal to acknowledge a materialist derivation of mind from matter its poignancy, and spells the death of transcendental philosophy in its encounter with matter.

Under guise, then, of renegotiating a relation between the I and nature, critical antiphysics produces a *Naturphilosophie without* nature. Conceived as a thoroughgoing reciprocity between organization and freedom, the relation between nature and the I is only more thoroughly severed: there are empirical animal-subjects that cannot attain to freedom, and free acts of an I without body. In brief, the Fichtean philosophy of the animal entails the admission into the unconditioned of the conditions of organic life.

3.4 ANTIPHYSICS AND THE GROUNDS OF SCIENCE

The philosophemes of a Kant, a Fichte and a Schelling have given the labours of the physician and the natural scientist a manifest and proper direction in our own day, just as the philosophemes of Empedocles, Democritus, Heraclitus and Aristotle did earlier. (Röschlaub, *Magazin zur Vervollkommung der theoretischen und praktischen Medizin*, 8.3 (1805): 473)

The physician Andreas Röschlaub attests to the 'valuable impetus that the philosophy of nature had given' to the sciences. Finding in particular that the *Wissenschaftslehre*, although 'Fichte's purpose was simply to ground cognition, nevertheless contained counsel as regards reworking the grounds of the special sciences' (1799: 43),[53] Röschlaub drew from it the foundations of a dynamic understanding both of 'the construction of the disease process' of the therapeutic practice: 'Just as the theory of nature in general must simply be the history of nature, so too nosology has only to exhibit one branch of the history of the nature of the organism' (*Lehrbuch der Nosologie*, 1801: vii). This history was not a developmental history of species, however, but an individual history of specific acts: a diagnostee was considered an archive from 'pragmatic history' (*W* I, 222; 1982: 198–9), that is, as a history of *actions*, while the diagnostician's 'experiments in perception' become actions oriented towards discovering the appropriate counteraction, in order to restore proportionality to an organism's 'excitability [*Erregbarkeit*]' in which, for a Brownian such as Röschlaub,[54] the 'constant activity of [the] organised parts' (*Untersuchungen über Pathogenie* (1800): vol. 1, 244) that was the 'vital process', exclusively consisted.

The basis of the Fichtean influence was his ontology, which swept aside the somatism on which mechanism depended, and replaced them with a 'new dynamics' (Tsouyopoulos 1978b: 91): 'to borrow Fichte's terms', wrote Röschlaub (*Magazin* 9.1 (1806): 51), 'there is no being other than life'. To Röschlaub, Fichte was not pursuing a formalist agenda, therefore, so much as a dynamist one, providing the ontology to supplant both the Aristotelian and the Kantian, with their primitive substances, their phenomenologies and their somatism; as such, it provided the necessary means to rework the equally somaticist, mechanical foundations of the sciences. As Fichte puts it in the first *Wissenschaftslehre*,

> If the science of knowledge were after all to possess a metaphysic, as a supposed science of things-in-themselves, and such a metaphysic were demanded of it, it would have to refer to the practical part of the system [for] it is this alone which treats of an original reality; and if the science of knowledge should be asked, how, then, indeed, are things-in-themselves constituted, it could offer no answer save, as we are to make them. (*W* I, 285–6; 1982: 251–2)

Insofar as the 'aim of all medical knowledge is practical' (1800: 4), Röschlaub had little trouble in converting the constant activity of the Fichtean formal-practical *Ich* into 'the ground of life', although that the 'not-I' became 'the activities brought forth in the external world' presented the same problem Fichte's organicism encountered: only an *Ich*, and not a 'world' or a 'nature', could produce acts (1800: 244). How far down the series of conditions, then, can Röschlaub's so-called 'pure history of nature' (*Magazin* 5.2 (1801): 320) reach?

Schelling's criticisms of Röschlaub in the *Annals of Scientific Medicine* are addressed to precisely this problem. The Brownians' quantitative analytics of 'excitability' constitute 'a merely formal construction of the condition of life' (VII, 276), and are therefore capable only of a formal history of nature. Moreover, since the determinants of 'excitability' are not sought in nature as such,[55] they seek its conditions in the organism alone, and are therefore capable at best of a restricted nature. Yet because organic life is itself a restriction of nature, to attempt such a natural history as Röschlaub proposes is to attempt to explain the whole as less than its part. Against this transcendental animal and the restricted dynamics it supports, therefore, Schelling argues 'Nothing happens in nature except by thoroughgoing restriction: nothing *just acts*.'[56] Accordingly, rather than explaining life, excitability is an empty concept: 'there is no excitability as such; rather, it is simply something determined' (VII, 208).

That Fichte's overtly 'pragmatic' or, better, *practicist* science of knowledge was so easily adapted by naturalists, however, demonstrates at once the virtue of his anti-somaticist, and anti-phenomenalist antiphysics, and the fatal decay of modern European *Wissenschaft* from *physis* to the ethico-teleological. What emerges on the one hand is a restricted naturalism consequent on Fichte's formal dynamics. As long as it remains thus formal rather than *genetic*, there can be no natural history, such as Röschlaub imagined. Indeed, the Fichteans' reasons for maintaining what Schelling diagnoses as 'the common deficiency of all modern European philosophy' (VII, 356; 1986: 30) consist in a need to maintain, on the other hand, the exclusive priority attached to human ideation and practice as guaranteed by a *natural order*, whether in the form of a 'plan of nature' (from Bonnet to Geoffroy de Sainte Hillaire), an 'organic continuum' (Leibniz, Herder), a transcendental and 'continuous geography' (Kant, *Ak.* IX, 161), 'a temporal cross-section of nature' (Windischmann, in Schelling 1969, 1: 109), or by runaway ethico-teleology: 'the earth is there for the sake of man' (Ritter 1984: 184).

Writing in Schelling's *New Journal for Speculative Physics* (1.1., 1802), physicist Karl Joseph Windischmann's 'Outlines for an Exposition of the Concept of Physics' finds organicism as the cause of this erroneously restricted nature. The 'great speed' with which 'the theory of the nature of organic bodies, commonly named *physiology*' had recently developed has also, due to 'unfamiliarity with the true essence of physics' amongst the natural scientists of organism, led to 'misconceptions and errors in the majority'. Windischmann's explanation of this does not seek simply to identify the errors themselves, but their philosophical source:

> *because* they hold it impossible to derive the laws of thought from the general concepts of matter, they allow a force in organic bodies that constitutes what is proper to them, and which leads in animals, and ultimately in man in particular, to *representating* [. . .]. Hence the concept of the *vital force*. (Windischmann, in Schelling (ed.) 1969, 1: 140; my emphases)

That vital forces, such as the Brownians hypothesized under the concept of 'excitability', arise in nature at all, means, for Windischmann's naturalism, that they do not exist in themselves, eternally as they are and act, as the Fichte-Hülsen hypothesis has it, but are rather 'determined by' (so Schelling) or generated out of the confluence of the same physico-chemical processes operative in nature in general. Since 'there can be no events in nature but the physical', the hypothesis of a 'vital force' leads to nothing more than 'an increase in words for an unknown thing' (ibid.: 141).[57] The reason, Windischmann asserts, for this hypothesis is less to do with the physics of nature, however, than with the isolation of the source of practical events *in nature* from the physico-chemical context, that is, of a 'rational human soul'. Completing Schelling's demand, in the *Ideas*, for a 'natural history of our mind' (II, 39; 1988: 30) in place of the Fichtean 'pragmatic history of the human mind' (*Wz* I, 222; 1982: 198–9), Windischmann therefore proposes a physics of our representing, if not of the Idea, in the form of a 'natural description [*Naturbeschreibung*] of thinking and the thought' (Windischmann, in Schelling (ed.) 1969, 1: 82).

While Windischmann opposes the restrictions imposed by Fichtean-Röschlaubian animality on nature, he equally opposes the ethico-teleological grounds for them, insofar as these lie in the expulsion of ideation from nature: the balance of the ethical and the physical in 'transcendental physics' (Schelling 1969, 1: 163) is out of kilter. Yet Windischmann does take two things from Fichte: firstly, the ascription to 'ethical science' of a 'protective and leading' role in the pursuit of 'the path of science' (Windischmann, in Schelling (ed.) 1969, 1: 91); and secondly, a *formalist* and *non-phenomenal* solution to the problem of the 'natural description' of ideation, with the relation between them being the task of the sciences as such to resolve. As regards the first, '. . . for its proper extension, ethics leads us into the field of physics, and enjoins us both to ceaseless progress therein, while always keeping the mind free from its mastery' (Windischmann, in Schelling (ed.) 1969, 1: 93). In consequence of this, and as for the second, Windischmann confesses that while he too 'first abandoned the *Wissenschaftslehre* with the prejudice that, as Kant too has explained, it is mere logic, with which one cannot flatter oneself to have explained reality' (ibid.: 111n), further study brought him to 'acknowledge its truth'. The truth in question concerns precisely Fichte's radicalized, ontologizing formalism, which Windischmann considers a necessary consequence of the fact that 'thinking can in no way be exhibited to the senses, and is not intuitable through vision, but only through itself' (ibid.: 82). Windischmann characterizes the resulting science of 'logic' as a non-phenomenal 'mathesis' which, by virtue of consisting in 'events in nature', constitutes in turn a *Naturbeschreibung*, that is, a description *by*, and not merely *of*, nature. Science, therefore, is

> not simply pure mathesis, as we might arbitrarily consider number, figure and their laws; rather we must strive for the eternal, omnipresently exhibited mathesis of nature itself, and search for its inalterable, all-structuring dimensions. Only in this way do we attain in physics . . . that order which nature itself follows in its developments. (Windischmann, in Schelling (ed.) 1969, 1: 106)

Although up to this point, Windischmann's venture is indeed 'analogous to my own', as Schelling notes in his 'Editor's Preface' (1969, 1: 79), their projects diverge on two counts. Firstly, a 'natural description' remains as distinct from a 'natural history' of the Idea for Schelling as these two designations were for Kant (*Ak*. V, 428n; 1987: 315n), insofar as the former implies nothing as regards time, and therefore priority. Secondly, Schelling and Windischmann differ as regards the matter of the ethical, an examination of which will reveal the ground of the first divergence. While Windischmann has indeed dispensed with the priority of 'recognition' to be accorded a merely phenomenalizing physics,[58] this is by according ethics the 'leading role' in physics. As he writes, the 'vital principles' and 'unwavering foundations' provided by the *Wissenschaftslehre* are to 'guide the researcher in scientific investigations of the ethical and the physical'. Windischmann's Fichteanism consists in ceding phenomenal recognition to practical *production*: 'Each man pursues physics only under the protection and lead of ethics, and is to exert all his force in gradually forming the world into a sphere of moral actions' (Windischmann, in Schelling (ed.) 1969, 1: 91). Openly subordinating science as such to the 'collective science of humanity' (ibid.: 93) which only then subdivides into physics and ethics, Windischmann continues to subject nature, as Schelling will describe Fichte's subordination of the same, to an 'economic-teleological principle':

> When we hear him [Fichte] speak, we do not know whether *he* is complaining more about the obstacle of nature, or the latter is regarding the obstacle of Fichte. It pressures him, hits him, gnaws at him from all directions, forever threatening and restricting his life [*W* VI, 369–70]; for this, he pays it back royally; for what is, in the end, the essence of his entire understanding of nature? It is that nature must be employed, used, and that it exists no further than it is thus employed; the principle in accordance with which he views nature is economic-teleological: 'It must be thus', he says (that is, we must appropriate nature), *so that* human life gains freedom through its own freedom. Now for this it is necessary that one subjugate natural forces to human ends [*W* VI, 370].[59] (VII, 12)

Schelling, by contrast, neither subjugates nature nor freedom to recognition, nor pretends to an 'elimination of the contradiction',[60] such as Windischmann (in Schelling (ed.) 1969, 1: 80) presupposes between the sciences of nature and the practical, as the ethical teleology of 'collective science of humanity' as such. Rather, it is a consequence of nature's *a priority* (III, 179; 2004: 198) that whatever 'freedom' might turn out to be, it cannot be confused with a merely *formal* deduction of its nature in accordance with the canons of teleology, but must instead, like the 'natural history of mind', be *genetic* (II, 39; 1988: 30). As Jules Vuillemin warns transcendentalists in philosophy and physics alike, 'the transformations to which contemporary physics has subjected the concept of the possibility of experience warn us that it is probably the most elusive concept in transcendental philosophy' (in Förster (ed.) 1989: 247). If therefore, as is often asserted, Schelling's is a transcendental philosophy of nature, it will not be one recognizable from the premises of Kanto-Fichtean transcendentalism. This is precisely the topic of 'On the True Concept of Naturephilosophy', which Schelling published as a contestatory response to Karl August Eschenmayer's 'Spontaneity = world soul', in the *Journal of Speculative Physics* (2.1., 1801), in which the physician undertook a critical commentary on Schelling's *First Outline of a System of Naturephilosophy* (1799) that opposed, even in its title, transcendental modernism to a Platonism bizarrely meshed with empiricism.

106

As is clear from its titular equation, Eschenmayer's essay attempted a critical reconstruction of Schelling's philosophy of nature along transcendental, that is, ethico-teleological lines. Drawing on the same problem Windischmann's concept of the 'collective science of humanity' set out to resolve, namely, 'what is the connection between *nature* and *concept*, *law* and *freedom*, *dead mechanism* and *vital mechanics*?' (in Schelling 2001: 233), Eschenmayer first attempts to recast a problem Schelling had formulated in the *First Outline of a System of Naturephilosophy* in the following terms: 'what is the universal source of activity in nature?' (III, 220; 2004: 158). Schelling's solution to this problem, like Windischmann's, begins by tracking back from the given fact of organic activity to its determinants or *conditions* in other – electrochemical – natural processes. Pursuing this 'unconditioning' or *unthinging* further, Schelling reaches the provisional conclusion that whatever the source of activity in nature might be, it must itself be something that is 'not objectively-knowable', something 'absolutely non-objective' (III, 219; 2004: 158).

It is due to Schelling's assertion of the *non-objectivity* of the source of activity in nature that Eschenmayer (in Schelling 2001: 234) characterizes the philosophy of nature as 'an *unthinged* empiricism [*einem unbedingten Empirismus*]'. It is *empiricism* in that it is 'unconditioned', i.e., in that it rejects transcendental philosophy's pursuit of the a priori conditions or principles that might conclude its inquiry. It is an 'unconditioned' empiricism for two reasons. Firstly, not only an empiricism without conditions, it is also an empiricism of the *unthinged*, because a 'thing' is by definition 'conditioned [*bedingt*]'. Secondly, it is 'only unconditioned', argues Eschenmayer, 'on condition that a *principle of becoming* is precluded'. The naturephilosopher, inseparable from unprincipled and unconditioned natural becomings, is therefore reduced to 'setting forth whatever natural principles happen now to be active', and can at best thereby show the *actuality*, but not a *source*, of activity in nature. Since no principle can be furnished by immersion in nature, Eschenmayer argues it must be sought in what rises above this 'non-objective' nature, namely in that 'originary principle' that turns the 'creative self' into 'the supersensible substrate' of nature. The remainder of Eschenmayer's essay therefore sets out a 'more detailed proof' of the retranscendentalization of nature in accordance with the formula: 'spontaneity = worldsoul' (Eschenmayer in Schelling 2001: 234). This elimination of nature by freedom is, writes Schelling (IV, 83), the '*clavis Fichteana*', the key to Fichtean philosophy.[61]

For transcendental philosophy, no *physics*, but only an *ethics* of the world-soul is possible, since the transcendental research into a principle of becoming leads not to material nature, but to vital consciousness, which bears such a principle within itself alone. Clearly indicating as much the conceptual distance between transcendental philosophy and naturephilosophy, as that between transcendental and Platonic physics, Schelling opens the 'True Concept' thus: 'Some, misled by the term "naturephilosophy", will think they should expect a transcendental deduction of natural phenomena' (IV, 82). As the *Ideas* had already demonstrated, however, a naturephilosophy remains inconceivable from the Kantian perspective, despite the best efforts of Schelling's naturalist contemporaries – and our philosophical ones – to overlook this. Rather than finding its limits at the threshold of a merely 'possible nature', as Kant's transcendentalism did, Schelling seeks instead to demonstrate the *actual* source of activity in nature, the *arche kineseos* of Platonic cosmogony. A transcendentalist such as Eschenmayer simply posits this source of all activity 'in the mind', while for the naturephilosopher, 'this is the product of something that actually lies within *nature itself* – the working *soul* of nature' (IV, 102). Issuing a rallying call to conflict over the nature of the world-soul, Eschenmayer therefore supplants 'being' and 'becoming' – the distributive matrix of Platonic ontology – with the Fichte-Hülsen ontology, which establishes 'being' in antithesis to 'activity', and proposes that all that is active in nature is intelligence, since nature *is* only insofar as it consists in the residua of exhausted force. Eschenmayer gives this ontology in the form of 'an absolute quantum of activity divided between two opposing powers (mind and nature), the more active in me, the more negation in nature, and inversely' (Eschenmayer, in Schelling 2001: 235–6).

Ultimately, however, since the I is enjoined to extend its activity to the greatest possible extent ('the whole universe *ought to be* . . .', as Fichte (*GA* II, 3: 247) put it), nature *is* accordingly *only as* the 'exhausted force' of activity. In effect the practical determination of nature amounts to its *ideal elimination*, which is what makes the transcendental philosophy into an eliminative idealism. For Schelling, however, as for Windischmann, intelligence consists in physical activity whose source is not the I, but rather nature, 'since I absolutely do not acknowledge two different worlds, but rather insist on only one and the same, in which everything, even what common consciousness opposes as nature and mind, is comprehended' (IV, 102).

Further stipulating that between the 'idealism of nature' and the 'idealism of the I', 'the former is the original, and the *latter* the derivative' (IV, 84), naturephilosophy 'constructs' (IV, 84) activity in mind *from* the primacy of activity in nature: 'The acts which are derived in the theoretical part of idealism are acts the simple powers of which exist in nature and are developed in the philosophy of nature' (IV, 92). Where for Windischmann, however, it was enough to propose a 'natural description of thought' (in Schelling 1969, 1: 82), a *Naturbeschreibung* (to which Kant (*Ak.* V, 417; 1987: 302) had stipulated the 'system of teleological concepts' belonged, rather than to 'natural science'), Schelling's claim reiterates the point made in the *Ideas* that a properly genetic philosophy requires a 'natural history of mind' (II, 39; 1988: 30). Fully in accordance with the principles of Platonic physics, the naturephilosophy pursues ideation from the perspective not simply of its 'former and ancient states', which transcendental archaeology of nature Kant had proposed as performing the proper functions of 'natural history' (*Ak.* V, 428n; 1987: 315n), but from that of their *becoming*. The priority of naturephilosophy over transcendental philosophy is Schelling's physicalist response to the Platonic problem of *genesis eis ousian*, the 'becoming of being' (*Phlb.* 26e9).

Accordingly, it is not the case that naturephilosophy is empiricist in the 'dogmatic' sense attributed to it by transcendental philosophy. Concerned with the becomings prior to mind, or nature, Schelling, in a passage from the *First Outline* to which the 'True Concept' refers, explains that whereas empiricism 'treats its objects *in being* as fixed and established', 'science on the contrary treats its object *in becoming*'. Unlike empiricism, moreover, 'Since science cannot concern anything that is a product, that is, a thing [*was Ding ist*], it must concern the *unthinged* [*dem Unbedingten*]; the primary inquiry of speculative physics [therefore] concerns the unthinged in natural science' (III, 283; 2004: 201–2, t.m.).

For Schelling's avowedly 'one-world' physics (IV, 102) the 'unthinged' cannot be an object restricted to ideation, since if it were, it would be a conditioned product of (thinking) nature. Schellingian dynamic physics – which its author claims Eschenmayer has falsely mistaken for the Kantian (cf. IV, 82), is therefore unconditioned with regard to its *objects* not insofar as it is an empiricism (although thirty years later, Schelling will return to a *Presentation of Philosophical Empiricism*, X, 225–86), but insofar as the unthinged, not *being a thing*, must be considered by a science of becoming, as the *First Outline* stipulates. Not only, therefore, is the naturephilosophy led by Platonic physics rather than by 'ethical science' (Windischmann, in Schelling 1969, 1: 81); like Platonic physics, because its research into the nature of the world-soul 'early lead[s] to the Idea of a self-organising matter' (II, 47; 1988: 35), so 'naturephilosophy . . . consider[s] . . . nature above all in its self-construction' (IV, 96–7).

Naturephilosophical science, which considers the unthinged in becoming, cannot therefore revert to the Aristotelian transmutation to which *Naturphilosoph* Carl Gustav Carus' odd substantive '*das Werdende*' (1944: 15) subjected it, giving it a substance 'of which being can be said' (XI, 362, condensing Aristotle, *Met.* 1017b10–15). Rather, just as Platonic physics insists that logic not merely be a formal approximation of a thing, but rather be 'of the same kind', *suggeneis*, as its object, so Schelling will reiterate as his science's inductive axiom,[62] *Gleiches Gleiches hervorruft*, 'like produces like' (VII, 281; cf. II, 219; 1988: 175; VII, 337; 1986: 8; XIII, 103). And since this 'like' cannot be like some *thing*, it must be an *unthinged* like, or an 'absolute identity', which 'never ceases to be what it is' (IV, 20). Thus Schelling completes the derivation of Platonic physics: by tracking the 'unthinged in nature', naturephilosophy seeks 'what never ceases to be what it is' in the 'boundless sea of diversity' (*Stat.* 273d9), the 'sea of becoming' (Carus 1944: 19). Naturephilosophy, then, led by 'guiding Ideas' (I, 353; 1994c: 69), is the science of 'the becoming of being'. Rather than pursue these Idea-attractors into a speculation unmixed with matter, however, the Ideas conduct ideation *in nature*, drawing the mind by 'the Idea of self-organising matter' (II, 47; 1988: 35). Accordingly, the pursuit of the Ideas, the becoming of being, amounts to a *natural* history that 'thinks nature in its freedom as it evolves along all possible trajectories':

Such a presentation of nature would only be *natural history* were it derived from nowhere other than from nature perceived in its *freedom*; this certainly does not imply that nature is *lawless*, because all its products have arisen by *deviation*, and a deviation precisely from an *ideal* [*Ideal*] whose limits it nowhere oversteps. (I, 469)

Schelling's guide in the natural history of the unthinged will be Carl Friedrich Kielmeyer, from whose *On the Proportions amongst the Organic Forces throughout the Series of Organisations* (1793) Schelling claims 'future times will doubtless reckon a new epoch in natural history' (II, 565). We will examine in particular the extent and limitations of Kielmeyer's dynamics in relation to the natural historical principles of his contemporaries, before returning to the attractor theory by which Schelling completes the physics of the Idea.

Notes

1 'Plato himself had a concept of nature or *physis*, by which he meant being as a whole. And since for him the Ideas are true beings, they are also nature in the strict sense' (Böhme 2000: 18).

2 Stipulating that by the term 'idealism' he understands 'nothing other than the meaning I have already given that term' in the *System of Transcendental Idealism*, Schelling distinguishes real-idealism from ideal-realism in the *Presentation of My System of Philosophy* (1801): 'Fichte . . . thought idealism as entirely subjective, and I, by contrast, as completely objective; Fichte's idealism could remain at the standpoint of reflection, and I, by contrast, posited Idealism from the standpoint of production' (IV, 109).

3 Jaspers' *Schelling* illustrates the effect of reintroducing Schelling into contemporary philosophy, which he clearly defines in terms of the transcendental: 'If Kant is our contemporary, then it is as if Schelling has undone the chains that held the human mind together [and that] are the expression of its finitude' (1955: 321). We shall see that in the naturephilosophical perspective Jaspers' book all but ignores, the damage is not confined to the transcendental; Schelling's naturalistic 'geocentrism' ungrounds the possibility of the reducibly transcendental.

4 It is Badiou's promotion of a formalist Platonism over the dominant Kantianism of contemporary philosophy (its criticality, its practicism) that makes this task 'necessary' (cf. Badiou 2000: 45ff). Although these remarks are made in the context of his discussion of Deleuze's 'univocity of ground', it is here pertinent to note that Badiou does not pursue this project through the overtly Schellingian thematic of 'ungrounding' pursued in *Difference and Repetition* (Deleuze 1994: 229–35, *passim*), but proceeds directly to the role of the 'virtual' in ontology. More pertinent still, however, is the problem of ground to which both Badiou and Deleuze contribute, although as we will see (in ch. 5, below), neither Badiou's *formalism* nor Deleuze's 'nature *and* freedom' (1994: 19) eliminate the antiphysics Kant grounded in that problem. See also the direct address to this problem that runs throughout Deleuze and Guattari's *What is Philosophy?* (1994), esp. ch. 2.

5 Amongst those who regard naturephilosophical Schellingianism as a simple 'extension of Kantianism over nature' are Knittermeyer (1929: 162), Jaspers (1955: 178, 286), von

Engelhardt (in Hasler, (ed.) 1981: 77–8), Bonsepien (1997: 147, 216, and in Hasler (ed.) 1981: 169–70), Peterson (2004: xiii–xxvii) and, in a qualified manner, Moiso (in Zimmerli, Stein and Gerten (eds) 1997: 203–74) and Beiser (2002: 509–10). This tendency is not new, however, and has persisted at least since Eschenmayer's 'Spontaneity = World Soul' (1801, in Schelling 2001: 233–72) and Windischmann's (1802) 'Outlines for a presentation of the concept of physics' (in Schelling 1969, 1: 78–160). Amongst those who reject this conception are Krings (1994: *passim*), Peetz (1995: 97) and Bach (2001: 33–4).

6   Both Kirchhoff's remark concerning Schellingianism's geocentrism (1982: 47) and Sandkühler's assertion that 'the real basis of the theory of the *Ages of the World* is modern geology' (ed., 1984: 21), present cases in point. This view is crucial to the present work.

7   Schelling repeats this point from a letter to Fichte (19 November 1800; in Schulte-Sasse (ed.) 1997: 75), where naturephilosophy is characterized as 'the physical proof of idealism'. See also, however, Schelling's contemporarily written preface to the *System of Transcendental Idealism* (III, 332; 1978: 3), which warns the reader not to expect 'a deduction of idealism from the primary objects [*Hauptgegenstände*] of nature'; while the latter may seem explicitly to contradict the 'physical proof' argument, the contradiction is removed with Schelling's rejection of a somatic basis in the Idea of matter, or in the matter of the Idea.

8   Harris's and Heath's translation of the *Ideas* (1988) persistently renders '*Vorstellungen*' and its cognates by 'idea', thus obscuring the eradication of the grounds of Kantianism with regard to nature in which the 'Introduction' consists.

9   It is precisely this that Jacobi unpicks by concentrating on the groundlessness of Kant's division between phenomena and noumena in the first edition of *Critique of Pure Reason*.

10   Strictly speaking, this is a citation not from Kant but from Fichte: 'Intellect and thing are exact opposites; they inhabit two worlds between which there is no bridge' (*W* I, 436; 1982: 17). However, Fichte identifies the *Wissenschaftslehre* entirely with the transcendental philosophy – 'my system is nothing other than the Kantian' (*W* I, 420; 1982: 4).

11   Although clear from the *Timaeus*, Plotinus makes the argument that 'matter too is an incorporeal' (*Enn.* III.6.vi) especially clear: 'Matter must be incorporeal – for body is a later production, a compound made by matter in conjunction with some other entity' (III.6.vii).

12   The *Prolegomena* calls one a 'naturalist of pure reason' who 'trusts himself to decide in matters of metaphysics without any science' (*Ak.* IV, 313–14; 1971: 74–5), thus emphasizing the dependence of transcendental metaphysics on physics.

13   This is why Kant argues only that force 'cannot be assumed to be actual' (*Ak.* IV, 524; 1970: 79) but cannot argue that forces *are not* actual; the modality (possible/actual) of 'objects' whose necessary conditions have not been given in deduction must necessarily remain undetermined.

14   The text gives '*einer anderen Natur*' here, which recurs at *Ak.* V, 335; 1982: 206. Elsewhere in the *Critique of Judgment*, morality is expressly characterized as 'a second, namely, a supersensible, nature [*eine zweite . . . Natur*]' at *Ak.* V, 275; 1982: 136. Since all nature is to be subordinated by teleology its purpose is to survive in nature, the *actuality* of this 'second' or 'other' nature is thus substantiated.

15   Kant breaks this rule when he writes: 'matter can receive more and other forms than it can get through mechanism' (*Ak.* V, 411; 1982: 296). For more on these issues, see Grant 2000b.

16   The statement of this natural dialectic of judgement runs: '*Thesis*: All production of material things is possible in terms of merely mechanical laws. *Antithesis*: Some production of material things is not possible in terms of merely mechanical laws' (*Ak.* V, 387; 1987: 267).

17   The stakes, therefore, of the sacrifice of the reproductive to the productive imagination, or of first to second nature, are high: the production of the new earth and the preservation of the 'cause of the world'.

18   Kant's mechanism is repeatedly apparent. In the *Universal Natural History and Theory of the Heavens* of the previous year (1755), for example: 'I hope to found on incontrovertible

111

grounds a firm conviction that the world recognises for its origin a mechanical development unfolding from the general laws of nature; and second, that the kind of mechanical genesis we have presented is the true one' (*Ak*. I, 334; 1981: 170). Metaphyics is grounded, methodologically and even ontologically, in mechanical physics for the precritical Kant: 'The true method of metaphysics is basically the same as that introduced by *Newton* into natural science . . . Newton's method maintains that one ought, on the basis of certain experience and, if need be, with the help of geometry, to seek out the rules in accordance with which certain phenomena of nature occur. Even if one does not discover the fundamental principle of these occurrences in the bodies themselves, it is nonetheless certain that they operate in accordance with this law.' (*Ak*. II, 286; 1992a: 259)

19 Edwards (2000: 120) discusses the *Physical Monadology*'s 'isolationist' concept of 'simple substances', a descriptor he ascribes to Kant's definition of the monad as capable of permanent independent existence: 'Bodies consist of parts, each of which has an enduring existence separate from the others' (*Ak*. I, 477; 1992a: 53). Although Edwards uses this definition (Proposition I of the *Physical Monadology*) to argue that Kant is not a corpuscularean, his argument is premised on a non-identity between substance and body from the perspective of the transcendental aesthetic in the *Critique of Pure Reason*: 'substance' is not *phenomenally* equivalent to 'body' insofar as the latter is 'a matter between determinate boundaries . . . [which] therefore has a figure' (*Ak*. IV, 525; 1970: 80). As Schelling notes, however, it is precisely the indivisibility and impenetrability of the simple substance that 'obliges' the mechanical philosopher 'to presuppose bodies, and with them, attractive and repulsive forces' (II, 196; 1988: 157), because such philosophers 'begin by presupposing the independence of matter in thought, and then afterwards in reality' (II, 195–6; 1988: 156–7).

20 'The substrate [*hypokeimenon*] is that of which the rest are predicated, while it is not itself predicated of anything else. Hence we must determine its nature, for the primary substrate is considered to be in the truest sense substance' (*Met*. 1028b36–1029a3).

21 Edwards (2000: 65–8) provides an account of the Leibnizian 'transition' project, as outlined in the concluding section of 'Critical Thoughts on the General Part of the *Principles* of Descartes' (1692): '[M]echanical principles and general laws of nature themselves arise from higher principles and cannot be explained by quantitative and geometrical considerations alone; there is rather something metaphysical in them . . . which is to be referred to a substance devoid of extension. For in addition to extension and its variations, there is in matter a force or a power of action by which the transition is made from metaphysics to nature, and from material to immaterial things.' (in Leibniz 1969: 409) While Leibniz's conception of metaphysics as dealing with dynamic phenomena and physics with mechanical ones might be mapped Kant's 'two kinds of bodies', the same distinction might equally be mapped onto Kant's *Transition*, insofar as the latter maintains an a priori division of labour between transcendental philosophy and physics, despite their stemming from a single 'material principle'.

22 Compare this with the evident Aristotelianism of the *Metaphysik Mrongovius* of 1782–3, thus immediately postdating the publication of the first edition of *Critique of Pure Reason*: 'Since the object of metaphysics does not lie in bodily and thinking nature, what is it then to which metaphysics applies? It must be an object beyond the senses. Metaphysics means beyond natural science, beyond the natural things <*meta ta physica*>, it means beyond physics <*trans physicam*>' (*Ak*. XXIX, 273; 1997: 130).

23 This version, as elsewhere in Kant's philosophy, is clearly indebted to Aristotle's verdict regarding the 'substantial existence of the Ideas' as given in the *Metaphysics* (1031b15–21): 'it is clear that if the Ideas are such as some hold, the substrate will not be substance; for the Ideas must be substances, but not involving a substrate'.

24 If, philosophically, Kant had been disappointed by the reception of the *Critique of Pure Reason*, it provided the impetus for a generation of physiological thinkers for a physicalist derivation of mind as a dynamic series of modifications of a single *Grundkraft*, or basic

force. See Hansen (1998) for a detailed account of the development of this school of physiology from Kant, and see my 'Kant after geophilosophy' (Grant 2000b), for the significance of such work regarding Kant's own, unfinished 'metaphysics of nature' (CPR Axxi).

25 Chemistry, Kant notes in the *Metaphysical Foundations of Natural Science*, is insusceptible to mathematical construction (*Ak*. IV, 468–9; 1970: 4–5), and therefore can only form an art composed of an empirical aggregate rather than the systematic articulation required of a science. Ten years later, however, in his preface to S. T. Sömmering's *Über das Organ der Seele* (1796), Kant is seeking to construct a materialist theory of mind on the basis of a 'dynamical [organization], based on chemical principles' (*Ak*. XII, 34). For a reconstruction of the process of Kant's 'chemical revolution', see Friedman 1992: 264–90. Mai Lequan provides a brilliantly concise outline of a reading of Kant's entire corpus as a 'chemical philosophy', in *La chemie selon Kant* (Paris: PUF, 2000).

26 The fuller passage runs: 'Analogy between attraction and light, where seeing precedes the light, and, if the former is not operative in space, then neither is the latter. Illumination in empty space. Double concept of reflection. Seeing is repulsive – like touch' (*Ak*. XXI, 24; 1993: 227). The passage, elliptical though it is, can be explicated as follows. Attraction is the *second* of the two original forces [*Urkräfte*], the first being repulsion. Both are necessary for producing matter, according to the *Metaphysical Foundations* (*Ak*. IV, 510; 1970: 59). This is because repulsive force, were it not checked by a contrary, attractive force, would 'disperse itself to infinity' (*Ak*. IV, 508; 1970: 56–7). Equally, the analogy runs, there is no seeing, which I provide, without light. Were light to precede seeing, there would be illumination in empty space – i.e., due to the absence of any receptivity, objective space without intuition – which is impossible. The conclusion drawn from the analogy is that, however, seeing is the primary constituent of intuitions, and is *physically* therefore repulsive, like touch, and indeed, all the forms of our sensibility. However, Kant adds the question of a 'double concept of reflection'. This is to get around the problem of making light merely objective and therefore secondary, as opposed to the subjective priority of seeing. Rather than objective light-matter, as it were, light is a product of my representations, coeval with my seeing what it reveals to me as the objective within representations. Thus, physically, the senses are repulsive, but are checked by the equally subjective positing of light as the objective element of my representations. The double concept of reflection is therefore the method proper to the deduction at once of the objectively physical and subjectively objective elements of my representations. The co-dependency of attraction (one of the original forces [*Urkräfte*] of physics, along with repulsion, according to the *Metaphysical Foundations*; *Ak*. IV, 516; 1970: 67) and light, and of seeing and light, is clear here. So too is the transcendental principle that seeing, i.e., an activity I perform.

27 What follows is condensed from version 2 of the 'Übergang 1–14' that make up the 'aether proofs' in the *Opus postumum*. For more detail, see especially Friedman (1992), who is heavily criticized and an alternative proposed in Edwards (2000), and the essays by Tuschling, Förster and Vuillemin in Förster (ed.) (1989). Förster (2000) provides an especially concise account of the problems and constitution of the aether proofs.

28 Even those who, like Edwards (2000: 153), argue, against Friedman's (1992: 328) account of the 'material principle' as 'hypothetical, not real', that the aether proofs are not simply proven 'in respect of form, but also . . . in respect of matter', do not undercut the significance of form and matter as principles of the transcendental account of nature. Förster (1989: 233–5) makes the same argument, making the *Transition* a continuation rather than a departure from the transcendental system, while opposing this view, Tuschling (in Förster (ed.) 1989: 206–7) argues that Kant's deduction of 'material possibility' (the possibility of the generation of bodies, rather than the identification of matter with bodies that undercut the *Metaphysical Foundations* and the *Physical Monadology*), while changing the character of transcendental idealism, is not yet a naturephilosophy.

29 As Tuschling (in Förster (ed.) 1989: 202) glosses the point, 'It is not the name but the function of this "material" that matters.'

30 The attributes Kant ascribes to this primary substance echo Aristotle's almost exactly: a 'somatic substance besides the four in our sublunary world' that is 'prior in nature' to those other bodies, and possessed of a 'continuous and eternal . . . revolutionary motion' (*Heav.* 369a30–b16).

31 Fichte makes the same point in his *On the Concept of the Science of Knowledge* (1794): 'The science of knowledge has therefore absolute totality. In it, the one leads to the all, and the all to one' (*W* I, 59).

32 A supposition amplified by Fichte himself. Kant's is a 'yet-to-be-completed whole, which is actually not yet available', he tells us (*W* I, 485; 1982: 57). Indeed, the entirety of §6 of the 'Second introduction to the science of knowledge' amounts to Fichte's claim to succession of the critical philosophy (*W* I, 468–91; 1982: 42–62). The prefatory note to the 'First introduction' leaves no doubt: 'I have long asserted and repeat once more, that my system is nothing other than the Kantian . . .' (*W* I, 420; 1982: 4).

33 *Wissenschaftslehre* is properly a project, rather than a single work. The 1794 edition translated (with modifications from 1798) into English as *The Science of Knowledge* (1982) is therefore only one of 13 versions that Fichte worked on between 1792 and 1813. See Fichte's *Werke*, Bde. I–II, IX–X.

34 All the more surprising, given the proximity of the projects of the *Opus postumum* and the *Wissenschaftslehre*, that Kant rejected Fichte's system as 'indefensible', since to Kant, it amounted to a 'vain effort [. . .] to cull a real object out of logic' ('Open letter on Fichte's *Wissenschaftslehre*, Ak. XII, 370–1). The terms of this verdict openly dismiss the central tenet of Fichte's system, regarding the actual identity of theoretical and practical positing, but, interestingly, do so in terms of the logical derivation of real things. This realist criticism of Fichte's transcendental-practical apparatus echoes Jacobi's criticisms of Kant.

35 Helmut Müller-Sievers (1997) offers a fine generative account of Fichte's procedure, principally through the text *Praktische Philosophie* (*GA* II, 3: 181–266). He argues that Fichte's model of generation is essentially the biological one of epigenesis, and the book is occasioned by what Müller-Sievers accounts an alarming reemergence of this paradigm in the concept of autopoiesis, as deployed in chaos theory, fractal geometry and non-linear dynamics on the one hand, but also in the human sciences on the other. In consequence, Müller-Sievers' account tends towards the critical rather than the constructive. While there is virtue in the biological approach, given Fichte's constant references to life and organism, the formally formative element of positing coupled with the power of abstraction yields a more mathematical model of generation than epigenesis on its own allows.

36 Heath and Lachs (in Fichte 1982) translate Fichte's '*Ich*' and '*nicht-Ich*' as 'self' and 'not self', tending therefore to objectify the terms of the logic, rather than deriving the object from the subject. Accordingly, 'I/not-I' will be used throughout.

37 Notwithstanding the categorical nature of the assertions Fichte makes on this point, both in the *Wissenschaftslehre* (1794) and in 'Propositions for the elucidation of the essence of animals' (1800), Fichte seems, in the *Foundations of Natural Right* (1797), to take up the challenge he posed the materialists in the 'First introduction' of the same year, namely, to demonstrate 'a continued passage from matter to mind or its reverse' (*W* I, 431; 1982: 13): 'Nature has destined the human being . . . for freedom, i.e., for activity' (*W* III, 211; 2000: 184).

38 Fichte sketches a one-world system in the *Praktische Philosophie* (*GA* II, 3: 241–3), where the two orders cut not between mechanical causality and freedom, but between cause and effect. Moreover, the temporal conjunctions between these orders are subject to variation, so that causes may either precede or succeed their effects, for the reflecting-acting I. This phenomenological solution, however, continues the evasion of physics, to which it poses more unsettling questions than that of the causal force of free actions.

39 Müller-Sievers (1997: 73–5f) offers an account of this same passage in the name of presenting Fichte's *Praktische Philosophie* as 'an energetic and ultimately practical philosophy' that compounds the practical with the physical. However, as we have argued

here, Fichte's logic is premised on the process of abstraction that cannot be reduced to physicality. As Fichte writes in the *Wissenschaftslehre*, 'all force in the physical world is a mere product of the I's imaginative power of bringing unity into the manifold according to a law of reason' (*W* I, 274; 1982: 242). While Müller-Sievers takes this as the law (for representational reason) of the insuperability of metaphor, the present account would emphasize the 'law of reason' as the *abstractive striving* that generates the system in the first place.

40 This passage is also cited by Friedman in his analysis of Kant's 'flowing quantities' in the latter's account of the continuity of space and time: 'Space and time are *quanta continua*, because no part of them can be given without being enclosed between limits (points and instants) . . . Points and instants are only limits, that is, mere places of their limitation' (CPR A169/B211). Friedman (1992: 55–95) offers an extended discussion of the problem at hand, by way of reconstructing Kant's geometry.

41 Müller-Sievers argues (1997: 85) that Fichte's Platonic account, in the *Foundations of Natural Right*, of the splitting of the sexes into 'complementary sexual difference . . . guarantees both the absolute productivity of natural drives and the naturalness of specific forms'. This account, which is determined to ground Fichte's generative system in biological epigenesis, ignores the conditioning of the 'formative force [*Bildungskraft*]' Fichte gives (*W* III, 305; 2000: 265) in the interests of borrowing a properly Schellingian account of nature as productivity to patch the whole of Fichte's conditioned absolute. Müller-Sievers therefore ignores Fichte's thesis concerning the purely imaginary status of forces in nature (*W* I, 274; 1982: 242), alongside the claim that it is only ideally that nature '*ought [soll]* to be an organised whole' (*GA* II, 3: 247).

42 Cf. Ayrault (1976: 280): 'If the first part of the *Ideen* [Herder's *Ideas for a Philosophy of Human History*] offers an exemplification of the Leibnizian law of continuity, the discovery [Goethe's discovery of the intermaxillary bone] exemplifies those laws in turn that make man the fundamental schema of the continuity of the animal kingdom: the detail of the osteological structure, to which he was then denied access, safeguards his original "difference" from the monkey.' Ayrault's argument is that the philosophies of nature of the early nineteenth century were simply explications of the naturalist and philosophical precepts expounded in *Sturm und Drang* Weimar.

43 'The body is thus actually a space desired by intuition' (letter to Schelling, 15 November 1800, in Schulte-Sasse 1997: 74). Kant makes a similar substantialist claim on the part of transcendental philosophy in the second *Critique* (*Ak*. V, 9n; 1993: 9n), and reiterates it in the *Critique of Judgment*, where he writes that desire is 'the power of causing, through . . . ideas, the actuality [*Wirklichkeit*] of the objects of those ideas' (*Ak*. V, 177n; 1987: 16–17 n18).

44 See Fichte's discussion of the *Bildungstrieb* in his *Praktische Philosophie* of 1795 (*GA* II, 3: 256–60). Fully in accordance with Blumenbach and Kant, Fichte writes: 'As concerns the source of this *Zweckmäßigkeit*, it is absolutely not here a question of whether there is a prime mover, a non-finite understanding, that has calculatedly determined the movement: we must seek such *Zweckmäßigkeit* in accordance with the striving of our power of judgment' (*GA* II, 3: 257). See the excellent discussion of Fichte, Blumenbach and the formative drive in Müller-Sievers (1997: 76–81).

45 Jardine (2000) gives Oken as an example of the fearful incomprehensibility of the *Naturphilosophisch* sensibility for contemporary science. The excellent Gould (1977) gives a sober outline of Oken's contributions to the sciences, in terms of both the latter's career as a scientist, and in his organizational achievements. Neither Jardine nor Gould, however, can resist targeting Oken's cumbersome system, not to mention his commitment to war as the ultimate end of the species. Oken is so embarrassing, that even the enormous (but indispensable) bulk of the supplementary volume on Schelling's *Naturphilosophie* cannot find room to mention him. His full name having been 'Okenfuß', it is as though he has been scapegoated for all *Naturphilosophie*'s speculative criminality.

46 Oken's translator, Alfred Tulk, renders *Naturphilosophie* as 'Physio-philosophy'. The German term is here replaced in the interests of continuity, despite the admirable grasp

Tulk's neologism maintains on the physics and the speculation.

47 For a lucid account of set theoretic number generation, see Barrow (2001: 164–71).

48 Oken's truly vast systematization of the All of nature begins with the science of the whole (mathesis), moves to the science of singulars (ontology) and finally the science of the whole of singulars (biology; 1847: 9).

49 That the generative series should *become parallel* suggests, as a denial of Euclid's fifth postulate, a non-Euclidean geometry, i.e., not a geometry of planes, but of curved surfaces. Oken certainly suggests this when he defines geometry as 'the doctrine of the sphere; for all forms are contained within the sphere. All geometrical proofs admit of being conducted through the sphere' (1847: 34). Carl Friedrich Gauss had published his non-Euclidian hypothesis that 'any geometry denying the parallel axiom [i.e., Euclid's fifth postulate] must have a particular length (for instance, a "curvature of space") associated with it' (cited in Pledge 1966: 180) in 1808, two years before the first edition of the first volume of the *Lehrbuch der Naturphilosophie* (Jena: F. Frommann, 1810).

50 On Stahl's vitalism, see Thomas S. Hall, *Ideas of Life and Matter: Studies in the History of General Physiology 600 BC–1900 AD* (2 vols, Chicago and London: University of Chicago Press, 1969), I: *From Pre-Socratic Times to the Enlightenment*: 351–66. Stahl noted the chemical corruptibility of bodies as an inherent property thereof, and found no adequate chemical or mechanical accounts of why some, i.e., living bodies, resisted this decay. The resistant principle is the soul, which is locomotive and sensitive, as well as rational. The core of the rational soul was to preserve the organism against corruption, and was thus teleological. In its chemico-mechanical irreducibility, in its efficacy without mechanical causality on the bodies whose locomotion, sensitivity and reasoning it governed, and in its purposive advancement of those bodies, Stahl's vitalism is indistinguishable from the Blumenbach-Kant *Bildungstrieb*.

51 There is more continuity between the *Lebenskraft* and the *Bildungstrieb* than is commonly supposed. A convincing case for Blumenbach as a synthetist of Enlightenment science, which valued both its mechanism and its vitalism, rather than as the trailblazer of romantic biology has however been made by Timothy Lenoir under the rubric of 'vital materialism'. See Lenoir, 'Kant, Blumenbach and vital materialism in German biology' (*Isis* 71: 256 (1980): 77–108).

52 A. L. Hülsen's 'Über den BildungsTrieb' appeared in the *Philosophisches Journal einer Gesellschaft Teutscher Gelehrten* Bd.9 (1800): 99–129. The *Journal* was edited by Fichte himself, along with the publisher Immanuel Niethammer.

53 Röschlaub dedicated Vol. 2 no. 1 of his *Magazin zur Vervollkommnung der theoretischen und praktischen Medizin* (*Magazine for the Improvement of the Theory and Practise of Medicine*) to Fichte in the following terms: 'I maintain the most profound respect for your undying service to true philosophy, and therefore to all the sciences.' On Röschlaub and Fichte, see Tsouyopoulos (1978a). Schelling's response to Röschlaub's reconstruction of the theory of disease was to found, with Adalbert Marcus, the *Annals for Scientific Medicine* in 1805 (it ran until 1808), and to devote some considerable content thereof to a critique of Röschlaub's attempts (VII, 271–88). On Schelling and the history of medicine, see Tsouyopoulos in Cunningham and Jardine (eds) (1990), along with her and Rothschuh's contributions in Hasler (ed.) (1981), von Engelhardt in Sandkühler (ed.) (1984), Gerabek (1996) and Wallen (1994).

54 Röschlaub translated John Brown's *System of the Arts of Healing* in 1768. For German Brownianism, see von Aesch (1966: 187–94), Snelders and Wetzels, in Cunningham and Jardine (eds) (1990), and Tsouyopoulos (1978b). For Schelling's criticisms of Brown, see *On the World Soul* (II, 505–7n), *First Outline of a System of Naturephilosophy* (III, 87–8n; 2004: 66n; II, 153–4; 2004: 111–12), in the 13th of the *Lectures on University Studies* (V, 335–43) and, most pointedly in the materials from the *Annalen der Medizin als Wissenschaft* (VII, 131–9, 245–88).

55 Rather, the Brownians are formalists precisely because they seek the conditions of life in

science alone. While therefore Schelling ironically praises Brown's antipathy to philosophy as a 'warn[ing] against any causal explanation of excitability', his 'restricting himself to the phenomenon, to excitability alone' demonstrates 'better judgment . . . than most of those who, before or after him, wished without enlisting a higher kind of cognition, to attain cognition of the essence of excitability' (VII, 262).

56 This is exactly how Schelling criticizes the concept of *Lebenskraft* or 'life force' in the *Ideas*: 'I maintain that life-force . . . is a completely self-contradictory concept. For we can think of force only as something finite. But no force is finite by *nature* except insofar as it is limited by one opposing it. Where we think of force (as in matter), therefore, we must also presume a force *opposed* to it' (II, 49; 1988: 37).

57 'For the natural scientist as such, there can be no other events in nature than the physical, and accordingly also in organic nature, nor can the chemical mode of operation anywhere cease to be chemical. Accordingly, what a force *opposing* the chemical or physical mode of operation (which are ultimately two names for the same object) means, is not so easy to understand . . . What may therefore be gained for natural science by way of the terms "vital force", "vegetal force", "animal" and "human" force, may be reducible to a mere increase in words for an unknown thing.' (in Schelling 1969, 1: 141)

58 Illustrating the philophical prestige accorded the criterion of 'recognition', Reinhard Löw describes Schelling's project thus: 'If modern, mathematico-physical philosophy of nature shows us a real-genetic image of actuality, which men are neither familiar with nor can form concepts of, then Schelling's transcendental construction characterized the countervailing interests of reason: how must nature be thought so as to conceptualize actuality on the one hand and on the other, so that man can understand himself as an intellectual and moral being? Hermann Krings has introduced the concept of *logogenesis* for such a construction.' (in Hasler (ed.) 1981: 103) This account might more accurately be applied to Windischmann's physics than Schelling's.

59 Schelling's most overt anti-Fichtean polemic, *Exposition of the True Relation of Naturephilosophy to the Improved Fichtean Theory* (1806), was spawned from a review (VII, 4–20) of Fichte's *Über das Wesen des Gelehrten* (Berlin 1806; W VI, 347–448, esp. 'Zweite Vorlesung', W VI, 360–71), to which I have inserted references in the cited passage.

60 The manner in which Windischmann's 'collective science' addresses the contradiction of nature and the (practical) ideal is uncannily reminiscent of Hegel's assessment of the 'inner identity' between Schelling's transcendental philosophy and the philosophy of nature: 'We have thus far set the two sciences in their inner identity against each other . . . Insofar as they are opposed to each other, they are . . . internally closed in themselves and form total-ities . . . [that] are at the same time only relative totalities, and as such tend towards the point of indifference' (Wz 2: 110–11; 1977a: 169).

61 Exactly as Hegel concludes in the *Difference* essay, the basal kind of Fichtean transcen-dentalism consists in the ethico-teleological sequence given through Fichte's transcen-dental animal: 'the Idea must absolutely dominate drive' *because* 'freedom must dominate nature' (Wz 2: 87–8; 1977a: 149), just as his formalism stems from the 'immediate deter-mination of nature by and for intelligence' (Wz 2: 81; 1977a: 143). Hegel's own *Philosophy of Nature* will however bear greater traces of Fichteanism than Schellingian naturephi-losophy: 'In man's *practical* approach to nature, the latter is, for him, something immediate and external; and he himself is an external and therefore sensuous individual, although in relation to natural objects, he regards himself as an *end*. A consideration of nature according to this relationship yields the standpoint of *finite* teleology. In this, we find the correct presupposition that nature does not itself contain the absolute, final end.' (1970: 4; Wz 9: 7)

62 Alcinous defines induction as 'any logical procedure which passes from like to like' and adds that 'induction is particularly useful for natural concept-formation [*phusike ennoia*]' (*Handbook of Platonism*, 158.1–3). It is Schelling's inductivism that Eschenmayer mistakes

for empiricism: 'This essay', i.e., the *Ideas for a Philosophy of Nature*, 'does not begin *from above* (with the establishment of principles) but *from below* (with experimental findings and the testing of previous systems)' (II, 56; 1988: 42).

CHAPTER 4

The Natural History of the Unthinged

That a phenomenon is explicated dynamically means: it is explicated from the original conditions of the construction of matter in general. It therefore requires no manufactured causes (such as specific matters, for example) beyond these universal grounds. All dynamic motions have their final ground in the subject of nature itself, namely in the forces of which the visible world is only the support. (IV, 76)

Schelling's most complete statement of naturephilosophy is the *Universal Deduction of the Dynamic Process* (1800). As its title implies, its object is to demonstrate the actuality of the dynamic succession of stages, the *Stufenfolge*, in nature. A 'deduction of the dynamic process', Schelling writes, 'therefore stands as a complete construction of matter itself' and so is identical to 'the highest task of natural science as a whole' (IV, 4). How the naturephilosophy reaches this point, however, is not by the transcendental route 'deduction' implies, but rather, consists in the naturalization of the transcendental. Insofar as this is the case, the *Universal Deduction* satisfies the inductive criterion of 'coincidence', by which nature is nature only insofar as it 'originally and necessarily, not only expresses, but even realizes, the laws of mind' (II, 55–6; 1988: 41–2). The naturalization of the transcendental is the topic therefore of chapter 5.

The present chapter is concerned with the naturalistic roots of the problem to which the naturephilosophy is the solution. This problem has its roots in the emergence of eighteenth-century dynamics. Although Schelling's sources are all too often simply presented as organicist, the roots of the emergence of dynamics lie in three crucial elements of late eighteenth-century physics, which Schelling described as 'an age of the universal palingenesis of all science' (2001: 45), philosophy included. Four interrelated problems in particular are crucial to understanding Schelling's dynamic philosophy: the genetic problem, the continuity problem from the perspective of time and from the perspective of causes, and the decomposability of matter.

The genetic problem at its most basic consists in the attempt to discover the elements from which natural phenomena are assembled; once discovered, the task is then to plot their recursion and mutation throughout each and every branch of the system of nature. If this is not done, the genetic problem is not resolved. Therefore, any solution to the genetic problem that counts only for one subset of natural phenomena is inadequate. The flashpoint of this particular issue consists in the gulf between organic and inorganic nature that was the legacy of mechanism, and was compounded in the late eighteenth century by the Kant-Blumenbach hypothesis by which organic nature assumes a natural autonomy, separated from inorganic nature by a gulf. Thus the continuity of causes – the problem to which Schelling devoted the *World Soul* – arises, and brings with it the continuity of time: if there is such a gulf as mechanists and 'teleomechanists' or 'vital materialists' such as Kant and Blumenbach maintain, then the generative series in the organic world is historically or genetically unrelated to that of the inorganic. It is in an effort to resolve a nature riven by temporal and causal gulfs that the genetic problem spawns dynamics in natural history.

4.1 'THE EARLIEST PROGRAMME OF GERMAN COMPARATIVE ZOOLOGY'[1]

I myself would like to derive all variation in the material of inert nature from a striving for heterogenesis, analogous to that in the organism, in the *soul* of nature. (Kielmeyer 1938: 56)

Why does Schelling (II, 565) reckon 'the advent of a completely new epoch in natural history' to have been opened by comparative anatomist Carl Friedrich Kielmeyer, Blumenbach's pupil and Cuvier's teacher in physiology? Gould (1977: 35) has argued that the theory of recapitulation, latterly called the 'biogenetic' or 'Meckel-Serres law', and of which Kielmeyer is amongst those credited with developing at the end of the eighteenth century, was an 'inescapable consequence of a particular biological philosophy'. Lenoir (1981: 159; 1982: 5–6), following Dietrich von Engelhardt's (1976: 5) 'threefold differentiation' of transcendental, metaphysical and scientific naturephilosophy, identifies the philosophy from which Kielmeyer begins as Kant's, and thus allots him to the first of these – oddly Linnean – classes. In this, Lenoir is disputed by Bach (2001: 239–41), and, more overtly, by Kielmeyer himself. Echoing the Platonizing grounds of Schellingian naturephilosophy, Kielmeyer begins his *Discourse On the Relative Proportions of the Organic Forces in the Series of Various Organisations* (1793) with a 'self-contemplating' and 'self-articulating' NATURE, derived from Plotinus (III.8.iv),[2] which declares itself opposed to the transcendental structures of possible experience, for any *single* organic system:

If I [NATURE] could only lead you outside space and time and with you, follow the developmental process where it departs from your [human] system, you would likely have to confess that it is no less artificial to be capable of death, which change you commonly do not esteem very highly, than to live. [. . .] And the consequence of all this is . . . that despite the destruction of individuals, the species survives; yet even this great new system of effects, the living species, I make advance along a developmental path over long periods of time, as you may most clearly perceive in your, human, species, and although you may see but a single moment in this history of your species, yet the early youth of your race is dawning over its childhood; although I might in time come to replace your race with another, new species, you need no explanation of this as yet. (Kielmeyer 1938: 64–5)

With this autonomous, autarchic nature, Kielmeyer sets the species-specificity of transcendental conditions of possible *experience* against the backdrop of a natural history full of extinction events. Crucially, the *timescale* of such events is 'large beyond all standard of sense' (*Ak*. V, 255; Kant 1987: 112): of the actual history of the developmental paths of species, individuals, and their organs (1938: 63), we see, NATURE tells us, 'but a single moment'. As regards therefore the multiplicity of species and the 'great machine of the animal kingdom' (1938: 65) itself, as regards the planets on which such great organic machines arise and the stars whose extinction eliminates them (1938: 66), finite human experience can provide no standard. Where transcendental philosophy sees only the finitude of space and time as necessary forms of intuition, NATURE announces their reality as necessarily extending beyond any and all 'possible experience'; where transcendental philosophy can only regard nature by analogy with purposes, NATURE announces 'I have none' (65); where transcendental philosophy extends into nature only so far as organism reaches, NATURE is a 'great machine [of] at least seven million wheels . . . linked only in time' that is itself 'so well accommodated into inorganic nature' (65) as though the one had supplied the want of the other. Where transcendental philosophy insists on the fixity of species, nature might extinguish humanity, as it already has the stars (66), and produce wholly 'new species' (65). If transcendental philosophy reaches its limit with a merely possible nature, actual NATURE confronts merely transcendental necessities with the stark inevitability of the eventual elimination of species whose experience is conditioned by them.

Hence Kielmeyer's judgement, in 'On Kant and German naturephilosophy' (1807), that a philosophy asserting that 'external nature . . . may be deduced from a priori principles . . . from the nature of our minds' is 'fundamentally based on a self-delusion' (1938: 236). Kielmeyer proceeds to catalogue not only Kant's 'significant failings' (1938: 244), but also those of transcendentalism as a whole, insofar as this 'explained as subjective not merely the formal in our knowledge of nature, but also the material'. By contrast, writes Kielmeyer, citing Schelling's definition of his own philosophical programme in 'True concept' (IV, 89), 'the system of the Real-idealists seems consistent to me' (1938: 248).

However, Kielmeyer's philosophical influences – whether those exerted on him by others, or by him on others – are unimportant when set against the philosophical consequences of his theory of recapitulation as regards the development of naturephilosophy as such. Schelling's engagements with the problems of the materiality of the Idea, of a natural history of the world-soul, the identity of the Idea, and of dynamic physics, acquire decisive new trajectories under Kielmeyer's core idea of recapitulation; the theory of the 'powers' or *Potenzen*, although derived initially from Eschenmayer (1797, cited II, 313–14n; 1988: 249n), acquire their doctrine of measurement from Kielmeyer. Even the geological philosophy of the *Philosophical Inquiries into the Essence of Human Freedom* (1809) and the *Ages of the World* (1811–15) has its first strata laid in the encounter with Kielmeyer.

Schelling's prognosis regarding the advent of a Kielmeyerian epoch is not made in regard to philosophy, but in regard to natural history. Since it is primarily his interventions in that field, in other words, to which Schelling draws our attention, we must begin by examining the difference introduced by *Kielmeyer's* account of the theory of recapitulation into the development and programmes of natural history.

4.1.1 The natural history of transcendental anatomy

Nowhere does the arbitrary nature of the isolation of metaphysics from physics become more apparent than in the development of natural history during the eighteenth century. Georges Louis Buffon, for example, bases the prospect of a 'system of natural history as a whole' on nature's embodiment of the Leibnizian law of continuity:[3]

> To make a system . . . everything must be contained within it; it is necessary to divide the whole into different classes, to separate these classes into genera, to subdivide these genera into species, and all according to an order into which some arbitrariness will necessarily enter. But nature works by unknown gradations, and in consequence it cannot completely lend itself to these divisions, since it passes from one species, and often from one kind, to another, by imperceptible nuances. (Buffon [1749] 1985: 166–7)

Applying 'the German Plato's' law of continuity directly to the problem not simply of 'making a system', which differentiates where nature integrates, but a system of natural *history*, Charles Bonnet's *Philosophical Palingenesis or Ideas on the Past and Future States of Living Beings* (1769) posits variation within, but not exceeding, fixed species:

> The same sort of progression which we discover today between the different orders of organized beings will no doubt continue to be observed in a future state of our globe. But it will follow different proportions, and these will be determined by the degree of possible perfectibility of each species. (Bonnet 1769: 202, cited in Gode von Aesch 1966: 64)

Again, precisely because even Leibniz's 'imperceptible nuances' are 'full of life' (Leibniz 1998: 259), Buffon argues that the divisions of any system of nature as a whole will necessarily cut through 'intermediary species' (1985: 167), and therefore defeat in advance the prospect of a system *of* natural history. Because Leibnizian nature consists in an infinite continuum formed of 'imperceptible nuances', Buffon's naturalist *must* become an historian rather than a systematist, since it is in the succession of individuals of the same species, the constant reproduction of like by like, that nature offers the naturalist the opportunity to cut with its temporalizing grain. A species, writes Buffon, is a 'constant succession and uninterrupted renewal of individuals' ([1753] 1985: 196). Hence, the units of division – classes, kinds, and species – enable a developmental approach to the variations as might occur within them, but cannot account for the differences between them. Natural history must follow the 'real succession [*suite*] of all beings' ([1753] 1985: 195).

Buffon's temporalizing solution provides Bonnet's problem: if species are not artifacts of arbitrary systems, but real, indivisible unities of nature, how is the continuity of nature to be maintained? For Bonnet, natural history follows not the catastrophic changes of nature, but rather the uniformity of the unchanging, partless 'souls', coeval with the cosmos, that constitute species. Rather than deny the reality of change in nature, Bonnet pursues the unfolding of these souls throughout the various 'epochs of nature', each separated from its preceeding and succeeding epochs by great natural upheavals. However, it is precisely because, given an organic continuum, all species *necessarily survive* such catastrophes that change can be charted, since they properly consist of nothing but the *complete* (not an evaluative, but a grammatical 'perfect') unfolding of species-souls across the epochs of nature. Bonnet does not so much add time to natural history, as subtract time from nature by infinitizing the unfolding of the organic continuum.[4] For Bonnet as for Kant, 'true history is nothing but a continuous geography' (*Ak.* IX, 161).

Between Buffon and Bonnet lie two problems, the first of which is the reality of time. If Bonnet offers a nature transcendentally insured against time and catastrophe, Buffon tracks time through the articulation of species' reproductive development and devolution. The second problem consists in their shared commitment to Leibnizian continuity and plenitude, which ultimately sets this continuum as a substrate underlying all change, so that species differ only as regards the reality of change upon it. While Buffon was sceptical as regards the prospect of a system that would provide a complete geography of the continuum, Etienne Geoffroy Saint-Hilaire, by contrast, abandoned a substantive continuum along with the reproductive mechanism, by which Buffon's nature fixes species, in favour of a 'plan of nature': 'It seems that all of nature has enclosed herself within certain limits and has formed all living beings on only one unique plan, essentially the same in its principle, but which she has varied in a thousand ways in all its accessory parts' ('Mémoire sur les rapports naturels des Makis Lemur, L.', cited Rehbock, in Cunningham and Jardine (eds) 1990: 144). Geoffroy's 'philosophical' or 'transcendental anatomy'[5] posited that although the ground plan 'had no physical existence in its pure state' (ibid.), nature itself consists of nothing more than its expression, 'varied in a thousand ways'. It is the task therefore of the transcendental anatomist both to express the unity of plan in its abstract form, and to chart its expressions as they cross from species to species, transforming them in the process. It is by reason of the problem of the instantiation of the plan of nature across all animal kinds – the One over many – that Geoffroy and the transcendental anatomists have been called 'Platonists' (Depew and Weber 1996: 37–9).[6] The 'same Animal' that Deleuze (1993: 144n) ascribes to Geoffroy consists in a great organism of 'natural relations' which the anatomist, tracking these relations across the organic kingdom, can demonstrate to unravel[7] the merely temporary variation in which alone 'species' consist, and at the same time, outline the animal-kind from which these derive.

Rejecting this one-over-many plan of nature, Geoffroy's opponent in transformism and Kielmeyer's student Georges Cuvier[8] overtly resuscitates the Aristotelian account of a fixity of species on functional or teleological grounds.[9] Reducing Aristotle's 'great kinds' to four, Cuvier operates a functionalist critique of any 'same Animal' on the grounds that, throughout the animal kingdom, nature has arrived at four *different* 'ground plans' that alone are functionally viable. Accordingly, the history of species consists in variation within these 'types': too much variation, or variation of the wrong sort (a horse with gills), and the animal becomes non-viable. As a result, 'Cuvier . . . presented the fixity of species as a pragmatic consequence of . . . the complexity of living things' (Bowler 1984: 108).

Cuvier, however, is not just a functionalist regarding organic forms, but also a realist as regards the divisions in his system of nature. He lays out the system of nature in his *Lectures on Comparative Anatomy* (1800): 'Every animal must be considered as a particular machine, having certain fixed relations to all other machines that together form the universe' (Cuvier 1800: 20, cited in Lenoir 1982: 64). History would be played out in each of the four domains to which the 'particular machines' belong, while Buffon's 'intermediary species' are eliminated, as are Geoffroy's transformist 'natural relations', by 'fixed relations'. Cuvier's relations are not fixed species-to-species, however, but rather *between* species. Cuvier therefore eliminated the continuum in favour of plans of nature – Cuvier's finite multiplicity, Geoffroy's infinite variation of the one. As Deleuze notes, anticipating the development of the 'fold',

> The great controversy between Cuvier and Geoffroy Saint-Hilaire concerns the unity of composition: is there an Animal in itself or an Idea of the universal animal – or do the sub-kingdoms introduce impassable gulfs between animal-types? [. . .] Can a Vertebrate[, that is,] be folded in such a manner that the two ends of the spine approach one another, the head moving towards the feet, the pelvis towards the neck, and the viscera arranged in the manner of Cephalopods? (Deleuze 1994: 215)

The philosophy of natural history from the seventeenth to the nineteenth centuries was structured around the problems of the reality as against the phenomenality of time; the abstract artificiality as against the physical actuality of the system of natural history; and the instantiation of the plan of nature. These are precisely the topics that Kant investigates: systems of natural history are either merely 'logical' and 'arbitrary', like the Linnean, or 'natural' both for the understanding (*Ak.* II, 429) and the reproductive order of nature, as in Buffon. Stimulated to further 'induction' (cf. 4.2, below) by the apparent syggeneity (the 'ancient doctrine' espoused by Plato, 'that like is known by like') or kinship of the order of nature and that of the understanding, Kant further considers a proto-Geoffroyian alternative: perhaps 'comparative anatomy', combing the orders of nature and under-standing, might reveal the 'basic outline [*Grundriss*]' from which nature 'was able to produce this great diversity of species'; perhaps, in consequence, our perceived analogies may be provoked by natures 'actually akin' to one another, or separated only by 'imperceptible nuances' on the graduated system of animal genera (*Ak.* V, 418; 1987: 304)? Yet Kant introduces a further problem for natural historians or 'archaeologists of nature': whether the latter, pursuing their researches, cannot but export their basically organicist prejudice even into the inorganic world. While Cuvier seems, that is, to introduce divisions or 'impassable gulfs' between animal-kinds where Geoffroy had only 'slight differences' (Deleuze 1993: 76), the contrast serves only to highlight the extent to which Geoffroy, like Blumenbach, acknowledges 'the immense gulf that Nature has appointed between animate and inanimate Creation' (Blumenbach 1782: 71; cited in *AA* Ergbd.1: 644). Kant reveals this with the following advice: the natural archaeologist is, the philosopher concedes,

> free to have that large family of creatures (for that is how we must conceive of them if that thoroughly coherent kinship among them is to have a ground [*Grund*]) arise from the traces that remain of nature's most ancient revolutions, and to have it do so according to all the natural mechanism he knows or suspects. He can make mother earth (like a large animal, as it were) emerge from her state of chaos . . . (*Ak.* V, 419; 1987: 304–5)

For Geoffroy and Kant, even the earth is an animal, against which the organized beings sprung from her lap are even 'less purposive creatures' (ibid.). For Kant, such excessive organicism can only be curtailed by the 'unlimited authority' that must, if 'insight into the nature of things' is to be possible at all,[10] be accorded mechanical over teleological explanation *wherever possible*. Meanwhile, although like all fixity-theorists before him, Cuvier was repeatedly taunted with his system's incapacity to explain the origin of species, the same applies to Geoffroy's transformism insofar as its groundplan merely segments 'the whole' that a system of nature, according to Buffon ([1749] 1985: 166–7), must necessarily include.

The transcendentalist's organo-somatism, the conflicts staged between Aristotelian and Platono-Leibnizian philosophy as this organo-somatism unfolds across eighteenth-century natural history, and the reduction of time to the a priori form of 'inner experience' alone, are all contested as the grounds of natural history. It is not simply against the former that Kielmeyer's intervention is decisive, however. Rather, it is his proposals for regrounding natural history that provoke Schelling's naturephilosophical development.

4.1.2 Physics and the animal kingdom

Kielmeyer's earliest sketches of comparative anatomy are striking in their insistence on a temporal nature. That science is to be furthered, according to Kielmeyer's 'On natural history' (1790),

> by research into how a determination of the causes and consequences may be given for developmental phenomena in general and for the variation of classes. Presented – by the integration of imperceptibly small and infinitely many changes – in periods of formation: (a) in the period of emergence; (b) in the period of further development and increase; (c) in the period of decline. (Kielmeyer 1938: 23)

This is because nature is conceived not as a body, a collation of bodies, nor a megabody or substrate, but rather in accordance with what is 'probably the first' concept of nature to have arisen, as 'including within it emergence, becoming, birth'. Moreover, such a concept, insofar as it is a concept, makes immediate reference to 'the laws in accordance with which humans arrange concepts in series', suggesting a parallelism between natural genetics and conceptual genetics. Yet this relation is more a causal relation than an analogical one, since according to Kielmeyer, 'thoughts are awakened by the *actus*, the emergence of a thing, or the causes of this change' (1938: 213–14): physical becomings are ideogenic.

Immediately, then, Kielmeyer's 'system-programme for biology' (Bach 2001: 87) establishes as it were the upper reaches of his science's remit, as pertaining to the natural laws of thought, or precisely the 'natural history of our mind' Schelling had proposed philosophy become (II, 39; 1988: 30). It further establishes that the grounds of this science are to be sought in time, in units of becoming or development, rather than in bodies. What ties it to the Leibnizian metaphysics underlying Buffon and Bonnet, and even to Geoffroy, according to Deleuze (1993: 144n; 1994: 185), is the reference to the formal means whereby this science is to be conducted, by 'the integration of imperceptibly small and infinitely many changes'. What differentiates Kielmeyer from these naturalists, however, is twofold. Firstly, integration yields not what Kant called a 'geographical continuum' (*Ak.* IX, 161), but rather a temporal plenum. Since Kielmeyer's 'object' is a natural history, the syggeneity of the latter term for the former is given if and only if nature itself *is* no object, but rather becomes, changes. Secondly, integration is necessarily a *formal* procedure because the timescales involved in natural becomings exceed the phenomenological capacity not only of individuals, but also of any and all species, insofar as these arise *in the course* of such developments. Kielmeyer states this clearly at the overture to the *Discourse* (1793), which explicitly compares time and space 'as they depart from the human system' against the 'single moment in the history of your species' to which the phenomenal capacity of its members is limited (1938: 64–5).

Kielmeyer's temporal plenum therefore offers a natural history that is properly genetic and ideogenic, and to that extent also non-somatic. Given, further, that time *necessarily* 'departs' from the systems of measurement to which it gives rise, the formalism of Kielmeyer's natural history is a necessary consequence of its anti-phenomenalism. Thus Schelling's praise for Kielmeyer is doubly understandable: firstly, as befits its recipient, it allots him not a *place* amongst the immortals, but an *epoch*, albeit one to be futurally determined. Secondly, the abrupt emergence of Kielmeyer's *Discourse* in the concluding argument of *On the World Soul* has as much to do with the 'new' physics of forces as it does with Platonic physics. Thus Schelling combines a natural principle, 'originally formless although susceptible of all forms' (II, 567) stemming from the theory of Platonic matter, with 'a principle of continuity of the anorgic and organic world'. Just as the 'universal continuity of all natural causes' to recover Plato's world soul for 'the physics of our own time', so Kielmeyer will later avow as his own theory of the 'productive cause of things' (1938: 214), the 'heterogenetic soul of nature' (1938: 56) alongside a process of integration that extends from 'the history of the terrestrial sphere' (1938: 210) to 'the laws in accordance with which humans arrange concepts' (1938: 214).

It is however in the detail of Kielmeyer's programme as well as in its macro-structure that a further determinant of Schelling's thinking emerges. That is, Kielmeyer's development of a 'Laplacian dynamics of animal organisation' (Lenoir 1981: 161) is to supplant the Aristotelian phenomenalism and somaticism covered by the field of 'natural history [as] the entire range of observable forms, from minerals to man' (Hankins 1985: 113). While it may seem obvious that the subject matter of natural history, more especially, of 'comparative anatomy', should indeed be animal bodies, two problems vitiate this understanding. Firstly, as Buffon had noted, the reality of species is only the phenomenalization of time, so in studying species and their reproductive capacities, the natural historian is seeking less for the specifics of these organizations than for their capacity to serve as such media for the study of nature as time. Secondly, even if it is assumed that bodies do provide the subject matter of natural history, the question *'which bodies?'* soon arises. For example, under the Buffonian conception, this question is answered: *reproducibility* is the selector for the study of the temporal order of nature. If, however, the same question is asked of Geoffroy, the response would be: *none or all*, since the task of the natural historian is to discover not the key animal amongst all that now exist, but rather the 'same Animal', the 'plan of nature', from the transformations of whose 'natural relations' all animal organization has derived. Finally, asked of a fixity-of-species theorist such as Cuvier or Bonnet, the answer would be: *not the animal, but its organization*, since it is ultimately the structures of animals that inform as to their 'kinds'.

The problem becomes more intensely debated, however, as it becomes more apparent that fixity of species is an error or an illusion. Kant reports, for example, the evidence unearthed by Petrus Camper to the effect that, amongst those 'natural revolutions' that eliminated species from the earth's series of organizations, no human remains are to be discovered (cf. *Ak*. V, 428; 1987: 315–16; *Ak*. XXI, 214–15; 1993: 66–7), indicating that precisely because of nature's historical upheavals, natural history cannot be premised on any such large meta-body as a species, or must, under pressure from Leibniz's 'law of continuity', extrapolate the gaps between the strata disinterred by nature's archaeologists in order to perfect the 'continuous geography' to which any 'true history' approximates (*Ak*. IX, 161), insofar as its object is to demonstrate the continuum.

Natural history confronts the problem of how to introduce order into chaos, or how to impose the uniformity or *continuity* of 'causes which can now be observed in action' onto the evident catastrophism of nature's timescape. In geology, for example, uniformitarians or actualists, proclaiming the phenomenological inscrutibility of beginnings and ends, developed the 'observable cause' as a methodological solution to the continuum of nature: since there are no currently observable catastrophic changes in causes, the geological naturalist must assume the same causes active now as have – given minor, non-catastrophic variations – always prevailed.[11] Projecting a natural history backwards from the time taken for a mountain to form certainly revealed deep time. As Depew and Weber (1996: 98, paraphrasing Gould 1977) note, however, 'It is obvious that the further you extend time, the less significant seems any event within it. Extend your perspective far enough and change smoothes itself out into a linear curve.' By forming their continuum from causes rather than bodies, the uniformitarians thus complete the geographization of natural history by means of a steady-state deep time.

Because, however, catastrophists such as Camper took evidence of species destruction, as this arose from the newly emerging fossil record, as evidence of past and probable future extinction events, these extended necessarily, to Kant's evident horror, to man. Since speciation is faster than geogony, Depew and Weber's curve has insufficient time to flatten out, and there emerges a discontinuity between the geological and organic continua, or a continuum such as Blumenbach found, riven by a 'gulf sunk by nature'. Either naturalists have to find a reducibly organic continuum to set alongside – or more usually, above – its geological counterpart, or integrate geogonic and biogenetic time. Buffon, to whose natural history the problem of time is central, was initially understood therefore not simply as a 'biocentric' naturalist with an 'account of generation', but rather as a *natural historian* attempting to present a 'cosmological, geological *and* general biological theory' (Sloan 1979: 122).[12]

Although therefore Kielmeyer is usually considered as reducibly a comparative anatomist or as a proto-biologist, his earliest outlines of 'Natural history' are equally refractive to any ascription of 'biocentrism' (Bernouilli and Kern 1926: viii), extending from 'humanity's ideational capacity' to the 'history of the globe' (1938: 210). From the outset of his *Rede*, time takes the upper hand over bodies of all sorts: stars, planets, terrestrial organizations. The consequences of considering Kielmeyer as a temporalizing natural historian will entail, amongst other things, that a distinction be made between a *linear* and a *non-linear* usage of the theory of recapitulation, to which we now turn.

4.1.3 *Linear and non-linear usages of the theory of recapitulation*

Although a meticulous examination of the traces of . . . natural devastations seems to prove (at least in Camper's judgment) that man was not included in those revolutions, yet he is so dependent on the other creatures on earth that, once we grant that a natural mechanism holds sway over the others universally, man too must be considered subject to it, even though his understanding was able to rescue him (for the most part, at least) from those devastations. (*Ak.* V, 428; 1987: 316)

4.1.3.1 *Linearity*

Kielmeyer's theory of recapitulation is often elided with the form this theory was given under the 'Meckel-Serres law', which states that *ontogeny recapitulates phylogeny*, or in Meckel's (1821) formulation, 'the development of the individual organism obeys the same laws as the development of the whole animal series' (cited in Gould 1977: 37). While ostensibly similar, Kielmeyer's formulation differs in important respects from Meckel's:

Since the distribution of forces in the series of organisations follows the same order as the distribution of forces in the various developmental stages of particular individuals, then it may be concluded that the force productive of these latter, namely the reproductive force, coincides in its laws with that force by means of which the series of various of the earth's organisations are called into existence. (Kielmeyer 1938: 93–4)

Where Meckel's law treats of individual organisms and whole animal series, Kielmeyer's treats, as his title announces, of *The Relative Proportions of the Organic Forces in the Series of Various Organisations, the Laws and the Consequences of these Proportions*. Kielmeyer's treatment of 'organizations' does not set the forces whose distributions form them between the somatic poles of individual and species. Were he to do so, Kielmeyer's dynamics would be as compromised as Kantian or Aristotelian dynamics by their assumption of a somatic nature. More importantly, the polar antithesis of large and small bodies (substrates and atoms, substance and concrete wholes) leads to the linear microcosm-macrocosm comparatism by which naturephilosophy has been so frequently parodied (sometimes, it should be said, by its own practitioners), as for example by Henri Milne-Edwards (1844), who makes explicit the assumption of a linear use of recapitulation underlying theses such as Oken's that 'Animals are only the persistent foetal stages or conditions of man' (1847: 491):[13] 'If [the lower animals] were in some way permanent embryos of the [higher], it would be necessary to admit, at least for the types, a progressive and linear series extending from the monad to man' (cited in Gould 1977: 37).

The linear use of the theory of recapitulation is responsible for what Oken called 'singulars' – the whole-in-the-individual in which the animate kingdom consists. Echoing Herder's 'primary form' and 'primary plasma' (1965: 98–9) and echoed in turn by Carus' 'primordial cells [Urzellen]' (1944: 49), Oken's own contribution to this theory consists in his account of the 'protoplasm' or mucus, the Urschleim: 'the primary organic is a mucus point' (1847: 188) from which all organic life is derived. Susceptible of all forms, the protoplasm is the matter of biology, producing plants, fishes, animals and humans. By Meckel's statement of the recapitulation theory, the development of individuals from protoplasm entails that they are made of it, and thus *contain and run through the whole of biology* with the production of each individual, from the lowest (the mucus point) to the highest (humanity). Recapitulation therefore establishes parallels between biological wholes and individuals, between protoplasm and man.

In partial contrast, Goethe's science of 'morphology', as a phenomeno-logical pursuit of 'pure form' (Goethe 1975: 25), seems, as Gode von Aesch notes, to 'discard the idea that it should be possible to discover actual specimens of the prototype' (1966: 147) or in Goethe's own terms, the *Urphänomen* (1977: 42), from natural history. Unlike Geoffroy's search for a non-phenomenal 'plan of nature', Goethe seeks only the 'metaphysics of phenomena' whose object, the 'particular', lies between the largest and the smallest, insofar as these exceed phenomenological access (Goethe 1977: 34). Polarized between 'the first physicochemical elements [and] their most intel-lectual expression in humanity' (1977: 45), morphology has less to do with morphogenesis than with the presumption of the reversibility of the 'ascending process' by which the phenomenon is generated ('*den Stufengang des Phänomens*', 1975: 396). By means, that is, of generating phenomena, the polar tension between the physicochemical and the intellectual is assumed equally to be 'following in nature's footsteps as thoughtfully as possible' (1975: 89): *what is produced in phenomena is the recapitulation of its production in nature*. Since, therefore, the phenomenon arises through the reciprocity of subject and object that forms Goethe's experimental method,[14] the polarity by which the phenomenon is generated is indissociable from the 'vegetal type' that will rise to the 'original plant [*Urpflanze*]' ([1790] 1975: 89), or the 'osteological type', the intermaxillary bone ([1795] 1975: 186–92) thus phenomenalized. Gode von Aesch accordingly identifies the immanent polarity attaching a physics to Goethe's phenomenology, when he writes of the *Urphänomen* that 'it no longer existed *apart* from its variations' (1966: 147, my emphasis). However, just as there is an ascending recapitulation of type into phenomenon, so there is an ascending recapitulation from the simple to the complex. On the first axis, between the physicochemical element and intelligence, in other words, there is an ascending differentiation of parts. To find the type of the crystal is therefore simpler than that of oxen (how many differentia are there not simply between the intermaxillary bones of ox and camel, but between those and other bones within the same system?); and insofar as it is a principle of morphology that 'the more similar the parts are to one another, the less they are subordinated to one another[, while t]he subordination of parts indicates a complete being' (1975: 56), the complex subordinates the simple in nature and in ideation.

It is precisely this kind of hierarchy that is common to linear usages of recapitulation, in which 'man expresses the ultimate purpose of nature's design' (Oken 1847: 663). The same goes for Ritter: although the universe is an animal (1798: 171) each part of which accordingly reciprocally interacts with every other, yet 'The earth is there for the sake of man. It is only his organ' (Ritter 1984: 184). And again for Fichte's universal animal (3.3), which carries animal reciprocity all the way down to 'every minute part', so that 'the entire universe *ought to be* an organised whole; and every minute part of this universe a whole in turn, belonging necessarily to this organised whole' (*GA* II, 3: 247). Yet in 'projecting the concept of myself into nature' (*W* XI, 362), the *Ich* nevertheless subordinates this as its body, with 'one force, one soul, one mind' (*W* XI, 366). The ethico-teleological project of the linear recapitulationists provides their uniformitarian response to the continuum problem. The extinction of species is no longer considered as a break in the chain of causes, but rather the application of the schema of life of the individual to nature as a whole. Parallelism – animal kingdom : man:: human foetus : animal kingdom (Oken 1847: 3, 492), or the *animal imperative*, is therefore driven by the problem of securing humanity from catastrophist species-extinction. Ironically, the distance travelled between Kantian strictures regarding the respective dominions of mechanism and teleology in natural science, on the one hand, and linear recapitulationism on the other, is best expressed in Schelling's *On the World Soul* (1798), although it conflicts with the basal dynamism to which his title refers:[15] 'Things are therefore not principles of the organism, but rather conversely, the *organism is the principle of things*' (II, 500). This is why Fichte's 'ought' provides the clearest expression of linear recapitulationism's response to the continuum; but it is equally the reason why the poles bound by the linear parallels of an Oken, a Herder, a Goethe, a Ritter and a Fichte are somatic-phenomenal. In the process, however, linear recapitulation, as is clear from Goethe's account of the phenomenological reversibility of 'nature's footsteps' in the 'ascending process of the phenomenon' (1975: 396), eliminates time, or reduces it to the measure of organization, which Schelling defines as 'an arrested stream of causes and effects . . . a succession that, *enclosed within certain limits*, reverts to itself' (II, 349). Thus linear recapitulationism is necessarily organicist: regardless of its objects' physicochemical make up (intermaxilliary bones, protoplasm), the more complex governs the less, elevating organization to the principle of nature.

4.1.3.2 The genetic problem

For linear recapitulationism, its somaticism is not the consequence of an a priori assumption, as is sometimes alleged. Rather, it is a response to a problem upon which depends the entire natural order. Carl Gustav Carus provides the necessary perspective on this problem:

> Whoever has grasped correctly how every basal form [*Grundform*] of the organism rests on innumerable recapitulations of the *one* basal form; and how that cell is the recapitulation of the first germinal seed [*Eikeim*]; and how even this is for that very reason always in turn the basal idea, actualised; or precisely therefore something living in itself; whoever grasps this, now considers with entirely different eyes the whole formed from all these recapitulations. (Carus 1944: 35)

The search for a basal form expressed in all natural production did not arise from a natural history designed to eliminate time, like Bonnet's or Cuvier's. Rather, once time becomes the focus of a 'real and physical' natural history, the question of the origin of organizations necessarily arises. Even Buffon therefore had his 'interior mould', his version of Aristotle's 'generative soul (*psyche gennetikos*)' (*Gen.An.* 736a19ff): 'There is in nature a general prototype in each species, on which each individual is modelled . . . The first animal, the first horse, for example, was the exterior model and interior germ, on which basis every horse ever born has been formed' (Buffon [1753] 1985: 188).

The Geoffroyan problem of the instantiation of the plan becomes the Romantic problem of the identification of the poles between which recapitulation etched its parallels. Goethe identifies the problem clearly, but answers it solely in methodological terms: 'the metaphysics of phenomena' locates its object as 'the particular lying in the middle' of the largest and the smallest (1977: 34). As Clark and Jacyna write, for recapitulationist natural historians,

> The stress upon comparative studies owed much to the movement in the early nineteenth century to ascertain the general laws of life and organisation. The romantic philosophy of nature . . . maintained that underlying the complexity of the living world there was simplicity. The most elaborate forms of organisation were developments of simple types; the 'highest' and

the 'lowest' organisms were therefore constructed upon a uniform plan. The task of the biologist was to identify the simple type of a given structure and to trace its progressive elaboration in the *scala naturae*, culminating in its fullest expression in humans. Jacob Henle, in a retrospective review written in 1846, described this as the 'genetic method [*genetische Behandlung*]' by means of which 'an entirely new field of research was opened up'. (Clark and Jacyna 1987: 21)

The genetic method couples the identification of the 'simple type' with the 'given structure'. Pursued empirically, this entails the identification of such a structure and the attempt to discover its type or 'basal element' (Clark and Jacyna 1987: 43). Pursued beyond empirical means, however, the problem of the reduction of nature to the phenomenal-somatic, which we have seen as consequent upon linear recapitulation, now becomes the basis from which recapitulation is linearized. The point is made clear in Carus' memoirs, *Denkwürdigkeiten und Lebenserrinerrungen* (2 vols, Leipzig 1855–6, vol. 1: 72), when he draws attention to the 'fact made known' by Oken, in *On Generation* [*Die Zeugung*], 1805, that

> there is an unmistakable parallel . . . between the history of human development from the *nicroscopic* ovum . . . to a final formation in the mature individual on the one hand, and the successive stages, on the other, from the *microscopic* infusoria by way of the tender and soft mollusc to the anthropoid animals (Carus, cited in Gode von Aesch 1966: 122).

Whatever was microscopic in organic form, Oken had, as yet,[16] no means of sensory access, but had instead to proceed on a speculative basis. The grounds of his speculation are governed by the same essentially somaticist search for the middle body between the largest (the continuum) and the smallest (the atom) as informed Goethe's phenomenology. The task of identification must also concede in advance the limits of a linear recapitulation theory to a class of phenomena to which the structure under investigation belongs. Thus, by parallelism, there must be an organic *Urtyp* of organic structure, a minerological one of mineral structure, and so on. To undo this linear reduction, the recapitulationist can either descend further in the 'genetic typing' of any structure, running the risk of vitiating the parallelism *at both the very large and the very small levels* and thus *losing all phenomenal orientation*; not to do so is to concede a nature irrevocably riven into kinds, such as Cuvier presented for the animal kingdom alone. Or the recapitulationist can abandon the organo-somatic phenomenalism that governs the linear use of that theory. The problem is aptly summarized by Novalis: 'Where is the primal germ, *the type of the entirety of nature* to be found? The nature of nature?' (1996: 440, my emphasis).[17]

Although there had been hints of non-linear recapitulation – Schubert's or Ritter's theories of the metals in the organic kingdom, for instance[18] – to produce a non-somatic and non-phenomenological, non-linear account of the recapitulation not of any primary body, cell, protoplasm or phenomenon at all, and to extend this across the entire domain of natural history, from the lithic to the ideational, from a dynamic rather than a somatic 'basal element', is therefore the task Kielmeyer's non-linear use of the recapitulation set itself.

4.1.3.3 Non-linearity: A new epoch in natural history

> Nature admittedly makes no leap; but it seems to me that this principle is much misunderstood if we try to bring into a single class things which nature has not only separated, but has itself opposed to one another. That principle says no more than this, that nothing which *comes to be* in nature *comes to be* by a leap; all *becoming* occurs in a continuous sequence. (II, 171–2; 1988: 133)

Although Kielmeyer is commonly considered to be just another microcosm-macrocosm Romantic recapitulationist,[19] as Lenoir (1981: 169) notes, Kielmeyer nowhere asserts 'that the series of beings is linear, so that the ontogeny of man recapitulates the phylogeny of the entire animal kingdom'. In place of the somatic poles of mega- and micro-bodies – protoplasm, foetus, man and world, substrate and atom, species and individual, substance and concrete whole, type and phenomenon, and so forth – by which the *linear usage of recapitulation* is maintained, the 'object' of Kielmeyer's *non-linear use of recapitulation* is *time*. Just as, that is, Buffon considered ' "species" [to be] an abstract general term whose object exists only in nature considered in the succession of time, in the constant destruction and equally constant regeneration of beings' ([1753] 1985: 196), so Kielmeyer's 'series of organizations' are not the *object* of natural historical explanation, but the *medium* through which time becomes momentarily phenomenal. Further, following the above-cited passage from 'On natural history' (1790), it is not a becoming *of* something that Kielmeyer assesses; rather, his 'system-programme' of comparative zoology measures different time-periods – the emergence, development and decline of (a) individuals, (b) species, (c) planets and (d) stars – against the integral of an 'infinite number of changes' (1938: 23).

Concerned with 'relative proportions of forces', Kielmeyer's method is necessarily comparative. Just as Schelling measures philosophical systems against 'true philosophical science that is the cognition of the All' (VII, 80), so Kielmeyer measures the 'relative proportions' of organizations against time, against becoming, because this affords the largest scale. Against time itself, the entire 'developmental history' of the animal kingdom traces only a 'parabolic curve' (1938: 28, 62, 65). Kielmeyer therefore repeats this comparatist procedure to take the measure of specifically organic systems; here, however, it is not the relative proportions of times to one another but rather that of forces, the most extensive of which in (and beyond, as we shall see) the organic kingdom is the *reproductive force*:

The reproductive force is by far the most universal, accounting for the greatest amount of force expended in organisations, and we may, by reason of its properties and characteristics, consider it a force distinct from nature's other products, although even this . . . may show that it too is generated from inorganic nature, and derivative of the forces there native. (Kielmeyer 1938: 81–2)

Good Platonist that Kielmeyer is, in both instances, comparison ensues between the greater and the lesser, the large and the small *as such*, not large, small and medium *bodies*. Rather, all bodies are intermediary media between imperceptibles. As regards the various organic series, therefore, it is not large and small *organisms* that matter, but rather the degree of reproductive force manifest in the production and continuation of their species. Nor is Kielmeyer particularly concerned to fix the existence of species, as Plotinian self-articulating NATURE, opening the *Discourse*, bluntly advised the professor's audience, in the Stuttgart Auditorium, some two hundred years ago:

despite the destruction of individuals, the species survives; yet even this great new system of effects, the living species, I make advance along a developmental path over long periods of time . . . [until] I come to replace your race with another, new species, you need no explanation of this as yet. (Kielmeyer 1938: 64–5)

Because Kielmeyer takes not space and bodies, but time and becoming, as the focus of natural history, the problem of the continuum of species – extant and extinct – is supplanted by that of the *filling of time*. 'It no longer disturbs' Kilemeyer, therefore, 'that nature makes leaps' (Bach 2001: 179), since the problem that concerns dynamic natural history is not species preservation, nor the continuity of natural forms, but rather the 'imperceptibly small and infinitely many changes' (1938: 23) by which 'time is filled' (1938: 61–2). Forces are not merely in, nor do they occupy, space, but rather *fill time*. From the standpoint of time, the great axis of becoming against which all other extensities are measured, Kielmeyer descends through the various 'developmental levels' of these forces, and each time compares the smaller against the larger, and never claiming their productivity exhausted or terminated in a perfect natural form. That nature speaks to us at all, as it says, *flatters* us insofar as nature must descend to the systemic-level of one of its products (1938: 66).

Kielmeyer's emergent system consists of two basal structures, and since each is a structure of becoming, we will refer to these as *kinds* (*gene*) in the sense given this term under Platonic physics. The first kind, like the Platonic, concerns 'the great and the small', which provides the innumerably and imperceptibly large measure (no product may phenomenologically retrospect the totality of time) against which all becomings are necessarily lesser, although these are larger still than the 'imperceptibly small' and the 'innumerably many'. At the level of measure, then, there is a threefold scale that exceeds phenomenality both in the direction of the infinite and the infinitesimal. In the middle, these basic unequal structures are recapitulated not at the level of bodies, but of forces. At this point, it is important to note that Kielmeyer specifies that *the largest measure* within the distribution of forces in organic nature, i.e., the *reproductive force*, is generated 'from inorganic nature, and derivative of the forces there native' (1938: 82).

The second of the Kielmeyerian kinds are given, in the *Discourse*, in the form of laws, but their necessity is a consequence of the extension of the differentia amongst the first kind to differentia amongst *forces*. As Kielmeyer writes, 'When it is a matter of proportions of forces, one must first consider the standard of measurement in accordance with which they may be compared as a whole and measured acording to their magnitude' (1938: 71). Since no particular body, macrobody (substrate, primal substance, aether, etc.) or microbody (protoplasm, intermaxillary bone, etc.), provides the 'standard of measurement' or 'basal element' of organic nature, the forces that define its specificity do not inhere in an isolably organic nature, but extend, as the first sketch of natural history testifies (1938: 210), to earth history. Kielmeyer's attempts to generate a 'threefold parallelism' (cf. Kielmeyer 1938: 203–9; Coleman 1973) at the level of forces, rather than at that of temporal scale, between the 'great system of operations' that is the animal kingdom, the individuals that populate that kingdom, and the system of earth history, rest on the *form* of the dynamic laws referred to, in the *Discourse*, as the 'plan of nature' (1938: 90). Each law describes a 'developmental level' as a structure emerging in the relative proportions of forces, taking the rough form, 'the more of these forces is developed on the one side, the more it is diminished on the other' (1938: 91),[20] and each level generates a layer of organization.

This is where the 'genetic problem' arises for Kielmeyer: what differentiates levels unless they are identifiable within organizations? And if these levels are so identifiable, what identifies an organization? Kielmeyer's answer is that an organization is not a body, but a 'system of operations'; an organization, that is, is a systematic 'net' of forces channelled into the maintenance and reproduction of specific activities. Accordingly, as Schelling specifies, 'What then is this developmental level? It is designated by a determined structure. But this determined structure is itself only the phenomenon. The real that grounds it is the inner proportion of forces which is originally found in every organization' (III, 54n; 2004: 43n). The basal element, in other words, consists in nothing other than the proportions of forces whose *phenomena* are determined structures, populating animal, mineral and noetic worlds with all kinds of bodies. This is why Bach, for instance, is wrong to describe Kielmeyer's science as a 'phenomenology of the organic' (2001: 294): Kielmeyer's dynamics does, it is true, make bodies of all sorts into phenomena, yet these phenomena are not the products of mind, but of forces. As Schelling puts it, still developing the implications of dynamic natural history in the early drafts of the *Ages of the World*, 'Whoever talks only about phenomena loses all necessary measure' (1946: 7). This is precisely why the 'Oldest programme of German comparative anatomy' (1790) stipulates that this science is rather an 'animal dynamics' (1938: 27), and why the *Rede* is concerned with the *Relative Proportions of the Forces*. Since, moreover, the particular body type is not the concern of Kielmeyer's dynamics as such, any parallelism it might establish is not a parallelism of bodies, but rather of forces: these proportions, the large and the small, are recapitulated at different levels throughout systems of organization, regardless of somatic type. This is why Kielmeyer responds favourably to Eschenmayer's suggestion that the parallelism of individual animals and animal series be extended to include geological organization or 'the developmental history of the earth' (in Kielmeyer 1938: 203), a suggestion that Steffens (1801) had already developed. But it is equally why the *Rede* not only descends to minerality, but also '*ascends*', to speak Okenian, to 'the forces assembled in the human mind'. The same laws, that is, that Kielmeyer establishes as regulating 'the distribution of forces in the series of organisations . . . in the different developmental stages of individuals', and 'calling into being . . . the different organisations on the earth' (1938: 93–4), also regulate the 'changes shown by the human mind, in its developmental periods, in the proportion of the forces assembled in it [. . .]. Here too', adds Kielmeyer, 'a similarity in the laws according to which the organic forces and the forces of the human mind change in their proportions can be observed' (1938: 99).

Kielmeyerian natural history marks a new epoch for Schelling not only insofar as it provides the basis for his early attempt, in the *First Outline of a System of Naturephilosophy*, at a solution to the 'genetic problem' in the form of 'dynamic atomism', but also insofar as this basis can be extended from *geogony* to the 'natural history of our mind' (II, 39; 1988: 30). Kielmeyer does not simply provide a new account of natural history, but also converts the principle of transcendental philosophy from the phenomenal and somatic nature to which Kant had tied it, to making the somatic into the phenomenal products of an a priori dynamics, thus naturalizing '*Scheinprodukte*' (III, 16)[21] without making the phenomenal-somatic coextensive with nature as such. It is because forces and not phenomena provide the necessary measure that Schelling proposes that continuity is not to be found between '*things* that nature has separated', but only in the sequences of 'coming to be' or 'becoming'. Products are discontinuities, acts separated by nature, *objects*; productivity *itself*, activity *to auto*, produces in a 'continuous sequence' (II, 171; 1988: 133) while necessarily remaining 'non-objective' or 'unthinged'. When therefore the *First Outline* engages the problem of the 'unthinged in nature' (III, 11; 2004: 13) because this cannot be sought in any finite product, the claim is not that nature is to be investigated in accordance with the ideal, but rather that 'materiality as such is not yet corporeality' (XI, 424). For nature conceived on the grounds of 'the basal science of dynamics' (II, 6; 1988: 5), the 'speculative physics' that pursues the 'unthinged in the natural sciences' (III, 283; 2004: 202) is not speculative because it pursues an Idea of nature rather than *nature itself*; rather, since *nature itself* cannot be assessed according to its somatic phenomena, but only according to its productivity, physics must necessarily abandon empiricism for an analogue of the constructivism deployed in nature. As Heuser notes, 'Schelling correctly understood that a universal theory of self-organisation may not presuppose objects, but that they must first be constructed from the nonobjective' (Heuser, in Zimmerli, Stein and Gerten (eds) 1997: 285).

The idea of nature's apriority, not simply in the sense of its necessity in order to generate *ideation* through the recapitulating sequence: geogony – magnetism – organization – neural net,[22] but also insofar as it ties the conditions expressed by these forces both to the production of the phenomena in question and to that of their ideation, transforms Schelling's conception of transcendental philosophy in its entirety. By virtue of attaching not to mind, as a discrete physical product, but to the 'nature that produces', (Plato, *Phlb.* 26e6; cf. Schelling 1994a: 48), apriority will become cognitively unavailable by virtue of the irreversibility of the excess of productivity over product. On the basis of 'the identity between the dynamic and the transcendental' (III, 451; 1978: 92), Schelling's *System of Transcendental Idealism* accordingly constructs the transcendental as a recapitulation of the irreversible disymmetry between productivity and product in nature, at the level of consciousness. Since in recapitulation, the same proportionality of forces as constructs the product at one level is recapitulated at another, the consequence of this in Schellingian transcendental idealism is that the conditions of productivity, the forces with the greatest extensity in thinking, can never be recovered in *consciousness* as product, which operates with forces of lesser extensity. Natural ideation, or *induction*, therefore provokes a transcendentalism consisting necessarily in construction.

In the form of the Schellingian problem of 'induction', Kielmeyer's system therefore achieves what the transcendental ethico-teleologists in philosophy and the linear recapitulationists and other uniformitarians in natural history could not: a non-somatic and non-phenomenal dynamic *physis* of ideation.

4.2 THE FACTORS OF PARALLELISM: THE DYNAMIC SUCCESSION OF STAGES IN NATURE

Several, not unknown, natural scientists acknowledge an unbroken graduated succession of stages or a chain, that leads from the rawest masses of unformed matter, by intermediary links, to the most perfect creatures. This so-called chain of nature, however, is a chimera. Between organized and inorganic bodies there is an immense gulf, unfilled by any intermediary body. [. . .] The concept of a progressive *Stufenfolge* of natural things can in consequence find no place in natural history, as Herr Blumenbach has already noted. (Girtanner 1796: 44)

That our experience has taught us no transformation of nature, no transition from one form or kind to another . . . is proof against this possibility, for . . . the alterations to which organic as well as inorganic nature are subjected may have happened in *far greater periods of time than our lesser time periods can provide a measure for*, and that are so great that until now no such experience has been lived through. (II, 349, my emphasis)

We now comprehend the problem: to determine *a priori* the various organic functions and their various possible proportions. Were this problem successfully resolved, then not only would this entail a *dynamic succession of stages* in nature as such, we would also have derived [*abgeleitet*] that very dynamic succession of stages *a priori*, elevating what was previously known as *natural history* into the *system of nature*. (III, 68; 2004: 53, t.m.)

Thus Schelling proposes to resolve the 'genetic problem' (cf. 3.4, above): an a priori determination – that is, a determination *from the first* – of 'the dynamic succession of stages', directly contravening the so-called 'Kant-Blumenbach research programme' or 'vital materialism'[23] represented by the above passage from Girtanner's *On the Kantian Principle in Natural History*. It is to be noted that the grounds for Girtanner's rejection of the 'chimerical' notion of the *Stufenfolge* – the graduated succession of stages in nature – consist in the very somaticism that prevented Kant's theory of dynamics ever reaching the level of a philosophy of nature (VI, 8). For such as Girtanner, there are only bodies and analogies between them. Accordingly, analogism and linear recapitulationism considered their task to be resolvable upon identification of the 'type – the basal element' of relations of similarity or organization, respectively (Clark and Jacyna 1987: 44), a dynamic philosophy can neither accept the primacy of an 'originary being' (III, 13; 2004: 14), nor, therefore, a primary body (a cell, a bone, a vesicle) from which others would derive. In place, therefore, of somatic prototypes, and following Kielmeyer's 'Oldest programme of German comparative anatomy' (1938: 13–29), Schelling's naturephilosophical works immediately succeeding the *Ideas* propose diverse means to complete the 'derivation' of this 'dynamic succession of stages' or *Stufenfolge*, an undertaking, states the *First Outline*, 'in which all the problems of naturephilosophy might well be combined' (III, 69; 2004: 53, t.m.).

These problems include the conceptual coordinates already established: being and becoming or the ontology of nature; phenomenality in nature, or the physics of appearances; induction and construction, or the mode of nature's self-articulation in ideation; and the relation of product to productivity, that is, the operations of a nature transcendental with respect to its products, but immanent with respect to its forces, or nature-as-subject. Further, however, insofar as our present purpose is to establish the grounds for the 'identity of the transcendental and the dynamic' (III, 452; 1978: 91)

139

announced in the *System*, this section is in particular concerned to set up the graduated series of stages that leads from 'nature's only primitives' (IV, 4) to the 'construction of the Idea' (V, 135). This alone gives the measure of a theory of nature that involves the universal amongst the multiplicity of particulars, and an idealism that does not eliminate nature as a precondition of its merely formal consistency. Before moving to Schelling's dynamics of the Idea, therefore, we will examine the two major attempts at determining that *Stufenfolge*, while exposing the problems combined in it.

In common with Kielmeyer's identification of 'the great and the small' in nature at the level of the *forces* operative therein, and at the level of *time*, consisting of the 'universal transformations of nature' (II, 347), Schelling takes the first step towards a '*Stufenfolge* of all organic beings' (II, 348) in *On the World Soul* (1798). The world soul itself, comprising the 'first' or 'originally positive force of nature' and a second, negative or 'restricting force' (II, 381), precisely echoes the *Timaeus*' soul of the world, which, Plato writes, comprises 'the being which is indivisible and remains always the same and the being which is transient and divisible in bodies' (*Tim.* 35a1–3). Here again we encounter the differentiation of 'materiality as such' from 'corporeality', repeatedly made by Schelling (cf. XI, 424). It is precisely because, on dynamic principles, matter exceeds divisible body that Plato, as Aristotle notes (*Phys.* 187a18–20), 'makes matter consist in the diversifying antithesis [of] the great and the small'. The immediate application of the diversifying antithesis in the context of *On the World Soul* is not to the identification of archetypes, but rather, again echoing Kielmeyer, to time. The grounds of this extension lie in the consequences of the removal of a priori somatism from the genetic problem. Thus, asked to comment on the prospect of a 'threefold parallelism' between the developmental stages in organizations (ontogeny), series of organizations (phylogeny) and earth history (geogeny), by Karl Joseph Windischmann, Kielmeyer responds favourably to the idea of thus extending the *Stufenfolge* through inorganic nature (as is evident from his own suggested programme to this effect in the 1790 text 'On natural history'),[24] while remaining sceptical concerning the prospects for the execution of such a programme. It is less his scepticism than the grounds of it that are of interest, however. In this regard, William Coleman correctly observes that 'Kielmeyer evinced no inclination to pursue the past on its own terms, that is, by means of stratigraphy and palaeontology', but is entirely wrong concerning the grounds of the disinclination, concluding that *since* Kielmeyer's interest lies in expanding the developmental series from ontogeny and phylogeny to geogeny, and since he rejects investigations of the past on its own grounds, so to speak, his evidentiary researches *must therefore* be 'directed entirely at living organisms' (Coleman 1973: 344). Yet the focii of Kielmeyer's inquiries are the problems of time, discontinuity, and the limits of phenomenality in nature. In consequence, the focus was always placed more on the proportions of forces expressed in bodies, than on bodies themselves, regardless of their nature. Explaining his reasoning to Windischmann, Kielmeyer enumerates the problems to be encountered in any such *Stufenfolge*: not only is the determinability of 'each parallel developmental moment of the earth and its organizations' practically untenable because

> a great many intermediary links have been lost from the series of organizations, which is now no longer complete and cannot be seen as the reflection of what was once present. This would practically mean that a progression through individual links could not be completed . . . but it is [also] highly probable that the series never was continuous. (Kielmeyer 1938: 206–7)

If the *Stufenfolge* can no longer be phenomenally encompassed, this may indeed be due to the ravages of time: 'species die out', as Buffon (1755: 62) succinctly put it, 'because time fights against them'. However, to the empirical difficulty that renders Windischmann's project uncertain of success, Kielmeyer adds an ontological dimension: rather than the empirical incompleteness presented by the oryctologists' fragmentary fossil record,[25] the problem consisted in the 'high probability' that *there never was a continuous series* of individual links in what Buffon, amongst others of those 'not unknown natural scientists' against whom Girtanner (1796: 44) inveighs, imagined to be a great chain operating by 'almost imperceptible degrees from the most perfect creature to the most formless matter' ([1749] 1985: 166). If the grounds of this discontinuity lie, according to Kielmeyer, in the discontinuous series of organizations, the combinatory that works to unite nature into a *Stufenfolge* cannot consist in bodies at all, but rather in forces. Thus, following up on an hypothesis made in the early 1790s, Kielmeyer announces that hope for a dynamically grounded threefold – or even multiple (Coleman 1973: 347) – parallelism might be grounded in the 'continuity' between 'the force' that *produced* the series of organizations, the sequence of stages in *individual* organizations, and that in the *series* of organizations, on the one hand, and that of 'magnetism' (1938: 204) on the other. Coleman's misconception is based on the same somaticist error as is Girtanner's: that continuity must be demonstrated across series of bodies, rather than across *becoming*. On the contrary, as Schelling notes in the *Ideas*, the principle that 'nature makes no leap' is misunderstood unless this is held to say 'that nothing which comes to be in nature comes to be by a leap; all becoming occurs in a continuous sequence' (II, 171; 1988: 133).

Thus, on the matter of the experiential or phenomenal accessibility of the great transformations undergone by nature, Schelling notes the 'lesser' timescale 'can provide no measure' for the 'greater' (II, 349), but provides no proof against 'universal transformation'. By referencing the great and the small in regard to 'heterochrony' – relative accelerations and retardations of 'infinite becoming' – Schelling not only draws overtly on Kielmeyerian sources, however, but equally pulls the resolution of the problem of 'nature's primitives' (IV, 4), in terms drawn from the *Universal Deduction*, beyond the reducibly spatial coordinates within which the antithesis of divisible and indivisible matter is played out in natural history. In a reversal of Kant's suppression of Buffonian progressive and regressive time in natural history, Schelling not only triumphs Kielmeyer's anti-phenomenological principles, but equally considers it a necessary consequence of combining somatic with temporal researches into the coordinates of the 'genetic problem', that the science 'previously known as natural history' be transformed, not into the achrony of Kant's proposed 'archaeology of nature', but into a 'system of nature' (III, 68; 2004: 53), and ultimately, into the 'system of times' investigated in the *Ages of the World* (1811–27).[26]

This is how the problem of phenomenality arises in the *Stufenfolge*. Firstly, the first and second forces of nature that combine to form the world-soul, being 'too large' for the domain of possible experience, cannot be deemed secondary to, but must be primary with respect to body. This being the case, physical reality consists of forces in motion that do not, *pace* Kant's *Metaphysical Foundations*, fill *space*, but rather fill time (Kielmeyer 1938: 61–2). The excess of time over natural production, underscored by Schelling's argument that what is phenomenally available cannot be held to determine the course of things past or future, since the timescale within which experience is possible is 'too small' with respect to that of natural transformations (everything from cosmogeny to phylogeny) to provide a measure. Schelling and Kielmeyer, with his denial of any continuity at the level of the series of organizations over time, commonly propose a phenomenal catastrophism, while equally maintaining a non-phenomenal *Stufenfolge*, the composition of which is dependent not upon phenomenal resemblance, as we have seen, but upon recapitulations of the proportionality of forces, on the one hand, and upon the construction of 'epochs' of becoming, on the other.

It is not the case that therefore Schelling argues all phenomenality is illusion. Rather, phenomenality is itself a natural production, having its a prioris not in mind, but in nature. As a result, naturephilosophy in no way proposes the elimination of empirical researches from the investigation of nature, but rather integrates such research at the phenomenal, or derivative level. This is why Schelling employs no 'principle of exhaustibility' to empirical theories of nature, such that if one is right, the others are wrong: empiricism cannot claim exhaustibility because, if consistent, it cannot rule out experiments or hypotheses whose results differ from one another. Accordingly, Schelling does not take sides between Newton's emanation theory of light and Euler's wave theory (II, 387–8). It is only when the natural sciences illegitimately transform empiricism into a limiting ontological principle that a nature reduced to bodies and phenomena emerges. This is why, contesting Eschenmayer on precisely this issue, Schelling insists that empiricism cannot be limited or restricted, but must be 'extended to the unconditioned' (III, 24; 2004: 22, t.m.), at which point empiricism can no longer operate in accordance with preconceived principles regarding the nature it investigates. However, it is crucial to demonstrating this integration that Schelling derive the empirical-phenomenal from the first force as 'the sole object of a higher science of nature'. Since this first force is the 'principle of all motion' (II, 382), while the second or negative force *retards* the first, their necessary union slows infinite becoming to the point of phenomenal production. Schelling's 'autocratic nature' (*Stat.* 274a6) again follows the principles Plato establishes in the *Philebus* (26e6) regarding the 'coming into being through the measures imposed by the limit' on the unlimited. That is, while nature itself is infinite becoming, such becoming is not yet phenomenal, even at the level of matter, which remains 'the darkest of all things' (II, 359; cf. II, 223; 1988: 179; VII, 360; 1986: 35) or 'invisible power' (II, 381), these forces constitute the conditions of possibility of phenomenal nature as such, without themselves being phenomenal. Thus: 'When this original-positive force is *infinite*, it flies far beyond the limits of *possible perception*. Restricted by the opposing [force], it becomes a *finite magnitude* – it begins to become an object of perception, or it manifests itself in *phenomena*' (II, 381).

In a breathtakingly fast overthrow of the entire transcendental structure Kant bequeathed his philosophical successors, the first pages of *On the World Soul* proceed from the production of phenomena as an act of the first force in nature, to their production as phenomena for finite intellects: as primary and positive, the first force is the 'one immediate object of intuition'. Nor even is this intuition located *in us*, but before and after us, it remains what is positive *in phenomena*. To complete the genesis of phenomena *for us*, Schelling pronounces the 'negative, retarding force' the 'cause of mere *sensation*'. Far from even this being intuitable for us within our phenomena, as perhaps the last vestige of humanism might hope, the retarding force can only be *inferred* (II, 382). To summarize: phenomena are products of natural forces, the positive of which is also the immediate *object* of intuition, the negative simultaneously the cause of sensation, and the product of an inference. The positive force, unlimited without retardation, is not devoted to the production of phenomena, or even of intuition, but courses precisely *wihout end* through the 'in discrete phenomena'.

Without going too far into the matter of the transcendental here (cf. 5, above), it is crucially important that the degree of Schelling's naturalism be noted. The 'Construction of matter' in the *Further Presentations from My System of Philosophy* (1802) goes so far as to stipulate that 'no philosophy at all exists without naturephilosophy' (IV, 424). Unless the tension between the physical and the ideal, in other words, is maintained at its highest; that is, unless philosophy is constantly held to the standard of the 'cognition of the All' (VII, 50), the force of the philosophy of the ideal evaporates entirely. Thus there is nothing remotely metaphorical in the presentation of chemistry as 'sensory dynamics' (II, 323–4; 1988: 257), which instead constitutes a challenge to the composition of thought. At the same time, however, phenomena are not dependent upon actual intuition events for their existence. Therefore the positive force, the 'principle of all movement', is the 'immediate objective of a higher theory of nature', which *On the World Soul* proposes to introduce: even the 'higher and lower' reiterates the diversifying antithesis by means of which measure is introduced into the immense. By retaining the positive and the first as the measure of everything subsequent that is a restriction, or better, a *retardation* of it, the *Sufenfolge* pursues this 'Proteus of nature' throughout the 'ever changing forms and innumerable phenomena', that is, through the 'discrete phenomena', in which it recurs. Innumerable phenomena are the necessary consequence of an infinitely outflowing force because, *qua* infinite, it is not exhausted by any possible number of productions, so no limit can be set to the number of production events to follow from productive nature. Thus at no point is the primary force *separate* from its retardations. It is first by virtue not of the order of the production of bodies, but rather by virtue of being the a priori condition under which alone restriction is possible.

It is accordingly inevitable that Schelling begins the derivation of the *Stufenfolge* with that phenomenon that displays most readily the *speed* and *generality* of the primary force – light, which 'moves itself with such force and speed that many have even doubted its materiality,[27] since it lacks inertia, that universal characteristic of matter' (II, 382). In the propagation of light, Schelling nevertheless argues that light is necessarily a 'material becoming' on two grounds. Firstly, if discrete 'matters' are composed of forces and forces necessarily compose matters, then 'any development, and any becoming is a matter, accompanied by its proper motion' (II, 382). Secondly, the 'first force' is not to be understood as 'limitless' or 'absolute', but rather in dynamic, and therefore changing relations with other forces, as 'the negative of their opposed force', but never the 'absolute negation' of the latter (II, 384). As Eschenmayer put the problem in *Propositions from the Metaphysics of Nature*,

> There is no absolute freedom or bondage of these forces in matter, for the concept of matter would thereby be eliminated. In an absolute freedom, the forces would be independent of one another, and an infinitely larger or smaller degree – that is, no degree at all – of matter would be present. In absolute bondage the gradation would likewise be eliminated and experience would be = 0. (Eschenmayer 1797: 8, cited in *AA* I, 6: 287n)

The point, in other words, is not to institute an ontological gulf between matter and force, but rather that forces constitute the 'maximum and the minimum' of any scale on which becomings are measured. 'It is the first principle of a theory of nature that no principle is to be seen as absolute, and to assume a *material* principle as the vehicle of every force in nature' (II, 386). Accordingly, Schelling will always distinguish, in considering any particular phenomenon – light, heat, gases, electricity and magnetism, as the first book of the *World Soul* runs – between the 'positive' and the 'negative matter' in that phenomenon. Light, for example, 'is no simple element', notes Schelling, but always the 'product' of a higher and a lower degree of elasticity or expandibility (II, 385). Between these never reached extremes, the positive force expresses endless becoming in the phenomenon, insofar as it is 'conceived in becoming' (II, 387), while its retardation by the negative force constrains the actions of the positive within the sphere of those phenomenal becomings. Accordingly, 'infinite becomings' are of two kinds: those that perpetuate the wholesale transformation of phenomena, and those that are particularized within phenomena. The world-soul, the 'cell' of these forces, is therefore what constructs the becomings of phenomena. As we shall see, this dynamic 'cellular' hypothesis will have far-reaching consequences in terms of the 'dynamic atomism' propounded in the *First Outline*.

That these becomings are infinite is evident at the level of phenomena, therefore, by the fact of their becoming. For instance, in charting the becomings of the phenomena of light, Schelling notes the extreme regionality of the point of contact between light-phenomena and a receptive organ, in which it 'causes' sensation. Since the light reaching us from the 'decomposition of the sun's atmosphere' (after Herschel 'has made this hypothesis probable to the highest degree', II, 387) can never be phenomenally recovered by any such organ, light phenomena as such far exceed their phenomenality for any receptive organ, so that the becomings in any such phenomenon must be conceived as 'in a state of development'. In other words, what phenomena are cannot be reduced to how they appear for any given apparatus of reception, technological or biological. This is why empiricism can never exhaust the phenomena, and why any attempt to restrict the ontology of nature to particular bodies is simply an extension of the limitations of the receptive apparatus onto nature, a 'transcendentalizing empiricism'.

What, then, is the 'dynamic cell' the *World Soul* derives? Its primary measure is the indeterminate or 'diversifying antithesis' of infinite becoming and infinite restriction. The positive and the negative, or the expansive and the retarding, being necessarily active in every phenomenon, determine the measure of these particular becomings by means of the highest force expressed therein (the 'great force and velocity' in the motions of light, for example; II, 382), and the forces therein subordinated to it, insofar as these reach a 'dynamic equilibrium' that is regional with respect to time, and variant within it (II, 387). Following Kielmeyer's example, Schelling expresses these regional and dynamic equilibria by means of laws of proportionality: 'when an extremely high . . . but finite degree of elasticity is generated, so too will be the phenomenon of a highly elastic matter . . . extended in a space proportional to the degree of that force' (II, 382). The primary 'diversifying antithesis' itself, however, is 'first' in the generation of phenomena. Schelling writes: 'These two forces, clashing or represented in conflict, leads to the Idea of an *organizing*, self-systematising *principle*. Perhaps this is what the ancients wanted to hint at by the *soul of the world*' (II, 381).

The world-soul, the primary diversifying antithesis in the *Stufenfolge* of nature, is so-called precisely because, while not *being* body, it is nonetheless matter; it is the 'darkest of all things' (II, 359) precisely insofar as it generates phenomenality. The *Stufenfolge* is derived, therefore, by combining the dynamic metrics of particular phenomena with the primary diversifying antithesis, or measuring the dynamics of phenomena against those of generation as such. The first step in any *Stufenfolge* is always therefore a 'self-organizing matter', as in the *Ideas* (II, 47; 1988: 35), the 'construction of matter' (III, 25; 2004: 23) in the *First Outline*, or the 'self-construction of matter' (IV, 4) in the *Universal Deduction*. The *World Soul* further qualifies this process as an 'outflowing . . . in *singular matters*' (II, 382). Not only, in other words, is no *phenomenon* in nature absolute, so that none can be taken as the type of all the others, or as the element recapitulated throughout one or many series; in addition, no matter is *singular*, but rather a composition of endless becomings: 'things', as Schelling puts it, 'are not simply *phenomena*, but an infinite succession of stages approximating *individuality*' (II, 500). In this process, the forces move between points of dynamic equilibrium, or the relative self-identity of a phenomenon, and points of decomposition, or the relative differentiation of a phenomenon. Dynamic equilibrium does not 'imprison' force in matter therefore, just as decomposition does not 'free' it, as Eschenmayer says, since in either case, matter and forces simply disappear. Rather, the *Stufenfolge* is the material succession of stages in the *approximation of identity* by phenomena.

That such approximations fall always and necessarily short of their attractor – the likeness to which they are akin, and that therefore calls them into being ('*Gleiches Gleiches hervorruft*', VII, 281) – is simply a given of dynamic systems, and follows immediately from the necessary absence of absolutes amongst natural products. Thus all Schelling's 'laws' take the form of proportional (and linear)[28] equations, as for example, in the retardation of light:

> since the degree of [a matter']s elasticity is of course finite, and the elasticity of every matter decreases in proportion as the space in which it expands is increased, thereby gradually lowering its elasticity until it reaches an equilibrium of forces relative to its degree of expansion, and thus makes *rest*, that is, a permanent state of matter, possible. (II, 383)

Or, from the *First Outline*,

> Since the tendency to evolution [the expansive force] is originally infinite according to the presupposition, it must therefore be thought as a force that would fill an infinitely large space in an infinitely small time. Let space rise to infinity, or time fall to infinity, then in one case we have $\infty/1$, in the other $1/\infty$, i.e., [in both] the infinitely large. Hence the expansive force runs, according to its nature, towards the infinitely large and represents therefore the positive factor in general. (III, 262–3; 2004: 188, t.m.)[29]

The problem, however, these 'experiments in dynamic physics' (IV, 114) are attempts to resolve consists in how 'the germ of an infinite evolution, the germ of an infinite decomposition into ever new products, was placed in the universe' (III, 258; 2004: 184, t.m.); how, that is, *individual* products ever arise. That is, having resolved the genetic problem by means of the decomposition of the whole, the question arises as to how what eighteenth-century physics referred to as 'the specific difference of matters' could have any reality whatever. At the level of matter itself, to acknowledge such specific differences would repose the genetic question for each such different matter: how could matter a, if different *in kind* from matter b, generate it?

To this problem, Schelling offers two distinct answers, one of which is predominant in the *World Soul*, but also recurs in the *First Outline*, and the other which occurs only in the latter work. The second of these solutions, which Schelling calls 'dynamic atomism', attempts to fix the problem of contingency with respect not so much to natural products as to productivity. We will examine it briefly below. The earlier and more widespread solution rejects the prospect of specific differences amongst matters in favour of the problem of 'real antithesis', which Schelling defines as 'only possible between things of one kind and of common origin' (II, 390).[30] Yet because nature as such originates from nothing other than the primary or diversifying antithesis of the forces, 'it is necessary', writes Schelling, 'to think all matter as *of one kind* with regard to its substance [*Stoff*]; for it is only insofar as it is homogeneous with itself that it is susceptible of bifurcation, that is, of a real antithesis. Yet every actuality already presupposes bifurcation' (II, 390). That real antithesis or endless bifurcations drive infinite decomposition therefore necessitates a 'universal identity of matter' at the level of kind, and this identity of matter is recapitulated as bifurcation in the production of particulars. 'Where there are phenomena', therefore, 'there are antithetical forces' (II, 390). Insofar, however, as this identity is recapitulated in the antithetical forces in every phenomenon, *they do not do so symmetrically*. Rather, bifurcation generates differences in kind *insofar as the really antithetical matters approximate the universal identity of matter*, thus driving further bifurcations, and demonstrating the 'infinite decomposition into ever new products' that marks the endless approximation of identity in matter. What therefore is recapitulated throughout a particular *Stufenfolge* is the whole in particulars, or identity. In other words, it is the *universal* that recapitulates itself *down into* the parts, which are in principle unlimited in form and number – matter is infinitely divisible – and hence unending in becoming. Schelling's first solution to the reality of antithesis is therefore: since no product is not derived from the recapitulation of the primary antithesis, all antitheses are real. Since, however, this is the case, then there can be no differences in kind, but only in degree.

Ultimately, these differences in degree are, as in Kielmeyer, relations of time to units of becomings, or, as the *First Outline* engages it, the problem of the infinitely fast evolution of nature. That is, 'to explain the retarding – or, in order that nature as such *evolves at a finite speed*, and thus exhibits everywhere determinate products (from a specific synthesis) – appears to be the highest problem of naturephilosophy' (III, 102–3; 2004: 77, t.m.). As a result of such quantitative differences, therefore, differences between times arise that are not reducible to real antitheses, but constitute, as it were, different 'ages of the world'. These will emerge in two forms: in the epochs and monuments of the *System of Transcendental Idealism*, by which Schelling completes the 'natural history of mind', and in the 'system of times' of the *Ages of the World* itself.

For the moment, however, it is now clear how the *Stufenfolge* works: in pursuing the infinite approximations of singularity that are phenomena, the forces endlessly recapitulate their primary diversifying antithesis – 'infinitely fast evolution' and retardation, as the *First Outline* puts it – in the infinite becomings that are not the becoming *of that phenomenon*, as though it constituted the goal of the whole process. Rather, as Schelling says, 'the immediate goal of nature in the process here described is only the *process itself*' (II, 514). Instead, the retardation of expansion is the *decomposition* of nature into multifold series of matters. As regards the genetic problem, therefore, *any unit*, any phenomenon *whatsoever* will do as a point from which to begin proportional dynamic analysis. As Schelling puts it in *The System of All Philosophy and of Naturephilosophy in Particular* (1804), 'no primary germ [*Urkeim*] is necessary that we must present as dispersed in the chaos, as if it had somehow fallen directly from the creator's hand. *Everything* is primal germ, or nothing is' (VI, 388).[31] Since, however, the *Stufenfolgen* are the real 'decomponents' of nature, Schelling's analyses, like Kielmeyer's, always begin from the very large. The 'physics of the all' is not therefore a plea for an exhaustive catalogue of 'the physics of all things', but rather the demonstration of the serial decomposition that is never finished. This is why the *World Soul* proceeds from the first, infinite force, insofar as this is decomposed by a second, retarding one. The implicit measure in this process is velocity, or time over distance. Hence the 'great force and speed' of light phenomena provide the means to *derive*, from the decomposition of the infinite force, *the phenomena thereby generated*. Thus, the work moves from the decomposition of infinite forces as matters, followed by the further decomposition of matters into the varieties of matter – calorific, gaseous, electrical, magnetic, organic, and so on. Consider, for example, Schelling's diagramming of the decomposition and recomposition of gases into organic matter:

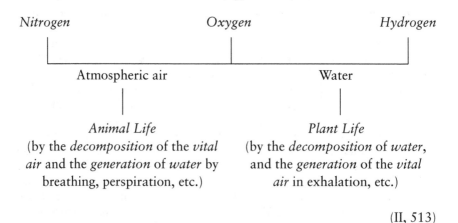

| *Nitrogen* | *Oxygen* | *Hydrogen* |

Atmospheric air   Water

Animal Life   *Plant Life*
(by the *decomposition* of the *vital* (by the *decomposition* of *water*,
air and the *generation* of *water* by and the *generation* of the *vital*
breathing, perspiration, etc.) *air* in exhalation, etc.)

(II, 513)

Issuing from an 'upstream' decomposition, as it were, whereby 'oxygen' is generated as the dynamic equilibrium reached between the decomponents of the higher system, the schema could equally well decompose further, into the organic systems into which the respiratory organs play their role, and even into the various means whereby such organs have been realized: gill, skin, lung, stomata. Thus in simple systems, such as polyps – internally undifferentiated aggregations of colloidal mass – the homogeneity of their parts enables them to replace lost members; 'how striking, by contrast', Schelling observes, 'the individuality of the organs in those organisms that *do not* replace lost members' (II, 531). Since no complex system can be produced by the simple iteration of one and the same 'basal type', or since no product is original in complex systems, every product consists in matters generated in the decomposition of higher, and itself decomposes into lower systems *without limit*. In other words, *infinite becoming* is not the liberation of force from *all limits of matter*, but rather a 'constant *individuation* of matter' (II, 532), an *infinite* individuation by means of the 'constant interruption and reproduction of the equilibrium of the negative principle in bodies' (II, 514), that is, by the progressive decomposition of nature. Just as the forces, in Eschenmayer's terms, are neither free nor bonded with respect to the matters they construct, the first, positive force is never completely 'free' of, or wholly 'enchained' by, the negative force. Ideally separable, therefore, they nevertheless lack *real* conditions of dissociability.

Two further consequences flow from Schelling's system of nature as its infinite decomposition. Firstly, since nature is not exhausted in any one series (quadrupeds, gases), or in any series of series (animal series, chemical series), naturephilosophy neither prescribes nor proscribes empirical natural science, since it does not take the place of the investigation of particulars, but derives these, serially rather than all at once, although not without a concern for 'amplitude',[32] from the physics of the all. Just as Rescher (2000: 26) invokes a 'law of natural complexity: *there is no limit to the number of natural kinds to which any concrete particular belongs*', so Schelling characterizes 'the presentation of the infinite in the finite' as 'science's highest problem' (III, 15; 2004: 15). He therefore extends a law of infinite complexity not only to natural kinds (the infinite number of possible decomposition-series in nature), but also to concrete particulars or *Scheinprodukte*, each of which must, he writes, contain 'infinity within itself' (III, 19; 2004: 18) in order to appear as nature. With both processes being unlimited a priori, naturephilosophy must therefore extend empiricism to the unconditioned precisely in order to generate nature from its *a priority* all over again. Rather than setting arbitrary limits to possible experience by deriving these limits from already *actual* experience, 'empiricism extended to the unconditioned' (III, 24; 2004: 22) recognizes that '[t]he transformations to which contemporary physics has subjected the concept of the possibility of experience warn us that it is probably the most elusive concept in transcendental philosophy' (Vuillemin, in Förster (ed.) 1989: 247). Naturephilosophy therefore favours the extremes to which Ritter subjected his body, in his 'galvanic self-experiments',[33] in order to generate new forms of possible experience over any rearguard humanist conservatism regarding the constitution of that experience *for us*. Reinhard Löw therefore is quite wrong to place Schelling's naturephilosophy at the service of humanism, combating the 'abstractions' of 'modern, mathematico-physical philosophy of nature'. Against these abstractions, however 'real',

> which men are neither familiar with nor can form concepts of, then Schelling's transcendental construction [of nature] fleshed out the countervailing interests of reason: how must nature be thought so as to conceptualise actuality on the one hand, *so that*, on the other, man can understand himself as an intellectual and moral being? (Löw, in Hasler (ed.) 1981: 103, emphasis added)

Löw here proposes that nature be subject firstly to a transcendental construction, and secondly that this be subject to an ethical reconstruction, exactly as Kant said 'second nature' should be produced (*Ak.* V, 314; 1987: 182). When, moreover, he proposes that 'familiarity' be adopted as a criterion in naturephilosophy's constructions, Löw undertakes to eliminate nature all over again, in accordance with the reassertion of the legislative authority not simply of theoretical, but primarily of practical reason. While we have already seen that 'nature as subject' 'ungrounds' the instantiability of *a priority* in mind, the effects of this thesis, although sketched in the *Ideas*' account of 'nature in all its multiplicity aris[ing] out of infinite [*endlose*] approximations to [an] X' (II, 219; 1988: 175, t.m.), and in the *World Soul*'s brief account of the concept as 'the fixed and resting monument of vanishing phenomena' (II, 516f), natural ideation only assumes centre stage with the *System of Transcendental Idealism*, to which we will shortly turn our attention.

The second consequence of the *Stufenfolge*, which demonstrates nature as infinite self-decomposition, is that since matter always expresses itself if not as an individual body, then as *series of bodies*, no series is ever exhaustive of nature as a whole. As Rescher notes, in Schellingian mode,[34] 'nature is vastly more complex than the human brain – if only because we ourselves are merely a minor constituent of nature itself' (2000: 22). This means that no necessity ever attaches to the series *produced* in nature, or those series derived through the *Stufenfolge*. All that is necessary is that 'nature IS *a priori*' (III, 279; 2004: 198); as the *Lectures on the History of Modern Philosophy* characterizes the naturephilosophical procedure, 'the first *being* [*Seyende*], the *primum existens*, as I have called it, is, therefore, at the same time the first contingency (original coincidence [*Urzufall*])' (X, 101; 1994b: 116). Since the approximation to being is precisely the product of becoming, however, the first existent or being (*Seyende*), or the 'ground', as the *Introduction to Philosophy* ([1830] 1989: 45) puts it, echoing the vocabulary of *On the World Soul* (e.g., II, 530: anything that is 'itself dependent on *contingent conditions*' is not 'absolute ground'). Thus the 'reproductive force', the *prius* of organized series for Kielmeyer, is no 'absolute, but a force *dependent on variable conditions*' (II, 532).

The contingency of being and the only ideal separability of the forces that Schelling presents as constituting the principles of nature, become the problems to be addressed in the third in Schelling's great trilogy of naturephilosophical works, the *First Outline*. Starting equally from the results of the *World Soul*, that nature produces by decomposition, or by the infinite inhibition of infinite production, the *First Outline* develops a theory of 'dynamic atomism' that are precisely the 'ideal factors' of nature, rather than real. Stemming from precisely the same problems as the *World Soul*, the later work nonetheless confronts precisely the instability of the contingent decomposition-series with respect to nature as such. On the basic problem of how particularity arises in nature, therefore, Schelling concedes that

> [t]he corpuscular philosopher has an infinite advantage over the so-called dynamic philosophers in that with his atoms, each of which has an original figure, he introduces something originally individual into nature, except these atoms, since they themselves are already products, cannot possibly be admitted as *primary* or *ultimate* in nature. The naturephilosopher, therefore, posits *simple actions* in their place, i.e., the *utlimate* in nature, as *purely productive* without being *product* (hopefully one has at least learnt from the transcendental method to think an activity *without a substrate* and *prior to any substrate*) – which (purely productive) activity exists admittedly only *ideally* in nature, since in infinite evolution, the simple can never arise, rather the All is still product to infinity. (III, 102; 2004: 76–7, t.m.)

It is not the problems this raises for physics – nor its sources in the Boscovich-Priestley 'point atoms' (cf. Crosland 1971: 210–13) – however, but the solutions it proposes for the transcendental philosophy that create the problem here. The 'units of activity' or natural monads effectively recover the Kantian project in the *Physical Monadology*, and do not serve to buttress the identity of forces in nature (the identity of which in any case lies in the construction of matter), but rather to identify units of natural activities with those of transcendental ones. In other words, although the advantage enjoyed by the atomist consists in locating the base of the genetic problem in non-decomposable bodies, in what sense would this constitute an advantage for naturephilosophy? Having demonstrated that the infinite decomposition of the universal is generative of particulars, where does the necessity for these transcendental buffers arise?

The basic flaw of the dynamic atoms lies not therefore in the role they play in naturephilosophy, but rather in the bridge they provide between naturephilosophy and the transcendental philosophy. By inserting 'simple actions' in place of simple bodies, the link between the construction of nature in philosophy and the naturalism of philosophical production ('all philosophy is productive', III, 351; 1978: 13) is simultaneously established as a continuity, and dissolved as production. That is, if 'all dynamic movement has its ultimate ground in the subject of nature itself, namely in the forces of which the visible world is merely their scaffold' (IV, 76), then supplanting the dynamic explanation by means of a wholly ideal one, *precisely undoes the 'parallelism between nature and intelligence'* (III, 331; 1978: 2) that it is the purpose of the *System of Transcendental Idealism* to unfold. The *System* (along with its naturephilosophical correlative, the *Universal Deduction*), as we shall see, constructs a more complex conception of nature than the *First Outline* does of the transcendental. In what follows, therefore, it is the actions of 'nature as subject' on the techniques of thinking that are at issue, since in one sense, in partial response to Vuillemin's point above, nature*philosophy* consists in a series of experiments in the provocation of thought forms by natural phenomena, or in the natural 'induction' of revolutions in thought – or, not to forget the point, in the *kosmoi noetois*, the worlds of intelligence.

Notes

1   So runs Kielmeyer's title for an unpublished sketch dating from 1790–93, predating the 'Oldest system-programme of German Idealism, (1796), whose uncertain authorship has caused it to be attributed, at various times, to Schelling (cf. Tilliette 1987: 26–43), Hölderlin, and Hegel. Frank (1975: 25–31) provides a more detailed account. See also Krell's translation and discussion of the text in *Owl of Minerva* 17 (1) (1985): 5–19.

2   'And Nature, asked why it brings forth its works, might answer if it cared to listen and speak: "It would have been more becoming to put no question but to learn in silence just as I myself am silent and make no habit of talking. And what is your lesson? This; that whatsoever comes into being is my vision, seen in my silence, the vision that belongs to my character who, sprung from my vision, am vision-loving and create vision by the vision-seeing power within me. The mathematicians from their vision draw their figures: but I draw nothing: I gaze and the figures of the material world take being as if they fell from my contemplation. As with my Mother (the All-Soul) and the beings that begot me so it is with me: they are born of a Contemplation and my birth is from them, not by their Act but by their being; they are the loftier reason-principles, they contemplate themselves and I am born."' (Plotinus III.8.iv) Schelling comments on this text in his 1806 polemic, *Presentation of the True Relation of Naturephilosophy to the Fichtean Theory, Improved* (VII, 78). Although it is commonly held that Schelling did not encounter neoplatonism until 1804, where it surfaces in *Philosophy and Religion* (cf. Peetz 1995: 133–4; Tilliette, 'Vision plotinienne et intuition schellingienne', 1987: 59 80), Harald Holz (1971) argues that Schelling was familiar with neoplatonism since 1798 (cf. Beiser 2002: 691n). Schelling's use of Plotinus' *kosmos neotos* in the *Timaeus* commentary (1994a: 30), of which Buchner notes, 'this concept is not found in Plato!' and refers to Plessing's commentaries as its possible source, at least suggests a second-hand acquaintance with neoplatonism even in 1794.

3   Leibniz's 'Specimen Dynamicum' (1695) discusses the law of continuity, 'which rules out changes taking place by leaps and bounds' as regards motion, which according to this law, consists in 'vanishingly small or minimal motion' (Leibniz 1998: 171). The *Principles of Nature and Grace* (1714) will deploy this to demonstrate that 'the whole of nature is full of life' (ibid.: 259).

4   Lovejoy (1964: 283–6) hesitantly grants the thesis that Bonnet may be accounted a 'forerunner of evolutionism' on the basis of his *perfectibility* argument: souls will achieve perfection once they have suffered the final natural revolution. If species are eternal, and suffer only that degree of perfectibility as is given to them in advance, then perfectibility only measures a state of the system immanent to it at any given time. As Geoffroy argued in 1833, Bonnet's theory postulated that 'organisms are and remain through the centuries what they have always been' (cited in Gould 1977: 18). Rather than continuing Darwin's canonization by having his forerunners failing to become him, Gould (1977: 17–28) offers a Bonnet heroically resisting phenomenalists and positivists alike.

5   *Philosophie Anatomique* is the title Geoffroy gives to a two-volume work in 1818–22, while his 'recapitulationist' successor in transformism, Etienne Serres, wrote 'Anatomie transcendente' in the *Annales des sciences naturelles* 21 (1830); both terms are used by E. S. Russell (1916), and are echoed by Lenoir (1981, 1982). Sloan 1992 calls the programme 'transcendental morphology' in order to include Goethe's science and Kant's philosophy.

6   Phillip Reid Sloan (1992: 26–7) makes an interesting case as to why Kant should be considered a Platonist. Based on Coleridge's differentiation of a 'sceptical' Kant from the 'true but secret teaching of Kant' in the *Biographia Literaria* (which Coleridge (1977: 88–94), in its briefest form, gives as the difference between the spirit and the letter of Kant's philosophy), Sloan cites Kant on the 'transcendental idea' as 'imposed by the very nature of reason itself' (CPR A327/B383–4) to argue that 'Kant held to the theory of the Divine Ideas of the Neoplatonic tradition', before applying this to the development of 'transcendental morphology' amongst the 'German anatomists'. Sloan thereby opposes the positivistic Kant encountered in the majority of historians of naturephilosophy. See Lenoir (1981, 1982), and Beiser (2002: 507–8, 684n) for the critique of the 'legacy of positivism' that besets Lenoir's Kant.

7   Deleuze makes more of the Leibnizian continuum underlying Geoffroy's 'unity of the plan of composition', making him 'one of the greatest philosophers of organic folding'. Yet Deleuze also makes Plato, for whom 'the forms are folded' (1993: 38) into a Leibnizian, answering, in so doing, the problem at the core of Geoffroy's trans-species natural connectivity. 'How', Deleuze asks (1993: 76), 'can the Many become the One? A great screen has to be placed between them. Like a formless elastic membrane, an electromagnetic field, or the receptacle of the *Timaeus*, the screen makes something issue from chaos, and *even if this something differs only slightly*.' For Deleuze, nature has always worked by imperceptible but thinkable differences.

8   On Cuvier's conflict with Geoffroy, see Appel 1987.

9   For Aristotle's *'megista gene'* or 'great kinds', see *History of Animals* 490b7–10, and see Depew and Weber's (1996: 33–50) account of this in relation to Cuvier. Depew and Weber oppose Cuvier's Aristotelian account to a parodically inadequate 'cookie cutter' model of Platonic physics they present Geoffroy and the *Naturphilosophen* as taking up, without noting Aristotle's own somatic corruption of the 'kinds' that underlie Platonic physics.

10   *Ak.* V, 417, 410; 1987: 303, 295, respectively. For further discussion of the collision of mechanical and teleological causal orders in Kant's riven philosophy of nature, see Grant 2000b: 44–52.

11   On catastrophism and uniformitarianism, see Gillespie (1996) and Gould (1987); for their concise summation of the problem, see Depew and Weber (1996: 94–8). For the statement of the uniformitarian principle, see James Hutton, 'Theory of the earth or an investigation of the laws observable in the composition, dissolution, and restoration of land upon the globe', *Transactions of the Royal Society of Edinburgh* 1: 209–305 (304), and Charles Lyell, *Principles of Geology*, abridged James A. Secord (Harmondsworth: Penguin, 1997): 16–17.

12   Sloan (1979: 148 n65) considers reviews and commentaries in Germany from 1750–54, following the publication of a German translation of Buffon's *Allgemeine Historie der*

Natur, Erster Theil in 1750, one year after Buffon's original. On the development of the concept of natural history from Buffon to Kant, Kielmeyer and Schelling, see Bach (2001: 200–32).

13 Oken is repeatedly singled out for abuse. To mention just two instances: Jardine (2000: 2) calls it a 'grotesque series . . . of deranged questions'; nor can Gould (1977: 39) resist, describing the *Lehrbuch der Naturphilosophie* (*Elements of Physiophilosophy*, 1847) as 'filled with bald, oracular pronouncements of the engaging sort that feign profundity but dissolve into emptiness upon close inspection. It is also responsible', he adds, 'for Oken's bad reputation as the most idle (if cosmic) speculator of a school rife with unreason'. However, what was held by Oken was not only held by him; Ignaz Döllinger, for example, equally holds that 'man, the pinnacle of the organic series, combines in himself all lower levels of organisation' (*Grundriss der Naturlehre des menschlichen Organismus.* Bamberg and Würzburg: Goebhardt, 1805, 10–11). So too Gottfried Reinhold Treviranus, generally more respected than Oken, not least because instead of calling his new science 'naturephilosophy' he coined the term 'biology' (1802), maintained, like Cuvier, that 'there were a certain number of "ground plans" in nature, by the "various combinations of which all other forms" arose. Because of this unity of type, Treviranus added, the "highest" and the "lowest" of nature's creations were bound together' (Clark and Jacyna 1987: 41).

14 See Goethe's *Experiment as Intermediary between Subject and Object* ([1793] 1975: 10–20), and Neubauer's essay on this 'theoretically foundational essay in Goethe's natural science' in Böhme and Schiemann (eds) (1997): 64–84.

15 Schelling writes (II, 381): 'These two conflicting forces conceived at the same time in conflict and unity, lead to the idea of an *organizing principle*, forming the world into a system. Perhaps the ancients wished to intimate this with the *world-soul*.'

16 Such access to the microscopic organic world would be supplied only in 1839, with the publication of Theodor Schwann's *Microscopical Researches into the accordance in the Structure and Growth of Animals and Plants.* Clark and Jacyna (1987: 387–8) provide a fascinating brief history of early microscopic ontology.

17 Ironically, Schelling criticizes Kielmeyer in almost identical terms to Novalis, although on the grounds of a perceived linearity in his account of the organic series in the *System of Philosophy as a Whole and Naturephilosophy in Particular* (1804): 'It is therefore false that the senses emerge in the same order in which the world of an organic being is extended. This law was also maintained by Kielmeyer in his *Discourse on the Relative Proportions of the Organic Forces.* Not only does natural history contradict him, however, so too does the necessary and universal type of all development.' (IV, 454)

18 Ziolkowski (1990: 31) cites Gotthilf Heinrich von Schubert: '"In general as I have shown elsewhere, the transition from the kingdom of minerals to that of plants and animals must in every respect be sought in the metals." Their combustibility hints at their chemical affinity with organic matter just as their color and shape imitate the higher organic world. "The whole kindgom of metals", he [Schubert] concludes, "seems to have arisen at the boundaries of two worlds, from the decline and deterioration of the anorganic, and to bear within itself the seeds of the new organic age."' (Schubert, *Ansichten von der Nachtseite der Naturwissenschaften,* 1808). Ritter, too, considered the metals transitional across Blumenbach's gulf, characterizing 'the universe as a second-order voltaic body' ([1810] 1984: 245), and making iron into the foetus of the inorganic world: 'All matters on the earth seem to be disintegrations of iron. Iron is the earth's core . . . and [is found] in the blood and in organic substances in general' ([1810] 1984: 78). In a report ordered by the Prussian government into the prospect of a chair in Animal Magnetism at the University of Berlin in 1816, Christoph Wilhelm Hufeland 'was convinced that every organism produces, in addition to warmth, also "a magnetic and still finer vital atmosphere" [*Journal für praktische Heilkunde* (March 1817): 129], and that "this animal magnetism is absolutely analogous to mineral magnetism, only in its living potency"' (cited

in Gode von Aesch 1966: 161). It is Heinrik Steffens who goes furthest in this direction, generating a much-cited dynamic chemistry of the inorganic and organic kingdoms in 'On the oxydation and deoxydation process on the earth' (in Schelling 2001: 93–110) and in the *Contributions to the Inner Natural History of the Earth* (1801), in which Steffens combines geognosy with chemistry and physics into a *Proof that nitrogen and carbon are the representatives of magnetism in the chemical series* (chs I–VI), before moving on to comparative anatomy and generation, where he argues that '*Blumenbach's Bildungstrieb* may explain ongoing generation, but not the *emergence* of vegetation and animalization' (1801: 279–80). See 5.1, below.

19 Jardine (2000: 33–43), Rehbock (in Cunningham and Jardine (eds) 1990: 147f), Snelders (1970: 196) and, although he remains unclear on the topic, Ayrault (1976: 300f), all present Kielmeyer as just another analogizer. Lenoir keeps company with Coleman (1973) and, most recently, Bach (2001: 239–41) in rejecting this view.

20 The full passage runs thus: 'The question of what then can be assembled as a Plan of Nature for the alterations of the relations of these forces from these individual laws can now be answered thus: the capacity for sensation is gradually suppressed through the series of organisations by stimulability and the reproductive force, and finally even the irritability of the latter weakens: the more the one is raised, the lower is that of the other, and at the very least sensibility and the reproductive force accommodate each other; further, the more of these forces is developed on the one side, the more it is diminished on the other.' (Kielmeyer 1938: 90–1)

21 Peterson (2004: 16) gives 'apparent products' for *Scheinprodukte*, which misses the consequence of phenomena being physically generated as nature's products, which understanding is key to Schelling's programme in the *First Outline*. See 4.2, below.

22 Kielmeyer, borrowing the concept from Johann Hermann's 'table of animal affinities', does not apply it only as a classificatory tool, as Hermann had, but speculatively considers it as the neuroanatomy of whole animal series, rather than individual products within a series: 'I had intertwined the nerves of one individual with those of the others into a net, and the impressions on the nerves of the one would be felt in the sensorium of the other' (1938: 64). See also Bach (2001: 102–3), citing Kielmeyer's mention of the net as a classificatory concept in the letter to Windischmann (1804). The problem concerns the instantiation of the plan of nature in nature. Cf. Chapter 5, above.

23 This is Lenoir's (1982: 4–5, 14) phrasing, and it is by this accommodation of Blumenbach the scientist to Kant the *crit*ical philosopher, that Lenoir makes his case for the rejection not simply of any actual, historical 'influence' of the naturephilosophers on the development, in particular, of the late eighteenth-century life sciences.

24 Of the XIV points specified in the prospectus of the programme opening Kielmeyer's 'On natural history', I–IV concern the concept of the science and the human mental powers operative within it, V offers the machine hypothesis familiar from the *Rede*, while VI–XIV extends from the 'history of the terrestrial sphere', its various strata and their cooperation, to an attempt at a graduated account of geogeny (Kielmeyer 1938: 211).

25 Oryctology is the late eighteenth century's term for what has been known, following Cuvier's successor at the Museum Nationale d'Histoire Naturelle, Ducrotayé de Blainville's coinage in 1834, as palaeontology. See Coleman (1977: 63ff), Appel (1987: 212) and Edwards (1976: 40–1).

26 It is usual to date the versions of the *Ages of the World* between 1811–15, since these are the versions comprised within the *SW* and Schröter's *Nachlassband* (1946). Apart, however, from the *Weltalter-Fragmente* (2002) of 1810–21, recently edited by Klaus Grotsch from Schelling's Berlin Nachlass, Siegbert Peetz has also published the *System der Weltalter* (2nd edn 1998) from Ernst von Lasaulx's transcriptions of Schelling's lectures in Munich from 1827–8. For all this, the *Weltalter* projects remain incomplete.

27 Jantzen and Kisser note, at *AA* I, 6: 283f, that one such sceptic was Girtanner, usefully echoing our counterpoint in this section. In his *Foundations of Antiphlogistican Chemistry*

(1795: 14), the Kantian writes: 'Light-matter is a merely hypothetically assumed *body*, the existence of which seems not yet to be proven. Perhaps light is not a specific matter, but rather a simple modification of caloric, by means of which it becomes capable of making a certain impression on *our visual organs . . .*' (emphasis added). Again we note the a priori somatism Girtanner shares with the other Kantians, as well as the requirement that phenomena be derived not from nature, but from their effects on the human mind or sensory apparatus. Who would have thought that a book with a title such as Girtanner's would expose the transhistorically arrogant humanism that lies at the root of the transcendental enterprise. As regards the speed of light, Galileo used torches, shutters and distant observers around 1600 in a failed attempt to measure it, while Descartes disagreed that light had a finite velocity. By the eighteenth century, however, through accumulating work from Römer (1676), supported by Halley, and Bradley (1729), although it was not until the mid-nineteenth century that the latter's findings were confirmed (cf. Pledge 1966: 69, 137; AA I, 6: 283n).

28 Schelling's 'equations' are linear insofar as, in Rescher's (2000: 23n) economical terms, they 'characterise a system whose functioning can be described by the smooth curves of everywhere differentiable equations. The behaviour of such systems is thus calculation-friendly and predictable.'

29 Further examples from the *World Soul* alone: 'as regards magnets', Schelling cites Daniel Bernouilli as having asserted that 'the absolute force of artificial magnets always increases as the cube root of the square of gravity, which amounts to the same as *in proportion to their surfaces*' (II, 482); or Sömmering on the effect of neurological complexity on the ethology of organs: 'voluntary movement in an organ increases with the number and size of its nerves' (II, 562), and so on.

30 Amongst the important variations of this proposition are the markedly Aristotelian: 'real antithesis is only thinkable where the opposing things are equally posited in one and the same subject', or its first edition, more dynamic variant, 'between *magnitudes* of the same kind' (II, 390).

31 Despite the Würzburg *System*'s apparent dismissal of the '*Urkeim*', the 1803 'Supplement to chapter 4' of the *Ideas* gives 'Matter [as] the general seed-korn [*Samenkorn*] of the universe, in which is hidden everything that unfolds in the later developments' (II, 223; 1988: 179). While this may seem to be an overt contradiction, no surprise perhaps to those who, following Hegel, consider that 'Schelling conducted his education in public' (*Wz* 20: 105), such a finding presupposes that the dilemma Schelling offers be resolved in the negative, rather than, as is consistent with both propositions, that *everything* is primal germ *because* (a) everything is matter, and (b) all matter is the matter of becoming, as we have seen in this section.

32 On 'amplitude', Rescher writes: 'our cognitive efforts manifest a Manichean-style struggle between complexity and simplicity – between the impetus to comprehensiveness (amplitude) and the impetus to system (economy)' (Rescher 2000: 37). Rescher's 'amplitude' corresponds to our 'extensity' (cf. 1.1, above).

33 For more on Ritter's 'galvanic self-experiments', see Ritter (1986: 101–4). I have briefly discussed these in relation to a physicalized transcendental in my ' "Philosophy become genetic": The Physics of the World Soul', in Norman and Welchman (eds) (2004: 142–4).

34 As a result of an unusual combination of ontological realism and epistemological antirealism, Rescher's contention that 'natural reality has an infinite descriptive depth' (2000: 26) entails, as he puts it, 'a precommitment to description-transcending features . . . is essential to our conception of what it is to be a real, concrete object' (2000: 31). In this, Rescher is close to Schelling's problems. Since Rescher's quasi-transcendentalism halts at 'descriptive inexhaustibility' and 'cognitive incompleteness', however, he introduces the same gulf between nature and ideation that prevented Kant from 'turning his account of natural science into naturephilosophy' (VI, 8). In other words, since it is the positive excess of the real over cognition, the irreducible localism even of a network of every extant

cognitive apparatus (real and artificial brains) with respect to nature, that *generates* such descriptive/cognitive deficits, then the necessarily asymmetrical relation of product to productivity is already an unacknowledged physics of the Idea.

CHAPTER 5

'What thinks in me is what is outside me':
Phenomenality, Physics, and the Idea

What am I thinking when I think what exists? (X, 303)

Schelling cannot simply abandon the transcendental. Kant and Fichte at the very least invented a new terrain for philosophical activity, but did not exploit it sufficiently; and Fichte, especially, showed a considerable grasp of the powers of abstraction. Such powers, since they are demonstrably actuable, require therefore a physical grounding to remove them from the 'unnature' the transcendentalists have established as taking the place, in 'all branches of culture and education' of nature (VII, 80). Between the *First Outline of a System of Naturephilosophy* and the *Introduction to the Outline* (both 1799), the *System of Transcendental Idealism* and the *Universal Deduction of the Dynamical Process* (both 1800), and the *First* and *Further Presentations from the System of Philosophy* (1801–2), Schelling will progressively work on the naturalization of the abstract, or the physics of ideation. The fundamental shift in the transcendental is achieved not simply by severing it from, or balancing it against, the naturephilosophy, as Eschenmayer (1801; cf. 3.4, above) presented it, but rather by demonstrating that the grounds of the finitude of transcendental reflection are not simply *logical*, as Hegel will present it (1801), but rather *physical*, and concern the relation between productivity and product. The transcendental is productive in the pursuit of conditions, but, having established such conditions *as* conditions, mere product when it accordingly determines a thought *as* thus conditioned. There is an energetic cost, in other words, to thought about thought. Hence 'the identity of dynamics and the transcendental', as the *System of Transcendental Idealism* has it (III, 452; 1978: 91).

It is in consequence of the derivative nature of the product with respect to productivity that Schelling's transcendentalism begins with the assertion: 'nature IS *a priori*' (III, 279; 2004: 198), but immediately raises the problem of how a nature can be thus a priori and, at the same time, 'unconditioned'. Accordingly, Schelling completely reinvents a transcendental philosophy that must reverse through the series of conditions until it discovers either the 'unconditioned [*das Unbedingte*] in nature' (III, 22; 2004: 20) that 'cannot be any *thing*' (III, 11; 2004: 13), or that nature *is* unconditioned. It is here that Schelling's attempt to generate a genetic philosophy from Platonism, to which project *On the World Soul* (1798) was the most recent contribution, joins forces with the philosophy of dynamics as emerging not simply from Boscovich and Priestley, but importantly, from Kielmeyer. For if nature *is* unconditioned, Platonic physics is eliminated. If on the other hand there is not so much an *unconditioned* as an *unthinged in* nature, then nature consists of 'a plurality of being and an infinity of not-being' (*Soph.* 256d9–e7).

Asserting the primacy of the physical, as Schelling's transcendentalism does against the Kanto-Fichtean primacy of the practical, is not simply a move within the history of transcendental philosophy, however, but entails a conjunction of naturephilosophy and the diverse branches of natural science. Nor does this mean that Schelling will cede philosophical authority to the natural sciences as regards nature, in the manner that Kant offers mechanical explanation 'unlimited authority' (*Ak.* V, 417; 1987: 303). It is precisely because this cession of *physis* to the sciences misconceives the *nature of nature* that its critical delimitation of metaphysics *by its border with physics* is premature on *naturephilosophical grounds*. Since it is this basic contention that Schelling claims strikes at the ethical heart of all modern philosophy, it is necessary, in order to test this thesis, to chart this obscure border – so natural to thought now that 'unnature' has taken the place of nature, and 'has been able to bear such bloom and fruits as the Fichtean philosophy' (VII, 80) – as it recurs in the 'various forms occurring in contemporary philosophy' (Hegel, *Wz* 2, 15ff; 1977a: 85ff), notably in Deleuze's account of natural ideation, and his general ontology, which inquiry, he writes, 'must embrace all the concepts of nature and freedom' (1994: 19).

If Schelling does not cede philosophical authority to the sciences, finally, nor yet does this mean that the naturephilosophy takes up the office of critical judge presiding over them. The 'reduplicative positing' (X, 103; 1994b: 117; 1989a: 50) evident in metaphysics conceived as the 'physics of physics', the logic proper to the 'double series' of transcendental science (III, 397; 1978: 49), points not to turning the 'doctrine of science' into 'philosophy about philosophy' (IV, 84), but rather that, like all 'true philosophical science', it pursue 'cognition of the All' (VII, 50). If it is not simply to provide analyses of phenomena that satisfy merely formal criteria, Schelling's Platonic measure of cognitive adequacy further requires that naturephilosophy be pursued in common with 'the thinking heads of the age' (III, 326; 2004: 232). Schelling is repeatedly overt, as in the Foreword to the *Annals of Medicine as Science* (1805), in proposing that naturephilosophy become a 'common labour' amongst 'philosophers and natural scientists of all kinds' (VII, 131).[1] Naturephilosophy, then, not only theoretically exceeds the transcendental, but also practically exceeds the isolated 'thinking head', the *Ich*, of the transcendental philosopher. Since, then, naturephilosophy must simultaneously pursue naturalistic investigations of the transcendental, or the physics of the Idea, alongside philosophical investigations of natural phenomena, no account of the naturephilosophy will prove adequate without an examination of the situation of natural history – the ground (not merely in the formal sense) of the genetic philosophy as Schelling develops this from

Plato – from which the naturephilosophy will develop beyond the remit of assessing the sciences from the perspective of their empirical input or their theoretical impetus alone.

5.1 THE SUBJECT OF NATURE ITSELF

An original antithesis of forces in the ideal subject of nature appears necessary to every construction. (IV, 5)

Anything whose conditions simply cannot be given in nature, must be absolutely impossible. (III, 571; 1978: 186)

Although we have pursued a dynamic succession of stages through nature, the genetic problem remains unresolved. What, that is, is the basal unit or 'subject' of recapitulation? All Schelling's solutions to this problem consist in various determinations of subjectivity in nature, and can be grouped initially into three: is 'nature as a whole . . . one and the same organisation' (II, 348), as the *World Soul* argues following the *Ideas* (II, 54; 1988: 40), or are there 'infinitely many' natural subjects, as according to the *First Outline*? The third consists in a non-linear and a linear variant of the combination of the previous two: either, that is, the subject of recapitulation is recapitulation itself, *regardless of the particularity of the product* (the identity thesis); or a 'universal world organisation' is the necessary condition of possible and particular 'self-organisation' (II, 482). As naturephilosophy or speculative physics, each hypothesis is conjointly a philosophical and a physical experiment: in the range of chemical decomposition and recomposition; in the constructibility of Boscovichian point-atomism; in the limits of recapitulationism, and in the nature of self-organization.

It is therefore important to note that the solutions Schelling proposes are to hold for *all* subjectivity. Even *Of the I* (1795), for instance, postulates an '*Urform*' or original form of the *Ich* as 'absolute identity' (I, 179; 1980: 83), that is rigorously non-specific as regards its actual instantiations, so that the *Urform* applies 'no matter what the *Ich* is' (I, 217; 1980: 110). This postulate is effectively reiterated in the *System of Transcendental Idealism*, where, since 'the concept of the *Ich* is merely the concept of becoming an object to oneself' (III, 366; 1978: 25), and since this corresponds to 'nature's highest aim' (III, 341; 1978: 6), 'self-consciousness' is simply 'nature . . . at its highest power [*Potenz*]' (III, 355; 1978: 14). From the other direction, for example, the *Ideas*, alongside its 'systematic overview of nature's operations' (II, 174; 1988: 136), pursues the 'natural history of our mind' (II, 39; 1988: 30) from the ground up, through chemistry as 'sensory dynamics' (II, 323–4; 1988: 257), echoing Ritter's self-experiments regarding the electrical alterability of the senses (1986: 101–4). If, as the *System* puts it, 'all philosophy must go about *either* to make an intelligence out of nature, *or* a nature out of intelligence' (III, 342; 1978: 7), the making in question is not arbitrary or voluntaristic, but naturalistic on both sides. That is, that 'nature IS *a priori*' (III, 279; 2004: 198) is the ground of all Schelling's transcendental experiments, regardless of which direction they take, whether 'animating laws of nature into laws of mind' or 'materialising laws of mind into laws of nature' (III, 352; 1978: 14, t.m.). A naturalized transcendental, having already been the subject of Reil's investigations into the *Grundkraft* from which the Kantian *Vermögen* or 'powers' derive,[2] was the research goal not just of Schelling, but constituted the dynamist vanguard of the late eighteenth century just as neuroanatomical materialism currently dominates the sciences of mind. Besides therefore being proof that 'a continuous galvanism accompanies the vital process in the animal kingdom', Ritter's 'autogalvanic' experiments are therefore attempts at a dynamic transcendentalism. Thus, 'optics is a transcendental chemistry in which we *see* matter' (1984: 139) or 'geometry whose lines are drawn in light' (III, 340; 1978: 6), while magnetism and electricity are the polar forces by which time and space arise (1984: 247). When therefore Schelling talks of 'the phenomena of electricity' (II, 131; 1988: 79), for example, both the phenomenality and the physics in effect define the naturalized transcendental: given nature's *a priority*, the forces that produce phenomena are not in us, but in things; were it not the case that physical forces create phenomena, how could they arise at all? The *System* makes the case plainly:

> The assumption that things are just what we take them to be, so that we are acquainted with them as they are *in themselves*, underlies the possibility of all experience (for what would experience be, and to what aberrations would physics, for example, be subject, without this presupposition of absolute identity between appearance and reality?). (III, 347; 1978: 10)

The phenomenon, in other words, does not hover above the thing in itself or coat it like a film, but is rather the identity of thing-in-itself and experience. The aim therefore of a natural science is 'to let nature act before our eyes, and to narrate what we observe as it strikes our senses' (II, 258–9; 1988: 207), and consciousness is '*filled* with the real object' (II, 269; 1988: 216).[3] Concomitantly, transcendental philosophy completes its task 'only if it can demonstrate this identity . . . in its own principle (namely, the *Ich*)' (III, 349; 1978: 12). This is why the two 'grounding sciences' of transcendental and naturephilosophy are 'necessary counterparts' of one another (III, 331; 1978: 3): its entire business is the demonstration or 'exposition' of identities, or of the 'coincidence of nature and mind' (II, 55–6; 1988: 41–2; cf. III, 339; 1978: 5), in which nature itself 'necessarily and originally' consists. By virtue of the predominance of Fichteanism in philosophy, the naturalistic side of Schelling's thesis of 'duplicity in identity' is most often overlooked in accounts of the transcendental philosophy, while the transcendental aspects of the naturephilosophy are hyped. Yet that there is a coincidence of nature's activities and those of intelligence is necessary if experience and knowledge are possible at all. Further, the cognition of the universe by which Schelling assesses philosophical adequation is not a reversible metric, as if the universe could be measured against 'our knowledge'. Since the 'final outcome of natural science' is 'the principle of transcendental philosophy' (III, 357; 1978: 17), i.e., the 'becoming an object to itself' that is 'the concept of the *Ich*' (III, 366; 1978: 25), the 'originality' of the naturephilosophy and the 'derivative' nature of the transcendental is clearly stipulated, from which it also follows that, from the point of view of philosophy's only measurement, the transcendental philosophy is regional with respect to the whole, and the *Ich* – which is 'merely the concept of becoming an object to oneself' – is a regional rather than a universal achievement of nature. Hence the *System*'s repeated emphasis on the 'limited nature of [its] whole task' (III, 355, 357; 1978: 14, 18): for Schelling, the knowledge is not transcendental insofar as it determines nature for consciousness; rather nature is transcendental with regard to the production and producing of intelligence. Since on no account 'can something that forms only the limitation of a science be made into the measure of the grounds of science in general' (V, 137), it is not the transcendental, but rather the naturephilosophy that is not the primary science of Schellingian philosophy, formally and materially. Nature is too large for finite reflective consciousness precisely because it is nature that generates it anew with each electromagnetic pulse.

In consequence, however, the *World Soul*'s overtly 'philosophically derived postulate' (II, 351) of 'nature as a whole' seems unwittingly to follow the Fichtean paradigm which, issuing the imperative: 'the entire universe *ought to be* an organised whole' (*GA* II, 3: 247), distributes the nature of this whole according to what Schelling identifies as a disjunction: '*either* A *or* B', where A = *Ich* and B = nature. Since Fichte denies intelligence in nature, the ethicism of its 'ought' strikes 'nature the final deathblow' (VII, 445). The reason Schelling posits 'nature as a whole' does indeed concern a subjectivity, although not of the transcendental or ethicizing sort. Although, that is, nature itself cannot satisfy its 'highest aim' of becoming an object to itself, it remains a subject, and subjectivity arises in nature. Again, the regionality of finite intelligence with respect to nature necessarily entails the regional exhibition of intelligence within it. What is at stake is therefore the 'subject of nature itself' (IV, 76) or 'nature as subject' (III, 284; 2004: 202), which, sourced from Kielmeyer's '*Ich* [*DIE NATUR*]' (1938: 64), follows its logic in the theory of recapitulation. Schelling hesitantly sets out the conjunction of that theory with 'nature as a whole' in the *Ideas*:

> Universal attraction and equilibrium have long been regarded as the law of the universe, and from then on every attempt to have the whole of nature act, even in subordinate systems, according to the same laws by which it acts in the system of the whole has been viewed as a valuable achievement. (II, 178; 1988: 141)

'Nature', in other words, is 'gathered up into a single whole' (II, 54; 1988: 40) insofar as the laws of the whole are also the laws of subordinate systems, so that the whole recapitulates itself in particulars. Again, the grounds of the *World Soul*'s 'whole nature' postulate are naturalistic. Accordingly, the subject of nature in the *World Soul* is a subject in permanent 'self-decom- position'.[4] This is why the *World Soul* follows through the decomposition of the first by the second force: in light (II, 387) and the decomposition of the 'solar atmosphere' from which it derives (II, 394); in air but not, following H. B. de Saussure's experiments, in water (II, 435); in oxygen (II, 441) all the way to its decomposition in animal respiration (II, 494–5) and in blood (II, 539). There are chemical, mechanical and electrical modes of decomposition. Galvanism is a mode of decomposition (II, 556). Finally, however, decom- position accounts for the emergence of specific matters, as, for example, electrical matter is 'decomposed oxygen' (II, 574).

The entirety of the *World Soul* is consumed by the decomposition of the first and second forces. The grounds for the 'philosophical postulate' of the infinite decomposability of matter are again naturalistic, and lie in chemistry: indecomposability was the means whereby Lavoisier maintained the atomism pioneered in chemistry by Boyle and Dalton, against the 'phlogistical chemists' such as Stahl, Schulzer and Brandis (*AA* Ergbd.1: 4–13), who 'wanted to eliminate the concept "element" from chemistry' (*AA* Ergbd.1: 15). In the *Elementary Treatise on Chemistry* (1789), Lavoisier argued that 'if we attach to the term "element" or "principle" of bodies the idea of a final term reached by analysis, all substances that have hitherto been indecom- posable by any means are "elements" for us' (cited in *AA* Ergbd.1: 13). Indecomposables, elements, thus obstruct the infinite decomposition of nature, grounding natural products in determinable individuals, and once more reducing matter to corporeality. Although he adopts oxygen as the 'basic material' of the 'vital air' (Novalis (1996: 300) even calls Schelling 'the philosopher of the new chemistry, the absolute oxygenist')[5] and as the 'acid- generator' after which function Lavoisier named it, Schelling opposes the antiphlogistical chemistry because it entails the existence of 'specific matters' that vitiate the 'self-construction of matter' (IV, 4) on which the dynamic philosophy is premised (cf. II, 347–8; IV, 76). Against the postulate of a priori individuated matters, therefore, the *World Soul* postulates in turn[6] that 'it is necessary to think all matter as homogeneous as regards substance; for only insofar as *it is homogeneous with itself* is it susceptible of a *bifurcation*, that is, a *real* antithesis' (II, 390).

Prior then to Kielmeyer's interventions, the grounds of Schelling's 'one and the same organisation' (II, 348) are the conflict regarding the chemical construction of matter: either analysis yields chemical simples, or matter is infinitely decomposable. When therefore Schelling stipulates that 'things are not the principles of organism, but rather conversely, *organism is the principle of things*' (II, 500), the claim is not simply the commonplace caricature of naturephilosophy as universal organicism, but rather for organ- ization, since 'the original disposition of matter to organisation lies certainly in the formative forces proper to matter as such' (II, 565). Accordingly, it is not from the sciences of the organic, but from 'chemical operations . . . from which alone we may conceive the formation of matter' (II, 498–9). In common with Fichteanism, or the philosophical determination of physics by ethics, as Windischmann's 'Exposition of the concept of physics' recommends (in Schelling 1969, 1: 91; cf. 3.4, above), what assertions of organicism omit is precisely the physicalistic ground of organization in the formation of matter, the omission of which is due entirely to the 'old illusion' maintained by the Kant-Blumenbach hypothesis: 'that organisation and life are inexplicable from natural principles' (II, 348).

The *First Outline*'s 'dynamic atomism' seems all the more surprising in this light, since, like the *World Soul*, it seeks 'to derive [*abzuleiten*] the dynamic graduated sequence of stages in nature' (III, 6; 2004: 6), but, by way of the dynamic atoms or 'simple actions', reverts to finite divisibility. The grounds of this hypothesis are twofold. Firstly, the *World Soul*'s 'nature as a whole' pursues an infinitely decomposable nature, a homogeneity of natural principles, and an infinitely divisible matter in order to ground what the *Ideas* calls 'the universal [*allgemeine*] law of bifurcation [*Entzweiung*]' (II, 254; 1988: 203, t.m.; cf. II, 21–2; 1988: 17). Yet the presumption of a primary substance, substrate or subject that *underlies* and precedes nature's *self-*decomposition, apparently implicit in this postulate, undermines the dynamics, the proportions and relations of the first and the second forces, with which the work begins. An Aristotelian trap is sprung on the *World Soul*'s *Stufenfolge*: *there must be*, runs the thesis, *a primary substance-substrate-subject (ousia, hypokeimenon) from which* 'formed substances' *derive, and in which the powers (dunameis) inhere*. Being-as-*ousia* thus undermines the primacy of dynamics, of the 'infinite becomings' that form the latticework of the Platonic kinds and Kielmeyer's 'net', to the precise extent that it *underlies* them as substance or subject. Since for Schelling as for Plato, the problem is not the being that underlies becoming, but rather the becoming of being, 'the concept of Being as something originary must be completely eliminated' from naturephilosophy. This is not to say that being as such is eliminated, but only an *originating* or primordial being; rather 'being itself is construction itself' (III, 12; 2004: 14, t.m.).

Secondly, however, although 'nature as a whole' amounts to a 'philosophical postulate', it is not reducibly a conceptual facilitator, but follows from the indissociability of the first and second forces. Were the forces dissociable, that is, there would be no decomposition or recomposition in nature, or, in the language of the *First Outline*, productivity would yield no products. Deleuze undergoes the same problem. Inverting the Platonic dictum that 'materialists, if at all intelligent, should speak of power rather than bodies', Deleuze makes the following claim: 'it is true, conversely, that intelligent dynamists must first speak of bodies, in order to "think" power' (1992: 257). The Eleatic Stranger's postulate that 'the definition of being is simply power' (*Soph.* 247e4), however, arises due to his criticisms of those materialists that identify 'body and substance [*soma kai ousian*]' (*Soph.*

246a9–b1) and thus restrict nature to the 'somatic [*somatoeides*]' (*Stat.* 273b5; *Tim.* 31b5). Since, ultimately, the basic science of Platonic as of Schellingian physics is neither somatics nor mechanics, but dynamics, bodies must be derivable from forces or the 'becoming' or 'construction' of being becomes an arbitrary formalism. Since Deleuze must be included amongst the 'intelligent dynamists', we must conclude that it is not on ontological grounds that this somatic primacy is constructed. And so it is. Just as *Difference and Repetition* sets out its ontological stall over Kantian faultlines when Deleuze announces 'this enquiry must embrace all the concepts of *nature and freedom*' (1994: 19, emphasis added), thus establishing an insurmountable ontological difference between the two 'domains', so too the dynamist turns out to be intelligent not in accordance with nature, but freedom: 'The theory of power according to which actions and passions of the body accompany actions and passions of the soul amounts to an ethical vision of the world' (1992: 257).

The 'embodied individual' is for Deleuze the locus of freedom, but at the cost of naturalistic consistency. Once again the conjunction of organovitalism and the 'ethical vision of the world' vitiates the project of a dynamic ontology from which actions issue, rather than a voluntaristic dynamism issuing from a somatic principle.[7] Although Schelling vehemently rejects the 'moralizing of the entire world that undermines life and hollows it out, a true disgust towards all nature and vitality except that in the subject, the crude extolling of morality and the doctrine of morals as the one reality in life and science . . .' (VII, 19), the problem Deleuze is operating on is common to them both. That is, without somatic principles, how is the actual determination of products and their series in nature to be philosophically accounted for; where, in other words, can the search for a basal and stabilizing resolution of the genetic problem terminate? Thus, where Deleuze introduces a body (thereby inheriting all the problems of the linear recapitulationists),[8] Schelling goes in the other direction entirely, initiating the search for the 'unthinged in nature' (III, 11; 2004: 11). As the *First Outline* makes clear from its opening enquiries into the nature of the unthinged, it is to *this* problem that the dynamic atoms or simple actions are a proposed solution. This is why the *First Outline* presents its version of Boscovich's 'point atomism' (cf. Crosland (ed.) 1971: 210–13) as 'ideal explanatory grounds':

As ideal explanatory grounds, we have posited in matter simple actions of indeterminate, that is, infinite, diversity. This explanatory ground is ideal since it is premised on something ideal, namely: that nature has evolved thus far from the simple. Were we to go further along this path, we would arrive at an atomistic system. However, due to its inadequacy, this system would in the end drive us back to the dynamic system. (III, 22n; 2004: 24n)

Dynamic atomism is conceptually therefore the direct antithesis of the *World Soul*'s 'nature as a whole', the naturalistic flaw which Schelling identifies as resting on the assumption of an 'already completed evolution'; were this the case, the 'universal decomposition of every product into its factors would leave nothing remaining as simple factors'. Hazarding the term 'original productivities', Schelling cannot affirm their existence in nature – and as such, 'they do not exist' – but only that they must be *thought* in nature 'in order to explain original qualities', qualities which constitute 'fixed point[s] from which nature can begin to form itself' (III, 22n; 2004: 24n). Schelling's own verdict on this antinaturalistic aberration, in the *On University Studies* (1802), is scathing: 'The true annihilation of nature is in any case that which makes it into a whole of absolute qualities, limits and affections, which as it were may be considered as ideal atoms' (V, 275).

Although Schelling gives as a reason for the physical non-existence of these 'ideal atoms' the formal one that were they assumed to be material, the imposition of limitations on the divisibility of matter would return the system to atomism, there is also a physical reason, namely, that the separability of productivities from products entails finite units of productivity that would then require an additional cause to assemble them into products. In attempting a solution to the problem of the determinacy of products in nature, or how 'plurality and individuality' arise within it, 'naturephilosophy acknowledges with the atomist, that there is an original manifold of individual principles in nature' (ibid.) – again directly opposing the *World Soul*'s postulate of 'the original homogeneity of all positive natural principles' (II, 351) – the *First Outline* introduces a symmetry break between the construction of nature and the determination of natural individuals in ideation.

The issue is not reducible to a 'bottom up' construction from simples to complexes (*First Outline*) as against a 'top down' decomposition of relative simplicity from massive complexity (*World Soul*), but rather concerns the relation of nature and ideation. Whereas the 'law of universal bifurcation' sufficed to *construct* the manner in which nature self-decomposed into relative individuals, the 'laws of mind' have not yet been demonstrated to be 'realised . . . necessarily and originally' by nature (II, 55–6; 1988: 41–2), in which 'expressing and realising' nature properly consists. Nor, similarly, does the introduction of the thinkable but non-physical 'original productivities' into nature achieve 'nature' as such. Schelling's famous declaration at the beginning of the *First Outline* – 'to philosophise about nature is to *create* nature' (III, 13; 2004: 13) – although grounded metaphysically in the objection to 'nature as a unique being originally present to us', remains unrealized by nature. This is especially clear in that Schelling invokes the 'simple actions' as 'fixed points or nucleii from which nature can begin to form itself' (III, 22n; 2004: 24n).

Yet in the stumbling passages in which dynamic atomism – 'neither dynamic . . . nor atomistic' (ibid.) – is outlined, the problem of natural individuation is precisely resolved by means of the emergence of natural subjectivity, or the putative 'self-forming' of nature. The 'Idea of a self-organising matter' (II, 47; 1988: 35) remained on the one hand an index of

a 'natural kind of philosophising (*autophysis philosophia*)' (XI, 258), while
on the other, an Idea, introducing the *auto* therefore into nature. Apart, that
is, from the formal reasons for Schelling's hypothesis, the simple action or
original productivity is explicitly said to be the 'nucleus [*Keim*]' around which
'nature can begin to form itself' (III, 22n; 2004: 24n). Thus, by way of the
various attempts to resolve the identity of the genetic element or basal type
(to which we return below), the necessity that the Idea is, as Böhme put it,
'nature in the strict sense' (2000: 18), is reintroduced, although not resolved:
in place of the 'intelligent dynamist's' body, such an Idea would introduce
'vortices and turbulences' into becomings (III, 18n; 2004: 18n). Or it would
do, were it not *reducibly* ideal: that the hypothesis is marked by renouncing
a physical solution to the genetic problem – to what Novalis aptly called the
search for 'the primal germ of nature' (1996: 440) – is consequent upon the
rejection of Kielmeyerian postulates. While proclaiming itself 'at one with
dynamic physics' to the extent that it grounds nature not in any 'smallest
material parts' but in activity, naturephilosophy differs from dynamics 'in the
prevailing sense of the term' in that 'it does not agree that the diversity of
matter consists in particular proportions of the forces' (III, 22n; 2004: 24n).
This is because 'neither the mechanism nor the ground of [the] succession
of stages has been discovered up to now' (III, 195n; 2004: 141n), and
insofar as this mechanism and ground are lacking, there is as yet no account
of the emergence and maintenance of specific differences in nature.

Following the *System*, which introduces its own method for the production
of particularity – one that, not accidentally, corresponds to Steffens'
procedure in his *Inner Natural History of the Earth* – the dynamic sequence
of stages will find its ground in the 'self-construction of matter' (IV, 4).
Despite the overtly idealist aberration that is the theory of dynamic atomism,
the *First Outline* therefore pursues the 'unthinged in nature' by other means.
Since this pursuit is neither naturalistically nor philosophically satisfied by
a 'not-in-nature' – because, that is, 'anything whose conditions simply
cannot be given in nature must be absolutely impossible' (III, 571; 1978: 186)
– the hypothesis of dynamic atomism is confined to a lengthy footnote, and
Schelling's 'experiments in dynamic physics' (IV, 114) continue. If the
'unthinged in nature' cannot be an object, it must therefore be a subject:
building therefore on the theory of the 'nature-subject' with which
Kielmeyer's *Rede* began (1938: 64f), the *First Outline*'s 'nature as subjectivity'
grounds the introduction of the Idea, the *auto kath'auto* or 'itself according
to itself', the unconditioned or unthinged, in nature. In brief, the philosophical roots of subjectivity belong to the line stretching from the Platonic
Idea, which is *auto kath'auto*, itself by itself, to the 'thing in itself', which
Idea 'had lost all meaning' in the Kantian philosophy (II, 33; 1988: 26).
Schellingian subjectivity is not therefore the eliminative subjectivism of its
Kantian variant, but reinstates the objectivity of the subjective. Accordingly,
when the *First Outline* specifies nature's *a priority*, its 'autonomy' and its
'autarchy' as grounding the naturephilosophy, 'nature as subjectivity' means
simply nature *itself*, nature *to auto*, that owes more to repairing the

Aristotelian rift in Platonic physics than to any post-Cartesian conception of subjectivity. Even *Of the Ich* (1795) is more concerned with the function of principles than with the content of reflection, and is more a theory of 'what is by itself', of the 'unthinged', or of 'absolute identity' (I, 178–9; 1980: 83), than a philosophy of reflective consciousness. Schellingian subjectivity is therefore neither substrate nor *Ich*, but rather the *itself*, the *auto*. The 'spiritual automaton [*geistige Automate*]' (IV, 342) or 'mental self-activity' (I, 357; 1994c: 72, t.m.) is *one* subclass of the 'itself', not its archetype or '*Urform*' (I, 177; 1980: 82).

In consequence, it would be a mistake to approach the relegation of *a priority* from mind to nature as though it were nothing more than the 'transfer of mind onto nature' or of 'the subjective onto the objective' (cf. Baum, in Sedgwick (ed.) 2000: 209) in a transcendental sense.[9] Precisely because such 'analogical'[10] processes maintain the a prioris thus transferred to be reducibly immanent to a transcendental *Ich* or a 'pre-eminent or transfinite mentality', no mention is made of the central characteristic, in Kielmeyer, Plotinus and Schelling, of subject-nature: productivity.[11] This is precisely what the *Introduction to the Outline of a System of Naturephilosophy* (1799) stipulates in this regard: '*Nature* as mere *product* (*natura naturata*) we call nature as *object* (with which all empiricism is concerned). *Nature as productivity* (*natura naturans*) we call *nature as subject* (all theory is concerned with this alone)' (III, 284; 2004: 202).

Merleau-Ponty observes that the 'nature-subject'[12] can be taken in two ways: the Kantian and the Schellingian (Merleau-Ponty 2003: 177). The first, as a 'hidden world' behind all those we inhabit, 'transcends every particular milieu' (von Uexküll 1965: 90); the second, that there is always an excess of reality over *our* phenomenological capacities. Since Merleau-Ponty's lectures (1956–60) on *Nature* lay down the groundwork for a steady ascent from '*phusis* to *logos* to History' (2003: 199) *à la* Herder, he does not pursue the grounds of the famous Schellingian thesis of the 'irreducible remainder' or unrecoverable ground (VII, 359–60; 1986: 34), and so misses the third prospect, which is its consequence: what makes nature a subject is, as Schelling puts it, its '*auto*': its 'autonomy', its 'autarchy' and its 'unthinged reality' (III, 17; 2004: 17). It is for this reason that 'nature as subject' is a priori with respect to its products: if the product – any 'organization' whatever – is merely 'an arrested stream of causes and effects', and therefore necessarily 'enclosed within certain limits', as the *World Soul* defines it (II, 349), these limits prohibit a priori the recovery of its production. There is a deficit of product with respect to productivity that marks a basic asymmetry between them; 'the particular is inadequate to the universal' (V, 139), as Schelling formalizes it.

In the *System of Transcendental Idealism*, therefore, where the problem of the subject is addressed through the 'limited nature' (III, 355; 1978: 14) of the *Ich*, which is 'merely the concept of becoming an object to oneself' (III, 366; 1978: 25), Schelling generates a dynamic rather than a reflective theory of subjectivity, premised on the same productivity–product asymmetry evident in 'nature as subjectivity': since 'the concept of the *Ich* is merely the concept of becoming an object to oneself' (III, 366; 1978: 25), productivity does not cease in the production of the product, but produces *serially*, reproduces it over and again. Unlimited productivity subjected to limits necessarily generates an infinite number of products, but *not all at once*. Hence in constituting the *Stufenfolge* not of 'nature as a whole' but of a single product, the *System* renounces Kielmeyer's 'integral of time' (Bach 2001: 179; cf. Kielmeyer 1938: 23, 61–2) along with the phenomenal continuum (cf. 4.1, above) for 'actions that constitute epochs' (III, 398; 1978: 50). Between products, that is, there is neither phenomenal nor temporal continuity, so that while becoming is infinite, it is not 'continuous', but generates a dynamic succession of stages in 'leaps' (cf. II, 171; 1988: 133), where each stage is the product of a power. Schelling's dynamics no longer deal with discrete magnitudes, but with powers. Self-conscious subjectivity, therefore, is simply the 'highest power' of the 'identity of subjective and objective we call nature' (III, 355; 1978: 14). Due, however, to the basal asymmetry between the subjective and the objective, or productivity and product, it is the *powers* of identity that are expressed in nature, rather than 'absolute identity', or identity itself. Moreover, identity must be constructed, not merely indicated, because although identity itself *produces* what Schelling calls 'coincidence', or Plato 'syggeneity' (the 'ancient doctrine', mentioned earlier, 'that like is known by like'),[13] the concept must be constructed in order not to recover, but to recapitulate the productivity of that identity at a higher power. Because, that is, 'all construction rests on the conflict between the absolutely universal . . . and the particular . . . the particular is inadequate to the universal' (V, 139). Therefore, the concept arising from the construction does not recover the original identity of productivity and product, but is blocked by 'limit-points in the recovery of absolute priority' (V, 137). At the same time, however, limit-points do not mark the failure of construction, but the emergence of a new product – the concept – that is a recapitulation of the asymmetrical identity of productivity and product. Thus, as Steffens astutely remarks in a review essay of Schelling's 'Recent naturephilosophical works', published in the *Journal of Speculative Physics*, all construction consists in 'approximations to productivity' (in Schelling 2001: 26), simply because no product can recover productivity itself, or the subject of nature *whole*.

The same thing applies to all construction – whether 'ideal', ontological (the identity of construction and being, III, 12; 2004: 12), or the 'self-construction of matter' (IV, 4). Thus in nature as in the ideal, 'nature in all its multiplicity arises from infinite approximations to this *X*' (II, 219; 1988: 175). It is because no particular construction – ideal or physical – adequates to the absolute productivity in which nature as subject consists, that approximations are 'infinite' and nature 'multiple'. Thus the pursuit of particularity in nature leads not to 'nature as a whole' nor to 'dynamic' or material atoms – nor indeed to 'things' of any kind, but to the 'unthinged in nature' (III, 11; 2004: 11), or nature as subject. Since, however productivity is indissociable from product, the basal unit of recapitulation is the 'identity of subjective and objective we call nature' (III, 355; 1978: 114); since, however product is irreversibly dependent upon productivity, the identity consists in the asymmetrical 'diversifying antithesis' of productivity and product, a proportion of the first and second forces, or of nature as subject and nature as object, the irreversibility of which is guaranteed by *actual* nature. Identity does not abolish or cancel a constant asymmetrical differentiation in nature, therefore, but rather consists in the constant recapitulation of the 'universal law of bifurcation'.

The subject of nature thus consists in the constantly reiterated identity of productivity and product: since productivity is indissociable from product (without which it would not be productivity, but a force with no effect, and therefore not a force at all), but since it is not reducible to any product or totality of products, the asymmetry of the identity is maintained only through constant productivity. Thus, as the *Introduction to the Outline* states, 'the product of productivity is a new productivity' (III, 324; 2004: 231); in other words, *nature as subject is self-recapitulating at different levels*. This is why, synthesizing the constant decomposition of 'nature as a whole' charted in the *World Soul* with the 'autonomous' and 'autarchic', unconditioned productivity of the *First Outline* and the theory of *to auto* derived from Platonism, the *Universal Deduction of the Dynamic Process* (1800) finally renders the basal unit of recapitulation as the dynamic process itself: 'The same phenomena that we conceive under the term "dynamic process", and which are the only primitives of nature, are nothing other than a consistent self-construction of matter, simply repeated at different stages' (IV, 4). Non-phenomenal and discontinuous, neither a universal substrate nor a somatic particular, but rather the generation of matter itself, the dynamic process paradigmatically requires construction, and in the construction produces the *auto* in which the identity of subjective and objective that the *System* calls 'nature' consists. In this construction, however, the entire nature of the transcendental is clarified, and with it, the solution to the materiality of the Idea that haunts Platonic physics.

Before turning to the account of the transcendental in which the relation between phenomenality and productivity is given the 'fullest possible exposition' (III, 331; 1978: 2), Schellingian naturephilosophy needs to be reset in the context from which the 'becoming of genetic philosophy' began (1.1, above). Contrary to what Böhme identifies as the 'widespread prejudice' (2000: 161–2) that asserts the impossibility of a Platonic physics, Plato does present the outlines for a dynamic physics that, as Whitehead notes (1964: 17), may better serve the conceptual environment generated by relativity physics than the Aristotelianism whose 'substratist' prejudices have governed the development of 'all natural philosophy, not just the part that became our physics' (Des Chenes 1996: 2). The *Timaeus* apart, Platonic physics remains in outline only, although the neoplatonists, and Plotinus in particular, developed it further; it is to this task that Schelling, against the defect common to all post-Cartesian philosophy 'that nature does not exist for it' (VII, 356; 1986: 30), and against in particular the 'ethical vision of the world' that has, in the name of metaphysics, supplanted nature, directs the entire naturephilosophical programme. Although Plato demonstrated repeatedly that becoming was thinkable from the standpoint of being, it is not only reciprocally necessary, if becoming consists not simply in degraded images (as in the current and false image of Platonism), but also in physical nature as *approximations of being*, that being be thought from the standpoint of becoming; rather, the consequence of this is that becoming becomes necessarily prior with respect to being if physical productivity has any reality at all. In this regard, to paraphrase Tillich's account of Schelling's theory of the powers, a naturalistic 'meontology' must ground ontology.[14]

5.2 THE DECOMPOSITION OF INTELLIGENCE

The transcendental philosopher says: give me a nature composed of antithetical activities, of which one reaches out to the infinite while the other tries to intuit itself in this infinitude, and from this I will bring forth intelligence for you. (III, 427; 1978: 72–3)

In the finite, there is only physical deduction, or, all physical deduction is finite. (Ritter [1810] 1984: 245)

The subject of nature itself, then, 'nature's only primitives' (IV, 4), constitute the dynamic process. Yet this is difficult for a transcendental subject to intuit, because regardless of whether or not it might contingently match experience, in fact it cannot do so, insofar as the dynamic process *itself* is necessarily non-phenomenal, while at the same time necessarily phenomenal in every product. Insofar as Schelling's *System of Transcendental Idealism* aims, by means of what the *Universal Deduction* gives as the subject of nature itself, to demonstrate, as the passage cited above shows, the potentiation of that subject of nature itself into a subject capable of becoming an object to itself, the philosophical focus shifts not in accordance with the nature of the subject treated, but in accordance with the means in which it is so. The specific difference between the two is therefore at one level quantatitive only – the 'identity of subjective and objective we call nature, in its *highest power* we call self-consciousness' (III, 355; 1978: 14) – although it is on this latter that the work concentrates. Rather than the concern with locating the subject, therefore, the subject of transcendental philosophy is circumscribed by what Schelling repeatedly calls the 'limited nature' of the project: to account for the 'identity of the unconscious activity that has brought forth nature and the conscious activity' (III, 349; 1978: 12). The problem is rather to account for continuity from the standpoint of products (concepts, experience, knowledge), the 'memorials and documents' (III, 331; 1978: 2), as it were, of the 'natural history of mind' (II, 39; 1988: 30), while at the same time to demonstrate the actuality of this continuity from the standpoint of production. Transcendental philosophy therefore consists of a 'double series' derived from a single, reiterated, productivity-product identity. This solution to the problem of the subject is therefore given by means of an entirely different approach to the pursuit of the dynamic process, one shared, as we shall see, with Steffens' geological researches.

In keeping with the 'double series', it is the purpose of this section therefore to pursue the dynamic process from nature to ideation, on the one hand, and from ideation to the subject of nature on the other, just as Schelling divides the philosophical sciences into two according to whether they follow one or the other trajectory: 'all philosophy goes about to make a nature out of intelligence or an intelligence out of nature' (III, 343; 1978: 7). It is vital, however, that the relations between the sciences, and between intelligence and nature, are neither symmetrical in the idea nor in nature, precisely because the latter retains ontological priority throughout – how could it be otherwise, unless mind creates nature? Since Idealism in particular is that philosophy from which such manufactory arrogance may be presumed, we cannot treat this problem as settled, however. Specifically, since the *First Outline* announces that 'to philosophise about nature is to *create* nature' (III, 11; 2004: 11), the problem explicitly recapitulates the ancient Platonic one of the materiality of the Idea. The physics of ideation has returned to contemporary philosophy (as Whitehead might have predicted) in Deleuze's work. Since he and Guattari (1994: 11), while heaping praise on what they consider Schelling's 'autopositing' concept, were also working on a 'philosophy of nature' (Deleuze 1995: 155), the *Ideas*' 'testing of systems' (II, 56; 1988: 42) must be extended to future as well as past ones, in order to expose the relative amplitude of these philosophies of nature, or the forces exerted by them. Since it is a core postulate of Deleuzo-Guattarian philosophy that 'a philosophy's power is measured by the concepts it creates' (Deleuze 1992: 321), so the emergent concepts of nature in that philosophy face a decisive test.

Of the claims most often made against the viability of the Schellingian philosophy in general, the most deranging and the most frequently made concerns the relation between the transcendental and the naturephilosophy. The high frequency with which it recurs is due in part to Hegel, who set the ball rolling in the *Difference* essay, announcing a fourfold equilibrium between the two parts of Schelling's philosophy (each with a subject and an object, the subject of the one science balancing the object of the other), and thus forecasting his own eventual sublation of these antithetical sciences in philosophical science as such. This is because Hegel's presentation of their 'inner identity', tending towards outward 'indifference',[15] is parasitic on their reconstruction as 'relative totalities . . . closed in themselves [and] opposed to each other' (*Wz* 2: 110–11; 1977a: 169). What is so damaging in Hegel's reconstruction is the assumption of symmetry in identity: for Hegel, identity is latent in opposition, while for Schelling, 'bifurcation' is dynamic in precisely the sense that it is symmetry breaking. Identity, in consequence, is not the recovery or 'integration'[16] of differences, but causes difference to proliferate. This is already evident in the *World Soul*, often mistakenly understood as simply the manifesto of organicism: while the first, productive force would result in nothing were it not for the second, retarding force, no product, as the retardation of productivity, can recover or absorb productivity as such, or all nature would consist of a single product, leaving productivity itself requiring an additional cause. As the *Universal Deduction* puts the point, dynamics requires 'no special, fabricated causes (specific matters, for example) beyond these universal grounds' (IV, 76). The emergence of identity is therefore consequent upon the symmetry break that is the relation of the forces or 'the subject of nature itself'. This is why the above-cited passage from the *System* gives the conditions of intelligence as lying in nature; clearly demonstrating that Hegel's assumption of the mutual isolation of the two sciences is false.

Directly contradicting the ideal stasis that governs the Hegelian presentation of the two basic sciences, Schelling never sets them in opposition as regards their object fields or boundaries, but plots them as antithetical '*trajectories*'[17] across the absolute, which is by definition open territory since if it had boundaries and limits, it would not be absolute, but relative to those limits. Moreover, the antithesis of 'trajectories' is itself derived from the *a priority* of nature, so that the ground of the antithesis is not simply ideal, but 'lies *in things*'.[18] The 'opposition of naturephilosophy and transcendental philosophy', Schelling makes clear in 'True concept', is therefore twofold, concerning trajectory, on the one hand, and more fundamentally, *priority* on the other. Therefore, of the two sciences, 'the former is the original, the latter derivative' (IV, 84): the ground of the transcendental, that is, is not itself transcendental, but physical, and even 'lies *in things*'. The transcendental philosopher does not simply 'ask' for 'a nature composed of antithetical activities', as though repeating Fichte's ultimately ungrounded 'choice' between idealism and dogmatism; rather the necessity of physical grounds is necessarily *imposed* on the philosophizing product (intelligence): 'anything whose conditions simply cannot be given in nature must be absolutely impossible' (III, 571; 1978: 186). When therefore the *System* programmatically states that idealism has as its task 'to make a nature out of intelligence' (III, 342; 1978: 7), this does not mean a reduction of nature to an artifact of intelligence; rather, idealism as Schelling conceives it entails the naturalization of ideality.

The *System of Transcendental Idealism*, clearly warning the reader, despite its title, that its transcendentalism is not to be mistaken for its Kantian variant, therefore begins not with any attempt to ground autonomous mind, but rather with 'nature's highest aim: to become an object to itself' (III, 341; 1978: 6). The transcendental must be considered from the outset then as giving the conditions not simply under which experience is possible for 'human and other finite intellects', as Fichte enigmatically put it (W I, 283; 1982: 249), but as determining the mode under which nature attains to intelligence, that is, becomes an object to *itself*. While everything that is has by definition become an object – that is, a phenomenal product – only a subject can become an object *to itself*. The object-becoming of the subjective and the subject-becoming of the objective form the two terminii therefore of transcendental and naturephilosophy, respectively, although the two sciences are not coterminous, but 'parallel'.[19] As the *System* notes, the two sciences 'can never merge into one' because intelligence itself introduces a symmetry break into nature. In place therefore of the unilinear development of nature to intelligence that is the 'necessary tendency of all natural science' (III, 340; 1978: 6), the *System* proposes different orders of production: history, for example, is 'second-order' nature (III, 333; 1978: 4), comprising therefore a productivity/product antithesis. Similarly, because it is only *in reason* that 'it becomes apparent that nature is identical from the first with what we recognize in ourselves as the intelligent and the conscious' (III, 341; 1978: 6), this identity is *ideal* precisely insofar as it is in the order of intelligence that the identity in question becomes phenomenal, so that 'philosophy is the only science in which this double series occurs' (III, 397; 1978: 49). Finally, therefore, the 'subject of nature itself' is not identical to the self-conscious subject, although both are subjectivities. A pattern reemerges: for Schelling, identity differentiates rather than integrates.

This is why, unlike Kant's transcendentalism, there is no single subject at the core of Schelling's philosophy, but rather a multiplicity of subjects: there is the transcendental subject, and an ideal *Ich* or its *Urform*, 'no matter what the *Ich* is' (I, 217; 1980: 110), and the 'autonomous . . . autarchic' (III, 17; 2004: 17) 'subject of nature itself' (IV, 76). In nature, matter is 'self-organising' (II, 47; 1988: 35) and 'self-constructing' (IV, 4), while nature is 'self-creating' (III, 401; 1978: 52) and 'self-recapitulating at different levels' (IV, 47); even the dynamic atoms, whatever the problems with the hypothesis in general, are presented as 'real individuals' or 'natural monads' (III, 23; 2004: 21). Amongst the subjectivities in the transcendental philosophy, knowledge is knowledge only 'insofar as it is grounded in itself, i.e., subjective' (III, 357; 1978: 18), a *Selbigkeit* without *Ichheit*, while 'the concept of the *Ich* is merely the concept of becoming an object to oneself' (III, 366; 1978: 25). The identity that is subjectivity does not therefore entail that all subjectivities are identical; rather, they differ only in degree, as the *System* explains: that 'absolute identity of subjective and objective we call nature which, at its highest power [*Potenz*], we call self-consciousness' (III, 355; 1978: 14, t.m.). This is also why, although a dynamic explanation has its 'ultimate ground in the subject of nature itself' (IV, 76), Schelling can simultaneously insist that while the two basic sciences do not merge, there is an 'identity of the dynamic and the transcendental' (III, 452; 1978: 91). Identity combines differentia into series that are themselves differentiated by powers. Identity is misconceived if it is considered as 'bringing into a single class what nature has . . . divided' (II, 171–2; 1988: 133); identity itself, as the *Exposition of My System* puts it, 'never ceases to be what it is' (IV, 120). Insofar, that is, as it is always what it is, identity is an 'autopositing' of *unlimited* quantity (= ∞),[20] while each autoposition differs according to its power. The quantity of identity is precisely what Schelling's *Potenzlehre* or 'theory of the powers' measures: on this view, the *extension* of identity (how many objects can be subsumed under it), is measured by the quantity of its effect (how much can be produced by its activity).[21] For example, when identity is predicated of nature, as when the *First Outline* defines it as 'absolute activity' (III, 16; 2004: 16), Schelling's concern is not to enumerate the elements in which that identity consists, since, as 'absolute activity', this would be an endless task, but to chart nature as productivity as it 'self-recapitulates at different levels' (IV, 47). The reason for this, as Schelling says, 'lies *in things*' (IV, 84), that is, in the nature of what Schelling calls 'phenomenal products [*Scheinprodukte*]'. That all products are phenomenal follows necessarily from nature as productivity: 'Productivity is originally infinite; thus when it achieves a product, this product is phenomenal only. Every product is a point of inhibition, but in every such point there is again the infinite' (III, 16; 2004: 16, t.m.).

Schelling does not therefore argue that all products are identical, but rather that every product recapitulates identity. There are therefore identities wherever there are products. We may therefore define identity as the contraction or retardation of the infinite in the finite, or productivity in the product. Due however to the basal disymmetry, or priority of productivity over product, identities are not given, but generated. Even the primitive cell of logical identity that Schelling takes from Fichte, the A=A, is not a perfected, analytic equilibrium of subject and predicate that eliminates their difference, but is a synthesis of 'identity in duplicity' (III, 373; 1978: 30), and thus comprises at least three factors: identity, duplicity and the copula. The more central the theory of identity becomes in Schelling's philosophy, therefore, the more factors it turns out to involve: under the magnetic schema of the *Exposition of My System*, for example, identity becomes a polar phenomenon, and its elements decompose into two pairs of antitheses:

$$\frac{\overset{+}{A = B} \qquad\qquad\qquad \overset{+}{A = B}}{A = A}$$

(*SW* IV, 137)

This schema can be read as asserting precisely the elimination of differentia, so that the lower term is the product of its factors, only on the basis that the magnetic line, the tension, is elided as a merely formal element of the equation; correcting for this, identity consists in the specific determinations of tension in magnetic phenomena. Rather than asserting the integration of differences, therefore, the schema posits the universality of magnetism, the 'first dimension = selfhood, *Ichheit*' (VII, 450) in nature. The physical basis of identity implicit in the magnetic schema is made explicit in the *Stuttgarter Privatvorlesungen* (1810), where Schelling writes of the completed schema of the powers, which runs thus:

$$\frac{A^3}{A^2 = (A = B)}$$

The first power [i.e., (A = B)] must in accordance with its nature precede the second [A²]; there is therefore a priority and a posteriority between the two powers; the real is *natura prius*, the Ideal *posterius*. The lower is of course posited before the higher . . . in regard to existence. (VII, 427)

The *Stufenfolge*, as we have seen, is the articulated system of nature's self-decomposition into products. A bifurcating decomposition is constant in Schelling's philosophy. In the *Ideas*, for instance, 'the form of subject-objectification bifurcates to infinity throughout the universe', finally '*seeming to lose itself in pure objectivity and corporeality*' (II, 146–7; cf. 1988: 114, t.m., emphasis added). Here already the basic structure and problems of a reconditioned transcendentalism is apparent: as *infinite*, bifurcation is not, but *appears* lost in objectivity and somatism, just as the *First Outline*'s '*Scheinprodukte*' are phenomenal precisely insofar as they are not simply 'remainders', but rather the repeated channels by which productivity is 'retarded' into particular forms. Since productivity would be finite if it were restricted within *a* particular form (man, cosmic animal, minerality), phenomenality is not the appearing *of* a thing, but rather productivity appearing as things. Nor are phenomena ontologically dubious: products are possible at all only insofar as infinite productivity is infinitely retarded; phenomenality, that is, arises only due to the necessary indissociability of productivity from products, so that 'the assumption that things are just what we take them to be' is a necessary one if experience is to be possible. It is important to note, however, that the identity in question is not itself phenomenal, but dynamic. The 'subject of nature itself' in which 'all dynamic explications of phenomena' terminate as their ground, manifests 'visible nature as merely its framework' (IV, 76). This dissymmetrical relation is typical of Schellingian identity: when the extensional set of identity is greater than one (= identity *itself*), identity itself is not identical to the factors of which it is posited.

When therefore Schelling treats specifically of self-conscious subjectivity, as with any other product, its generative ground cannot be recovered whole, since it extends 'down' to the subject of nature in which 'all dynamic movement has its ground' (IV, 76). Just as with the contortions to which the *Stufenfolge* in general subjects time, so too the continuous production of 'the concept of becoming an object to oneself', or the *Ich*, does not recover an unbroken continuum since it is not composed of one. Like the subject of nature, or the 'form of bifurcation into subject and object that prevails endlessly in the universe' (II, 146–7; 1988: 114), the 'self-decompos[ition] . . . of an ideal *Ich* . . . into a subjective and an objective' (III, 425; 1978: 63). Rather, such a subject must first construct itself as 'approximations to productivity' (Steffens, in Schelling 2001: 26). Because such constructions, however, are necessarily finite and multiple, the philosophical history of the subject can be composed only of 'those actions which constitute epochs' in the subject's history. Moreover, as noted earlier, Schelling's conception of history does not consist in the narration of a past, but only in the *production of a future*. In other words, the basal asymmetry that prevents the subject recovering its ground means that the *Ich* can intuit itself as productivity only by making itself into a product, but in intuiting itself as product, it remains productivity. Its history, therefore, is not recoverable, since it consists in the production of new actions. In the language of the *System*, 'self-consciousness is the lamp of the whole system of knowledge, but casts its light ahead only, not behind' (III, 347; 1978: 18). In other words, the history of self-consciousness is not recovered in 'becoming an object to oneself', but *deposited* in the series of productions of such objects as it becomes. Contrary therefore to Ritter's judgement that Schelling does not address the polarity of time, but only of space, a portrait of time in transcendental philosophy emerges that has little to do with the 'inner sense' to which Kant consigned it. It is precisely the irreversibility of the time of productivity that necessitates the history of self-consciousness be introduced into it as a 'symmetry break', so that time *issues from* production, rather than underlying it or integrating it into some great continuous series, or 'chain of being'. The general thesis is far-reaching, and will eventually find its way, via Steffens, into the 'system of times' that constitutes the *Ages of the World*: time emerges with product series, or with the emergence of a subject in general, and extends only so far as its 'epoch-making' is sustained.

Following the 'History' essay, in which Schelling argued '*that history in general only exists* where there is an *ideal* and an *infinite multiplicity of deviations from it*' (I, 469), the *System* is explicit concerning the symmetry-breaking introduction of such 'progressivity' (III, 592; 1978: 202) into the series of times. At one level, the system of times is precisely produced by the 'absolute interruption of the succession' with which philosophy begins (III, 396; 1978: 48). In part, it is this that is responsible for the trajectory difference between the two basic sciences, of nature and intelligence. The necessary priority of the former over the latter would entail, at its limit, that the emergence of any subjectivity whatever recover all the natural series, from the self-construction of matter up, before any history could be generated. Since 'the whole object of this [transcendental] philosophy is nothing else but the *action* of the intellect according to determinate laws', and since this action can only be grasped in a further action – that of intuiting these actions – transcendental philosophy consists in a 'constant producing of these original acts of the intellect . . . and a constant reflect[ion] upon this production'. It is because 'all philosophy is productive' (III, 350–1; 1978: 13) that the 'lamp of the whole system' points 'ahead only, not behind' and this irreversibility thus acquires its proper significance: transcendental reflection does not recover, reflect or copy anything, but rather produces constantly. Productivity extends both to reason itself, and the product, i.e., the *Ich*. While reason remains 'a mere play of higher forces, of necessity unknown to us' (III, 273–4; 2004: 194), the *Ich*, according to the *Treatise Explicatory*, remains a product:

By virtue of this original construction, the philosopher obtains indeed a product (the *Ich*); however, this product exists nowhere outside of the construction, just as the straight line postulated by geometry exists only to the extent that it is originally constructed and is nothing outside of this construction. (I, 448; 1994c: 135, t.m.)

A first asymmetry in transcendental productivity thus arises, consisting in the redistribution of time following from the 'originality' of construction: the construction is original in the sense that it does not exist prior to the construction. 'Originality', in other words, attaches not to the construct, but to the constructing; it is not simply the sudden advent of a new item in a *preexisting* succession that forms originality, therefore, but rather the production of a new time series immanent to the constructing. This is why Schelling will refer to the 'beginning of all philosophizing' as an 'absolute interruption of the succession' (III, 396; 1978: 48): importantly, what would be better termed 'originativity' does not eliminate the succession it interrupts, but differentiates it into systems. As the *System* puts it, 'time is not something that flows independently of the *Ich*; the *Ich itself* is time conceived in activity' (III, 466; 1978: 103).

Similarly, the spatiality of the construction is generated rather than pregiven – hence the line is its own spatiality, or has a degree of *extensity*. Similarly, when mathematics constructs its objects, for example, 'there is a cube in this portion of space', this means that 'in this part of space my intuition can be active only in the form of a cube' (III, 408; 1978: 58). It is because the mathematician assumes space in which to construct, rather than constructing that space 'originatively', that Schelling constantly constrasts geometrical and philosophical construction. The (Euclidean) geometer, that is, is not concerned to construct space as such, but only the constructs within it (the cube), while the philosopher, by contrast, is concerned only 'with the act of construction itself' (III, 350; 1978: 13). Accordingly, while the geometer's constructs may be empirically presented, the philosopher's cannot, and to that extent have no spatial dimensions. This is because the philosopher's construction is not the construction of an object at all, but of the subject, since the philosopher's concern with 'the act of construction itself . . . is an absolutely internal thing' (III, 350; 1978: 13). Since it does not determine a space, the measure of construction is *extensity* rather than extension. Schelling defines extensity as 'not merely spatial size in the object, but [as] determined by intensity, in a word, by what we call *force*. For the intensity of a force can be measured only by the space in which it can diffuse itself without becoming equal to zero' (III, 468; 1978: 105).

What, then, does extensity measure? Firstly, the amplitude of a construction. When, for example, the *System* announces its aim of 'the exposition of idealism to its fullest extent' (III, 331; 1978: 2), it explicitly undertakes to 'produce the world' (III, 349; 1978: 12) without ceasing to produce the 'concept of becoming an object to itself' or the *Ich*. Since 'infinite extensity = dissolved *Ich*', construction is necessarily finite both with respect to its task, and with respect to the limits imposed upon it. Extensity also therefore measures the reiterability of the *Ich*, the 'monuments and documents' by which, in its construction, it becomes an object to itself, and the *integration* of the series of acts 'into which the one act of self-consciousness evolves' (III, 397; 1978: 49). Constructibility (approximation to productivity) therefore provides an important measure of the finite integration of series. As the *System* puts it, 'boundedness (extended to infinity) is thus the condition under which alone the self as self can be infinite' (III, 384; 1978: 39). It is for this reason that the history of self-consciousness is punctuated by 'epochs', with each iteration-series beginning with the 'absolute interruption of the succession' (III, 396; 1978: 48). Therefore, the forces articulated in construction constitute the amplitude of the subject that is its necessary by-product: since "absolute extensity" amounts to the infinite diffusion of force, its construction entails 'the dissolved *Ich*' (III, 467; 1978: 104). Forces, however, are not the primitives of the *Ich*, but of nature; insofar as there is dynamic motion at all, such motion has its ground 'in the subject of nature itself'. Since the *Ich* is a by-product of construction rather than its cause, what is it that constructs in construction? Heuser, commenting on Schellingian construction, clarifies the nature of self-construction: 'For Schelling, nonempirical intuition is no longer restricted to space and time, but is the intuition of "absolute activity", i.e., the intuition of the activity of the original self-construction, with which alone space, intuition and time are posited' (in Zimmerli, Stein and Gerten (eds) 1997: 286). Self-construction, that is, is not simply the construction *of* a self or an *Ich*, but the *auto* of construction *itself*. It follows therefore that although extensity measures the amplitude of construction in intuition, it does not attach solely to construction in intuition, but also takes place in non-intuiting self-construction, that is, in nature as such. Thus 'length as such can only exist in nature in the form of magnetism, or magnetism as such is conditioned by *length* in the construction of matter' (IV, 10), insofar as force thereby constitutes length as polar tension. That such forces are necessary in the self-construction of matter is further given from the stipulation that 'space', considered as the geometrical substrate, 'originally has no direction' (III, 477; 1978: 111), since this is only given in construction which, by introducing a break in directionless space, creates extensity. As the *Universal Deduction* demonstrates, therefore, magnetism, electricity and chemistry construct extension from forces. The constructions of the *Ich* are therefore 'second-order processes' insofar as they are 'recapitulations . . . of those first-order processes that produce their reproducing nature' (IV, 43). Heuser, seizing on precisely the non-phenomenal in construction, presents Schelling's account of 'symmetry breaking' in construction as in nature as offering important methodological insights for thinking through contemporary non-linear dynamics. Her claim is, in short, that 'speculative naturephilosophy' has strong links with mathematical physics, which 'have something to do with the possibility of *a priori* constructions in physics' (in Zimmerli, Stein and Gerten (eds) 1997: 277). Heuser's unusually positive account of naturephilosophy in effect proposes that naturephilosophy and mathematical physics alike conduct conjoint investigations of the transcendental conditions of the construction of ideation and nature alike. In so

179

doing, therefore, Heuser *transcendentalizes naturephilosophy*. Schelling, however, operates in precisely the opposite direction:

> The regularity in all the movements of nature, for example, the sublime geometry applied to the movements of the celestial bodies, is not explained by the fact that nature is the most perfect geometry; but inversely, by the fact that the most perfect geometry is that which nature produces. By this mode of explanation the real becomes transposed into the ideal world and its movements transformed into intuitions that persist in our intuitions alone, and that correspond to nothing outside us. (III, 271–2; 2004: 193)

This point is made explicitly and repeatedly from the outset of the *System* that transcendental philosophy is completed *if and only if* it *demonstrates* the 'absolute identity of subjective and objective we call nature' (III, 356; 1978: 17), or the 'identity of the unconscious activity that has brought forth nature and . . . conscious activity' (III, 349; 1978: 12). Schelling's physics is non-phenomenal not in order to segregate it from the dross of experience, but because *productivity is non-phenomenal*, while products are phenomena. The identity to be established is therefore not between phenomena, but the productivities they approximate. Hence the philosopher's interest in geometry lies not in its constructions, but in the constructing in which it consists. Recalling the *Meno's* figures in the sand, the *System* proposes its own account of the geometry lesson: 'Geometry proceeds . . . not from theorems, but from postulates. In that the most primary construction therein is postulated, and the pupil himself left to bring it forth, it is dependent from the start on self-construction. – So too with transcendental philosophy' (III, 371; 1978: 29).

In Plato's dialogue, Meno is said to 'recall' geometry from 'before he was a human being' (86e4), thus precisely recovering the soul from eternity. Schelling's geometry student, by contrast, seems not to be being asked to 'recall' anything at all, but rather to construct the geometrical figure from postulates, a construction necessarily accompanied by and dependent on a self-construction, an absolute interruption in the phenomenal that Schelling calls *abstraction*. Since the philosopher, however, unlike the mathematician, is not concerned with the construct, but 'with the act of construction itself' (III, 350; 1978: 13), the same dynamic asymmetry of productivity and product arises in transcendental philosophy as in nature. Yet the *System* establishes from the outset that there is a 'parallelism of nature and intelligence', each with its own science that can never merge into one. The grounds for this stipulation concern, as we have seen, the asymmetrical relation between them, in that natural productivity is necessarily prior to its products. Yet the parallels meet in the 'identity of the dynamic and the transcendental' (III, 452; 1978: 91). The identity is repeated in the *Universal Deduction*:

> To physics, the dynamic is precisely what the transcendental is to philosophy, and dynamic explanation in physics means precisely what

transcendental explanation means in philosophy. Explaining a phenomenon dynamically means exactly that it has been explained *from the original conditions of the construction of matter in general*: its explanations therefore require no special, fictitious causes (for example, individual matters) beyond those universal grounds. All dynamic movements have their final ground in the subject of nature itself, namely in the forces of which the visible world is only the framework. (IV, 75–6; emphasis added)

The self-construction of the subject is therefore the recapitulation of the subject of nature itself at the level of conscious production. Thus the *System*'s nascent geometer is asked to *recapitulate* the productivity of nature in ideation. In a passage that *involves* everything the *System* gradually *evolves*, Schelling explains:

If philosophy's first construction is the imitation of an original, all its constructions will likewise be merely such imitations. So long as the *Ich* is apprehended in its original evolution of the absolute synthesis, there is only one series of acts, that of the original and necessary acts of the *Ich*; as soon as I interrupt this evolution, and freely project myself back to its starting point, there arises for me a new series, in which what was necessary in the first series is now free [. . .]. Philosophy therefore is nothing else but the free reproduction, the free recapitulation of the original series of acts into which the one act of self-consciousness evolves. (III, 397; 1978: 49)

Again, exactly as the *Universal Deduction* defines the dynamic process that is the 'subject of nature itself' as the 'the constant self-construction of matter, simply recapitulated at different levels' (IV, 4), the system here asserts the 'identity of the transcendental and the dynamic' (III, 452; 1978: 91). The 'free recapitulation' of self-construction that constitutes the history of self-consciousness is free in the sense the 'History' essay stipulates, that is, susceptible of an '*infinite multiplicity of deviations*' (I, 469), rather than free in the sense of lawlessness; or in the sense that Cantor ascribed to mathematics: the ontological insufficiency of the merely 'potential' existence of the Aristotelian infinite demanded mathematics construct actual infinites, and fill being with 'manies too big to be ones'.[22] Free construction, therefore, is free in the sense that it exploits the powers of the abstract in order to bring things into being:

Being (objectivity) is always merely an expression of a limitation of the intuiting or producing activity. There is a cube in this portion of space, means nothing else but that in this part of space my intuition can be active only in the form of a cube. The ground of all reality in cognition is thus the ground of limitation independent of intuition. (III, 408; 1978: 58)

This is a major innovation in Schellingian transcendentalism. It is precisely because productive intuition is 'free' to the extent that it is not bound to the reproduction of an antecendent existent, that it effects the becoming of being. The transcendental is therefore neither a reflex of reality, nor a screen dividing finite rational intelligence from it, but is nature potentiating itself in new acts, new forms, new phenomena, and new concepts: transcendental philosophy is the physics of ideation turned experimental.

If, by means of the transcendental, Kant undertook a 'critique of natural cognition' (*SW* XI, 526), Schelling's specifically transcendental philosophy accordingly renaturalizes the transcendental, and grounds it in the a prioris inherent in the 'logic of nature' (*SW* XIII, 102–3): 'nature IS *a priori*' (*SW* III, 279; 2004: 198). 'Genetic thinking', Schelling's 'most extreme problematic', according to Jaspers (1955: 149), was already being primed in *Of the I*: 'The finite *Ich* must strive to produce [*hervorbringen*] in the world what is actual in the infinite' (*SW* I, 242; 1980: 127, t.m.).[23] The *Ich* cannot limit the genetic problem to the recovery of the 'monuments and documents' of its own becoming (*SW* III, 5; 1978: 2), since the extent of its *productive* task is not determined by any finite measure. The regionality of the *Ich* to becoming as such constitutes an insuperable barrier preventing any recovery of the infinite in consciousness, and therefore creates the conditions under which thought is nothing other than production, by means of the *same* infinite productivity by which not only it, but nature itself, becomes (mind has a 'natural history', *SW* II, 39; 1988: 30). Reflection is not only regional in regard to natural production, but even to natural production insofar as it occurs as ideation. This asymmetry is constitutive of the *System of Transcendental Idealism*, Schelling's most overt and continuous transformation of transcendental philosophy: 'Self-consciousness is the lamp of the whole system of knowledge, but it casts its light ahead only, not behind' (*SW* III, 357; 1978: 18). This genetic asymmetry, however, does not renege on the task set the *Ich* in *Of the I*; rather, it is insofar as it retains the productive imperative of the genetic task that it 'materializes the laws of mind into laws of nature' (*SW* III, 352; 1978: 14). The *System*'s 'theory of productive intuition' does not therefore consist solely in the production of phenomena for, but rather in mutations of, consciousness. Productive intuition is not a free production; rather, intuition, 'a modification of my being' (*SW* II, 217; 1988: 174), is determined by the intuited: ' "There is a cube . . ." means nothing other than . . . my intuition can be active only in the form of a cube' (*SW* III, 408; 1978: 58). The objective determination of productive intuition (ideation) means that due to the constitutive asymmetry of consciousness with regard to nature, when 'the naturephilosopher puts himself in the place of nature' (Schelling 2001, 1: 192), the demands made on the *Ich* finally produce 'a new species equipped with new organs of thought' (1989a: 57).

Notes

1   See also the Foreword to the *Journal of Speculative Physics* (1.1, 1800; 2000: 5): 'I ask all the thinking heads that participate in naturephilosophical inquiries, to secure the highest interest in this *Journal* by sharing their ideas.'

2   On Reil and Kant, see Hansen (1998) and Grant (2000b). For a subjectivist take on Reil's transcendentalism as 'a tributary of Kantianism', see Ayrault (1976: 303).

3   In this regard, the crucial text is the 'Philosophy of chemistry in general' in the *Ideas* (II, 257ff; 1988: 202ff).

4   The case is restated in the *First Outline* (III, 257–8; 2004: 184, t.m): 'It must here be deduced a priori, what elsewhere [in the *World Soul*] was demonstrated by induction, that one and the same universal dualism disappears from magnetic polarity and reappears in electrical phenomena, finally even in chemical heterogeneities, and ultimately again emerges in organic nature. The question is therefore how that one antithesis has extended into so many and various antitheses. If magnetism produced the first antithesis in nature, then thereby at the same time the germ of an infinite evolution placed the germ of that decomposition into ever new products in the universe.'

5   Wetzels (1971: 47) equally notes Schelling's oxygenism in an unusually positive assessment of the naturephilosophy, albeit at the cost of the usual organicism: 'One does not do justice to Schelling's *Naturphilosophie* by pointing only to its hypothetical and speculative, even mystical traits. Schelling's writings amply document an astonishing ability to make use of the latest discoveries in contemporary scientific research . . . Oxygen, which only recently had been made the basis of a new theory of combustion by Lavoisier, served Schelling as primary evidence of life in what used to be called inorganic nature. The decisive role that "fire-air" or "life-air" played in rust formation, breathing and blood circulation made oxygen the very elixir of life in his organic universe.' Sandkühler (1998: 90) again echoes Novalis' claim: 'Schelling sees oxygen as the principle of all chemical attraction, and that is, as the principle of binding and dissolution, as the universal agent [that] may indeed grow to become the universal system of nature.' Textual support for Schelling's chemical transcendentalism is not hard to find: from the sixth chapter of Book 2 of the *Ideas* to its conclusion, the subject matter is the chemical construction of matter, for instance, while chemistry is the basis of parts III to V of the *World Soul*; even the otherwise inexplicable inclusion of the literature review appended to that work is concerned in the main with researches in chemistry, as is a large chunk of the conclusion to the *First Outline*.

6   'The authority for assuming all positive natural principles as homogeneous, is only philosophically derived. Without this *postulate* (I presuppose that one knows what a *postulate with a view to a possible construction* is), it is impossible to construct the first concepts of physics, for example, the theory of heat. Idealism, which philosophy is gradually introducing into all the sciences (it has long since become dominant in mathematics, especially since Leibniz and Newton), still seems to be little understood.' (II, 351)

7   It is, of course, axiomatic for Deleuze, especially when writing about Spinoza or Nietzsche, that the body *does not know* what it is capable of, so that the actions issuing from it are opened by their indissociability from bodies, rather than delimited in advance by it. In effect, Deleuze achieves this through his transcendental empiricism, borrowing Spinoza's affectibility–power ratios to demonstrate a body's capacity for becoming (1992: 218). Again, as he writes in *Nietzsche and Philosophy*, 'what defines a body is the relation between dominant and dominated forces' (1983: 40). Nor does Deleuze specify *which* body here, leading to a certain 'transmigratability' in the constructions of 'becoming-animal' (Deleuze and Guattari 1988), or the becoming body of thought, as Deleuze and Guattari report Thales' thought becoming-water, Heraclitus' becoming-fire, and Epicurus' becoming-atomic (1994: 38, 220).

8   To this extent, Badiou (1997: 64ff) is correct to level the charge of organo-vitalism against Deleuze, although he is entirely wrong to ascribe this to an Aristotelianism on the part of his subject, as against his own Platonism. If Deleuze's ethical ontology does operate with an animalizing imperative, it does so in partial compliance with the universal 'visible, living creature' presented in the *Timaeus* (92c) which Badiou's self-styled Platonism conveniently omits.

9   Schelling's *Timaeus* commentary, on which Baum is leaning for his account of 'The beginnings of Schelling's philosophy of nature', does indeed state that 'the key to explaining the entire Platonic philosophy is the observation that *he everywhere transfers the subjective onto the objective*. Thus there appears in Plato (already extant before him, however) the proposition that *the visible world is nothing but a reproduction of the invisible*' (1994: 31). The key to understanding Schelling's evident conflation of the Kantian and Platonic philosophies here is, however, that he misconstrues reproduction as the linear repetition of 'higher types' (the Ideas), and thus transfers the *phenomenal* onto the *ideal*. Fortunately, this error, as we have seen, does not persist throughout the Schellingian philosophy.

10   The clearest, but not the only, expression of this 'analogical' understanding of naturephilosophy is given by Hans-Jürgen Treder (in Sandkühler (ed.) 1984: 333): 'the concept of "equation [*Gleichung*]" that Schelling and Ritter took over from mathematical physics was made into a synonym for proof by analogy, making the subjective cohere with the objective. This making-coherent of the subjective and the objective *per analogiam*, replaced the insight that a mathematical equation must be the subjective copy of an objective natural lawfulness.'

11   'Transfinite mentality' is Vater's suggestion for characterizing the position of Schelling's conception of the unconscious in relation to the 'classical philosophy of transcendence as seen in Plotinus or Spinoza' on the one hand, and 'the kind of material transcendence of Will or Being over its finite forms, voiced by Schopenhauer, Nietzsche, and in our day, Heidegger' (in Schelling 1978: xxxiii).

12   The term is von Uexküll's (1965: 90): 'The role played by nature as object in different milieux is eminently contradictory. Were we to gather together its objective characteristics, we would be faced with chaos. Nevertheless, all these milieux are borne and sustained by the totality that transcends every particular milieu. Behind all the worlds to which it gives birth, hiding, yet eternally present, the subject: nature.'

13   (VII, 337; 1986: 8). Although Schelling first explicitly articulates the principle 'like produces like [*Gleiches Gleiches hervorruft*]' in the *Annals of Medicine as Science* (1805; VII, 281), it is operative in the *Ideas'* conception of 'the necessary coincidence of nature and mind' (II, 55–6; 1988: 41–2), where, echoing the Platonic concept of 'syggeneity' (cf. 2.2, above) whereby 'the logics will be akin to their diverse objects' (*Tim.* 29b3), it acts as a principle of the naturalized transcendental: 'what after all can work upon the mind other than itself, or that which is akin to its nature' (II, 219; 1988: 175). The Middle Platonist Alcinous, in his *Handbook of Platonism*, defines the concept as 'any logical procedure which passes from like to like . . . Induction is particularly useful for activating natural concept formation [*physike ennoia*]' (158.1–3; 1993: 10). Since, however, Alcinous' definition arises in the context of an investigation of 'how our reasoning power [*dunamis*] works on the physical level' (154.18; 1993: 5), Schelling's usage of the principle in the investigation of the 'natural history of our mind' (II, 39; 1988: 30) repeats Alcinous' concerns exactly.

14   Tillich describes the *Potenzlehre* as 'an ontology of what is not' (cited in Snow 1996: 201).

15   Even in this early, supposedly Schellingian phase, Hegel betrays the seeds of the *Phenomenology's* infamous 'night in which all cows are black' (1977b: 9), insofar as the inner identity of the antithesis of merely relative totalities is said in the *Differenzschrift* to 'tend towards indifference'. In 'The eternal and necessary bond between philosophy and physics' (Grant 2005), I argue that whatever the appearances, Hegel praises Fichte under Schelling's name, and criticizes Schelling under Fichte's.

16 Hegel follows Fichte in his integrationist account of differences. In the first edition of *Concerning the Concept of the Wissenschaftslehre*, Fichte makes overt – if selective – use of integral calculus to intuit the free space of the transcendental *Ich*: 'a question for mathematicians: Is not the concept of straightness already included in the concept of a line? Is there any other sort of line except a straight one? Is the so-called curved line anything other than a stringing-together of infinitely many points which are infinitely close to each other?' (W I, 64n; 1988: 120–1n).

17 'Certainly, the reason that I have opposed naturephilosophy and transcendental philosophy, and have sought to bring the latter about in a wholly other trajectory than the former, lies in *things*', writes Schelling (IV, 83), and further underscores the ontological realism in which both 'basic sciences' are grounded when, discussing Eschenmayer's criticisms of the 'idealistic method of explanation or rather construction' in the *First Outline*, 'nothing of the sort is to be found in naturephilosophy as I have established it'. The *System* itself is simply 'the idealist construction of nature' (IV, 84). 'True concept' is as clear a manifesto of naturephilosophy as could be wished for, providing the reader bears in mind that it is Eschenmayer's Fichteanism that Schelling's response attacks.

18 See also the *System*'s treatment of the same issue: 'there is a significant reason lying deep within the matter itself, why the author has opposed this science to transcendental philosophy and completely separated it therefrom' (III, 332; 1978: 3).

19 Emmanuel Cattin (2001: 127–8) argues the Hegelian case for the symmetry of the two sciences on the basis of the *System*'s 'parallelism': 'The geometric metaphor is strict, indicating the irreducibility of an opposition grounded in the thing itself: the internal division of philosophy is governed by the double series at the level of the *Sache* itself [. . .]. In these conditions, the complete exposition of transcendental idealism is more fundamentally – philosophically – incomplete: in effect, philosophy is double. But this doubling, not unparadoxically, provides precisely the form of its unity: transcendental philosophy and philosophy of nature expose two inversely identical series.' That is, according to Cattin, the two sciences can, geometrically speaking, be translated one into the other. Apart from mistaking Schelling's for Kant's 'thing in itself' (cf. II, 33n; 1988: 26n; III, 347; 1978: 10), in direct contravention of this case, Cattin also acknowledges Schelling's insistence that the doubling 'is only exposed and proven in the ideal series', but turns the grounding of both series in the 'real series' into a mere paradox rather than a demonstration of the naturalism of naturephilosophy and the resulting regionality of consciousness to it. Failure to note this transforms any philosophy into subjective idealism.

20 As we shall see, the quantity of identity becomes crucial to Schelling's *Potenzlehre* or 'theory of the powers', which works precisely on the exponents or powers of any given identity. A, A^2, A^3, as the sequence runs.

21 I borrow the phrasing from Beiser (2005: 86), discussing the Leibnizian *vis viva* or 'living force': 'We must measure this power, Leibniz maintained, not in terms of extension – the *quantity of motion* (the velocity times the size of the object) – but in dynamic terms – the *quantity of effect* (how much can be produced by its activity).'

22 Georg Cantor, *Grundlagen einer allgemeinen Mannigfaltigkeitslehre* (Leipzig: Treubner, 1883). For Cantor's contestation of the merely potential infinite, see Moore 2001: 117ff. Cantor's typology of infinites included the 'absolute infinite' or 'inconsistent totalities . . . manies too big to be regarded as ones'. Of the Absolute as such, Cantor wrote: 'the Absolute can only be acknowledged and admitted, never known, not even approximately' (cited in Moore 2001: 128), echoing the Schellingian account of intellectual intuition.

23 A further early account of the 'genetic philosophy' is given in the *Treatise Explicatory of the Science of Knowledge*: 'In that transcendental philosophy views everything objective from the first as *nonexistent*, because its first principles are *genetic*, it is directed by nature towards *becoming* and *animation* by which both mind and world

become and develop' (*SW* I, 403; 1994c: 104, t.m.). The problem remains a constant in Schelling, culminating in the 'generative [*erzeugende*] dialectic' of the *Philosophy of Mythology* (*SW* XI, 330).

CHAPTER 6

Dynamic Philosophy, Transcendental Physics

Being is the content of pure thinking only as power. Now power, as it were, is by nature on the point of making the leap into Being. By the nature of its content therefore thought is drawn outside itself. For what has made the transition to being is no longer merely the content of thought. (XIII, 102)

Schelling does not think 'concepts'; he thinks forces and thinks from positions of the will. (Heidegger 1985: 111)

Given that the Eleatic Stranger, whom Deleuze (1992: 257) renames 'the Intelligent Dynamist', proposes that 'being is nothing other than power' (*Soph*. 247e3–4), it would be surprising had Plato not attempted the parallel approach to resolving the vexed problem of the 'matter of the Ideas', as Plotinus (VI.6.vi) puts it: in place of the somatism he criticizes (*Stat*. 273b5; *Tim*. 31b5), Plato therefore asks: with what 'powers' is something 'endowed by nature' (*Phil*. 29b7; cf. *Tim*. 49a4–6)? Intelligent dynamists and Platonists alike, therefore, consider the 'indeterminate dyad' to comprise the conjunction of being and becoming in the *kinds*, or the 'combination of unity and multiplicity, or plurality' that Schelling identifies as a Platonic 'concept of nature [*Naturbegriff*]' (1994a: 36): it is evident in the *Sophist*'s definition of kinds as comprising 'plurality of being and infinite not-being' (256e8), and in the *Philebus*' 'infinite kind [*tou apeirou genos*]' to which 'all things that become more or less' belong (24e7–8).

Schelling, arguing that the 'content of pure thinking' is Being as power, is likewise a philosopher of forces (although not on the reducibly volitional grounds Heidegger slightly desperately suggests). Following Kielmeyer's indication that a derivation of 'the laws in accordance with which humans arrange concepts' (1938: 214) is to be expected from the laws of dynamics, Schelling therefore undertakes to provide that derivation. When therefore the *System* postulates 'the identity of the dynamic and the transcendental' (III, 452; 1978: 91) as grounding the parallelism of nature and intelligence, the entirety of the ancient problem of the matter of the Ideas comes with it. Schelling's basic assumption is that the construction of objects follows identical series in ideation as in matter: the introduction of a limit into the unlimited (first act), the object-becomings of the construct as repeatedly divided by this limit (second act), and the object-becoming-to-itself of the construct now recapitulating this division in itself (third act), i.e., between forces. At each stage, the decomposition of intelligence parallels that of matter, while at no stage is the asymmetry of the process eliminated.[1]

The *System*'s identity postulate, echoed in the *Universal Deduction* (IV, 76), has, like the 'diversifying antithesis' in which the materiality of the Ideas was said by Aristotle to consist, at least two elements, with one addressed in each work according to its subject. The *System* therefore pursues this identity in terms of the transcendental; here again, the identity decomposes into two forces: firstly, 'what we call reason is simply a play of higher natural forces unknown to us' (III, 273–4; 2004: 194), and secondly, the matter of intuition, whether the chemical intuition of the *Ideas* (II, 323–4; 1988: 257), the electrical sensibility of the *System* (III, 452; 1978: 91), or the magnetic *Ichheit* of the *System of Philosophy as a Whole* (VI, 398, 455). Accordingly, Schelling crosses the two sciences: from the 'basic science' of philosophical dynamics, a transcendental physics emerges.

We will see below that physics is precisely the domain of the transcendental insofar as its remit is finite phenomena; at the same time, however, the transcendental, as Schelling repeatedly stresses, the production of phenomena, presupposes a necessary conjunction of matter and intuition, without which experience is inconceivable. Thus the *Universal Deduction* similarly proposes that sensation is electrical, as Ritter's autogalvanic experiments demonstrate, and as Schelling reports in the *World Soul* – 'apply zinc to the nerves and silver to the muscles, you get excitation; reverse the procedure, and the organism is at rest', and so forth (II, 559–60). Matter, therefore, subjected to repeated potentiations in 'self-recapitulating nature', is necessarily coincident with intuition, so that 'the human is not only idealist in philosophers' eyes, but also in the eyes of nature itself' (IV, 76): it is, in other words, Schelling's hypothesis that *realism concerning the Idea* follows from the physical grounds of idea-generating organizations, or intelligence. In many ways, Schelling's naturalistic realism offers a counterpoint to the eliminativist strategy in contemporary neurophilosophy: *if* ideation is electrochemistry, electrochemistry grounds, rather than undermines, all ideation. Therefore, to eliminate one ideation (that has its electrochemical grounds) in favour of another cannot be grounded in physics.[2] Hence Schelling's late definition of myth as still 'a kind of philosophy', only 'unconscious, naturalistic, *autophusis philosophia*' (XI, 258), or '*nature itself philosophizing*'. Myth is of course preconceptual, but precisely in the sense that the potentiation of the *autophusis* generates concepts. Forces, as we shall see, subject the concept to other tests.

That the identity of the two sciences therefore retains rather than eliminates their basic asymmetry is further given when the *Universal Deduction* considers the parallel modes of explanation in transcendentalism and dynamics: in their reversion to ground as explanatory strategy, philosophy and physics are indeed identical – hence the seconding of the philosopher's assertion that philosophy is 'nothing other than physics, just *speculative* physics' (III, 274; 2004: 194) by Ritter: 'philosophy is nothing other than physics' (1984: 247). Yet because 'a phenomenon dynamically explained means exactly that it has been explained from the original conditions of the construction of matter in general' (IV, 76), philosophical grounds are necessarily parasitic on physical ones. Concerning the apparent egalitarianism of the *System*'s distribution of trajectories between the two basic sciences – 'all philosophy must go about *either* to make an intelligence out of nature, *or* a nature out of intelligence [i.e., transcendental philosophy]' (III, 343; 1978: 7) – the *Universal Deduction* concludes: 'the *true* direction . . . is that which *nature itself* has taken' (IV, 78). When Hegel attempts the presentation of Schellingian identity, he botches it royally: 'Everything is in *one* totality only: the objective totality and the subjective totality, the system of nature and the system of intelligence are one and the same' (1977a: 166). Where Hegel posits an 'identity of becoming and being' (1977a: 172), Schellingian identity potentiates the differentiation of its elements, precisely because it is not simply numerical or extensional identity, but rather power. As the *Exposition of My System* (the work on which Hegel bases his account of Schelling) states: 'the essence of absolute identity, insofar as it is the immediate ground of reality, is *force*' (IV, 145). Due in turn to the identity of the dynamic and the transcendental, the nature of this force can be specified: 'In magnetism, we see clearly in all nonorganic nature alone, what is equally characteristic of nature as a whole; namely identity in duplicity and duplicity in identity (what differently put, is termed polarity)' (III, 253n; 2004: 181n). Polarity is not therefore a merely formal arrangement of antithetical elements, but is the specific instantiation of tensions in the 'primal antithesis extending throughout all of nature in infinite bifurcations' (III, 219; 2004: 148) that is nature. Absolute identity is identity *involved* to zero, to the 'lack of reality in intuition' (IV, 6), at which point not even 'quantitative difference can be thought' (IV, 347), or *evolved* to its highest power, which is 'self-consciousness' (III, 355; 1978: 14) or intelligence. Because therefore magnetism is the 'first dimension of self-construction', 'objective self-consciousness' or the '*Ichheit* of nature' (VI, 398, 455), its potentiation is constant throughout nature and ideation: 'everything that is, is identity itself' (IV, 120).[3] While 'the acts which are derived in the theoretical part of idealism are acts the simple powers of which exist in nature and are set out in naturephilosophy' (IV, 92), naturephilosophy amounts to 'the most elaborate experiment in the exposition of the theory of the Ideas and the identity of nature with the world of Ideas' (II, 69; 1988: 52). The identity of the dynamic and the transcendental therefore lies not in any procedural similarities, nor in any essential 'likeness' of the two sciences, but in identity itself, that is, in self-fracturing identity at the base, at the level of the forces.

Schellingian identity therefore takes the synthetic place of the analytic disjunction of intuition and matter in Kant. Accordingly, there is no barrier or screen between intuition and nature *in itself* ('to what aberrations would physics otherwise be subject . . .?', III, 347; 1978: 10), so that 'all our knowledge is originally empirical' (III, 528; 1978: 151) and if knowledge at all, then knowledge of reality. Key to this as regards transcendental philosophy is the non-equivalence of subjectivity and *Ichheit*, although this non-equivalence is simply a potentiated or intensified consequence of the primal antithesis of productivity and product in nature. Indeed, it is only because of this that the transcendental non-equivalence can be sustained: the *Ich* is a product, 'merely the concept of becoming an object to oneself' (III, 366; 1978: 25), in which the producing is never exhausted. To turn, as it were, from the product and form a concept of the producing does not complete the intuition, but renders the producing a product itself produced by another producing, thus leaving an 'irreducible remainder' of forces that cannot be resolved into the product. Thus the production of the *Ich* consists in a repetition of the asymmetrical relation of forces at the highest power, so that the *Ich* is no transcendental atom or 'universal thought-molecule', as Novalis suggested (1996: 593), but a potentiation of the antithesis between productivity and product, or 'the identity of subject and object we call nature' (III, 355; 1978: 14).

Dynamic identity has a long history, stemming from the '*aoristas duas*', the 'diversifying antithesis' or 'indefinite dyad', the 'purely dimensional not-anything that occupied in Plato's system the place taken by . . . matter in Aristotle' (Wicksteed and Cornford, in Aristotle 1970, I: 40n). Identity, like matter, cannot be intuited, because it is necessarily universal. Thus, while 'all our knowledge is originally empirical' (III, 528; 1978: 151), the sensible is shot through with 'force, the nonsensible in objects' (II, 219; 1988: 175). Universals such as force, matter and identity are not sensible, although they generate intuition; yet they remain intelligible precisely because their universality is real, not merely logical. Due to the identity thesis, force is the '*material [Stoff]* of the universal' (XI, 313),[4] where the universal is not simply a *logical* entity, but rather, 'the Universe itself' (VI, 184; 1994c: 175). Non-intuitable but thinkable by the involution (depotentiation) of the powers to indifference, the Idea of matter, for instance, entails that 'every-thing is midpoint' (VI, 255) precisely because products arise *between* these poles and disappear at the limit, 'which is indicated in intuition simply by zero or absolute lack of reality' (IV, 6). Objects and intuitions are real transcendentals, with their grounds in 'self-constructing matter, simply recapitulated at different stages' (IV, 4). What is recapitulated is identity: the physically magnetic antithesis of the forces. Even 'the empirical magnet must', Schelling writes, 'be considered the indifference point in the total magnet' (IV, 379). The Schellingian diversifying antithesis therefore diversifies along the vertical axis of recapitulation or the determination of forces, and along the horizontal axis of transcendentalization, the intro-duction of the limit into the unlimited, or the determination of objective intuition.

The history of the diversifying antithesis does not end with Schelling. Deleuze takes it up in characterizing Platonic becoming – the 'hotter and the colder', the 'younger becoming older than the older, the older becoming younger than the younger' – but proposes an entirely different solution to the problem to the matter of the Ideas. 'We recognise', writes Deleuze, 'this Platonic dualism.'

> It is not at all the dualism of the intelligible and the sensible, of Idea and matter, or of Ideas and bodies. It is a more profound dualism hidden in sensible and material bodies themselves. It is a subterranean dualism between that which receives the action of the Idea and that which eludes this action. It is not the distinction between the Model and the copy, but rather between copies and simulacra. Pure becoming, the unlimited, is the matter of the simulacrum insofar as it eludes the action of the idea and insofar as it contests both model *and* copy at once. Limited things lie beneath the Ideas; but even beneath things, is there not still this mad element which subsists and occurs on the other side of the order that Ideas impose and things receive? (Deleuze 1990: 2)

In specifying the 'mad element' contesting both orders and their relations as the 'matter of the simulacrum', Deleuze introduces a subordinate differential series that evades the metrics of the Idea, which imposes order as though stemming from practical designs, a proto-*Statesman*, indeed. Just as Heidegger correctly locates the preeminence of forces in Schellingian intelligence, but mistakes their origin in a will, so Deleuze approaches the coordinates of Platonism with a view to usurping the 'justice' or the just that is to be consequent upon the Ideas' induction into matter. In percolating through the orders, the mad element and its series – the series of claimants to philosophy, for example, that the Eleatic Stranger tracks down in the *Sophist*, whose indistinctness causes the Stranger to proliferate his collecting and dividing – makes the receiving matter too turbulent to take the impress of the Idea. Now Deleuze conceives of this turbulent matter exactly as does the *Statesman*, as a 'boundless sea of diversity' (273e1), or as the *Timaeus*' 'nature which receives all bodies' (50b7). Where Plato adds, however, that this nature 'never takes on the permanent impress of any' such body, Deleuze adds an activity to this impassivity, so that as 'pure becoming', it 'eludes the action of the Idea'. Locating the 'indeterminate dyad' therefore in 'sensible bodies', the Intelligent Dynamist posits a more profound multiplicity that lies under the ground of limited bodies and the grounding of the Idea.

For Deleuze as for Schelling, limited objects are exceeded on both sides by the forces and actions of matter and Idea. What differs between the two accounts is on the one hand, the focus of the forces, and on the other, the nature of the Idea. Concerning the first, for Deleuze, the teeming subterranean multiplicity of becomings have as their antithesis the unshakeable vertical radiance of the solar One, in a struggle over the determination of sensible bodies and the balance of powers between those exercised through them, and those exercised upon them. For Schelling, by contrast, the becoming of being consists in passages and transitions, while identity consists in potentiations and depotentiations, determining the limited thing as a power of the unlimited, while limited things are in turn 'approximations of productivity'.

Forces are antithetical all the way up, therefore, and do not only become so in phenomenal antitheses (the empirical magnet). In consequence, Schelling's problem is not the excessive burden of determination on becoming, but rather the extent to which determination can be at once constructed *in general* and *in particular*. The *System*, taking only a single series (the production of the *Ich*), manages the latter precisely by turning away from the former, while the naturephilosophical works manages the former without attaining to particular products. It is in an endeavour to resolve this therefore that Schelling turns first to the 'identity system', and then, following Steffens, to geology. Deleuze, by contrast, makes sensible bodies into the regional focus of antithetical actions stemming from different sources, or different subjects, to speak Schellingian. In consequence, the differentiating natures of the Idea and of pure becoming are given only in sensible bodies. The Deleuzian antithesis, therefore, consists in the attempt to determine the nature of ground. Emergent therefore from this engagement is a third common problem, which we shall address below: that of transcendental geology.

To a certain extent a variation on the same themes as the last problem, the determination of the nature of the Idea in each philosopher could not be more different. Deleuze and Guattari define the Idea as 'objectively possess[ing] a pure quality' and therefore 'not something other than what it is', while limited things, by contrast, are 'always something other than what they are' (Deleuze and Guattari 1994: 30). Praising Plato as 'master of the concept', Deleuze and Guattari criticize the ethics of Plato's creation of the concept: 'he creates concepts but needs to set them up as representing the uncreated that precedes them' (1994: 29). This is precisely the meaning Deleuze attaches to the Nietzschean formula of reversing Platonism, which must mean, he writes, 'to bring the motivation of Platonism out into the light of day, to "track it down" – the way Plato tracks down the Sophist' (Deleuze 1990: 253). The problem here is not that this ethicization demeans the Royal 'objectality' of the Idea *as* Plato constructs it, with all his elevated language; rather, it is the elision of the problem of the matter of the Idea. In other words, the attempt to reverse Platonism results in the maintenance of a 'subterranean' form of two-worlds metaphysics. The same problem can be glimpsed in the otherwise minimal characterization Deleuze gives of the 'philosophy of nature' on which he and Guattari were working, 'now that any distinction between nature and artifice is becoming blurred' (1995: 155): artifice is, as is usual, here considered as belonging to the order of construction, which would not be suspicious were it not for a nature assumed construction-free. Again, this is not simply an issue of retrospecting a golden age of 'natural nature' prior to its artificialization; rather it concerns the distribution of construction. Schelling's naturalism concerning self-organization has no problem acknowledging that the 'self-construction of matter' entails that matter is both the agent and the object of construction, as well as the groundwork for the construction of all subjectivity, insofar as this consists in the *Selbigkeit* of the *auto* that, while it necessarily precedes the *Ichheit* of consciousness, does not require to become this in order to be 'subjective'. On these lights, Deleuze cuts construction off at its roots, in order to bootstrap a reducibly political ethology of the artificial.

At issue here, then, is the scope of naturephilosophy, divided by the most persistent of its detractors. Rather than the Hegelianism against which Schelling is often pitted (Frank 1975, Bowie 1993), it is rather Fichteanism that troubles naturephilosophy. When therefore, in the context of Nietzsche's thought (never far from Deleuze's concerns), Deleuze asks of the forces, 'Which is the reactive? Which the active?' (1983, *passim*), two events pass simultaneously. First, the grounding of Nietzschean physiology, which pursues the constitution of the thinker as a diagnosis of the thought ('what is the motivation?'); and second, due to the argument that reactivity is not by origin, but rather becomes other than the active, the objective is the maximal expansion of the sphere of activity, and the progressive transmutation of the reactive into the active. Although not set against nature, as the first edition of *On the Concept of the Science of Knowledge* defines the 'not-*Ich*' (W I, 65; 1988: 121), the implication is clear: that *ethos* is to determine *phusis* presents the stakes of the artificialization of nature for Deleuze. It is no accident then that Alliez, writing on Deleuze, has recently called for a philosophical reopening of the Fichte case (cf. 2004: 30n). The intelligence of the Intelligent Dynamist does indeed therefore consist in the 'ethical vision of the world' (1992: 257); that it is a vision of the *world*, however, enables Deleuze to resolve Schelling's problem regarding the determination of particularity (sensible bodies): what determines the nature of bodies is the character of the forces acting through or on them. For this reason, there can be no physics of ideation in Deleuze.

Given this, it might have seemed surprising that Deleuze and Guattari single out the 'philosophical reality' of the Schellingian 'autopositing' or 'autopoietic concept' (1994: 11) for praise, were it not for the fact that, as they are careful to stipulate in their exemplification of Plato, the Idea is there said to be a concept. Schelling does not, that is, present the concept *itself* as 'self-positing'; rather the Idea is the autopostulate – albeit in a limited sense – and the concept its grasp in reflection, where it becomes a 'purely formal concept' (II, 198; 1988: 158). Hence Schelling's repeated insistence on the limited nature of the concept: 'there are concepts only of objects, of what is limited and sensibly intuited' (I, 401). We have already noted, for instance, that the concept of the *Ich* is a *product*, and consists precisely and only in 'becoming an object to oneself'; the producing of the concept is not therefore autonomous, but requires construction in order to become so. Amongst the initial concerns of the *System*, therefore, is the problem of how 'presentations, arising freely and without necessity in us, pass over from the world of thought into the actual world, and can obtain objective reality' (III, 347; 1978: 11). Just as the first moment of subjectivity is, however, given in the self-construction of matter, so that nature is precisely the subject-object the potentiation of which becomes self-consciousness, so too the concept does not arise from nothing, on two counts. Firstly, as noted, natural subjectivities are everywhere in nature; as in the *Parmenides*, 'everything thinks' (132c8), albeit to a limited extent.

Secondly, the concept is a synthesis of thought and thing, just as intuition is the coincidence of matter and sensation; 'all our knowledge is originally empirical precisely because concept and object arise for us unseparated and simultaneously' (III, 528; 1978: 151). Accordingly, concepts 'still have the real outside themselves' (X, 139–40; 1994b: 144). From this identity of concept and intuition, the transcendental philosophy arises; but the concept can also be potentiated through construction. Emphasizing its productivity, Schelling will later characterize construction as 'the dialectical method', which is 'not demonstrative, but generative [*Erzeugend*]' (XI, 330), just as the *Ideas* asserted that the synthetic procedure 'allows the concept to arise . . . and to find the ground of its necessity in its own origin' (II, 214; 1988: 172). Further potentiated or 'evolved', the concept becomes the 'Idea, which is the infinite concept, the concept of the universe' (VI, 185; 1994c: 173), something which itself 'oscillates between the infinite and finitude . . . Products of this kind are what we call Ideas as opposed to concepts' (III, 558–9; 1978: 176). Even at the highest power, the Idea recapitulates the basal syntheses of the concept, or the primal antithesis of identity.

Along with this synthetic aspect of the concept, which guarantees the physical immanence of the transcendental, it is in its finitude that the nature and function of the concept become apparent. Rather than any autopositing character, it is the concept's insertion into the series of the real, on the one hand, and its reduplication, on the other, that provides the first axis of its dynamic nature. The *System* constantly emphasizes that the *Ich* is nothing other than the concept of becoming an object to oneself, that is, it is insofar that the *Ich* is conceived that it is actualized. Since the *Ich* arises as construction in the 'sole organ of transcendental philosophy', i.e., *inner sense* (III, 350; 1978: 13), the synthesis it performs corresponds to no intuitable content other than the constructions of which it is the by-product. Thus the *Ich* arises punctually and serially, rather than constituting a subject in the Aristotelian sense of substrate (*hypokeimenon*). This is why the *Ich* has 'epochs': it is originally no continuum, but must be integrated into one. It is not simply, however, as a guarantee of the identity or persistence of a particular empirical *Ich* that this reduplicative or recursive positing is thus integrated; rather, the other element synthesized in the *Ich* as concept is the constructions undertaken of concepts in general, so that the number of iterations of the *Ich* in any given series corresponds to the extensity of the concepts thus constructed. This is why Schelling makes a fuss about the *System*'s experiments in 'the exposition of idealism *to its fullest extent*' (III, 331; 1978: 2, t.m.): every philosophical construction undergoes the test of the *extensity* of its concepts. So too the quantity of its bifurcating power, that is, the extent to which the ideal *Ich* is capable of successive decomposition into particulars, yields the *intensity* of the concept, and consists therefore in the measure of the largest differential of which that bifurcating power is capable. Thus, in sensible intuition, the 'recursive' or 'reduplicative positing' (X, 103; 1994b: 116; 1989a: 49–50), reiterates the physical immediacy of the synthetic concept. Rather than establishing an identity of concept and nature, the identity consists in the coincident nature of their constant bifurcations. This is why 'there is only quantitative difference between the Ideal and the real' (VI, 209). The *Potenzen* or 'powers' of the concept therefore provide the method of integration proper to the constructions in which philosophy necessarily consists. At its highest potentiation, the concept undergoes something of a phase-shift: 'the Idea, which is the infinite concept [or] the concept of the universe' (VI, 185; 1994c: 173).

The titling therefore of the *Exposition of My System* and the *Further Expositions* does not simply indicate the 'setting forth' of that philosophy, but provides an approximation to productivity of that philosophy. In these works, Schelling makes, as it were, the sustained evolution of philosophical activity into a principle of philosophy in general. It is not so much the 'patient exposition of the absolute' that, according to Châtelet (1993: 139), marks the 'ambition' of Schellingian philosophy, therefore, as the constancy of its unfolding and the maximal integration of its concepts. Hence the sometimes bewildering density of the Schellingian conceptual landscape: the profusion of its concepts attests to the degree to which its constructions 'approximate to productivity', as Steffens astutely notes (in Schelling 2001: 26).

While this provides one test of the concept, and makes some sense of Heidegger's assertion that 'Schelling does not think concepts; he thinks forces' (1985: 111), there are two further dimensions of the concept to which its finite nature fits it. The first of these dimensions concerns the construction of particularity: the problem confronting the diverse derivations of the *Stufenfolge* in the naturephilosophy is, in effect, the problem identified in the 'History' essay concerning the theoretical intransigence of a nature whose *only* necessity is productivity, rather than the nature of its products. In other words, because no necessity, but only dependency, can be attached to physical particulars, how can their organization into *particular* product-series be explained? Hence the importance of the conjunction of the *finite* concept and the *finite* product in intuition: that 'there are concepts only of objects, of what is limited and sensibly intuited' is premised on the inductive principle that 'like is known by like' (VII, 337; 1986: 8), or that 'like *produces* like [*Gleiches Gleiches hervorruft*]' (VII, 281). Thus, the declaration of the concept's finitude is grounded in this inductive principle: just as, that is, 'freedom is known by freedom, activity by activity' (I, 401), so the finite concept conceives only the finite product. The identity therefore of matter and Idea consists in their constant disjunction, so the solution to this ancient problem by inductive means further resolves the problem of the construction of physical particulars.

Thus indissociably alloyed to particulars, the concept cannot 'grasp' becoming other than by its disintegration and reintegration into series of successive positings of the concept. Thus the final dimension of the dynamics of the Idea following from the finite nature of the concept paradoxically concerns the transitional nature of the thinking of being as power. With this, our exposition of Schellingianism is brought to an end. Thus, while Beierwaltes emphasizes the importance Schelling attaches to the 'grasping [*begriffen*]' that occurs in the concept [*Begriff*], entailing that this grasping is not an act of mind alone, but that there is something to grasp, an 'in itself' that is thus grasped, his assertion that there arises a 'grasping of the Idea' is false. The Idea arises as a potentiation of the concept, and as such, remains 'nothing other than syntheses' (II, 64; 1988: 48), whose poles are the ideal and the real as such, rather than particular ideations and particular products. That the Idea does not therefore have objects as such as its 'object' means that they take as their *objective* the 'unthinged'. But without things, what is there for thought to seize upon, what is the function of the concept? It is one of Schelling's greatest innovations in the concept 'Idea' to have replaced the relation of thought and thing with that of absolute and relative *motion*, or the unlimited becomings of nature. Already indicated in the truly strange notion of the 'speed of evolution' in the *First Outline* (III, 15; 2004: 15), Schellingian transcendentalism becomes progressively consumed by specific relations of motions, with relations of thought to the absolute:

> The absolutely mobile . . . which is continually an other, which cannot be held onto for a moment, which is only in the last moment . . . is actually thought – how does this relate to thought? Obviously not even as a real object of thought; for by 'object' one understands something which keeps still, which stands still, which remains. It is not really an object, but rather the mere *material* of thought that runs throughout the entire science; for actual thinking expresses itself only in the progressive determination and formation of what is in itself indeterminate, never self-identical, always an other-becoming. (X, 150–1; 1994b: 152, t.m.)

Hence Schelling's condemnation of the 'purely formal concept' engendered by reflection, consisting merely of projections onto the walls of the cave of consciousness: the concept is by its nature incapable of a grasp of becoming, although susceptible itself *to* becoming (potentiation).

The key element in the construction of the Idea therefore consists not of thinking *what* the construction is *of*, but rather the *nature of the movements produced thereby*. Every motion of thought draws lines across the medium of the Absolute, against which it is necessarily measured. Nor therefore are these simply harmless or ontologically innocent compositions, but the means by which 'a being becomes' (X, 150; 1994b: 152, t.m.). This, finally, is how Schelling satisfies the paradoxical Platonic rubric of the 'becoming of being', or the generation of the Ideas. Having seen, in other words, how a dynamic physics includes the Idea, what becomes of the character of the Idea?

> The emergence into being [*Erzeugung*] of such patterns or visions is a necessary moment in the great development of life. And while these are certainly not to be thought of as physical substances or as empty genera [*Gattungsbegriffe*] nonetheless neither are they to be thought of as finished and available, existing without motion and as it were standstill forms [*Formen*]; they are Ideas precisely because they are eternal Becomings,

ceaselessly in motion and generation [*denn eben darum sind sie Ideen, dass sie ein ewig Werdendes und in unaufhörlicher Bewegung und Erzeugung sind*]. [. . .] The generation [*Erzeugung*] of these archetypes [*Urbilder*] is a necessary moment . . . so these archetypes outflow from the interior of creative nature. (VIII, 289–90; 2000: 66–7)

When therefore Deleuze and Guattari write of the Platonic 'concept of the Idea' that it contains a bad faith paradox of temporality, being by nature 'prior to every concept', while the concept has time inserted into it, 'but a time that must be Anterior' in its construction (1994: 29), they fail to think the 'becoming of being' that is the central challenge of Platonic physics. The Schellingian solution, however, consists in this: the Idea is the eternity of motion phenomenally and physically serialized as 'always becoming' (*Tim.* 27e9), just as nature is infinite productivity serialized in products.

We come then to the final problem raised by the confrontation of Schelling and Deleuze, which concerns the nature of ground.

Notes

1   Schelling repeats these series, which appear in the *System* in the 'General note upon the first epoch' (III, 450–4; 1978: 90–93), in 'True concept': 'We will again see in the remaining three senses the recapitulation that happens only in the higher powers of the three moments of reconstruction – magnetism, electricity and the chemical process' (IV, 101); and again in the *Universal Deduction*: 'When the dynamic phenomena present themselves to us in the second power of productive nature, we see a still higher power active in organic nature. Therefore, just as magnetism presents the second power of the first moment, so *sensibility* is again the higher power of magnetism (from which it is already clear that as little as this can be a simple function, it instead presupposes duplicity as condition). In the same way, in *irritability* is a higher power of electricity, but in the *formative drive* a higher power of electricity is active.' (IV, 73)

2   This is because the metaphysics of eliminativism are complex, involving an epochal or futuralizing Nietzscheanism and a radically synthetic theory of constitutive identity construction: neurolinguistic identities do not simply represent the fruit of epistemological and empirical researches, but trigger a gestalt-shift and reinvent the world. Folk psychology is condemned therefore for its lack of physicalist imagination, rather than any missing physical grounds – what philosopher could disagree?

3   The 'True concept' is emphatic on this point: 'In naturephilosophy, I never depart from this identity of the ideal-real, I constantly maintain the two in their original combination; and the pure subject-object from which I begin is precisely simultaneously ideal and real at 0 potency. Only from this does the ideal-real at the higher power – the I – emerge for me, in which regard the *pure* subject-object is already objective.' (IV, 87)

4   'As we have seen, the third has the highest claim to being the existent. But since it cannot be what it is for itself, but only in reciprocity with the other, it can be said precisely of it that it only *can* be the existent for itself, that it is a potency of the existent. But is the whole that is necessarily generated in thought really the existent? Yes, but only in outline, only in the Idea, not actually. Just as every individual element only *can be* the existent, so the whole is indeed the existent, but the existent equally *is* not, but only can be. It is the schema of the existent, not it itself, the *material* of the actual Idea, not it itself, actually, as

197

Aristotle says of the dynamis in the universal: it is only the *material* of the universal.' (*SW* XI, 313) Schelling is here citing Aristotle, *Metaphysics* 1087a17: '*e men dunamis os hyle* [*tou*] *katholou*', which Tredennick gives as 'the potentiality being, as matter, universal'.

CHAPTER 7

Conclusion: Transcendental Geology

If we wanted to speak of a history of nature in the true sense of the word, we should have to picture nature as though, apparently free in its productions, it had gradually brought forth the whole multiplicty thereof through constant departures from a primordial original; which would then be a history, not of *natural objects* (which is properly the description of nature), but of *generative nature itself*. (III, 588; 1978: 199)

I hold nature and history to be utterly distinct things. (Eschenmayer to Schelling, VII, 145)

At the outset of the *Critique of Judgment*, Kant combines the results of the previous critiques, in the domain of the metaphysics of nature and knowledge, on the one hand, and in that of will and the practical, on the other: 'there must be', he writes, threatening a return to all those early essays on geology,[1] 'a ground uniting nature and freedom' (*Ak.* V, 176; 1987: 15). It is a measure of the unfinished task this problem represents that Badiou has recently repeated it: 'the rethinking of the univocity of ground is a necessary task for the world in which we are living today' (2000: 46). Elsewhere declaring 'the philosophy of or as nature' to be a 'contemporary impossibility' (1997: 64), Badiou therefore dismisses the Schellingian solution to this problem, and the traces of it he locates in Deleuze. As Eschenmayer remarked in his critique of Schelling's *Philosophical Inquiries into the Essence of Human Freedom*, the proposals concerning ground contained therein amount to 'a complete transformation of ethics into physics' (in Schelling VIII, 150). Rather than the naturephilosophical solution, therefore, Badiou favours the set-theoretic ontology pioneered by Oken, but crucially, claims this approach as a return to 'classicism' in philosophy, against the 'criticism' that has governed it since Kant. Notwithstanding Badiou's protestations in this regard, Kantian coordinates – 'world' in both its natural and its ethical aspect, and the problem of ground – continue nevertheless to determine the problem to which he proposes this ardent mathesis as a solution.

Similarly, the Deleuzian diversifying antithesis consists in the domains of nature and freedom that form the necessary poles of ontological inquiry. Repeating the determinants of Kant's third *Critique* while differentiating significantly from it, the Deleuzian antithesis, in contrast to the worldly urgency Badiou attaches to 'rethinking the concept of ground', does not seek a ground in which they are united, but rather an *ungrounding* that affects the world. The antithesis therefore proposes neither a one-world physics, as does Schelling, nor an imperative that the physical be determined by the ethical, as does Fichte, but a one-world transcendentalism in 'the upper and lower reaches of this world' (1994: 135). 'The laws of nature', writes Deleuze, 'govern the surface of the world', while a 'transcendental or volcanic spatium' troubles its depths (1994: 241):

> Depth is *like* the famous geological line from NE to SW, the line which comes diagonally from the heart of things and distributes volcanoes: it unites a bubbling sensibility and a thought which 'rumbles in its crater'. Schelling said that depth is not added from without to length and breadth, but remains buried, like the sublime principle of conflict that creates them. (1994: 230; my emphasis)

Thus locating the transcendental in the upper *and* lower regions of this world, the volcanic spatium is formed by sudden and convulsive transections of depth and height, which dimension lies perpendicular to a surface which, although governed by the laws of nature, is in no way distinct from the 'prodigious domain of the transcendental' (1994: 135) that erupts through it.

Although Deleuze indicates the source of this conception in Schelling – so unjustly maligned by Hegel, he claims (1994: 190–1) – his account differs on two counts from it. Firstly, Schelling is citing Steffens' 'On the oxydation and deoxydation process of the earth' (in Schelling 2001: 95–110), and is concerned with earth-history or 'scientific geology' (IV, 508):

> If . . . we take a volcanic zone that encircles the earth, beginning approximately at 22° to 23° latitude N, and ending at 15° to 16° latitude S (for every indication shows that the physical equator – like all land – extends further northwards than the mathematical equator), then all the volcanoes that do not lie in this zone, lie in the north towards the *eastern*, in the south towards the *western* hemisphere. (Steffens, in Schelling 2001: 101)[2]

The question therefore arises as to the nature of the 'likeness' Deleuze reports between the transcendental dimension of depth and this 'famous geological line'. When, for example, Schelling, in his editor's foreword to Steffens' essay, suggests that amongst the consequences to be hoped for from such geological researches are that some relation may be discovered 'between the expressions of terrestrial magnetism variant in proportion to variation in extent, and the lines characterised by volcanic chains over the body of the earth' (IV, 509), the likeness involved in such correspondences is not ideal or analogical, but physical. Volcanic depth and the chemistry of eruption do not therefore differ from the surface force of magnetism in nature, but precisely in dimension. Connections therefore between the chemical and the magnetic terrestrial processes will therefore 'lead us to a proof of the dynamic succession of stages in the construction of every real product in general' (ibid.). For Deleuze, meanwhile, the ground of the differentiation of the transcendental and the empirical dimensions of volcanism is itself transcendental or, as Deleuze names it in order to cement the distinction, 'groundlessness': 'Something of the ground rises to the surface without assuming any form, but, rather, insinuating itself between the forms; a formless base, an autonomous and faceless existence. This ground which is now on the surface is called depth or groundlessness' (1994: 275).

Secondly, therefore, the nature of the Schellingian transcendental is, as we have seen, as different from the Deleuzian as from the Kantian: the earth itself, as a productive product, is to that extent a natural transcendental or a *Scheinprodukt*. For Schelling, the transcendental is not a domain at all, but consists in physical series of products susceptible of potentiation, yielding the series for all products: forces – phenomenal product – idea. Accordingly, Schelling locates the base of the problem in the earth:

> The conflict between the axes of absolute and relative cohesion could hardly be settled otherwise than by the production of the *diagonal* of the two directions. We have no analogue amongst the known processes for the process of this production, which is that of the eruption and unleashing of the indwelling third dimension. [. . .] In this regard, I can rely all the more securely on what was demonstrated . . . by Steffens[, namely,] that *all volcanoes in the north lie to the eastern, in the south towards the western, hemispheres.* For what else does this relation express than the diagonal we have provided, and a *polarity of earth in depth*? (IV, 504–5)

In response to the problem of ground, therefore, we have two transcendentalisms: for the Schellingian transcendental, as for dynamics, grounding consists in explicating or evolving the phenomenon to 'the original conditions of the construction of matter itself' (IV, 76). It is to this that Deleuze adds the further, although equally Schellingian, dimension of *ungrounding*. Accordingly, the object (the surface of the world) does not require grounding until it has been ungrounded by transcendental volcanism. Thus 'to ground is to determine the indeterminate' (1994: 275), or all determination takes place on indeterminate grounds: 'ground is assigned only in a world precipitated into universal ungrounding' (1994: 202). 'How disappointing!' Deleuze exclaims, to find 'everything ungrounded instead of solid ground' (1994: 200). We recognize this ungrounding from the 'mad, subterranean element' that arose in the ungrounding of the Idea-thing relation in Deleuze's 'reversal' of Platonism. Ungrounding, the opening up of things to the turbulences beneath them, is like a Plutonian version of the Neptunist deluge: everything is fiery, rather than aqueous, demanding construction. This, as Deleuze concludes, 'is the circle that metaphysics makes . . . of the physical or *phusis*' (1994: 292). The function of the transcendental, as universal ungrounding, is to multiply the topologies of which metaphysics makes physics capable.

Since Deleuze borrows overtly from Schellingianism in the construction of transcendental volcanism and the rethinking of the concept of ground, the two transcendentalisms are strikingly similar. Other than the shared geological sources, for example, Deleuze notes that the ideal 'enjoy[s] the double property of transcendence and immanence in relation to the real' (1994: 189), just as the Schellingian concept 'still has the real outside itself' while being susceptible of potentiation to the Idea. In accordance with the Schellingian method, however, the question arises as to the comparative extensity of a transcendental that invents topologies, just as Cantor's free mathematics invents infinities, on the one hand, and the dynamics of the transcendental Schelling proposes. Since for Deleuze the transcendental is the ungrounding of *phusis* and *ethos*, or of nature and freedom, and since it is the basic claim of Schellingian idealism that the one condition that 'anything whose conditions cannot be given in nature must be simply impossible' (III, 571; 1978: 186) is non-eliminative, the test of that system is the freedom of which it is capable. Further, there is the problem of matter. While by avoiding or exacerbating the Kantian trajectory (where is the ground that unites nature and freedom?) by way of ungrounding, Deleuze maintains the antithesis of nature and freedom, and thus does not determine the one by the other, this comes at the cost of regionalizing matter with respect to ideation, on the one hand, and freedom, on the other, and therefore risks the elision of nature altogether, much as Hegel sought to eliminate the geological organism from philosophy. If this argument is borne out, then we reach the surprising conclusion that *only a non-eliminative idealism is capable of the philosophy of matter*.

As we have seen, Eschenmayer remains critical of Schelling on broadly Fichtean grounds. Therefore, his account of Schelling's solution to the freedom problem is instructive. In an exchange of letters on the subject of Schelling's *Philosophical Inquiries*, Eschenmayer's remarks are as instructive as they counter contemporary understandings of the so-called 'philosophy of freedom':

> your essay on human freedom seems to me a complete transformation of ethics into physics, a consumption of the free by the necessary, of feeling by understanding, of the moral by the natural, and above all a complete depotentiation of the higher into the lower order of things. (VIII, 150)

We can imagine Eschenmayer's shock: why does this work on the subject of freedom contain so much geology? Why is the *turba gentium* (VII, 380; 1986: 58), the world-disorder or species-riots, presented as the ground of freedom? The source of Eschenmayer's criticisms, however, lie in Schelling's insistence that if there is to be freedom, it must arise in nature as its 'final, potentiating act' (VII, 350; 1986: 24). Just as the *System of Transcendental Idealism* took a single product-series (the 'evolving' of the *Ich*),[3] the *Inquiries* takes geogony, or earth-becoming, as its transcendental 'midpoint' from which to attempt the retrospection of 'generative nature'. Hence the abridged 'ages of the world' that follows the 'forces of the deep [that] ruled upon the earth' to their first and second 'divisions', each stage divided from the others by reversion to chaos, the becoming-barren of the earth, and the *turba gentium* itself, that overflows 'the creations of primeval time' and deposits a second time (VII, 379–81; 1986: 56–8), obliterating its precursor. The first foundations of the 'series of times' that forms the core of the *Ages of the World* project, which consumed Schelling's philosophical activity following the *Inquiries*, is set down in the freedom essay; not because this text, taken as the inception of the philosophy of freedom, marks the abandonment of naturephilosophy and the transition to the Ideal (which Schelling was always advertising, but never achieved), but because the consequences of the dependence of transcendental physics on dynamic naturalism impose upon Schelling's reconditioned transcendentalism the demand that the All be grounded in the 'subject of nature itself', i.e., in the forces. Accordingly, the more disorderly the phenomenon, the darker and more abyssal the ground. This is why the inquiry into *human* freedom must (a) specify the attachment of this power of infinite evolution to a finite phenomenon (human), and (b) consider the ground of such a freedom as derivative of the 'self-operation of the ground' or the 'will of the deep' in the geological series: the potentiating series through which such a freedom must (repeatedly) evolve must therefore present the *expression of geological potencies* in practical intelligence. Hence the *System*'s postulate that 'the activity whereby the objective world is produced is originally identical with that which is expressed in volition' (III, 348; 1978: 11–12).

Thus, where a Fichtean such as Eschenmayer could assert that 'I hold nature and history for utterly distinct things' (VIII, 146), a Schellingian such as Steffens argues that 'history must itself become nature . . . if it wanted to be affirmed as nature, that is, in every aspect of its being' (1908: 176). Accordingly, following the 'History' essay, this *Inquiries*' confrontation with the historicity of 'generative nature' (as opposed to a history of objects, III, 588; 1978: 199) not only draws the only possible conclusion from the naturephilosophical investigations of generative nature – that is, that natural history is not charted a priori as a sequenced mechanism following 'necessary laws', but a posteriori, in a nature that 'evolves along all possible paths' (I, 467, 469); it also demonstrates therefore that the 'final potentiating act' that is the natural production of freedom has as its consequence the 'ungrounding' of nature, and in two ways.

The first ungrounding follows from the theory of the subjectivity of nature as a priori in respect of its productivity. While, that is, nature as productivity does not appear itself, but always appears in products, its subjectivity – its autonomy and its self-sufficiency – consists in its forces. Accordingly, the natural historians' attempt to derive a history 'not of *natural objects* . . . but of *generative nature itself*' (III, 588; 1978: 199) entails *involving* the universal bifurcations in which the universe consists, since the dynamic subjectivity of nature is no 'cosmic animal' because organization is already an evolved product of the 'original antithesis of forces' (IV, 5).

Natural history becomes the attempted retrospection therefore of a system of infinitely bifurcating forces that must work from a product that is transcendental with regard to the forces that produce, maintain and reproduce it. The grounding of the transcendental product in dynamics thus ungrounds it in natural history, insofar as this is considered a universal, rather than a particular science. Thus ground is always the ground of something, never ground in general, since the latter is *Ur-* or *Un-grund* (VII, 406; 1986: 87). For a truly dynamic philosophy, that is, since productivity necessarily precedes product, 'there must be a being before all basis and before all existence, that is, before all duality at all; how can we designate it except as "primal ground"or rather as the "groundless"?' (VII, 406; 1986: 87).

The 'intuition of an unfathomable past' (X, 393) becomes increasingly formative as Schelling's geologism develops through the *Inquiries* and the *Ages of the World*:

> The oldest formations of the earth bear such a foreign aspect that we are hardly in a position to form a concept of their time of origin or of the forces that were then at work. Everything that surrounds us refers back to an incredibly deep past. The Earth itself and its mass of images must be ascribed an indeterminably greater age than the species of plants and animals, and these in turn greater than the race of men. We see a series of times in which one always follows another and the following always covers over the foregoing; nothing original ever shows itself, a mass of strata laid one upon the other; the labour of centuries must be stripped away, in order finally to reach the ground. (1946: 11–12)

If therefore ground is always and irrevocably particular, then natural history can investigate the grounding of ground, but, again in virtue of the nature of the subject of nature, 'nothing original ever appears itself'. In brief, the transcendental phenomenon has a physical ground, but physical ground is a product of the dynamic ungrounding that *precedes* it as the subject of nature itself. The 'intuition of an unfathomable past' (X, 393) is the phenomenon of an 'abyss of forces' (III, 324n): just as the *Ich* cannot retrospect its own construction, the construction of particularity cannot reverse along the 'infinite deviations' that generated it, but only along the extensity of its series that ground it. Natural history yields the irreducibly regional physics of the transcendental within universal ungrounding.

When therefore Schelling discussed the possibility of history in 1798, it was not because nature is the domain of mechanical law that it could not furnish a subject of history, but rather because the productivity–product relation is irreversible, so that neither an *Ich* can retrospect its own, nor can all nature be retrospected from a single, generative series. At each 'crisis' artic-ulating the ages of the world, as the *Inquiries* famously puts it, the researcher confronts the 'irreducible remainder that cannot be resolved into reason by the greatest exertion but always remains in the depths' (VII, 359–60; 1986: 34). As opposed to Deleuze's recapitulation of Schellingian transcendental geology, therefore, the *depths are not the transcendental, but rather the transcendental is the surface of the world, while both are physical.*

Where then does this leave Schelling's philosophy of freedom? As we have seen, it is not because nature is the realm of mechanical laws that it is not a subject of history, but because genesis is irreversible. In consequence, as Schelling writes, the freedom at issue is not that which eludes physical causation, but rather that which eludes regularity, or which breaks from the system, although it is only in introducing a break in the series that it becomes part of the system; what applies for nature potentiated into self-consciousness, that is, for the natural history of mind, applies equally to geology: each attempt to retrospect the conditions of its production, each *deduction,* in other words, generates new series that 'light only forwards', or generate new *epochs.* Natural history is precisely that science that generates epochs in the universal unground, running from nature to ideation. When therefore Deleuze inverts the 'common order' of ground and conse-quent, writing 'ground [is] assign[ed] only in a world precipitated into universal ungrounding' (1994: 202), he takes the assigning of ground to be that action that required transcendental preparation, the ethology, in other words, of thought, which becomes an ethological series in the action, gener-ating the circuit of freedom from transcendental ungrounding, just as metaphysics makes a circle of *physis.* The diversifying antithesis therefore remains, and becomes accordingly an antithesis produced by a prior diver-sifying. Since for Schelling, by contrast, epoch-construction entails *maximizing the extensity of ideation in phusis,* it cannot take *physis* as such as its object, but rather *particular nature's* or transcendental objects. Each exhibits powers and forges actions, generating new species and 'new organs of thought' (1989a: 57). Natural history consists therefore in the investigation not of the properties but the powers of physical transcendentals as nature 'evolves along all possible paths' (I, 460). Natural freedom consists in the unlimited actions of the naturesubject, which is why, for the transcendental geology that is the *Philosophical Inquiries,* its subject is 'the will of the deeps'.

Finally, having pursued the naturephilosophy's capacity for freedom, it is important to note that insofar as these remain the coordinates of metaphysical adequacy, the continuing efficacy of the Kantian problematic is confirmed for contemporary philosophy; in such a case, and other things being equal, Schelling is not a forerunner of anything, but a precursor of philosophical solutions, or 'experiments in dynamic physics', yet to come.

Notes

1   Kant's geological essays, in order of publication: 'Examination of the question whether the earth has undergone an alteration of its axial rotation' (*Ak.* I, 183–91); 'The Question of the age of the earth, considered physically' (*Ak.* I, 193–214); 'On the causes of the tremors on the occasion of the misfortune that befell the countries of Western Europe towards the end of the previous year' (*Ak.* I, 417–27); 'History and natural description of the most

remarkable occurrence of the earthquake that shook a large part of the Earth at the end of the year 1755' (*Ak*. I, 429–61; the most overt as regards outlining a geological sublime. See in particular *Ak*. I, 455–61); 'Continued reflections on the recently experienced terrestrial convulsions' (*Ak*. I, 465–72). To this must also be added the essay 'On Volcanoes on the moon' (*Ak*. VIII, 67–76), which appeared thirty years on, and well into the 'critical' period, in 1785, in which Kant defends the 'universal ocean' of the Wernerian Neptunists against the igneous or volcanic causes of the terrestrial process by such as Hutton. By the *Critique of Judgment* (1790), however, Kant will reject the Neptunist account on the grounds that 'we cannot regard water, air and earth as means for the accretion of mountains . . .' (*Ak*. V, 425; 1987: 312).

2   Steffens reports his discovery of a 'concurrence between the lines that indicate inclination in Halleis' and Lambert's maps with the lines that run through the stretch of volcanoes on the northeastern part of our earth towards the north, and on the southwestern part of our earth towards the south' in a letter to Schelling of 26 July 1799 (Fuhrmans 1973: 178). In addition to Schelling's citation of this schema in the *Further Expositions from the System of Philosophy*, Hegel uses it as the ground of a political-historical geography in his *Philosophy of Nature* (1977a: 285), where the Old World is particularized by opposition to the New, into Africa as the 'lunar principle', Asia's 'cometary eccentricity', and Europe, as the 'consciousness, the rational part, of the earth'. Hegel rounds off this very rational explanation of the opposition of Old and New Worlds in the following manner: 'The division of the world into continents is therefore not contingent', thus relinquishing the maintenance of the concept to techtonic contingency.

3   'Philosophy is nothing else than . . . the free recapitulation [*Wiederholung*] of the original series of acts in which the one act of self-consciousness evolves [*in welchem . . . sich evolvirt*]. In relation to the second, the first series is real, while the second is ideal in regard to the first' (III, 398; 1978: 49, t.m.).

Bibliography

1. Editions of Schelling's works

Schellings sämmtliche Werke (*SW*), ed. K. F. A. 14 vols. Schelling, Stuttgart and Augsburg: J. G. Cotta'scher Verlag, 1856–61. This edition is reproduced, in a new arrangement, by: Manfred Schröter, six primary volumes and six supplementary volumes. München: Beck, 1927, where *SW* pagination is retained, as also in the most recent selection: *F. W. J. Schelling. Ausgewählte Schriften*, ed. Manfred Frank, 6 vols. Frankfurt am Main: Suhrkamp, 1985.

Friedrich Wilhelm Joseph Schelling, Historisch-kritische Ausgabe (*AA*), *im Auftrag der Schelling-Kommission der Bayerischen Akademie der Wissenschaften*, ed. Hans Michael Baumgartner, Wilhelm G. Jacobs, Jörg Jantzen and Hermann Krings. Stuttgart-Bad Canstatt: Frommann-Holzboog, 1976f. Reihe I: Werke, II: Nachlass, III: Briefe.

2. Works not included in SW

(1946 [1811–13]) *Die Weltalter: Fragmente, in den Urfassungen von 1811 und 1813.* (*SW* Nachlassband), ed. Manfred Schröter. Munich: Beck.

(1969 [1802–3]) *Neue Zeitschrift für spekulative Physik Erstes Heft. Drei Stücke in einem Band.* Photoreproduced Reprint of the Tübingen edition 1802–3. Referenced by issue (1–3) and original pagination. Hildesheim: Georg Olms.

(1977 [1841–2]) *Philosophie der Offenbarung* (*Paulus-Nachschrift*), ed. Manfred Frank: Frankfurt am Main: Suhrkamp.

(1989a [1830]) *Einleitung in die Philosophie* (Schellingiana Band 1), ed. Walter E. Ehrhardt. Stuttgart-Bad Cannstatt: Frommann-Holzboog.

(1994a [1794]) *Timaeus* (Schellingiana Band 4), ed. Hartmut Buchner. Stuttgart-Bad Cannstatt: Frommann-Holzboog.

(1998 [1827–8]) *System der Weltalter*, ed. and introduced by Siegbert Peetz. Frankfurt am Main: Klostermann.

(2001 [1800–1801]) *Zeitschrift für spekulative Physik*, 2 vols, ed. Manfred Durner. Hamburg: Meiner.

(2002a [1810–21]) *Weltalter-Fragmente* (Schellingiana Band 13), 2 vols, ed. Klaus Grotsch. Stuttgart-Bad Cannstatt: Frommann-Holzboog.

3. Schelling in English

(1942) *Ages of the World* (1815), trans. Frederick de Wolfe Bolman. New York: Columbia University Press (repr. 1966; New York: AMS Press).

(1966) *On University Studies*, trans. E. S. Morgan, ed. Norbert Guterman. Athens, OH: Ohio University Press.

(1984) *Bruno: Or, On the Natural and the Divine Principle of Things*, trans. Michael Vater. Albany: State University of New York Press.

(1978) *System of Transcendental Idealism*, trans. Peter Heath. Charlottesville: University Press of Virginia.

(1980) *The Unconditional in Human Knowledge: Four Early Essays (1794–1796)*, trans. Fritz Marti (includes *On the Possibility of a Form of All Philosophy* [1794]; *Of the I as Principle of Philosophy, or on the Unconditional in Human Knowledge* [1795]; *Philosophical Letters on Dogmatism and Criticism* [1795], 'New deduction of natural right' [1796]). Lewisburg: Bucknell University Press.

(1986) *Philosophical Inquiries into the Essence of Human Freedom*, trans. James Guttmann. Chicago: Open Court.

(1988) *Ideas for a Philosophy of Nature*, trans. Errol E. Harris and Peter Heath. Cambridge: Cambridge University Press.

(1989b) *The Philosophy of Art*, trans. Douglas W. Stott. Minneapolis: University of Minnesota Press.

(1994b) *History of Modern Philosophy*, trans. Andrew Bowie. Cambridge: Cambridge University Press.

(1994c) *Idealism and the Endgame of Theory: Three Essays by Schelling*, ed. and trans. Thomas Pfau (includes *Treatise Explicatory of the Science of Knowledge* [1797–8], *System of Philosophy in General and Naturephilosophy in Particular* [1804], Part 1, and *Stuttgart Seminars* [1810]). Albany: State University of New York Press.

(1997) *Ages of the World* [1813], trans. Judith Norman, with an essay *The Abyss of Freedom* by Slavoj Zizek. Ann Arbor: Michigan University Press.

(2000) *Ages of the World* [1815], trans. Jason M. Wirth. Albany: State University of New York Press.

(2002b) *Clara*, trans. Fiona Steinkamp. Albany: State University of New York Press.

(2004) *First Outline of a System of the Philosophy of Nature*, trans. Keith R. Peterson. Albany: State University of New York Press.

4. Works on Schelling

Bach, Thomas (2001) *Biologie und Philosophie bei Carl Friedrich Kielmeyer und F. W. J. Schelling* (Schellingiana Band 12). Stuttgart-Bad Canstatt: Frommann-Holzboog.

Baum, Manfred (2001) 'The beginnings of Schelling's philosophy of nature', in Sedgwick ed. (2000) 199–215.

Baumgartner, Hans Michael (ed.) (1975) *Schelling*. Freiberg und München: Alber.

—— and Harald Korten (eds) (1996) *Schelling*. München: Beck.

Beach, Edward Allen (1994) *The Potencies of God(s)*. Albany: State University of New York Press.

Beierwaltes, Werner (2002) 'The legacy of neoplatonism in Schelling's thought', *International Journal of Philosophy* 10 (4): 393–428.

—— (2003) 'Plato's *Timaeus* in German idealism: Schelling and Windischmann', in Reydams-Schils (2003).

Bonsepien, Wolfgang (1997) *Die Begründung einer Naturphilosophie bei Kant, Schelling, Fries und Hegel. Mathematische versus spekulative Naturphilosophie*. Frankfurt am Main: Klostermann.

Bowie, Andrew (1993) *Schelling and Modern European Philosophy*. London: Routledge.

Cattin, Emmanuel (2001) *Transformations de la métaphysique. Commentaires sur la philosophie transcendentale de Schelling*. Paris: Vrin.

Courtine, Jean-François (1990) *Extase de la raison. Essais sur Schelling*. Paris: Galilée.

—— and Jean-François Marquet (eds) (1994) *Le Dernier Schelling: raison et positivité*. Paris: Vrin.

David, Pascal (1998) *Schelling: De l'absolu à l'histoire*. Paris: PUF.

Di Giovanni, George (1979) 'Kant's metaphysics of nature and Schelling's *Ideas for a Philosophy of Nature*'. *Journal for the History of Philosophy* 17: 197–215.

Di Giovanni, George and H. S. Harris (eds) (2000) *Between Kant and Hegel*. Indianapolis: Hackett.

Durner, Manfred, Jörg Jantzen and Francesco Moiso (1994) *Wissenschaftshistorischer Bericht zu Schellings naturphilosophischen Schriften 1797–1800. AA Ergänzungsband zu Werke 5 bis 9* (cited as AA Ergbd.1). Stuttgart-Bad Cannstatt: Frommann-Holzboog.

Ehrhardt, Walter E. (1977) 'Nur ein Schelling', in *Studi Urbinati di Storia, Filosofia e Litteratura*, 51: 111–22.

—— (1984) 'Die Naturphilosophie *und* die Philosophie der Offenbarung. Zur Kritik materialistischer Schelling-Forschung', in Sandkühler (ed.) 1984: 337–59.

Esposito, Joseph L. (1977) *Schelling's Idealism and the Philosophy of Nature*. Lewisburg, PA: Bucknell University Press.

Fischer, Kuno ([1895] 1923) *Schellings Leben, Werke und Lehre*. Heidelberg: Winter.

Frank, Manfred (1975) *Eine Einführung in Schellings Philosophie*. Frankfurt am Main: Suhrkamp.

—— and Gerhard Kurz (eds) (1975) *Materialen zu Schellings philosophischen Anfängen*. Frankfurt am Main: Suhrkamp.

Fuhrmanns, Horst (ed.) (1962–75) *Schelling: Briefe und Dokumente*, 3 vols, I (1962), II (1973), III (1975). Bonn: Bouvier.

Gerabek, Werner E. (1996) 'F. W. J. Schelling und die Medizin der Romantik. Bemerkungen zur Würzburger Zeit (1803–6) des Philosophen', *Würzburger medizinhistorisches Mitteilungen* 14: 63–72.

Gower, Barry (1973) 'Speculation in physics: The history and practice of *Naturphilosophie*', *Studies in History and Philosophy of Science* 3 (4): 301–56.

Grant, Iain Hamilton (2000a) 'The Chemistry of Darkness', *Pli* 9: 36–52.

—— (2004) 'The physics of the world soul', in Norman and Welchman (2004) 128–50.

—— (2005) 'The "eternal and necessary bond between philosophy and physics": A repetition of the difference between the Fichtean and Schellingian systems of philosophy', *Angelaki* 10 (1): 61–77.

Gregory, Frederick (1983) 'Die Kritik von J. F. Fries an Schellings Naturphilosophie', *Sudhoffs Archiv* 67: 145–57.

Hasler, Ludwig (ed.) (1981) *Schelling. Seine Bedeutung für eine Philosophie der Natur und der Geschichte.* Stuttgart-Bad Cannstatt: Frommann-Holzboog.

Heckmann, Reinhard, Hermann Krings and Rudolf W. Meyer (eds) (1985) *Natur und Subjectivität. Zur Auseinandersetzung mit der Naturphilosophie des jungen Schelling.* Stuttgart-Bad Cannstatt: Frommann-Holzboog.

Heidegger, Martin (1985) *Schelling's Treatise on the Essence of Human Freedom*, trans. Joan Stambaugh. Columbus: Ohio University Press.

—— (1988) *Schelling: vom Wesen der Menschlichen Freiheit*, in *Martin Heidegger Gesamtausgabe* II: 42. Frankfurt am Main: Klostermann.

—— (1991) *Die Metaphysik des Deutschen Idealismus. Zur erneuten Auslegung von Schelling: Philosophische Untersuchungen Über das Wesen des Menschlichen Freiheit und die damit zusammenhängenden Gegenstände*, in *Martin Heidegger Gesamtausgabe* II: 49. Frankfurt am Main: Klostermann.

Heuser-Kessler, Marie-Luise (1996) *Die Productivität der Natur. Schellings Naturphilosophie und das neue Paradigma der Selbstorganisation der Naturwissenschaften.* Berlin: Duncker & Humblot.

Hoffe, Otfried and Annemarie Pieper (eds) (1995) *F. W. J. Schelling. Über das Wesen der menschlichen Freiheit* (Klassiker Auslegen Bd. 3). Berlin: Akademie Verlag.

Holz, Harald (1971) 'Die Beziehung zwischen Schellings Naturphilosophie und dem Identitätphilosophie in den Jahren 1801/02', *Philosophisches Journal des Görresgesellschaft* 8: 270–94.

Horstmann, Rolf-Peter and Michael John Petry (eds) (1986) *Hegels Philosophie der Natur.* Stuttgart: Klett-Cotta.

Jantzen, Jörg (ed.) (1998) *Die Realität des Wissens und das wirkliche Dasein.* (Schellingiana Bd. 10) Stuttgart: Frommann-Holzboog.

Jaspers, Karl (1955) *Schelling: Grösse und Verhängnis.* München: Piper.

Kirchhoff, Jochen (1982) *Schelling.* Hamburg: Rowohlt.

Knittermeyer, Heinrich (1929) *Schelling und die romantische Schule*. München: Reinhardt.

Krell, David Farrell (1998) *Contagion: Sexuality, Disease and Death in German Idealism and Romanticism*. Bloomington and Indianapolis: Indiana University Press.

Krings, Hermann (1982) 'Die Konstruktion in der Philosophie. Ein Beitrag zu Schellings Logik der Natur', in J. Stagl (ed.) *Aspekte der Kultursoziologie*. Berlin: Riemer.

—— (1994) 'Genesis und Materie – zur Bedeutung der "Timaeus"- Handschrift für Schellings Naturphilosophie', in Schelling (1994a).

Küppers, Bernd-Olaf (1992) *Natur als Organismus. Schellings frühe Naturphilosophie und ihre Bedeutung für die moderne Biologie*. Frankfurt am Main: Klostermann.

Lawrence, Joseph P. (1989) *Schellings Philosophie des ewigen Anfangs: der Natur als Quelle der Geschichte*. Würzburg: Königshausen and Neumann.

Mischler, Sibille (1997) *Der verschlungene Zug der Selle. Natur, Organismus und Entwicklung bei Schelling, Steffens und Oken*. Würzburg: Königshauser und Neumann.

Moiso, Francesco (1986) 'Die Hegelsche Theorie der Physik und der Chemie in ihrer Beziehung zu Schellings Naturphilosophie', in Horstmann and Petry (1986) 54–87.

Mutschler, Hans-Dieter (1997) *Spekulative und empirische Physik. Aktualität und Grenzen der Naturphilosophie Schellings*. Stuttgart: Kohlhammer.

Norman, Judith and Alistair Welchman (eds) (2004) *The New Schelling*. London and New York: Continuum.

Peetz, Siegbert (1995) *Die Freiheit im Wissen. Eine Untersuchung zu Schellings Konzept der Rationalität*. Frankfurt am Main: Klostermann.

Peterson, Keith R. (2004) 'Translator's introduction' to Schelling 2004.

Planty-Bonjour, G. (ed.) (1979) *Actualité de Schelling*. Paris: Vrin.

Risse, Guenter B. (1972) 'Kant, Schelling and the early search for a philosophical "science" of medicine in Germany', *Journal of the History of Medicine and Allied Sciences* 27: 145–58.

—— (1976) 'Schelling, *Naturphilosophie*, and John Brown's system of medicine', *Bulletin of the History of Medicine* 50: 321–34.

Sandkühler, Hans Jörg (ed.) (1984) *Natur und geschichtlicher Prozess. Studien zur Naturphilosophie Schellings*. Frankfurt am Main: Suhrkamp.

—— (ed.) (1998) *F. W. J. Schelling*, 2nd edn. Stuttgart: Metzler.

Schlanger, Judith E. (1966) *Schelling et la réalité finie*. Paris: Presses Universitaires de France.

Serres, Michel, ed. (1994) *Geschichte der Wissenschaft*. Frankfurt am Main: Suhrkamp.

Snow, Dale E. (1996) *Schelling and the End of Idealism*. Albany: State University of New York Press.

Steinkamp, Fiona (1994) 'Schelling's account of primal nature in the *Ages of the World*', *Idealistic Studies* 24: 173–90.

Tilliette, Xavier (1970) *Un philosophie en devenir. 1: Le système vivant, 1794–1821. 2: La dernière philosophie*. Paris: Vrin.

—— (1987) *L'Absolu et la philosophie. Essais sur Schelling*. Paris: PUF.

Tsouyopoulos, Nelly (1978a) 'Der Streit zwischen F. W. Schelling und Andreas Röschlaub über die Grundlagen der Medizin', *Medizinhistorisches Journal* 13: 229–45.

Wallen, Martin (1994) 'Schelling's dialogue of health in *Philosophical Inquiries into the Nature of Human Freedom*', *Studies in Romanticism* 33: 201–21.

Warnke, Camilla (1998) 'Schellings Idee und Theorie des Organismus und der Paradigmawechsel der Biologie um die Wende zum 19. Jahrhundert', *Jarhrbuch für Geschichte und Theorie der Biologie* 5: 187–234.

Wirth, Jason (2003) *The Conspiracy of Life: Meditations on Schelling and His Time*. New York: SUNY.

—— (2005) *Schelling Now: Contemporary Readings*. Bloomington, Indiana: Indiana University Press.

Zimmerli, Walter Ch., Klaus Stein and Michael Gerten (eds) (1997) *'Fessellos durch die Systeme'. Frühromantisches Naturdenken im Umfeld von Arnim, Ritter und Schelling*. Stuttgart-Bad Cannstatt: Frommann-Holzboog.

Zizek, Slavoj (1996) *The Indivisible Remainder: An Essay on Schelling and Related Matters*. London: Verso.

5. Other Works

Adickes, Erich (1924–5) *Kant als Natuforscher*, 2 vols. Berlin: Walter de Gruyter.

Aesch, Alexander Gode von (1966) *Natural Science in German Romanticism*. New York: AMS Press.

Alcinous (1993) *The Handbook of Platonism*, trans. and commentary John Dillon. Oxford: Oxford University Press.

Alliez, Eric (2004) *The Signature of the World*, trans. Elliot Albert and Alberto Toscana. London: Continuum.

Ameriks, Karl (ed.) (2000) *The Cambridge Companion to German Idealism*. Cambridge: Cambridge University Press.

Ansell Pearson, Keith (1999) *Germinal Life: The Difference and Repetition of Deleuze*. London: Routledge.

Appel, Toby A. (1987) *The Cuvier-Geoffroy Debate: French Biology in the Decade Before Darwin*. New York: Oxford University Press.

Aristotle (1968) *The Metaphysics*, 2 vols, trans. Hugh Tredennick. Cambridge, MA: Harvard University Press.

—— (1970) *Physics*, 2 vols, trans. P. H. Wicksteed and F. M. Cornford. Cambridge, MA: Harvard University Press.

—— (1986) *On the Heavens*, trans. W. K. C. Guthrie. Cambridge, MA: Harvard University Press.

Ayrault, Roger (1976) *La genèse du romantisme allemand*, 2 vols. Paris: Aubier.

Badiou, Alain (1992) *Manifesto for Philosophy*, trans. Norman Madarasz. Albany, NY: State University of New York Press.

—— (1997) 'Deleuze, *The Fold: Leibniz and the Baroque*', in Paul Patton (ed.) *Deleuze: A Critical Reader*. Oxford: Blackwell: 51–69.

—— (2000) *Deleuze: The Clamor of Being*, trans. Louise Burchill. Minneapolis: University of Minnesota Press.

—— (2004) *Theoretical Writings*, ed. and trans. Ray Brassier and Alberto Toscana. London: Continuum.

Barnes, Jonathan (1987) *Early Greek Philosophy*. Harmondsworth: Penguin.

Barrow, John D. (2001) *The Book of Nothing*. London: Vintage.

Beiser, Frederick (1987) *The Fate of Reason: German Philosophy from Kant to Fichte*. Cambridge, MA: Harvard University Press.

—— (2002) *German Idealism: The Struggle against Subjectivism 1781–1801*. Cambridge, MA: Harvard University Press.

—— (2005) *Hegel*. London: Routledge.

Bensaude-Vincent, Bernadette and Isabelle Stengers (1996) *A History of Chemistry*, trans. Deborah van Dam. Cambridge, MA: Harvard University Press.

Bernouilli, Christoph and Hans Kern (eds) (1926) *Romantische Naturphilosophie*. Jena: Eugen Diederichs.

Blasche, Siegfried (ed.) (1991) *Übergang: Untersuchungen zum Spätwerk Immanud Kants*. Frankfurt am Main: Klostermann.

Blumenbach, Johann Freidrich (1781) *Über den Bildungstrieb und das Zeugungsgeschäft*. Göttingen: J. C. Dieterich.

Böhme, Gernot (2000) *Platons theoretische Philosophie*. Stuttgart and Weimar: Metzler.

—— and Gregor Schiemann (eds) (1997) *Phänomenologie der Natur*. Frankfurt am Main: Suhrkamp.

Bowler, Peter J. (1984) *Evolution: The History of an Idea*. Berkeley: University of California Press.

Boyle, Robert ([1661] n.d.) *The Sceptical Chymist*, ed. M. Pattison Muir. London: Dent.

—— (1991) *Selected Philosophical Papers of Robert Boyle*, ed. M. A. Stewart. Indianapolis: Hackett.

Brisson, Luc and F. Walter Meyerstein (1991) *Inventer l'univers: le probleme de la connaissance et les modeles cosmologiques*. Paris: Les Belles Lettres.

Brock, William H. (1992) *The Fontana History of Chemistry*. London: Fontana.

Bruno, Giordano (1988) *Cause, Principle and Unity*, ed. R. J. Blackwell and Robert de Luca. Cambridge: Cambridge University Press.

Buffon, Georges Louis Comte de (1755) *Histoire de la nature*, vol. V. Paris: de l'Imprimerie Royale.
——(1985) *Histoire Naturelle*, ed. Jean Varloot. Paris: Gallimard.
Carus, Carl Gustav (1841) *Zwölf Briefe über das Erdleben*. Stuttgart: J. G. Cotta'scher Verlag.
——(1856) *Organon der Erkenntniss der Natur und des Geistes*. Leipzig: Breitkopf & Härtel.
——(1944) (ed.) Hans Kern, *Geheimnisvoll am lichten Tag: Von der Seele des Menschen und der Welt*. Leipzig: Reclam.
Châtelet, Gilles (1993) *Les enjeux du mobile. Mathématique, physique, philosophie*. Paris: Seuil.
Clark, Edwin and L. S. Jacyna (1987) *Nineteenth-Century Origins of Neuroscientific Concepts*. Berkeley: California University Press.
Clark, William, Jan Golinski and Simon Schaeffer (eds) (1999) *The Sciences in Enlightened Europe*. Chicago: University of Chicago Press.
Coleman, William (1971) *Biology in the Nineteenth Century*. Cambridge: Cambridge University Press.
——(1973) 'Limits of the recapitulation theory: Carl Friedrich Kielmeyer's critique of the presumed parallelism of earth history, ontogeny, and the present order of organisms', *Isis* 64: 341–50.
——(1977) *Biology in the Nineteenth Century*. Cambridge: Cambridge University Press.
Coleridge, Samuel Taylor (1977) *Biographia Litereria*. London: Dent.
Collingwood, R. G. (1945) *The Idea of Nature*. Cambridge: Cambridge University Press.
Cornford, Francis MacDonald ([1935] 1997) *Plato's Cosmology: The Timaeus of Plato*. Indianapolis: Hackett.
Crosland, M. P. (1971) (ed.) *The Science of Matter*. Harmondsworth: Penguin.
Cunningham, Andrew and Nicholas Jardine (eds) (1990) *Romanticism and the Sciences*. Cambridge: Cambridge University Press.
Danielson, Dennis Richard (2000) *The Book of the Cosmos: Imagining the Universe from Heraclitus to Hawking*. Cambridge, MA: Perseus.
Davy, Humphrey ([1802] 1982) *On Geology*. Madison: University of Wisconsin Press.
Deleuze, Gilles (1983) *Nietzsche and Philosophy*, trans. Hugh Tomlinson. London: Athlone.
—— (1990) *The Logic of Sense*, trans. Mark Lester and Charles Stivale. London: Athlone.
——(1992) *Expressionism in Philosophy: Spinoza*, trans. Martin Joughin. New York: Zone.
—— (1993) *The Fold: Leibniz and the Baroque*, trans. Tom Conley. London: Athlone.
—— (1994) *Difference and Repetition*, trans. Paul Patton. London: Athlone.
—— (1995) *Negotiations*, trans. Martin Joughin. New York: Columbia

University Press.

Deleuze, Gilles and Félix Guattari (1988) *A Thousand Plateaus*, trans. Brian Massumi. London: Athlone.

—— (1994) *What is Philosophy?* trans. Graham Burchell and Hugh Tomlinson. London: Verso.

Depew, David J. and Bruce H. Weber (1996) *Darwinism Evolving: Systems Dynamics and the Genealogy of Natural Selection*. Cambridge, MA: MIT.

Des Chenes, Denis (1996) *Physiologia: Natural Philosophy in Late Aristotelian and Cartesian Thought*. Ithaca: Cornell University Press.

Diels, Hermann and Walter Kranz (1952), *Die Fragmente der Vorsokratiker*. Berlin: Weidmann.

Echelard-Dumas, Marielle (1976) 'Der Begriff des Organismus bei Leibniz', *Studia Leibniziana* 8 (2): 160–86.

Edwards, Jeffrey (2000) *Substance, Force and the Possibility of Knowledge*. Berkeley: California University Press.

Edwards, W. N. (1976) *The Early History of Palaeontology*. London: British Museum.

Ellis, Brian (2001) *Philosophy of Nature*. London: Acumen.

Engelhardt, Dietrich von (1976) *Hegel und die Chemie*. Wiesbaden: Guido Pressler Verlag.

Eschenmayer, Karl August (1797) *Säze aus der Natur-Metaphysik auf chemische und medicinische Gegenstände angewandt*. Tübingen: Fues.

Faraday, Michael (1839–55) *Experimental Researches in Electricity*, 3 vols. London: Taylor.

Fichte, Johann Gottlieb (1962–) *Fichte-Gesammtausgabe der Bayerischen Akademie der Wissenschaften*, ed. R. Lauth and H. Jacob, cited as *GA*. Stuttgart-Bad Cannstatt: Frommann-Holzboog.

—— (1971) *Fichtes Werke*, ed. Immanuel Hermann Fichte, cited as *W* (11 vols). Berlin: Walter de Gruyter.

—— (1979) *Attempt at a Critique of All Revelation*, trans. Garrett Green. Cambridge: Cambridge University Press (*W* V).

—— (1982) *The Science of Knowledge*, trans. Peter Heath and John Lachs. Cambridge: Cambridge University Press (*W* I).

—— (1988) *Early Philosophical Writings*, ed. and trans. Daniel Breazeale. Ithaca: Cornell University Press.

—— (2000) *Foundations of Natural Right*, trans. Frederick Neuhauser. Cambridge: Cambridge University Press (*W* III).

Fine, Gail (1993) *On Ideas: Aristotle's Criticism of Plato's Theory of Forms*. Oxford: Oxford University Press.

Förster, Eckhart (ed.) (1989) *Kant's Transcendental Deductions: The Three Critiques and the Opus postumum*. Stanford, CA: Stanford University Press.

—— (2000) *Kant's Final Synthesis: An Essay on the Opus postumum*. Cambridge, MA: Harvard University Press.

Friedman, Michael (1992) *Kant and the Exact Sciences*. Cambridge, MA:

Harvard University Press.

Gaukroger, Stephen (2002) *Descartes' System of Natural Philosophy*. Cambridge: Cambridge University Press.

Gerson, Lloyd P. (ed.) (1996) *The Cambridge Companion to Plotinus*. Cambridge: Cambridge University Press.

Gillespie, Charles Coulston (1996) *Genesis and Geology*, 2nd edn. Cambridge, MA: Harvard University Press.

Girtanner, Christoph (1796) *Über das Kantischen Prinzip für Naturgeschichte*. Göttingen: Vandehock & Ruprecht.

Gloy, Karin and P. Burger (eds) (1993) *Naturphilosophie im deutschen Idealismus*. Stuttgart-Bad Cannstatt: Frommann-Holzboog.

Goethe, Johann Wolfgang von (1975) *Goethes Werke* Bd. 13: *Naturwissenschaftliche Schriften*, ed. Dorothea Kuhn and Rike Wankmüller. Munich: Beck.

—— (1977) *Schriften zur Naturwissenschaft*, ed. Michael Böhler. Stuttgart: Reclam.

Gould, Stephen Jay (1977) *Ontogeny and Phylogeny*. Cambridge, MA: Harvard University Press.

—— (1987) *Time's Arrow, Time's Cycle*. Harmondsworth: Penguin.

Grant, Iain Hamilton (1997) 'At the Mountains of Madness', in Keith Ansell Pearson (ed.) *Deleuze and Philosophy: The Difference Engineer*. London: Routledge.

—— (2000b) 'The Physics of Analogy', in Jones and Rehberg (2000) 37–60.

Hackforth, R. (ed. and trans.) (1955) *Plato's Phaedo*. Cambridge: Cambridge University Press.

Hall, Thomas S. (1969) *Ideas of Life and Matter: Studies in the History of General Physiology 600 BC–1900 AD*, 2 vols. Chicago: University of Chicago Press.

Hankins, Thomas L. (1985) *Science and the Enlightenment*. Cambridge: Cambridge University Press.

Hansen, LeeAnn (1998) 'Metaphors of mind and society: The origins of German psychiatry in the revolutionary era', *Isis* 89: 387–409.

Harman, P. M. (1982) *Energy, Force, and Matter: The Conceptual Development of Nineteenth-Century Physics*. Cambridge: Cambridge University Press.

Hegel, G. W. F. (1955) *Lectures on the History of Philosophy*, trans. E. S. Haldane and F. H. Simson, 3 vols. London: Routledge, Kegan and Paul.

—— (1968) *Gesammelte Werke*, ed. Hartmut Buchner and Otto Pöggeler. Hamburg: Meiner.

—— (1970) *Philosophy of Nature*, trans. A. V. Miller. Oxford: Oxford University Press.

—— (1975) *Hegel's Logic*, trans. W. Wallace. Oxford: Oxford University Press.

—— (1977a) *The Difference between Fichte's and Schelling's Systems of Philosophy*, trans. H. S. Harris and Walter Cerf. Albany: State

University of New York Press.

—— (1977b) *Faith and Knowledge*, trans. Walter Cerf and H. S. Harris. Albany: State University of New York Press.

—— (1977c) *Phenomenology of Spirit*, trans. A. V. Miller. Oxford: Oxford University Press.

—— (1986) *G. W. F. Hegel Werke in zwanzig Bänden*, ed. Eva Moldenhauer and Karl Markus Michel, cited as *Wz* 1–20. Frankfurt am Main: Suhrkamp.

Heidegger, Martin (1996) *The Fundamental Concepts of Metaphysics: World, Finitude, Solitude*, trans. William McNeill and Nicholas Walker. Bloomington: Indiana University Press.

Herder, Johann Gottfried (1965) *Ideen zur Philosophie der Geschichte der Menschheit*, ed. Heinz Stolpe. Berlin and Weimar: Aufbau.

Houlgate, Stephen (1998) *Hegel and the Philosophy of Nature*. Albany: State University of New York Press.

Humboldt, Alexander von (1997) *Cosmos*, 2 vols, trans. E. C. Otté. Baltimore: Johns Hopkins University Press.

Hutton, James (1788) 'Theory of the earth; or an investigation of the laws observable in the composition, dissolution and restoration of land upon the globe', *Transactions of the Royal Society of Edinburgh* 1: 209–305.

Inge, William Ralph (1923) *The Philosophy of Plotinus*, 2 vols. London: Longmans, Green and Co.

Jacobi, Friedrich Heinrich (2000a) *Über die Lehre des Spinoza im Briefen an den Herrn Moses Mendelssohn*, ed. Marion Lauschke, Klaus Hammacher and Irmgard-Maria Piske. Hamburg: Meiner.

—— (2000b) 'Idealism and Realism', in Brigitte Sassen (ed. and trans.) *Kant's Early Critics: The Empiricist Critique of the Theoretical Philosophy*. Cambridge: Cambridge University Press, 169–75.

Jacyna, L. S. (1983) 'Immanence or transcendence: Theories of life and organization in Britain, 1790–1835', *Isis* 74: 311–29.

Jardine, Nicholas (2000) *The Scenes of Inquiry*. Oxford: Oxford University Press.

Jones, Rachel and Andrea Rehberg (eds) (2000) *The Matter of Critique: Readings in Kant's Philosophy*. Manchester: Clinamen.

Juarrero-Roqué, Alicia (1985) 'Self-organization: Kant's concept of teleology and modern chemistry', *Review of Metaphysics* 39: 107–35.

Kanitscheider, Bernulf (1984) *Moderne Naturphilosophie*. Würzburg: Königshauser und Neumann.

—— (1996) *Im Innern der Natur. Philosophie und moderne Physik*. Darmstadt: Wissenschaftliche Buchgesellschaft.

Kant, Immanuel (1929ff) *Kants gesammelte Schriften*, cited as *Ak*. (29 vols). Berlin: Königlich Preussische Akademie der Wissenschaften.

—— (1968) *Werkausgabe*, ed. Wilhelm Weischedel (contains German translations of Kant's early Latin texts), cited as *WA* (12 vols). Frankfurt am Main: Suhrkamp.

—— (1969) *Universal Natural History and Theory of the Heavens*, trans.

W. Hastie. Ann Arbor: University of Michigan Press.

—— (1970) *Metaphysical Foundations of Natural Science*, trans. James Ellington. Indianapolis and New York: Bobbs-Merrill.

—— (1971) *Prolegomena to any Future Metaphysics that will be able to Present Itself as a Science*, trans. Peter G. Lucas. Manchester: Manchester University Press.

—— (1981) *Universal Natural History and Theory of the Heavens*, trans. Stanley L. Jaki. Edinburgh: Scottish Academic Press.

—— (1987) *Critique of Judgment*, trans. Werner S. Pluhar. Indianapolis: Hackett.

—— (1992a) *Theoretical Philosophy 1755–1770*, trans. David Walford and Ralf Meerbote. Cambridge: Cambridge University Press.

—— (1992b) *Conflict of the Faculties*, trans. Mary J. Gregor. Lincoln: Nebraska University Press.

—— (1993) *Opus Postumum*, trans. Eckhart Förster. Cambridge: Cambridge University Press.

—— (1997) *Lectures on Metaphysics*, trans. Karl Ameriks and Steve Naragon. Cambridge: Cambridge University Press.

—— (1998) *Critique of Pure Reason*, trans. Paul Guyer and Allen W. Wood. Cambridge: Cambridge University Press.

—— (1999) *Correspondence*, trans. Arnulf Zweig. Cambridge: Cambridge University Press.

Kanz, Kai Torsten (1991) *Kielmeyer-Bibliographie. Verzeichnis der Literatur von und über den Naturforscher Carl Friedrich Kielmeyer (1765–1844)*. Stuttgart: Verlag für Geschichte der Naturwissenschaften und der Technik.

Kielmeyer, Carl Friedrich (1938) *Natur und Kraft. Kielmeyers gesammelte Schriften*, ed. F. H. Holler. Berlin: Kieper.

Knight, David M. (1970) 'The physical sciences and the Romantic movement', *History of Science* 9: 54–75.

—— (1975) 'German science in the Romantic period', in Maurice Crossland (ed.) *The Emergence of Science in Western Europe*. London: Macmillan.

—— (1995) *Ideas in Chemistry*. London: Athlone.

Krafft, Maurice (1993) *Volcanoes: Fire from the Earth*. London: Thames and Hudson.

Krell, David Farrell (1985) 'The oldest program towards a system in German idealism', *Owl of Minerva* 17 (1): 5–19.

Lacoue-Labarthe, Philippe and Jean-Luc Nancy (1988) *The Literary Absolute: The Theory of Literature in German Romanticism*, trans. Philip Barnard and Cheryl Lester. New York: State University of New York Press.

Lambert, Johann Heinrich ([1761] 1976) *Cosmological Letters on the Arrangement of the World-Edifice*, trans. Stanley L. Jaki. Edinburgh: Scottish Academic Press.

Leibniz, G. W. (1969) *Gottfried Wilhelm Leibniz' Philosophical Papers and Letters*, ed. and trans. Leroy A. Loemker, 2nd edn. Dordrecht: Reidel.

——(1998) *Philosophical Texts*, ed. Richard Francks and R. S. Woolhouse. Oxford: Oxford University Press.

Lennox, James G. (2001) *Aristotle's Philosophy of Biology*. Cambridge: Cambridge University Press.

Lenoir, Timothy (1980) 'Kant, Blumenbach and vital materialism in German biology', *Isis* 71: 77–108.

——(1981) 'The Göttingen School and the development of transcendental *Naturphilosophie* in the Romantic Era', *Studies in the History of Biology* 5: 111–205.

——(1982) *The Strategy of Life: Teleology and Mechanics in Nineteenth-Century German Biology*. Dordrecht: Reidel.

Lequan, Mai (2000) *La chemie selon Kant*. Paris: Presses Universitaires de France.

Levere, Trevor H. (2002) *Poetry Realized in Nature*. Cambridge: Cambridge University Press.

Lloyd, G. E. R (1970) *Early Greek Science: Thales to Aristotle*. New York: Norton.

Lovejoy, Arthur O. (1964) *The Great Chain of Being*. Cambridge, MA: Harvard University Press.

Lyell, Charles (1997) *Principles of Geology*, abridged James E. Secord. Harmondsworth: Penguin.

Lyotard, Jean-François (1991) *Leçons sur l'Analytique du sublime*. Paris: Galilée.

Maimon, Salomon (1970) 'Weltseele', in *Philosophisches Wörterbuch, oder Beleuchtigung der wichtigsten Gegenstände der Philosophie, in alphabetischer Ordnung* [Berlin: Unger, 1791]: 179–208, in Valerio Verra (ed.) *Maimons gesammelte Werke* III. Hildesheim: Georg Olms Verlag: 203–32.

Marenbon, John (1988) *Medieval Philosophy*. London: Routledge.

Martin, Henri (1841) *Études sur le Timée de Platon*, 2 vols. Paris: Ladrange.

Marx, Karl (1993) *Grundrisse*, trans. Martin Nicolaus. Harmondsworth: Penguin.

McFarland, J. D. (1970) *Kant's Concept of Teleology*. Edinburgh: Edinburgh University Press.

Merleau-Ponty, Maurice (1970) *In Praise of Philosophy and Other Essays*, trans. John Wild, James Edie and John O'Neill. Evanston: Northwestern University Press.

—— (2003) *Nature*, ed. Dominique Séglard, trans. Robert Vallier. Evanston: Northwestern University Press.

—— (2004) *The World of Perception*, trans. Oliver Davis. London: Routledge.

Meyer-Abich, Klaus Michael (1997) *Praktische Naturphilosophie. Erinnerung an einen vergessenen Traum*. München: Beck.

Mohr, Richard D. (1985) *The Platonic Cosmology*. Leiden: Brill.

Moore, A. W. (2001) *The Infinite*. London: Routledge.

Müller-Sievers, Helmut (1997) *Self-Generation: Biology, Philosophy and Literature around 1800*. Stanford: Stanford University Press.

Mutschler, Hans-Dieter (2002) *Naturphilosophie*. Stuttgart: Kohlhammer.

Newton, Isaac (1974) [1692] *The Mathematical Papers of Isaac Newton*, ed. D. Whiteside. Cambridge: Cambridge University Press.

Novalis (1987) *Werke*, ed. Gerhard Schulz. Munich: Beck.

—— (1996) *Werke 2: Die Christenheit oder Europa und andere philosophische Schriften*, ed. Rolf Toman. Köln: Könemann.

—— (1997) *Novalis: Philosophical Writings*, ed. and trans. Margaret Mahoney Stoljar. New York: State University of New York Press.

Oersted, Hans Christian (1852) *The Soul in Nature*, trans. Eleonora and Joanna B. Horner. London: Bohn.

Oken, Lorenz (1847) *Elements of Physiophilosophy* [*Lehrbuch der Naturphilosophie 1802–11*], trans. Alfred Tulk. London: Ray Society.

Omnès, Roland (1999) *Quantum Philosophy*, trans. Arturo Sangalli. Princeton: Princeton University Press.

Ospovat, Alexander M. (1967) 'The place of the *Kürze Klassifikation* in the work of A. G. Werner', *Isis* 58: 90–95.

Palmer, John (1999) *Plato's Reception of Parmenides*. Oxford: Oxford University Press.

Paul, Fritz (1973) *Henrich Steffens: Naturphilosophie und Universalromantik*. München: Fink.

Plato (1975) *Timaeus*, trans. R. G. Bury. Cambridge, MA: Harvard University Press.

Playfair, John (1805) 'Account of the late Dr James Hutton', *Transactions of the Royal Society of Edinburgh* 5 (3): 39–99.

Pledge, H. T. (1966) *Science Since 1500: A Short History of Mathematics, Physics, Chemistry, Biology*, 2nd edn. London: HMSO.

Plotinus (1966–88) *Enneads*, 7 vols, trans. A. H. Armstrong. Cambridge, MA: Harvard University Press.

—— (1991) *Enneads*, trans. Stephen MacKenna. Harmondsworth: Penguin.

Poggi, Steffano and Maurizio Bossi (eds) (1994) *Romanticism in Science: Science in Europe 1790–1840*. Dordrecht: Kluwer.

Popper, Karl (1972) *Objective Knowledge*. Oxford: Oxford University Press.

Prigogine, Ilya and Isabelle Stengers (1984) *Order out of Chaos*. London: Flamingo.

Proclus (1997) *Commentaries on the* Timaeus *of Plato*, trans. Thomas Taylor. Whitefish, MT: Kessinger. Cited as *In Tim.*

Rehbock, Philip F. (1983) *The Philosophical Naturalists: Themes in Early Nineteenth-Century British Biology*. Madison: University of Wisconsin Press.

Rescher, Nicholas (2000) *Nature and Understanding: The Metaphysics and*

Method of Science. Oxford: Oxford University Press.

Reydams-Schils, Gretchen J. (ed.) (2003) *Plato's Timaeus as Cultural Icon*. Notre Dame: University of Notre Dame Press.

Ritter, Johann Wilhelm (1798) *Beweiss, daß ein beständiger Galvanismus den Lebensprozeß im Thierreiche begleite*. Weimar: Industrie-Comptoir.

—— (1800) 'Beweis, daß die Galvanische Action oder der Galvanismus auch in der Anorgischen Nature möglich und wirklich sey', in *Beyträge zur näheren Kenntniss des Galvanismus*, Bd. 1 Jena: Frommann.

—— (1984) *Fragmente aus dem Nachlasse eines jungen Physikers* [Heidelberg: Mohr und Zimmer, 1810], ed. Birgit und Stefan Dietzsch. Hanau: Müller & Kiepenheuer.

—— (1986) *Entdeckungen zur Elektrochemie, Bioelektrochemie und Photochemie* ed. Hermann Berg and Klaus Richter. Leipzig: Akademische Verlagsgesellschaft Geest & Portig.

Rothbart, Daniel and Irmgard Scherer (1997) 'Kant's *Critique of Judgment* and the scientific investigation of matter', *Hyle: An International Journal for the Philosophy of Chemistry* 3: 65–80.

Rueger, Alexander (1995) 'Brain water, the ether and the art of constructing systems', *Kant-Studien* 86: 26–40.

Rupke, Nicolaas (1998) ' "The end of history" in the early picturing of geological time', *History of Science* 36: 61–90.

Sallis, John (1999) *Chorology: On Beginning in Plato's* Timaeus. Bloomington: Indiana University Press.

Schlegel, Friedrich (1991) *Philosophical Fragments*, trans. Paul Firchow. Minneapolis: University of Minnesota Press.

Schrödinger, Erwin (1954) *Nature and the Greeks*. Cambridge: Cambridge University Press.

Schulte-Sasse, Jochen *et al.* (eds) (1997) *Theory as Practice: A Critical Anthology of Early German Romantic Writings*. Minneapolis: University of Minnesota Press.

Schulz, Walter (1968) *Briefwechsel Fichte-Schelling*. Frankfurt am Main: Suhrkamp.

Sedgwick, Sally (ed.) (2000) *The Reception of Kant's Critical Philosophy*. Cambridge: Cambridge University Press.

Sloan, Phillip R. (1976) 'The Buffon–Linnaeus Controversy', *Isis* 67: 356–75.

—— (1979) 'Buffon, German biology and the historical interpretation of biological species', *British Journal for the History of Science* 41: 107–53.

—— (1992) 'Introduction: On the edge of evolution', in Richard Owen, *The Hunterian Lectures in Comparative Anatomy*. London: Natural History Museum.

Snelders, H. A. M. (1970) 'Romanticism and *Naturphilosophie* and the inorganic natural sciences 1797–1840: A survey', *Studies in Romanticism* 9: 193–215.

Snider, Eric (1989) 'Scientific philosophy and philosophical method in

Fichte', *Metaphilosophy* 20 (1): 68–76.

Spinoza, Baruch (1996) *Ethics*, trans. Edwin Curley. Harmondsworth: Penguin.

Stauffer, Robert C. (1997) 'Speculation and experiment in the background to Oersted's discovery of electromagnetism', *Isis* 48: 33–50.

Steffens, Heinrik (1800a) 'Rezension der neuren naturphilosophischen Schriften des Herausgebers', in Schelling (2001) 7–36, 167–88.

—— (1800b) 'Über den Oxydations- und Desoxydations-Prozeß der Erde', in Schelling (2001) 93–110.

—— (1801) *Beyträge zur Innere Naturgeschichte der Erde*. Freyberg: Craz.

—— (1908) *Lebenserinnerungen aus dem Kreis der Romantik*, in Auswahl [from Heinrik Steffens, *Was Ich erlebte*, 10 vols, Breslau: Joseph Max und Kompanie, 1840–4] hrsg. von Friedrich Gundelfinger. Jena: Eugen Diederichs.

Stone, Alison (2005) *Petrified Intelligence: Nature in Hegel's Philosophy*. New York: State University of New York Press.

Strickland, Stuart (1995) 'Galvanic disciplines: The boundaries, objects and identities of experimental science in the era of Romanticism', *Journal of the History of Science* 33: 449–68.

Taylor, A. E. (1929) *A Commentary on the* Timaeus *of Plato*. Oxford: Oxford University Press.

Thom, René (1978) 'Morphogenèse et imaginaire', *Circé* 8–9, Paris: Les Lettres modernes: 7–90.

Thomson, D'Arcy Wentworth (1966) *On Growth and Form*, ed. J. T. Bonner. Cambridge: Cambridge University Press.

Troxler, Ignaz Paul Vital (1985) *Naturlehre des menschlichen Erkennens*. Hamburg: Meiner.

Tsouyopoulos, Nelly (1978b) 'Die neue Auffassung der klinischen Medizin als Wissenschaft unter dem Einfluß der Philosophie im frühen 19. Jahrhundert', in *Berichte zur Wissenschaftsgeschichte* 1: 87–100.

Uexküll, Jacob von (1965) *Mondes animaux et mondes humaines*. Paris: Denöel.

Wallace, William (1894) *Prolegomena to the Logic of Hegel*, 2nd edn. Oxford: Oxford University Press.

Watkins, Eric (ed.) (2001) *Kant and the Sciences*. Oxford: Oxford University Press.

Wetzels, Walter D. (1971) 'Aspects of natural science in German Romanticism', *Studies in Romanticism* 10: 44–59.

—— (1973) *Johann Wilhlem Ritter: Physik im Wirkungsfeld der deutschen Romantik*. Berlin: Walter de Gruyter.

Whitehead, Alfred North ([1920] 1964) *The Concept of Nature*. Cambridge: Cambridge University Press.

Windischmann, Karl Joseph (1802) 'Grundzüge zu einer Darstellung des Begriffs der Physik', in Schelling (1969), 1: 78–160.

—— (1805) *Ideen zur Physik*. Würzburg: Göbhardt.

Wright, M. R. (1995) *Cosmology in Antiquity*. London: Routledge.

Zammito, John H. (1992) *The Genesis of Kant's* Critique of Judgment. Chicago: Chicago University Press.

Ziolkowski, Theodor (1990) *German Romanticism and Its Institutions*. Princeton: Princeton University Press.

Index

CPSIA information can be obtained
at www.ICGtesting.com
Printed in the USA
LVHW082140251219
641698LV00006B/438/P

9 781847 064325